PERSONALITY DEVELOPMENT AT PREADOLESCENCE

Explorations of
Structure
Formation

Personality Development at Preadolescence

*Explorations of
Structure
Formation*

by
RILEY W. GARDNER

and
ALICE MORIARTY

University of Washington Press
Seattle and London

Preface

THE STUDY described in this book is grounded in an orientation to individuality that stems from psychoanalytic theory on the one hand and academic psychology on the other. As such, it is part of a programmatic attempt to employ concepts and methods from both theoretical realms and to bridge gaps between them, as well as to extend our understanding of individual differences in both areas. This orientation to individuality implies no arbitrary distinction between the rich insights into personality organization that are part of the yield of psychoanalysis and results of methodologically rigorous laboratory explorations of some of the major aspects of behavior relevant to adaptation, such as attention, concept formation, perception, and memory formation. When viewed from an orientation toward individuality, with its inevitable requirement of concepts of behavioral structures, developments in these two areas of psychology lead naturally to hypotheses concerning relations between the aspects of structuring that have been explored in each. Accomplishment of this long-range goal requires that adequate structural concepts be developed to account for individual differences in various aspects of adaptive behavior.

The concept of cognitive control, originally formulated by George Klein, provided a framework for the conceptualization of drive modulation per se in terms of relatively enduring constellations of cognitive operations that mediate the expression of intentions in certain classes of external stimulus conditions. As such, the cognitive control concept paralleled the older concept of defensive structures, but diverged from the defense concept in dealing with regulation of drive expression, rather than the resolution of conflicts between drives. Historically, the concept of

v

cognitive control emerged in part under the impetus of Freud's late emphasis upon individual heredity as a potential precondition shaping the formation of behavioral structures in the course of learning and maturation. Hartmann's elaboration of Freud's general point concerning conflict-free aspects of mental organization was an immediate precursor of the approach to one class of individual differences in terms of cognitive control.

Since Freud had consistently conceptualized defense mechanisms as enduring constellations of cognitive operations, the cognitive control concept provided a natural bridge between individuality in defense functioning and individuality in other areas of cognitive behavior. This natural bridge has been effectively employed in several earlier studies of relations between defenses and controls in adults.

The cognitive control dimensions thus far tentatively differentiated (conceptually and experimentally) from the vast array of individual differences deal with only a few major aspects of control. Many other aspects remain to be explored, and many important problems concerning the nature and development of behavioral structures, the actual role of heredity in structure formation, the relation of structure to drive, and so forth, are as yet all but untouched. A first task would seem to be the isolation of meaningful aspects of control, investigation of their relations to other aspects of personality organization, and exploration of some of the variegated patterns of developmental change that may characterize different aspects of control and defense. Although current studies of control structures are quite limited in this programmatic sense, the aspects of control thus far explored cover a sufficient range of behavioral phenomena to be useful in systematic explorations of relations between controls and other aspects of personality organization. Such studies have already proved fruitful in respect to selected defenses and various intellectual abilities (which are also referable to structure formation). Prior to the present study, however, a systematic approach to the development of such groups of cognitive structures had not been attempted. The fruitfulness of the concepts in earlier work with adults, including the vast contribution of Herman Witkin and his associates to our understanding of the articulation of certain aspects of experience, seemed to provide the preconditions for a study of major structural features of personality organization at preadolescence. Such a study promised a rather large yield of information relevant to some of the unresolved issues shared by psychoanalysis and academic psychology concerning structural differentiation at preadolescence and personality changes from preadolescence to adulthood. Such a study also promised a rich harvest of new information concerning the development of specific controls, defenses, and other structures, their degrees of emergence, and their interrelations at preadolescence. In addition to these important yields relevant to general issues concerning personality development, such a study gave promise of new information concerning broad-scale personality change between early and late preadolescence, indications of the effects of belief orientations on personality development, and answers to a host of additional questions.

With these general purposes in mind, two research groups at The Menninger Foundation—the Longitudinal Study Project directed by Lois B. Murphy and the Cognition Project directed by the first author—joined forces in a study of preadolescent behavior. The sixty children studied were drawn from a larger group of children studied in infancy by Sibylle Escalona, Mary Leitch, and others (see, e.g., Escalona and Leitch, 1953; Escalona and Heider, 1959). About half these children have been studied extensively since that time in a longitudinal program of testing and observation. The earlier work of Lois B. Murphy and her associates with these children (see, e.g., L. Murphy, 1962), including the development of effective ratings of children's behavior, was of signal importance to the study. By freeing skilled persons from already heavy research commitments, Dr. Murphy made several of the major forms of assessment possible. Without her theoretical and practical contributions, the study could not have been performed.

The cognitive control procedures, the defense assessments, and some of the ratings of over-all behavior were made by members of the Cognition Project. The WISC, TAT, Rorschach, and Holtzman Inkblot Test procedures were administered by members of the Longitudinal Study Project. The second author also made extensive ratings of each child's over-all behavior during administration of the WISC and TAT.

A number of other persons made significant contributions to the study. First among these is Gardner Murphy, Director of Research at The Menninger Foundation, whose constant support, encouragement, and stimulation provided an ideal context—ideational as well as practical—for this study and many of the earlier studies that led to it. His broad view of psychological problems, combined with his tutorial and administrative "green thumb," have been major factors in the evolution of a wide-ranging research department at The Menninger Foundation in which such collaborative studies have occurred in ever-increasing numbers. His penetrating comments on the design of the study and the formulations presented in this book were also of great assistance to the authors.

Several of our colleagues contributed their special skills to various aspects of the study. By so doing, they made it possible to maintain strict independence of ratings and test performances at several critical points in the design of the study. Robert I. Long's skilled administration of all the cognitive control procedures insured that this major group of variables was carefully and effectively assessed. Dr. Long's extensive earlier contributions to the work on cognitive controls and prior experience with procedures employed to measure them in adults made his services invaluable, especially with respect to the more complex control procedures, whose intricacies demand psychological sophistication and experimental precision. Mrs. Gail Bishop performed independent ratings of behavior in the laboratory testing situation and later did much of the scoring of various procedures. Mrs. Pitsa Hartocollis administered the Rorschach Test. Mrs. Rosalie Mayman administered the Holtzman Inkblot Test, which was scored under the supervision of its author, Wayne Holtzman. Dr. Holtzman also performed invaluable service as our principal consultant with respect to the design of the study and the approaches to data analyses. Robert Schoen, who has made major contributions to earlier studies of cognitive control in the area of categorizing behavior, analyzed the children's categorizing performances. He also developed new scoring schemes for certain aspects of these performances in the present study, as did Allen Willner. Mr. Schoen also lent his talent with clinical tests to the assessment of tolerance for unrealistic experiences and the conceptual distance of TAT stories from the physical properties of the pictures. Leander Lohrenz, who has been deeply involved in work on cognitive controls of attention and memory formation, served similar functions with respect to the measurement of leveling-sharpening and other controls at preadolescence. Mr. Schoen and Dr. Lohrenz also provided valuable detailed comments on earlier versions of this report.

The extensive statistical work involved in the study was performed by, or under the supervision of, The Menninger Foundation's chief statistician, Miss Lolafaye Coyne, whose contribution to the study was of immeasurable importance. Miss Coyne was the principal statistician in all the earlier work on cognitive controls and related variables done at The Menninger Foundation. Her intimate knowledge of the cognitive control procedures and the scores for them (some of which she was instrumental in developing), her skill with electronic computers, and her advice on the design of the study and the measurements involved should all be recognized here. Arnold Janousek, then assistant director of the Computation Center at the University of Kansas, and Rex Coffman, a representative of International Business Machines, facilitated her work with computers at the Kansas State Highway Department in Topeka, Kansas, and the Boeing Aircraft Corporation in Wichita, Kansas. In addition to the other services she performed, Miss Coyne applied her considerable talents as a reader to preliminary drafts of the entire manuscript.

Mrs. Marie Smith, of the Longitudinal Study group, performed multiple services in making the longitudinal data available for this study and in typing preliminary drafts of some of the case study material. Mrs. Karen Falley typed preliminary drafts of several chapters. Mrs. Charrel Wessel's patient devotion to the typing of drafts of the entire manuscript was of invaluable assistance. (Since this was written, the help of Mrs. Elaine Malinovitch has been invaluable in the final preparation of the material for publication.)

The financial support of The Menninger Foundation and the United States Public Health Service (portions of Research Grants M-4093, M-2454, and M-5517, as well as research career program award K3-MH-21,936 to the first author) are gratefully acknowledged.

Thanks are also due the following publishers for permission to quote copyrighted material: *American Journal of Psychology;* Basic Books; Child Development Publications; Harper and Row; Hogarth Press; *International Journal of Psycho-Analysis;* International Universities Press; Alfred A. Knopf, Inc.; McGraw-Hill Book Company; Norton Press; *Perceptual and Motor Skills; Psychoanalytic Quarterly, Inc.;* The Journal Press; University of Texas Press; and Williams and Wilkins Company.

RILEY W. GARDNER, PH.D.

The Menninger Foundation
Topeka, Kansas
June, 1967

Contents

PERSONALITY DEVELOPMENT AT PREADOLESCENCE

Explorations of Structure Formation

1 An Approach to Individuality at Preadolescence

FROM THE ego-psychological point of view, the problem of individual personality organization can be approached in terms of the nature of structure formation, including the number of relatively permanent behavioral structures, their hierarchical organization, and their place in the total equilibration process that is the individual organism. This statement in no sense denies the importance of heredity as a determinant of innate drive or apparatus characteristics, the probability that innately determined stages of maturation are involved in structure formation, or the likelihood that such related characteristics of the individual organism as its characteristic drive levels or over-all sleeping and waking activation levels are important determinants of the nature and employment of the structures that evolve during development. Neither does it deny the usefulness of the hypothesis that a more or less integrated set of "themes" comprising an "ego identity" (Erikson, 1950) provides direction and organization to the employment of the total array of behavioral structures that could be called the "ego."

Truly comprehensive exploration of personality organization at any stage of development obviously demands the employment of several types of approaches, of which the structural approach is but one. A study directed primarily toward major forms of cognitive structures and related behavioral structures is therefore a necessary but insufficient precursor to ultimate understanding of the patternings of individual behavioral organization commonly subsumed under the term, "personality."

With one notable exception, major theories of human behavior have not included the kinds of structural concepts that could provide the basis for a theory of individuality of personality organization. The exception is, of course, psychoanalytic theory, in the evolution of which such structural concepts have played a prominent role. Except for reference to the concept, "ego," we shall not concern ourselves here with Freud's tripartite concept of mental organization ("id-ego-superego") in any detail, although the forces and functions involved in Freud's conceptions of the id and superego are intimately intertwined with the development of ego structures and their place in personality organization. Hartmann, who has provided two excellent papers on the concept of the ego and the history of its development in Freud's work (Hartmann, 1950, 1956a) has noted that the term "ego" itself is perhaps best defined as "a substructure of personality . . . defined by its functions." As he pointed out, no comprehensive catalogue of ego functions has ever been attempted. Beres (1956, p. 171) has pointed out that "A complete listing of ego functions would be extremely difficult and perhaps not even feasible at this time." He has, however, discussed in detail seven major groups of ego functions: relation to reality; regulation and control of instinctual drives; object relationships; thought processes; defense functions of the ego; autonomous functions of the ego; and the synthetic function of the ego. Each of these groups of ego functions finds representation in one or more forms in the present study. Beres has also noted the complex interrelations of ego functions to the totality of personality in the ongoing stream of behavior. As he put it (p. 171), "one cannot deal with any aspect of ego activity without involving the total personality."

Freud's (e.g., 1933) major emphasis concerning ego organization was upon functions relevant to adaptation to external reality, e.g., perception, thinking, and action, in the sense that these involve the delay and rerouting of drives in accommodation to external conditions. The ego so defined was a central feature of Freud's hypotheses concerning structure formation and can be understood as a semiautonomous array of relatively enduring, organized clusters of functions (i.e., structures) that arise out of the adaptive necessity of mediating the expression of drives with respect to conditions in external reality. The primary concern of the present study is with such component ego structures as defense mechanisms, cognitive controls, intellectual abilities, and certain other presumably enduring patternings of behavior that contribute to the uniqueness of the individual by shaping his adaptive behavior into an individualized "style" of regulating the expression of drives and affects, cognizing experience, and defending awareness against potentially anxiety-producing impulse derivatives. It is at this level of conceptualization that empirical work can currently be most effectively performed and at which certain key aspects of the problem of personality organization can be approached most fruitfully. At this level of conceptualization, principles can be adduced that are quite general, but that also exemplify the extreme complexity of individuality. This level of conceptualization also seems most directly relevant to the individual's moment-to-moment mediation of internal and external stimulation as he performs the acts that define his modes of adaptation. And this is a level of conceptualization at which links between psychoanalytic theory and general psychology may be conceptualized and subjected to empirical test. This general point of view seems to be supported by work already performed on the ways that dimensions of individual differences called cognitive controls relate to defenses, intellectual abilities, and other aspects of personality organization in adults. Hartmann (1956a, p. 436) has noted that "Freud's structural hypotheses represent the closest and most systematic approximation to his early aim of a general psychology. The implications of this for a synthesis of psycho-analytic thought with other fields of knowledge have so far been only partly realized." The present study represents one kind of approach to some of that unfinished work.

The concept of defense, discussed in greater detail in Chapter 10, was for many years the only structural concept of this kind given extensive consideration in psychoanalytic theory. That is, no other structural concepts were developed to account for the constellations of cognitive operations that differ from individual to individual and that are presumably vital not only to his effective equilibration of forces within and without himself, but also to his very survival.

Defense formation, both in its defensive and adaptive senses, was conceived by Freud as a *sine qua non* of the relatively orderly group behaviors that are at the core of civilization. The formation of enduring constellations of cognitive operations in the service of defense was assumed to evolve from the interaction of the individual with his ecology, particularly the parental persons involved in his earliest experiences of frustration and gratification of innately determined drives, i.e., his earliest encounters with the necessity for psychic activity, including structure formation, as a means of adapting his behavior to fit conditions in internal and external reality. Developmentally, defense formation was presumed to proceed from the physical and mental anlage of earliest experience through a series of maturational stages dictated by evolution, and to continue to change, albeit at a reduced rate, throughout the life of the individual. The physical apparatuses involved in drive and cognition were also assumed to be dictated by the individual's heredity, as Freud (e.g., 1937) emphasized, particularly in his later writings.

In spite of the usefulness of defense constructs in clinical work and their extensive employment in this field for many years, important questions remain unanswered concerning the formation of these structures and the developmental changes they undergo. Some of these questions have not been answered because the relevant investigations require assessment of these and other cognitive structures in sizable groups of persons whose behaviors are observed under carefully controlled conditions. This kind of study is ordinarily denied the practicing clinician, however much his clinical experience may contribute to understanding of the particular constellations of cognitive operations involved and their relations to other relatively enduring structures in individual persons. Because of the special conditions of therapeutic interaction, certain kinds of information concerning behavioral structures are also difficult to obtain in clear form in the clinic. The oft-repeated dictum that defenses undergo radical changes at and following puberty, because of the easily observed increase in sexual and other drives, may serve to exemplify this point. A full-scale test of this hypothesis and of the related hypothesis that defenses and other cognitive structures are organized in simpler ways before puberty than after requires evaluation by groups of longitudinal and cross-sectional studies that cannot ordinarily be performed in the clinic.

The present study is one such attempt. It is focused on major facets of the structuring of behavior at preadolescence and on comparisons of certain of the findings with results of earlier explorations with adults. The study is organized around assessments of the following major aspects of individual consistencies in a single group of sixty children: cognitive controls; defense mechanisms; general characteristics of ego organization; major intellectual abilities; performance consistencies in the Holtzman Inkblot Test; behavior in a clinical testing session; and behavior in a laboratory testing session. In spite of the sizable numbers of tests and ratings involved, and the varieties of behavior sampled, this approach to personality organization at preadolescence is clearly incomplete. The study may nevertheless be unique in the number and types of personality structures dealt with and in the detail with which certain aspects of cognitive structuring can be compared in preadolescents and adults.

The Problem of Structure Formation

The term "controlling structures" is employed in this book to refer to automatized patterns, programs, or strategies of behavior involved in the shaping of drive expression. Rapaport (1957, p. 158) referred to such generalized structures, and other cognitive structures (e.g., memory organizations) as "tools of cognition." Klein (1958) has noted the relationship of the group of regulatory structures called "cognitive controls" to Gordon Allport's (1935) concept of "instrumental attitudes." The most general purposive feature of all such controlling structures is to achieve drive expression in ways that accommodate the individual to reality. All such structures are, therefore, mechanisms of reality contact.

Rapaport (1959, p. 94) pointed out that the structural point of view in psychoanalysis originated in recognition of the fact that the relation of drive to overt behavior is a highly variable one:

> It was observed that drives do not unequivocally determine behavior in general, nor symptom formation in particular. In contrast to the drive processes, whose rate of change is fast and whose course is paroxysmal, the factors which conflict with them and codetermine behavior appeared invariant, or at least of a slower rate of change. The observation of these relatively abiding determiners of behavior and symptom seems to have been the foundation on which the concept of structure was built.

As noted earlier, the defense mechanisms, presumed to serve the purpose of shaping and modifying the expression of conflicting drives, were the first such controlling structures to be conceptualized. The cognitive control concepts referred to throughout this study are a second group of structures operating at what appears to be the same general level in the hierarchy of structures involved in personality organization. The major intellectual abilities can also be conceptualized as controlling structures. Certain defenses, in fact, have direct implications for the evolution of "ability" structures, and one dimension of cognitive control seems to overlap with an important dimension of individual differences conceived of as an intellectual ability by Thurstone and others (see Gardner, Jackson, and Messick, 1960). Some cognitive controls also seem to have implications for defense employment. Although these and other possible controlling structures may differ in their origins, in their developmental changes, and in the particular adaptive purposes they serve, they seem to have similar positions in the structural hierarchy. Each group can, for example, be conceived of as a set of "intervening variables" that are intimately linked to drives, but which at the same time give patterned regulation to drive expression in ways that involve accommodation to reality conditions. Each group adds its bit to the total pattern of individual consistencies that gives each personality its unique characteristics and in part accounts for its recognizability over time.

The total realm of cognitive structures formed in the course of development is, of course, not limited to the kinds of controlling structures that are the primary focus of this study. The enduring patterns of cognitive functions formed through the coaction of constitutional and experiential phenomena range from simple motoric patterns and single memories to the kinds of higher-order structures that presumably give over-all direction to an individual's life style.

Rapaport (e.g., 1951b; 1960b) sought an answer to the problem of structure formation in an elaboration and explication of Freud's theory of attention cathexis. This has led to a program of work on learning and attention that involves some intriguing hypotheses and valuable results (see, e.g., Schwartz and Rouse, 1961). That is, the postulates Rapaport derived from Freud's theory of attention cathexis have led to a fruitful program of research. Whether or not the theory itself—with its assumption that the distribution of a "pool" of cathectic energy is essential to structure formation, the assumption that drive cathexis is transformed into attention cathexis, and so forth—is viable is perhaps another matter, as discussed in more detail in another section of this chapter.

One of the most intriguing groups of questions concerning the formation of the broad range of enduring structures involved in personality development is the role of learning in structure formation and the suitability of current learning theories for explanations of structure formation. Rapaport found all current theories wanting and set in motion the program of research referred to above in a first attempt to develop a more adequate theory of learning. It should be noted here, however, that there is considerable evidence of the relevance of learning as such to several of the aspects of cognitive behavior dealt with in the study. Recent demonstrations of learning in respect to attentional behaviors (see, e.g., Solley and Murphy, 1960; Binder and Feldman, 1960; and Santos, Farrow, and Haines, 1963) are valuable additions to this body of knowledge.

It seems obvious that all learning involves structure formation. It is less obvious, however, that all structure formation involves learning. Hartmann's (1939) emphasis on the constitutional structural characteristics of the apparatuses employed in cognition is relevant here, and much further work may be required to resolve such general issues.

Although some of the major questions concerning developmental changes in controlling structures are as yet unanswered, these patternings of behavioral organization, which lead to one broad class of individual consistencies, are presumed to be relatively enduring aspects of personality organization. In the case of adults, what Rapaport called the "slower rate of change" of these constellations of operations, as compared to the rate of change in drive processes per se, is clearly demonstrable. The stability of adult defense organization, for example, has been documented and redocumented in clinical experience (see, e.g., Rapaport, 1958). Within the normal and neurotic range, the impressive feature of the individual's defense organization is, in fact, its remarkable resistance to change. Much of the "work" of psychoanalysis and psychotherapy is attributable to the tenacity with which previously formed constellations of defense are maintained.

The relative temporal consistency of intellectual abilities, cognitive controls, and several other structural aspects of personality organization has also been demonstrated. Important questions remain, however, concerning differences in total personality organization at different age levels and the degrees of developmental change particular structures undergo. Time-honored controversies, for example, surround such problems as the degree of homogeneity versus heterogeneity of structural organization characteristic of different age levels. Such questions as the following become relevant here: Are children's structural organizations understandable in terms of fewer constructs than adults, or does children's behavior exemplify a greater number of (unintegrated) organizational parameters? At what stage of development are the main outlines of adult personality organization discernible? Do defense structures and their interrelational patterns undergo large-scale reorganization at and following puberty in every individual? Comprehensive answers to these and a considerable number of related questions await large-scale longitudinal studies. A study of several major features of personality organization at preadolescence, plus a step-by-step comparison of the results with earlier findings for adults, can, however, provide new information relevant to several of these general questions and a number of more specific ones.

In the realm of cognitive dimensions referred to as "cognitive controls," basic questions related to those listed above concern the individual consistencies in test performances which led to their acceptance as dimensions of cognitive organization. It is of theoretical importance, for example, whether individual consistencies in adult categorizing behaviors also characterize children. It is also important to theory whether the cognitive controls postulated thus far are as independent of each other in children as they seem to be in adults. One often expressed point of view suggests that fewer dimensions of cognitive control may be discernible in children's behavior than in adults'. Another common view would suggest, however, that *more* organizational principles are involved. The present study provided a first opportunity to explore relations between the organization of cognitive controls in preadolescence and adulthood.

Cognitive controls are assumed to be patterns of response that mediate between drive and intention on the one hand and external reality on the other. As noted by Gardner, Holzman, Klein, Linton, and Spence (1959), however, adult cognitive controls also appear to exist in their own right, as relatively autonomous aspects of cognitive organization that may be used to a greater or lesser degree because their exercise is pleasurable in and of itself. Interests, hobbies, and so forth, are common arenas for the expression of such autonomous tendencies. The statement that the ego as a whole is "a cohesive structure in its own right" (Gill and Brenman, 1959, p. 182) is also applicable to such specific features of ego organization as cognitive controls.

Other unanswered questions about cognitive controls concern their place in over-all personality organization. The following questions exemplify some of the relevant issues: How independent are controls of defenses? To what extent do cognitive controls actually involve "conflict-free" (Hartmann, 1939) aspects of cognitive organization? Are the cognitive controls postulated thus far characterized by equal situational generality? What are the relationships of different cognitive controls to affective and interpersonal behavior? Are different aspects of cognitive control determined to different degrees by the individual's heredity?

Only a few of the important unanswered questions concerning structure formation were approached in the present study. These and many more questions must be answered, however, before our understanding of the total array of structures involved in personality organization is complete.

Several groups of recent theoretical contributions referred to in this book (e.g., those of Hartmann, Rapaport, Erikson, and others) are necessary to the ultimate evolution of an effective theory of structure. For the most part, these recent developments are extensions of points of view stated but not explicated by Freud. As Klein (1958) has noted, other advances of equal or greater significance for the ultimate development of structural concepts are evident in the work of Hebb (1949), F. H. Allport (1955), and Piaget (e.g., 1953). In the passages below, we shall summarize briefly an additional, and perhaps more radical, revision of earlier psychoanalytic formulations that may also be essential to the development of an effective theory of structure.

The Energy-Structure Duality Reconsidered

One of us (Gardner, in press, 1967) has suggested that psychoanalytic explanations of cognitive phenomena in terms of energies on the one hand and structures on the other is uneconomical and leads to ineffective and potentially misleading formulations. To assume, as Freud and many subsequent psychoanalytic theoreticians have, that reality-attuned secondary-process thought involves special sets of control structures *and* a "transformed" type of energy seems logically indefensible. In the paper referred to, the point is developed rather extensively that recent discoveries in neurophysiology, particularly those exemplified in the work of Hernández-Peón and his associates (e.g., Hernández-Peón, 1959, 1961; Hernández-Peón and Scherrer, 1955), not only indicate the untenability of concepts of energy transformation (e.g., "neutralization," energy transfer, and so forth), but also delineate the nature of the apparatuses involved in the facilitation and inhibition of neural processes. The discovery that different neural structures are involved in the facilitation of neural activity on the one hand, and its inhibition on the other, plus the recent articulation of the hierarchical (cortical-midbrain-peripheral) organization of the neural controls of facilitation and inhibition involved in attention and perception provides a neurophysiological basis for a structural theory of cognition that is effectively focused on the *patterning* of regulation. This new stance toward the mediation of inner and outer reality must, of course, take cognizance of the intensity of activation and many other relevant variables. As discussed in detail by Gardner (in press, 1967), conceptualization of cognitive processes in terms of hierarchical patterns of facilitation and inhibition also implicates, at a superordinate level, a concept of progressive over-all organismic equilibration involving complex systems of "feedback." It is at this critical theoretical juncture that the suggested recasting of the psychoanalytic energy-structure dualism seems to mesh most effectively with recent developments in neurophysiology. An application of some of these developments to the specific problem of individual differences in the selectivity of attention is offered in Chapter 3.

The point of view outlined briefly here would also exclude the traditional view (see Rapaport, 1959) that structure formation is essentially a process which involves the "binding" of energies and which is rooted in the interactions of original and transformed energies (e.g., the "binding" of cathectic energy by means of countercathexis).

There are many, of course, who feel that a metapsychology need not conform to developments in related fields, however valuable the new insights may be for adequacy and economy of theory. Effective interplay between observations in psychology and such related fields as neurophysiology is, however, a necessity for theoretical progress. One of us (Gardner, in press, 1967) has argued that only by means of such continuous feedback—between different areas of science and between clinical and experimental psychology—can theories of personality (i.e., theories that account for *individual* consistencies in behavior) advance effectively. This subject has been discussed in some detail in the paper referred to. Suffice it to say here that such enduring arrangements of cognitive processes as defense mechanisms and cognitive controls can be conceptualized more economically and effectively in terms of organismic equilibration by patterned controls of facilitation and inhibition than in terms of older psychoanalytic concepts involving parallel energic-structural explanations. That Freud conceptualized in terms of forces and counterforces, that he constructed tentative "hydraulic" models of energy distribution, and that he extended his energic formulations to include the notion that instinctual energy is transformed into "neutralized" energy by the psychic apparatus is attributable to the scientific milieu in which he worked. Theoretical economy and the ever-present need to modify theory in conformance to related discoveries now underscore the importance of discarding these redundant energic-structural constructs. The energic constructs required are of a simpler and more limited nature and involve no assumptions about the transformation or transportation of energies.

The point of view expressed here is in no way incompatible with the extensive observations of psychoanalysts leading to the postulations of such cognitive structures as defense mechanisms, nor with the defense *operations* thus far postulated. Our disagreement is solely with current assumptions about the causal factors involved in these operations.

The Development of Controlling Behavioral Structures

Psychoanalytic theory states that three main groups of forces are involved in ego development: the instinctual drives (dictated by evolution and varying with the specific heredity of the individual); factors in external reality; and the innate and maturational characteristics of the physical apparatuses involved (Hartmann, 1952).[1] Freud's (1937) late emphasis upon the possibility of congenital variations in the ego provided a place for hereditary apparatus characteristics in ego development, particularly defense development. The interaction of these three sets of factors are assumed to account for the development of the mediational behavioral structures subsumed under the concept "ego."

Beres (1956) is among those who have succinctly presented the general concept of the ego as an organized constellation of mediating structures. As he put it (pp. 169–70):

The over-all function of the ego is to mediate between the instinctual drives and external reality, and this utilization of a mediating device is a specifically human attribute. In this sense the ego is unique to man and serves a group of functions which, in lower animals, are accomplished by the direct action of the "instincts." Freud . . . speaks of the ego as "an intermediary between the id and the external world." Hartmann, Kris, and Loewenstein . . . also point up the mediating function of the ego and indicate the importance of distinguishing between "instinctual drive" of man and "instinct" of animals. This distinction is relevant to the present discussion because the instinct of the animal is biologically adapted to respond directly to environmental stimuli, whereas the instinctual drive of man requires the intervention of the ego before it finds appropriate discharge.

It should be emphasized here that a conception of evolutionarily dictated maturational changes, as well as changes attributable to learning, is an essential component of this general conception. Evolution of the species and the specific heredity of the individual are thus conceived of as dictating both the nature of inborn ego apparatuses and (under normal environmental conditions) maturational changes that include, but are not limited to, several stages of development.

Hartmann *et al.* (1946) have spoken of the earliest stage of ego

[1] Excellent discussions of ego development have been provided by a number of authors, e.g., Fenichel (1945a); Hartmann (1939, 1950, 1952); Hartmann, Kris, and Loewenstein (1946); Jacobson (1954); Rapaport (1960a).

organization as an "undifferentiated stage" from which both the ego and the id later emerge. Hartmann (1952, p. 17) later noted that the

Earliest stages of ego development can be described as a process of differentiation that leads to a more complete demarcation of ego and id and of self and outer reality; as a process that leads from the pleasure to the reality ego; as the development of the reality principle; as the way leading from primary narcissism to object relationships; from the point of view of the sequence of danger situations; as the development of the secondary process, etc.

A key postulate in this group is that, given adequate constitutional and experiential bases, ego functioning changes during development from primary-process to secondary-process forms (see, e.g., Freud, 1900). That is, the "reality principle" (Freud, 1911a) comes gradually to dominate mental activity. A critically important assumption is that behavioral structures are formed when there are obstacles to immediate drive gratification (see Rapaport, 1959). When the impediments result from conflicts between drives, some of the preconditions for the emergence of defensive structures are met. Other secondary-process structures are also formed during development, however, as reality-attuned modulation of drive expression is an adaptive necessity whether or not internal conflict is involved.

Among the hallmarks of primary-process thinking are its inclusion of such primitive, drive-dominated, nonrational operations as condensation and displacement. Even in the infant, however, the employment of the hereditarily given drive-free and conflict-free apparatuses of cognition limits the degree of initial dominance of thought by the primitive patterns of control involved in primary-process thinking. As Rapaport (1958) has noted (following Freud), no thought process is characterized by "primary-process" operations alone. During early childhood, the progression toward dominance of waking consciousness by the more refined controls producing "secondary-process" thought is marked by maturational stages that add new and qualitatively different facets to thought organization. By latency and preadolescence, thought is ordinarily guided primarily, but not exclusively, by the reality principle. Detailed developmental studies employing these concepts are lacking, however.

Rapaport (1960a, p. 239) has pointed out that "The conception of the secondary process changes radically . . . when in *Totem and Taboo* Freud attributes a unifying, connecting, and rationalizing synthetic function to it." We shall hear more of this synthetic function of the constellation of structures Freud termed the "ego" in a subsequent chapter. Rapaport's point, and it is an important one, is that the concept, ego, by virtue of its synthetic function, came to include the view that secondary-process thinking is to some degree autonomous both of drive and of reality (see also Hartmann, 1939; Rapaport, 1958). In other words, secondary-process thinking is no longer conceived of (Rapaport, 1960a, p. 239) as "a mere superimposition upon the primary processes by the dire necessities of reality." As Rapaport (1960a) also points out, Freud's somewhat contradictory statements about the origins of secondary-process thought can be understood most accurately by assuming that he gradually became more aware that secondary-process functioning is not simply the product of clashes between drives and reality, but also involves innately given features of the apparatuses involved in ego functioning (see, e.g., Freud, 1937). These developments in Freud's work have been elaborated upon by Hartmann, Rapaport, and others in major contributions to current ego-psychological points of view. Hartmann (1939), for example, has spelled out the concepts of inborn ego structures of primary autonomy from drives and conflicts, and acquired ego structures of secondary autonomy. Rapaport (1951a, 1958) has expanded upon the relative autonomy of the ego as a whole from drives on the one hand, and reality on the other. Gill and Brenman (1959) have developed a concept of over-all ego autonomy.

Erikson (1950, p. 208) has added to earlier discussions of the synthetic function of the ego his view that ego synthesis is the individual's "way of mastering experience" and is intimately tied to the problem of group identity. These and a number of other recent contributions have broadened the scope of the ego-psychological approach to personality organization, and provided new concepts or enriched older concepts, such as the notion of ego strength, in ways that lead to improved assessments of ego organization. We shall discuss ego autonomy and ego strength in much more detail in a chapter devoted to the assessment of defense mechanisms and general characteristics of cognitive organization. Let us note here only that these recent contributions have made it possible to view the problem of structure formation in new ways that may be of particular value to studies of developmental changes in personality organization.

Development as Sequential Stages

Erikson (e.g., 1950, 1956) has expanded the original psychoanalytic conception of maturational stages rooted in dominance changes among the erogenous zones by constructing a developmental scheme that involves the resolution of a series of crises. Successful resolution of the focal crisis at each stage is necessary, Erikson postulates, for effective resolution of the focal crisis at the next stage. Adult ego strength is thus closely tied to the effectiveness of crisis resolution at each preceding stage. As Erikson puts it (1950, p. 233): "At any given stage of the life cycle the solution of one or more nuclear conflicts adds a new ego quality, a new criterion of ego strength." The crises involved in successive stages of development are outlined by Erikson in the following parallel series: oral sensory stage: trust vs. mistrust; muscular-anal stage: autonomy vs. shame and doubt; locomotor-genital stage: initiative vs. guilt; latency stage: industry vs. inferiority; puberty and adolescent stage: identity vs. role diffusion; young adult stage: intimacy vs. isolation; adult stage: generativity vs. stagnation; mature stage: integrity vs. disgust, despair.

As discussed in greater detail in subsequent chapters, the Midwestern children of the present study seemed somewhat inhibited, dutiful, and lacking in exuberant spontaneity at preadolescence, although they had not appeared so in their preschool evaluations. In Erikson's terms, these children as a group seemed, at preadolescence, to show a moderate limitation of autonomy and an inadequate resolution of the earlier crisis over guilt attached to aggressive exploration of the external world. Although the study includes only very limited data on characteristics of the parents, and although detailed studies of values and attitudes in the Midwestern subculture involved are lacking, it is our impression that this tendency toward inhibition, although a sign of partial ego weakness, is also adaptively effective in that it represents a key characteristic of the subculture itself, which can be described as strongly religious, conventional, motorically oriented, and somewhat nonintellectual. This tendency toward inhibition at preadolescence, which seems in part to be an age-related form of matching behavior to the values and personal orientations of parents and other associates, shows itself as less than optimal ego development primarily in relatively unstructured situations. As a group, these children's limitations are most apparent in situations requiring flexibility and originality of approach, or in situations in which either ambiguity or conflicting reality factors require active, autonomous imposition of order. Their rather dutiful industriousness makes them appear more adequate in structured procedures than in the Rorschach Test or the Thematic Apperception Test, which leave the organization of responses largely up to the individual. Tendencies toward industry without originality, persistence without flexibility, and compliance without affective spontaneity are among the general impressions upon which the study staff were in most complete agreement.

These impressions are recorded here because of our view that they provide a limited but necessary context for the studies of particular aspects of personality organization, and the integration of these aspects, that are described in this book. The patterning of defenses in the group as a whole is undoubtedly determined to a significant extent by the subculture's orientation toward acceptable and unacceptable behavior. The studies described here should, therefore, be replicated in other subcultures and other cultures. In Chapter 15, we shall argue, in fact, that intercultural comparisons of patterns of organization—including studies of hereditary influences on these patterns—are a necessity for understanding of personality development.

In terms of the stages of intellectual development postulated by Piaget, latency and preadolescence comprise the late portion of the "stage of concrete operations" and the early portion of the "stage of formal operations." The latter stage, at about eleven to twelve years, culminates the progression from infantile sensory-motor intelligence to adult thinking that includes reasoning in terms of hypotheses and propositions (see the excellent summary of these stages of intellectual development by Piaget, 1962). Whether or not the ages Piaget gives for the transition from concrete to formal operations fit the children of the present sample is unknown. It seems likely, however, that some of the younger children (who are nine and ten years old) differ notably from some of the older children (who are eleven to thirteen years old) in the features of intelligent behavior Piaget describes. Although no tests of the stages described by Piaget were employed in the present study, quantitative and qualitative features of certain test performances discussed in subsequent chapters may parallel Piaget's observations.

A Psychoanalytic View of Preadolescence

Anna Freud's description of the latency period is particularly apt and provides a still more general setting for our considerations of the specialized aspects of development represented by controlling structures. After describing the ego organizations of little children in general terms, she states (1936, pp. 157–58):

In the course of a few years the situation alters. The latency-period sets in, with a physiologically conditioned decline in the strength of the instincts, and a truce is called in the defensive warfare waged by the ego. It now has leisure to devote itself to other tasks and it acquires fresh contents, knowledge and capacities. At the same time, it becomes stronger in relation to the outside world; it is less helpless and submissive and does not regard that world as quite so omnipotent as heretofore. Its whole attitude to external objects gradually changes as it surmounts the Oedipus situation. Complete dependence on the parents ceases and identification begins to take the place of object-love. More and more the principles held up to the child by his parents and teachers—their wishes, requirements, and ideals—are injected. In his inner life the outside world no longer makes itself felt solely in the form of objective anxiety. He has set up within his ego a permanent institution, in which are embodied the demands of those around him and which we call the superego. Simultaneously with this development a change takes place in the infantile anxiety. Fear of the outside world looms less large and gradually gives place to fear of the new representatives of the old power—to super-ego anxiety, anxiety of conscience, and the sense of guilt. This means that the ego of the latency-period has acquired a new ally in the struggle to master the instinctual processes. Anxiety of conscience prompts the defence against instinct in the latency-period, just as it was prompted by objective anxiety in the early infantile period. As before, it is difficult to determine how much of the control over instinct acquired during the latency-period is to be attributed to the ego itself and how much to the powerful influence of the super-ego.

With puberty comes a notable increase in drive tension that may have extensive effects on ego organization, that strains defenses and other controlling mechanisms, and that begins to orient the child (although often not consciously) to the problem of his ego identity, including his relation to the identity of his group (see Erikson, 1950). Anna Freud (1936, pp. 158–59) has also stated the problem of drive control at puberty with unusual clarity:

The physiological process which marks the attainment of physical sexual maturity is accompanied by a stimulation of the instinctual processes, which is carried over into the psychic sphere in the form of an influx of libido. The relation established between the forces of the ego and the id is destroyed, the painfully achieved psychic balance is upset, with the result that the inner conflicts between the two institutions blaze up afresh.

At first there is very little to report on the side of the id. The interval between latency and puberty—the so-called prepubertal period—is merely preparatory to physical sexual maturity. So far, no qualitative change has taken place in the instinctual life, but the quantity of instinctual energy has increased. This increase is not confined to the sexual life. There is more libido at the id's disposal and it cathects indiscriminately any id-impulses which are at hand. Aggressive impulses are intensified to the point of complete unruliness, hunger becomes voracity and the naughtiness of the latency-period turns into the criminal behavior of adolescence. Oral and anal interests, long submerged, come to the surface again. Habits of cleanliness, laboriously acquired during the latency period, give place to pleasure in dirt and disorder, and instead of modesty and sympathy we find exhibitionistic tendencies, brutality and cruelty to animals. The reaction-formations, which seemed to be firmly established in the structure of the ego, threaten to fall to pieces. At the same time, old tendencies which had disappeared come into consciousness. The Oedipus wishes are fulfilled in the form of fantasies and day-dreams, in which they have undergone but little distortion; in boys ideas of castration and in girls penis-envy once more become the center of interest. There are very few new elements in the invading forces. Their onslaught merely brings once more to the surface the familiar content of the early infantile sexuality of little children.

Aspects of Preadolescent Behavior Explored in the Present Study

The major group of measures included in the present study are procedures used in earlier studies of adults focused on relations of cognitive control structures to defense mechanisms (Gardner *et al.*, 1959; Holzman and Gardner, 1959; Gardner and Long, 1962a) and intellectual abilities (Gardner *et al.*, 1960; Gardner and Schoen, 1962). The major areas of cognition dealt with in the control measures are the articulation of certain aspects of experience, including the capacity to attend selectively; the extensiveness of attention deployment in perceptual decision-making tests involving size judgments; spontaneous conceptual differentiation in free categorizing (in the present study, of objects and pictures of persons), including grouping behaviors, the types of concepts employed in categorizing, the conceptual distance represented by S's "stance" toward the objects, and related aspects of concept formation; the nature and degree of control of overlearned but momentarily irrelevant motoric responses; the degree of interaction of new percepts and related earlier memories; and tolerance for unrealistic experiences. Each of these aspects of cognitive control has been explored in several earlier studies of adults, the results of which suggest that they are important aspects of cognitive organization not previously conceptualized and not reducible to defense functioning.

Some of the control principles explored thus far are predictably related in complex ways to particular defenses in adults, raising important new questions concerning the origins of defense mechanisms.

One of the most intriguing questions concerning the development of cognitive structures concerns the developmental priority (if priority exists) of individual differences in the basic psychological functions dealt with in cognitive control research and defense structures. Gardner *et al.*

(1959) and Holzman and Gardner (1959) have reasoned that basic cognitive differences in memory formation, categorizing, scanning, selectiveness of attention, and so forth could serve as preconditioners of defense formation. Leveling in memory formation, for example, may be a necessary but insufficient condition for the emergence of repression as a pervasively used defense structure. This point, which finds its theoretical basis in the work of Freud (1937) and Hartmann (1939), has nowhere been better stated than by Hartmann (1950, p. 83):

It might well be that the ways in which infants deal with stimuli—also those functions of delaying, of postponing discharge mentioned before—are later used by the ego in an active way. This active use for its own purposes of primordial forms of reaction we consider, as you know, a rather general characteristic of the developed ego. This hypothesis of a genetic correlation between individual differences in primary factors of this kind and the later defense mechanisms (apart from those correlations that we think exist of defense mechanisms with other developmental factors, with the nature of the drives involved, with the danger situation, etc.) is intended as an appeal to further investigation by those analysts who have the opportunities for conducting longitudinal developmental studies on children—I think that it should be accessible to direct verification or refutation.

Answers to these kinds of questions require new types of studies that include, among other things, assessment of the importance of heredity to individual controls and defenses. If, for example, leveling (i.e., a high degree of assimilation among percepts and relevant memories) should prove to be relatively high in hereditary determination, the relationship of leveling to extensive use of repression in adult women may be determined by a constitutional leveling tendency that comprises one of the basic cognitive dispositions involved in repression. The development of procedures that adequately sample cognitive controls and are applicable to infants and young children will also be required to explore important questions concerning the constitutional bases and the sequential emergence of cognitive structures out of the coaction of hereditary and environmental factors. The obvious anticipation is that individual differences in some controls and defenses will be strongly determined by differences in the physical apparatuses involved in cognitive functioning dictated by heredity, whereas others will be primarily learned (Gardner, 1965).

Like the cognitive control principles, the defense structures assessed in the present study include only part of the potential realm of such structures. The control variables studied were dictated by the fact that earlier work has been done with adults that provides a basis for exploration of particular aspects of cognitive structuring at preadolescence. Many other potential aspects of cognitive control are as yet unexplored.

The selection of defenses from the larger arrays postulated by various psychoanalytic theorists was designed to maximize the number of major, well-defined, and extensively studied defenses assessed, but was limited by the kinds of data available. Turning against the self, for example, was not included because other kinds of observations than those included in the present study were considered necessary for adequate assessment.

The intellectual abilities included are two of the most widely known and extensively studied. They involve individual differences in verbal skills on the one hand and in "performance" skills on the other. The latter involve the capacity actively and effectively to articulate stimulus configurations, visual-motor coordination, and so forth.

As conceptualized here, controls, defenses, and intellectual abilities clearly involve relatively enduring personality structures. In the case of the intellectual abilities, rather voluminous evidence is already at hand (see, e.g., Erlenmeyer-Kimling and Jarvik, 1963) to indicate that general intelligence and at least some major specific abilities (see also Vandenberg, 1962) are determined, under normal environmental conditions, to rather striking degrees by heredity. Although results are more equivocal for verbal ability, the "performance" skills clearly involve high degrees of hereditary determination.

In addition to the measures of cognitive controls, defense mechanisms, and intellectual abilities, the present study included responses to the Holtzman Inkblot Test (Holtzman, Thorpe, Swartz, and Herron, 1961). This test also invokes enduring patterns of behavior that, like response to the Rorschach Test, appear to involve relatively complex sets of determinants. In one sense, the HIT can be considered a test of perceptual organization in response to complex stimuli. As such, it could involve the cognitive control of field-articulation, which is known to be related to several aspects of response to the Rorschach Test. Since concept formation and other aspects of cognitive functioning are also involved, it seemed possible that new implications of controls, defenses, and abilities might become apparent through inclusion of responses to the HIT among the data of the present study.

Ratings of behavior in the clinical and laboratory testing situations were included to introduce into the study individual difference dimensions that have not been explored previously in relation to cognitive controls, defenses, and abilities. Major aspects of each child's over-all response to these distinctly different situations—including the "openness" of his behavior, his curiosity, the activeness of his stance toward external reality, the over-all accuracy and effectiveness of his adaptive behavior, and key aspects of his relationship to adult male and female examiners—were evaluated by means of the two sets of ratings. The assessment of these and related aspects of behavior in the two situations therefore provided for assessment of relationships between the previously studied structural variables and new areas of behavior. As such, these sets of ratings promised to extend understanding of the broader implications of cognitive controls, defenses, and intellectual abilities and to serve the critical function of aiding in further assessment of the realms of predictive applicability of these structural concepts. A major purpose of the study—evaluation of the generality of defense operation—was thus significantly enhanced by inclusion of these variegated ratings of over-all behavior in the two settings. As indicated in Chapters 9, 11, and 12, inclusion of these ratings, in spite of their limitations, seemed to serve each of these purposes surprisingly well. The new-found correlates of individual differences in conceptual differentiation, for example (see Chapter 12), mesh effectively with related earlier findings and generate new hypotheses concerning this aspect of cognitive control. The new evidence (see Chapter 11) concerning the predictive limitations of defenses is also deemed valuable, especially in that it complements other evidence in the study pointing to the remarkable complexity of personality organization and the conceptual pitfalls inevitably attending any assumption that a single variable or type of variable can account for much that is adaptively important in individuality.

Since the use of ratings is often decried as methodologically unsound, special note should be made here of the reasons for including this type of measure in the study. The first determinant of their use was, of course, the obvious value of assessing aspects of the children's behavior that could be assessed as easily in no other way. The second determinant was the past success of both cooperating research teams with the use of carefully formulated ratings by experienced raters or by novices who are given adequate pretraining in the intended meanings of each rating and preliminary practice in the application of each rating to observed behavior or to test protocols. This point is spelled out in greater detail in Chapter 9, which describes the observational rating variables and results of analyses of these ratings.

Some Implications of the Methods Employed in the Study

The scope of the study is exemplified by the variety of assessment methods employed. These ranged from laboratory tests involving apparently simple size judgments to ratings of each child's position, relative to the other children, on some notably global dimensions. The fact that earlier work on cognitive controls has suggested the relevance of limited groups of behaviors measurable by laboratory procedures to other aspects of personality organization is in itself intriguing. It is less than fifteen years since Klein and Schlesinger's (1949) pointed query: "Where is the perceiver in perceptual theory?" Prior to that time, most work on basic cognitive functions, including perception, was oriented toward the establishment of general laws applicable to all persons.[2] As Klein and Schlesinger so aptly foresaw, individual variations previously conceptualized as experimental "error" and otherwise ignored have proved to be meaningful individual differences reflecting cognitive structuring. It is thus worthy of a passing historical note that the present study was designed to include laboratory measures of attention-perception, concept formation, memory formation, and other aspects of cognitive behavior with the confident anticipation that individual differences in these functions are related in meaningful ways to defense mechanisms, aspects of interpersonal behavior, the general integrity and adaptive effectiveness of personality organization, and the like. The totality of structures that comprises personality organization can no longer be conceived of as a core of dynamically interrelated functions and a periphery of autochthonous functions that are largely independent of the individual's personality.

The work on cognitive controls has also contributed to a heightened awareness of the fruitless arbitrariness of conceptualizations that draw sharp lines between such aspects of cognition as memory, concept formation, attention, perception, and thinking. The work on cognitive controls, particularly controls of attention deployment (e.g., Gardner, 1959, 1961a; Gardner and Long, 1960a, b, d, 1961a, 1962b), as determinants of perception and the nature and organization of consciousness (Gardner, 1961c, 1962) has contributed its bit to the breakdown of these arbitrary distinctions. The work on relations between memory formation and perception, under the general heading of leveling-sharpening, has provided further evidence in support of this point of view. The work showing that a laboratory test of the selectiveness of perception (via the selectiveness of attention) can be used to predict individual differences in learning and recall in one type of learning situation (Gardner and Long, 1961b; Long, 1962) provides even more striking evidence in favor of this view. As pointed out by various authors, any act of perception is also an act of at-

---

[2] In a valuable paper on genetics and individuality, Hirsch (1962) has summarized earlier points of view concerning individual differences.

tention deployment, an act of memory formation, an act affected by prior memory formation, an act affected by concept formation in the form of prior memory organization, and so forth. The work on cognitive controls has helped to extend these general principles to individual differences, where they are no less relevant and even more critical to effective prediction.

A key ingredient in the gradual—and as yet quite limited—progression toward such findings lies in a persistent attempt to conceptualize the mental operations, or processes, involved in various aspects of cognitive structuring. All such process concepts are inevitably inadequate at the present time. We have no fully articulated concept of what occurs in the mind when a person categorizes things or people, when an idea or an affect is repressed, or when attention is directed here, rather than there, in a complex perceptual field. The recent advances in neurophysiology referred to earlier have brought us many steps closer to understanding of certain mental operations, but much more eludes us than falls within our grasp. In spite of these obvious limitations, attempts to conceptualize the specific kinds of cognitive operations involved in various behaviors have led to some of the discoveries in this new area of individual-difference studies and have helped to break down certain of the untenable earlier distinctions referred to above. An attempt at process analysis of performance in embedded figures tests in terms of attentional selectivity, for example, led to successful prediction of individual differences not only in learning and recall and in the experiencing of one class of illusion-producing stimuli, but also in performance in tests designed to measure "induction" (Gardner *et al.*, 1960). Analogous work directed by process hypotheses on a more general level led, in the work of Witkin, Dyk, Faterson, Goodenough, and Karp (1962), to the refinement of an original hypothesis concerning field-dependence–independence into a hypothesis concerning the articulation of certain aspects of experience that has demonstrable validity in a remarkably broad range of situations.

The general question concerning the place of cognition in personality organization is no longer "Are individual consistencies in 'peripheral' behaviors (perception *et al.*) related to personality organization?" but "What aspects of the total hierarchy of behavioral structures involved in personality organization are involved in perception (or any other aspect of cognition), under what conditions are they relevant, and what are the relationships of these structures to other structures?"

2 Outline, Subjects, Methods

Outline of the Study

THE OVER-ALL design of the study can best be glimpsed from a brief description of the methods used to assess the six major aspects of preadolescent individuality dealt with—cognitive controls, performance in the Holtzman Inkblot Test (Holtzman *et al.*, 1961), intellectual abilities, general aspects of response to a clinical testing situation, analogous aspects of response to a laboratory testing situation, and defense mechanisms and general characteristics of ego organization. Each of these areas is represented in the study by from ten to seventy-five scores or ratings for each child's behavior.

The cognitive control principles postulated thus far are represented by a large block of scores and ratings based primarily on laboratory tests of such basic aspects of cognition as attention, perception, memory formation, and categorizing. The cognitive control concepts and the measurement methods employed are discussed in Chapter 3. The control test performances of boys versus girls, younger versus older children, and the present sample of children versus samples of adults tested earlier are discussed in Chapters 4 and 5. Chapter 6 contains descriptions of the cognitive control factors obtained for the present sample as compared to those obtained for earlier samples of adults.

Scores for performance in the recently developed Holtzman Inkblot Test were included as the second block of data (Chapter 7) because of the valuable information this procedure yields concerning responses to a group of inkblots designed to include systematic variations of form, color, shading, and so forth.

The third block of data (Chapter 8) consists of subtest scores for the

Wechsler Intelligence Scale for Children, which are used to obtain indices of two major aspects of intellectual ability.

The fourth and fifth blocks of data (Chapter 9) consist of seventy-five ratings of the children's behavior in the clinical testing situation and twenty-three ratings of their behavior in the laboratory setting.

Assessments of defense mechanisms and general aspects of ego organization (Chapters 10–11) comprise the sixth block of data.

Differences between the performances of boys and girls and younger and older children are considered in detail in the chapters dealing with blocks two through six. These chapters also contain detailed results of the methods applied to reduce each of these blocks of variables to its major dimensions.

Interrelations among scores representing the child's position on the major behavioral dimensions represented by each of the six blocks of data, plus a few additional variables, were explored in a subsequent analysis (Chapter 12). The exploratory final analysis was designed to provide the most general view possible in this study of over-all patternings of personality organization at preadolescence in this subculture. The factors yielded by this final analysis thus represent higher strata of the hierarchy of personality organization than the factors or scores representing more limited areas of behavior.

The availability of extensive longitudinal study material on approximately half the sample made it possible to select pairs of boys and girls high and low in general ego strength for case studies of personality development (Chapters 13–14). It is in these case studies that the reader will find included the variables considered in most minute detail with respect to individual children. It may be here that the meaningfulness of the factors and factor scores will be most apparent to the reader unfamiliar with such approaches to individual differences. The fact that the preadolescent results for individual children appear not only to mesh with their unique histories but also to reveal or clarify additional facets of their personality organizations seemed to lend further credence to the usefulness of the concepts and methods that formed the framework of the study.

Major findings of the study are summarized and their implications discussed in Chapter 15. Some of the major types of additional information necessary for improved understanding of personality development are outlined there.

The Subjects of the Study

The subjects of the study were sixty Midwestern children (twenty-nine boys, thirty-one girls) aged nine to thirteen. The great majority of the children were born in Topeka, Kansas. A few were born in smaller towns nearby. Topeka is a rapidly growing community whose population has increased from about 90,000 in the years of the children's births to about 130,000 at the time this preadolescent study was performed. Forty-five of the children have spent all their years in Topeka or its environs. Fourteen of the additional children were living in roughly comparable Midwestern communities at the time of the study. The one remaining child returned to Topeka from a larger city in Michigan to participate in the study.

Twenty-eight of the children (fourteen boys, fourteen girls) had been seen by members of the longitudinal study group in infancy and at preschool age (see, e.g., Escalona and Heider, 1959). Two of the clinical tests of the present study (Thematic Apperception Test and Rorschach) were included in the preschool battery. During the latency period, twenty of these children (ten boys, ten girls) were also given the WISC. The thirty-two remaining children had not been tested or observed since infancy. Participation of all sixty children in the present study was arranged by a member of the longitudinal study staff. Participation in the study was voluntary, and no fees were paid to subjects.

All but one of the sixty children were living with at least one natural parent at the time of the study. Twenty-four boys and twenty-seven girls had lived uninterruptedly with both natural parents from birth to the time of the present study. Four boys and one girl whose mothers had remarried following divorce or death of the father were living with their mothers and stepfathers. One girl was living with her mother, who had been divorced but who had not remarried. The mothers of two girls and one boy had died prior to the study. One of these girls was living with her father and stepmother. The other girl was living in her second foster home. The boy was living with his father, who had remarried but had subsequently been divorced.

Two pairs of brothers, two pairs of sisters, and one brother-sister pair were included in the sample.

The families of forty-eight children (twenty-three boys, twenty-six girls) attend Protestant churches, the families of twelve (six boys, six girls) attend the Catholic church (see Chapter 12).

The boys and girls of the sample were closely matched in age and IQ, number of children in the family, and birth order, and were not significantly different in social status.[1] The average WISC IQ is in the bright normal range, the dispersion from average to superior. The occupational levels of the fathers ranged from laborer to professional.

Ecological Factors Affecting the Sample:
The Plains States Subculture as a Developmental Context

The sixty children of the present study had spent all, or nearly all of their lives in or near Topeka, Kansas, an area that represents a synthesis of the "Midwestern" and "Post-Frontier" subcultures. A few of the children had reached puberty, a number seemed to be anticipating this great change in their life cycle in various ways, and a number of others seemed to exemplify the latency syndrome described by Anna Freud. The specific referents of anticipations concerning puberty varied considerably from child to child. Common examples included doubts and fears based upon past failures, anxiety about growing up, depression over the imminent loss of the protective mantle of childhood, specific anxieties concerning the change from an elementary school to a larger and more socially complex and demanding junior high school, anxiety about unresolved problems concerning sexual and personal identity, and the like. All of these, and a number of other problems and anticipated problems, are apparent in one or another of the sets of test protocols and observations included in the study.

As a group, these children's position in the life cycle—which could be characterized as a somewhat apprehensive stance toward incipient change—may have contributed to the impression of behavioral inhibition and affective constriction referred to earlier in terms of the kinds of developmental crises outlined by Erikson. It could be, however, that mild constriction is an especially prominent form of reaction to impending adolescence in children of this subculture. In view of the distrust of drive forces implied by this tendency toward constriction, adolescence may be a particularly frightening prospect to children of this subculture. Their group identity includes strong moral and religious values (with associated emphasis on the goodness and badness of various behaviors), an almost defensive emphasis on the virtues of hard work in the form of useful activity, a distrust of passivity and intimacy, and a related tendency to overvalue interpersonal distance and independence.

[1] The socioeconomic status index included dwelling area, father's occupation, and source of income (see Chapter 12).

Among the other outstanding features of the subculture from which the sample was drawn are two referred to by Barker and Barker (1961) in describing a smaller community in the Topeka area: the importance of the average person to the others in his community; and (p. 474) the "egalitarianism of the different age groups. . . ." Although these take slightly different forms in Topeka than in the community described by Barker and Barker, they are nonetheless significant. In addition to the partial leveling of class boundaries attributable to its post-frontier status, Topeka is small enough so that the importance of the functions performed by persons engaged in different occupations is more apparent—and the individual involved more highly valued—than in a metropolitan area. The special emphasis upon individuality and the recency of gross social mobility dependent upon industriousness, cleverness, and related factors also contributes to this appreciation of the individual adult and the individual child. Parents of this area seem, in fact, greatly concerned about the individuality of their children and to value the concept that each person should be dealt with as a unique entity.

It should be noted here that there are gross differences in socioeconomic status in the families of the children and that these differences are clearly evident in the organization of the social groups in which the families are involved. The interesting thing is that rich and poor alike value the notion that an individual adult or child should be judged on his own merits. The contrast between the naturalness with which these children relate themselves to authority figures (in spite of their general inhibitedness and tendency toward conformance) and the frightened hyperconformance of children in a more sternly authoritarian subculture was dramatically evident in a recent comparative study of performance in a free categorizing test by a subgroup of these preadolescent children and a group of preadolescents in Guadalajara, Mexico (Mercado, Diaz Guerrero, and Gardner, 1963). It is entirely possible, however, that children of another United States subculture, in which conformance is less valued, would show even greater effective autonomy and independence in such test situations.

Our statements about the subcultural emphasis on individuality may seem incongruous in the light of our statements concerning inhibition, conservativism, and conformity. This discrepancy appears, however, to be a major feature of the children's milieu. The individual is highly regarded, but he is evaluated within the limited framework described above. Carrying one's individuality to the extreme is consistently frowned upon; moral and political values are remarkably homogeneous; codes of behavior are, in general, rather rigidly defined, and a tendency toward "black-white" thinking concerning standards of behavior is apparent in the milieu as a whole. Expressive freedom is thus rather firmly controlled as to acceptable forms. In terms of ethical and political beliefs, the prevailing ideational setting is saturated with the "status quo" and yields minimal rewards for rapid or extensive change. The subcultural tendency toward an anti-intellectual bias is also apparent in these children's milieu, although to a lesser degree in this sample than in the subculture as a whole.

Although these remarks about the subcultural milieu may reflect some of its most outstanding characteristics, there are gross differences between families in each of these variables. In addition, there are subgroup differences in conformity and related variables that are associated with religious affiliation. Expressions of these differences consistently impressed the examiners in certain aspects of test performance and in the quality of extra-test relationships. These latter differences are also evident in the quantitative analysis of over-all cognitive organization reported in Chapter 12.

The general features of the subculture, which seem to typify these children's post-frontier environment, are offered primarily as major impressions only. Documentation of such points was not a subject of this study but could well be an additional central focus of more comprehensive approaches to personality organization at preadolescence.

The Administration of Tests and Rating Procedures

Fifty-six of the children were given the laboratory tests within one month of the clinical tests. For two children, the interval was about four months, for one child, six months, and for the remaining child, eight months. Observations of the children's behavior during the three hours of laboratory testing were made by an independent rater, who was situated so that she could not observe the subject's test performance per se (see Chapter 9). This rater evaluated aspects of behavior overlapping, in part, with those evaluated by the clinical tester.

The ratings of major defense mechanisms and general aspects of cognitive organization were made by an experienced rater (RWG) in a blind analysis of the typed WISC, TAT, and Rorschach protocols. At the time of these assessments, this rater had no knowledge of the children's performance in any of the other situations. The variables and the method of assessment employed are described in detail in Chapter 10.

The Choice of Variables for Statistical Analyses

Several of the groups of scores and ratings selected for use in the present study were drawn from larger clusters of relevant variables used in earlier studies of adults. In the case of the cognitive control dimensions assessed, tests were selected to provide the best scores available at the time of the study to represent all the major dimensions of control explored to that time (see Chapter 3). The seventy-five ratings based on the children's behavior in the clinical testing situation were chosen from the much larger number of preschool ratings made on twenty-eight of the children. Selection of ratings was based on the following criteria: (1) the feasibility of adequate rating on the basis of observations in the clinical testing session alone; (2) the adequacy and usefulness of each rating in the earlier studies; and (3) the presumed relevance of each rating to the other variables included in the present study (see Chapter 9). Most of the twenty-three independent ratings made on the basis of behavior in the laboratory were subsequently chosen to match ratings of performance in the clinical testing situation. A few additional ratings were also employed because of their special relevance to behavior in the laboratory.

The selection of ratings of major defenses and general aspects of ego organization was dictated by the psychoanalytic literature on these aspects of personality organization and the feasibility of performing each of these ratings on the basis of performance in the WISC, TAT, and Rorschach (see Chapter 10).

The scores used for the Wechsler Intelligence Scales for Children (Chapter 8) and the Holtzman Inkblot Test (Chapter 7) were those employed by the authors of these tests. In the latter case, slight modifications were dictated by the available literature on these scores.

Methods of Data Analysis

Means and sigmas of all major scores and ratings were compared (by means of t tests or analysis of variance) for boys versus girls, younger versus older children,[2] and, whenever possible, all the children versus

---

[2] The group of younger children consisted of thirteen boys and seventeen girls, the group of older children of sixteen boys and fourteen girls. The interaction of sex and age does not even approach significance ($p < .50$), so that the slight imbalance of boys and girls in these groups was assumed to have had little, if any, effect upon the results reported in subsequent chapters.

adults tested in earlier studies.[3] The other data analyses were performed for the entire sample. The decision not to present analyses of patterns of individual consistency (by means of correlation and factor analysis) separately for boys and girls in the cases of all blocks of data was dictated by the unreliability of such analyses with small samples, the exploratory nature of the study, and the striking fact that preliminary analyses of correlations for the sexes separately, among variables included in each of the six major blocks of data, revealed a significant number of different correlations in the case of one block only—the ratings of defense mechanisms and general characteristics of ego organization. The matrices for boys and girls were not significantly different in the case of the cognitive control scores and ratings, HIT scores, WISC scores, clinical ratings, or laboratory ratings.

The analysis of differences between boys and girls in the correlations among the defense and general ratings showed that six (13 per cent) of the forty-five correlations were significantly different, whereas two or three such differences would be expected by chance. Intercorrelations among these ratings are therefore presented for the sexes separately, as well as combined, in Chapter 11.

The lack of sex differences in five of the six blocks of data was an asset to effective interpretation of the results of the study in that nearly all the data could be analyzed for the entire sample. Correlation matrices and factor analyses based on samples of thirty *S*s have proved valuable when used cautiously in initial exploratory studies (e.g., Gardner *et al.*, 1959) but are grossly inadequate for the kinds of problems concerning personality organization posed in the present study. The total sample of sixty boys and girls can, in fact, be considered a minimum number for the achievement of reliable results. In the case of several of the major blocks of data, especially the ratings of behavior in the clinic, when the numbers of variables were greater than the total sample size warranted, they were reduced to appropriately small numbers by rational methods before correlations and factor analyses were attempted.

The general absence of significant differences between the sexes in correlations within five types of data also serves as a caution against too ready acceptance of apparent sex differences in behavioral patterning. This group of findings is among the most significant results of the present

[3] The pooled samples of adults tested earlier were generally quite large. The smallest subsample used in any individual analysis was thirty. The largest sample used was 362.

study and has important implications for developmental studies. Even in the case of the defense mechanisms and general characteristics of ego organization—in which sex differences in the patterning of variables would seem most likely—the number of correlations significantly different for boys and girls is quite small.

Each major block of data (i.e., control principle scores and ratings, WISC scores, HIT scores, ratings of behavior in the clinical testing situation, ratings of behavior in the laboratory testing situation, ratings of defense mechanisms and general characteristics of the ego) was reduced to its major dimensions by factor or cluster analysis. This approach was dictated by the obvious unlikelihood that the number of behavioral variables accounting for the common variance in any of the blocks of data was as large as the number of scores or ratings included. In the case of the cognitive control scores, factor analysis also made it possible to compare the behavioral dimensions involved in preadolescents' performances with those involved in adult performances in the same procedures, as indicated by results of earlier studies.

In each of the five factor analyses, the highest correlation was inserted in the diagonal cell as a communality estimate. This choice of diagonal-cell values is compatible with the conservative approach to factor analysis adopted throughout the study. The principal axis method of factoring was applied to the five blocks of data meeting the basic criteria for this type of reduction to major dimensions (e.g., logical and statistical independence of variables). Factoring was terminated when the estimated common variance was accounted for. The factors obtained in each case were rotated by the normal varimax method (Kaiser, 1958). This rotational method, which produces orthogonal (i.e., uncorrelated) factors, was employed in preference to a method yielding oblique (i.e., correlated) factors because of the unreliability of oblique solutions with relatively small samples. Use of the normal varimax method thus represented a conservative approach to factor structure and relations among factors appropriate to the sample size and the exploratory nature of much of the present study.

In the case of the defense and general ratings, some of which are presumed to be correlated (i.e., are not logically independent), although separate sets of cognitive operations are involved, factor analysis was obviously not an appropriate method. A clustering technique was therefore employed, which led to the selection of ratings to represent major clusters.

Factor scores were computed for each factor obtained for each block of data. These factor scores were weighted linear combinations of all the scores or ratings in each matrix in standard-score form. The matrices of beta weights used were obtained by post-multiplying each matrix of factor loadings by the inverse of the correlation matrix. This method produces the most accurate factor scores for the method of factoring used throughout the study (see Harman, 1960, pp. 228–348). These factor scores, with a few additional scores, were employed in the analysis of individual consistencies linking the six types of data that is described in Chapter 12. Factor scores were also obtained as measures of individual differences in the factors yielded by this final analysis. These factor scores were employed in the analyses of case study material presented in Chapters 13 and 14. It should be noted here that the principal axis factors are uncorrelated, but the factor scores are not necessarily uncorrelated. Principal axis factors were obtained in this study so that only the common variance in each block of data would be dealt with at the factor level. In some cases, this can result in artifactual correlations between factor scores (this artifact is essentially attributable to the use of an estimate of score communality in the diagonal cells of the correlation matrices, rather than 1.00, as would be done in one of the two principal components methods). In general, these artifactual correlations between factor scores within the various blocks of data were low and apparently of minor importance in determining the nature of the factors derived in the final analysis of relations between factor scores and additional scores described in Chapter 12.[4]

Brief Summary of the Nature of Factor Analysis in Such Studies

For the reader unfamiliar with factor analysis as a means of reducing a correlation matrix to major dimensions of individual consistency, a brief descriptive summary may be helpful. The essential rationale for this use of factor analysis is straightforward and basically simple. In the present study, a set of selected scores or ratings from any one block of data was first intercorrelated. That is, a statistical index of the degree of association between each score or rating and each other score or rating was obtained. The matrix of intercorrelations was then factor analyzed.

---

[4] Detailed tables of all the results referred to in this book can be obtained from the American Documentation Institute. Order Document 9565 from the Chief, Photo-duplication Service, Library of Congress, Washington, D.C. 20540, ADI Auxiliary Publications Project, remitting $12.50 for photoprints, or $4.25 for 35 mm. microfilm.

That is, a mathematical analysis was performed that yielded an appropriately smaller number of dimensions than the original number of scores or ratings and that could appropriately reproduce the original correlation matrix. These dimensions were then "rotated" in order to satisfy certain criteria (i.e., simple structure) and to aid in their psychological interpretation. In the present study, rotations were performed "analytically," that is, by a purely mathematical method involving no subjectivity on the part of the experimenters.[5]

Each score or rating included has a "loading" on each factor. The loading indicates the correlation of the score with the factor. A test score or rating that is an excellent measure of a factor will have a high loading. A score or rating that is less effective, or a score determined by two or more factors, will have a lower loading. If a test score is determined by other behavioral factors, its loading may be negligible. The uninitiated reader may understand the meaning of a rotated factor more easily if it is explained that, under ordinary circumstances, he could anticipate at least the major factors to be derived from a correlation matrix by inspecting the matrix for clusters of intercorrelated scores or ratings. If he found that six scores were correlated substantially with each other but with none of the other scores, he could confidently anticipate that a factor would emerge representing this cluster. The factor, incidentally, would be a more appropriate index of the individual differences involved than the individual scores because it represents the dimension of individual consistency producing the correlations among the scores. Factor analysis is thus a mathematical method for clustering scores that have common elements. A "factor" is a dimension of individual differences on which each individual in a study can be placed. In the present study, factor scores were computed for each child for each factor derived from each block of scores or ratings. It was these factor scores, plus several important additional scores, that were factor analyzed in the final analysis in order to provide the broadest possible glimpse of individual consistencies in the entire sample of children.

[5] The slight adjustment of the WISC factors obtained by this method (Chapter 8) is a minor exception to this rule.

3 Cognitive Control Structures and Their Measurement at Preadolescence

THIS CHAPTER contains brief descriptions of each of the cognitive control concepts employed and the methods of assessment used in the present study. Relevant literature on cognitive controls is referred to, but no attempt is made here to comment on all the studies that involve, or that have been purported to involve, these individual differences. Some of the reports omitted are valuable but not directly relevant to the central issues of conceptualization and measures. Others involve less-than-adequate measurement of controls and other features of no direct relevance to the present study.

Earlier studies of individual consistencies in adult samples, some of which are summarized in this chapter, led to the postulation of a number of dimensional principles of cognitive control. Individual differences on these dimensions represent consistent strategies of executing particular intentions under particular classes of stimulus conditions (see Gardner *et al.*, 1959, chap. i). One group of the earlier studies referred to in this chapter was focused on the situational generality of particular control principles. Other groups were focused on relations between pairs of controls, e.g., the leveling-sharpening and field-articulation controls as determinants of different facets of response to special size estimation tests. Still other studies were focused on relations among several control principles and among these and intellectual abilities. Understanding of some of the controls and their consequences in cognition also required the strictly experimental studies referred to at various points. Additional studies have dealt with such related questions as cultural differences in the dimension of cognitive control called conceptual differentiation (Mercado *et al.*, 1963). A study has also been performed to assess the reliability of criterion scores for several cognitive controls. Earlier indications of high intra-test reliabilities were supplemented in that study by satisfactory reliability coefficients for a three-year period, in spite of the fact that a number of the subjects had experienced gross changes of life situation (Gardner and Long, 1960e).

Contrary to anticipation, major revisions of the adult test procedures were not required in order to elicit effective participation and response by the preadolescent children of the present study. Pilot studies revealed that children of this age group could perform meaningfully and with a high degree of task involvement in all of the procedures used earlier with adults. Because of the obvious advantages of using identical methods for adults and children, procedural variations were kept to a minimum. The size estimation tests employed were given exactly as they were to adults tested earlier. This was also true of the sorting tests employed to measure conceptual differentiation, as well as most of the other procedures. Among the few minor variations in procedure was the practice of prompting the children, when necessary, to write down a size judgment of each of the squares in the Schematizing Test, and, in one case, writing down the responses of the child, who called them out.

The experimenter who administered the laboratory tests of cognitive controls reported the consistent impression that he was testing "little adults." In spite of the frustrations the children inevitably met in some of the relatively difficult procedures (e.g., the Embedded Figures Test), the experimenter was impressed by the degree of ego involvement, persistence, and poise shown by most of the children in the laboratory procedures. The one or two obvious exceptions were children who were independently rated quite low on ego strength (see Chapter 10). Even these children, however, were able to participate in the laboratory tests of cognitive controls in a meaningful way. Special care was taken, however, to insure that each child fully understood what he was to do in each of the procedures. The fact that all the laboratory tests were individually administered made this a minor problem for an experienced administrator, but could have been a serious problem if the group tests used as alternate measures in some studies of adults had been employed.

Leveling-Sharpening

When an individual perceives sequential stimuli that he experiences as similar, each new stimulus interacts with the memory matrix representing the preceding stimuli. Gestalt psychologists (e.g., Köhler, 1923;

Lauenstein, 1933) have referred to this interaction as a mutual "assimilation" among perceptual processes and memory traces. This kind of assimilation presumably alters both the perception of the new stimulus and the memories of relevant earlier stimuli in the direction of greater similarity. It should be emphasized that this kind of interaction occurs only if the person experiences a new stimulus as relevant to the sequence of experiences. Assimilative interaction also occurs only when the sequential stimuli fall within a limited range of objective similarity. Beyond this limited range, contrast effects occur. Some of the most intriguing unanswered questions in this area of individual differences concern relations between assimilation effects and contrast effects of the kind dealt with extensively by Helson (1964) in his development of adaptation-level theory.

Studies of individual consistencies in assimilation were begun by Holzman and Klein (Holzman, 1954; Holzman and Klein, 1954) and referred to by them as individual differences in "leveling-sharpening." Levelers are those who show relatively great assimilation, sharpeners those who show relatively little. This use of the term "leveling-sharpening" is, of course, distinctly different from earlier uses by Wulf (1922) and others. The Holzman and Klein studies seemed to show consistent individual differences in performance in the Schematizing Test (a procedure described below in which squares gradually increasing in size are presented in a natural and two random orders, following an earlier procedure developed by Hollingworth, 1913) and performance in visual, auditory, and kinesthetic time-error tests. A subsequent study (Gardner et al., 1959) included a kinesthetic time-error test and seemed to confirm the earlier result.

Studies by Smith and Klein (1953) and Gardner et al. (1959) have suggested that levelers tend to show "cumulative" patterns of interference in the Color-Word Test described later in this chapter. This finding may be referable to levelers' greater difficulty with tasks requiring rapid shifts of set.

Recent studies of leveling-sharpening have been focused on the implications of these individual consistencies for performance in learning and recall tests. In one study (Gardner and Long, 1960c) it was shown that performances in the Schematizing Test, used as a criterion measure of leveling-sharpening, allow prediction of the nature and number of errors in a classical learning situation involving highly similar words. In a second study, Holzman and Gardner (1960) showed that sharpeners are superior to levelers in recall of a story heard years earlier and not intentionally committed to memory. In a third study (Gardner and Lohrenz, 1960), groups of relatively extreme sharpeners and levelers were shown to be remarkably different in the number of elements accurately recalled and the number of contaminated elements produced when a story was passed from one member to another of each group in the fashion employed in "rumor" experiments. The story produced by the last member of the chain of levelers contained many fewer accurate elements and significantly more contaminated elements than did the story produced by the last member of the sharpening chain. In another recent study, Gardner and Long (1960e) demonstrated the reliability of Schematizing Test performances over a period of three years, in spite of the fact that the nature of the Schematizing Test precludes fully effective retesting.

It should be noted here that a series of attempts in the first author's laboratory to show relationships between individual consistencies in leveling-sharpening and individual consistencies in visual and kinesthetic aftereffects failed to produce any indication of the hypothesized relationship, possibly because of the fact that kinesthetic and visual aftereffects, at least as measured by the procedures used by Wertheimer (1955), are not individually consistent across these modalities (Gardner, 1961b). In addition, aftereffects in both modalities were shown to be unreliable over a period of six months. These studies were undertaken because time errors and related phenomena could presumably be explained as a function of either assimilation theory or Köhler's satiation theory (see, e.g., Köhler and Adams, 1958).

Gardner and Lohrenz (1961) recently showed that intensity of attention is one determinant of assimilation among sequentially presented members of pairs of visual designs, and among the pairs as well. This finding suggests that the level of activation research summarized by Duffy (1962) may be relevant to performance in the Schematizing Test, because of the presumed relationship between level of arousal and intensity of attention in the waking state.

A series of recent unpublished studies by Gardner and Lohrenz is focused in part on further exploration of relations between leveling-sharpening and field-articulation as determinants of learning and recall. These unpublished studies also include a considerable variety of forms of the Schematizing Test. It will be obvious to the reader that the original form of the test, employed in the present study, can be improved upon in several ways as a measure of assimilation. For example, having *S*s judge the sizes of sequentially presented squares in terms of inches introduces individual differences in number schemata that are irrelevant to measurement of assimilation. Recent studies have also included other percentages of increment in the stimulus materials employed. In the original Schematizing Test, the increments in the lengths of one side in the series of fourteen squares were approximately 20 per cent. In one recent version of the test, these differences were reduced to 14 per cent in an attempt to eliminate contrast effects in the responses of a few subjects in each of the earlier samples. One more refined form of the Schematizing Test developed in these recent studies employs these 14-per-cent increments in stimulus sizes and also provides for still more effective control of the visibility of the background on which the squares of light are shown. It is obvious, of course, that without such experimental control, the subject can judge the square sizes by reference to the size of the background (which has always been all but eliminated in this test by presenting the white squares in a completely dark room). In this series of recent studies, experimental control for the enhancement of brightness that occurs with increase in the sizes of projected squares of light was also added. Other changes in these still experimental procedures are also relevant to interpretation of the results of the original procedure used in the present study. These include the transition from response in the form of numbers to response in the form of marks made by the subject upon lines, to indicate the apparent size of each of the squares.

In spite of the flaws in the original Schematizing Test procedure, it has seemed to produce meaningful assimilation scores for adult subjects. In several studies (e.g., Gardner *et al.*, 1959, 1960), this dimension of cognitive control has appeared to be predictably independent of the field-articulation principle and the other principles included in the present study.

Among the more interesting recent findings concerning leveling-sharpening is Livant's (1962) demonstration that levelers show more primitive forms of simplification of grammatical structure in the recall of two kinds of verbal material.

A number of studies purportedly dealing with leveling-sharpening (e.g., Berkowitz, 1957; Lutzky and Schmeidler, 1963; Santostefano, 1964) as defined in the earlier reports referred to above have not included the Schematizing Test or have involved variations in this test procedure that could have gross effects on performance. Although these studies are valuable in their own right, their relevance to the concept of leveling-sharpening as defined by Holzman and Klein cannot yet be determined.

The Schematizing Test

This test has been described in several previous reports (e.g., Gardner *et al.*, 1959). The subject, sitting in a completely darkened room, judges the sizes of 14 squares ranging in size from approximately 1 to 14 inches in a preordained sequence of 150 judgments. At the beginning of the test, the five smallest sizes are presented in ascending order, then in two random orders. Each stimulus is presented for three seconds, with an eight-second interval in which the subject writes down his estimate of the size of that square in inches. Following presentation of the first series of stimuli in this fashion, the smallest stimulus is dropped, and the sixth stimulus in order of size is added. These five stimuli are then presented in the same way as the first five. This procedure is repeated until the range of fourteen square sizes has been traversed.

Major scores for this test have included a ranking-accuracy score, which consists of the percentage of correct ranks attained by the subject in the entire test when ranking is considered within each subgroup of five stimuli (see Gardner *et al.*, 1959). A second major score, the increment-error score, has recently been improved upon by development of a lag score (Gardner and Long, 1960b) consisting of the difference between the slope of the approximately straight line fitted to the logarithms of the subject's mean judgments for the ten series and the slope of the straight line fitted to the logarithms the actual stimulus sizes. The increment-error score used earlier is heavily dependent upon the mean of the first series, which careful inspection of earlier data indicated may well be the most unstable series for most subjects.

In previous samples of adults, the ranking-accuracy score has been correlated to a modest, but significant, degree with the increment-error and lag scores, which are highly correlated. Presumably, each score represents the effects of assimilation upon the perceived sizes of the stimuli. It is clear, however, that the accuracy score also involves other determinants. The lag score thus seems more justifiable as a measure of assimilation.

Extensiveness of Scanning

The original hypothesis concerning individual consistencies in extensiveness of scanning arose out of observations of individual consistencies in constant errors in several tests (e.g., Schlesinger, 1954; Gardner *et al.*, 1959, 1960). Recent studies of extensiveness of scanning have been focused primarily upon extensiveness of scanning per se, in the form of the number of looks at standard and comparison stimuli and a variety of other measures of scanning behavior in a cluster of size estimation tests. In these recent studies, apparent magnitude was presumed to be, in part at least, a consequence of extensiveness of scanning. These studies include a direct test of Piaget's centration hypothesis (Gardner and Long, 1962a). As pointed out by Gardner (1959), Piaget's theory of the relationship between attention deployment and the apparent relative magnitudes of stimuli involves, among other variables, the relative sizes of the stimuli, as well as the pattern and duration of cumulative centrations upon them. Additional studies by Gardner and Long (1960a, b) concerning centration effects showed clearly that standard stimuli tend to be overestimated as compared to variable comparison stimuli in the case of the inverted-T illusion and a comparable illusion involving reversed-L figures. Gardner (1961a) demonstrated a relationship between constant error in size estimation tests and such errors of the standard, which he experimentally disentangled from the illusion effect.

Presumed consequences of scanning strategies suggested by these earlier studies were explored in greater detail in two recent studies by Gardner and Long (1962a, b). In the first of these studies, electronic recordings and visual observations of eye movements provided detailed measures of a variety of aspects of the actual scanning behavior of subjects in various size estimation tests. Remarkable individual consistencies were observed in the scanning strategies of female adults. Extremely extensive adult scanners were also shown to use the defense mechanisms of isolation or projection to a greater degree than limited scanners. In the size estimation test employed by Gardner (1959, 1961a), which was also used in the earlier studies of apparent magnitude referred to above, a predicted relationship was found between extensiveness of scanning and subjects' constant errors in judgments of complex stimuli. In addition, it was shown that this relationship does not obtain in judgments of simpler stimuli that induce smaller numbers of interacting illusions.

Silverman, who has discussed the potential importance of cognitive controls of attention to theory and research on the broad group of disorders called "schizophrenia" (Silverman, 1964a), has recently shown that extensive scanning, inferred from size estimation performances, is more characteristic of paranoid than nonparanoid schizophrenics (Silverman, 1964b).

In the present study, visual observation was used to obtain several key scanning measures isolated in the studies by Gardner and Long. By employing two experimenters, one of whom operated a telegraph key attached to a moving tape, it was possible to record the total judgment time (i.e., the time in seconds between the subject's opening his eyes to begin adjustment of the comparison stimulus and his closing his eyes to indicate satisfaction with his judgment); the number of looks at the standard stimulus; the redundant scanning time (i.e., the time he spent "checking" his judgment after his final adjustment of the comparison stimulus); and some of the other major scores in the cluster so clearly indicating a syndrome of scanning consistencies in Gardner and Long's studies of adults.

Size Estimation Test I

This test was identical to a size estimation test with 40 mm. disks used in earlier studies of adults, except that two judgments rather than four were required (the very high reliabilities found in the preceding studies of adults suggested this time-saving reduction). For the first judgment, the comparison light circle was set 10 mm. below the size of the standard, i.e., at 30 mm. For the second judgment, it was set 10 mm. above, at 50 mm. The standard (i.e., constant) stimuli used were the gray, heavy gray, and black disks used by Gardner and Long and employed in several earlier studies.

The scanning scores used were mean judgment time (i.e., the mean time between opening the eyes and completion of the last adjustment); mean number of centrations upon the standard stimulus during judgment time (in this test, almost exactly equal to mean number of centrations upon the comparison stimulus); mean time per centration during judgment time; mean number of adjustment stops; and mean redundant scanning time (i.e., the time between the last adjustment stop and closing the eyes). Mean constant error was computed for the two judgments of each disk and the total of six judgments of the three disks.

Size Estimation Test II

The second scanning study by Gardner and Long (1962b) indicated that scanning scores for judgments of a 50 mm. black disk under the conditions of Size Estimation Test I are significantly correlated with scanning scores for a similar test in which the stimuli produce various illusions, and therefore bring into play the independent field-articulation control principle, relevant to the selectivity of attention. In view of this fact, the second type of test was also included in the present study, as Size Estimation Test II. The scanning scores were presumed to represent the extensiveness of scanning control principle. The illusion-effect scores were presumed to represent the field-articulation control principle. The study by Gardner and Long seemed to delineate with a high degree of specificity the different effects of the two control principles upon apparent magnitude in such situations.

The stimuli judged in the experimental conditions of this test were a 30 mm. circle enclosed in a 45 mm. circle; a 45 mm. circle enclosing outward-pointing arrows; and the 45 mm. circle enclosing the 30 mm. circle. The first and last judgments are affected by the Delboeuf illusion. The stimuli were drawn in black India ink on white cardboard backgrounds four and one-half inches (horizontal) by nine inches (vertical). One ascending and one descending judgment were made of each stimulus from starting points 10 mm. below and above the actual size.

Similar control judgments were made subsequently of the 30 and 45 mm. circles.

The illusion-effect scores were residual scores consisting of the difference between each S's actual score and his predicted score. The predicted score was based on the regression of constant error for that figure in the experimental condition on constant error in the control condition.

The scanning scores for the control and experimental conditions were the same as those derived from Test I.

Field-Articulation

An extensive array of studies of individual consistencies in the articulation of experience was recently summarized by Witkin *et al.* (1962). This dimension of individual differences is characterized by a remarkable degree of situational generality and seems to have many of the qualities of a capacity or ability. This hypothesis is supported by the findings of Gardner and his associates (1960) and others indicating its intimate relationship to the intellectual ability factor of "flexibility of closure" earlier defined by Thurstone, which was explored in a large group of earlier studies of intellectual abilities (see, e.g., the summary by French, 1951). A study by Goodenough and Karp (1961) confirmed the corollary anticipation that criterion field-articulation scores are correlated with Block Design, Object Assembly, and Picture Completion subtest scores of Wechsler's Intelligence Scales for Children.

Studies of individual consistencies in field-articulation performed in

The Menninger Foundation laboratories have been focused primarily upon relations to intellectual abilities; prediction of response to illusions requiring selective attention to relevant versus irrelevant stimuli; and prediction of individual consistencies in learning and recall situations requiring selective attention to relevant versus irrelevant stimuli. Gardner and Long (1961b) and more recently Long (1962) have demonstrated a relationship between performance in Witkin's Embedded Figures Test and both learning and recall in classical memory situations employing similar stimuli. It is the high degree of similarity, apparently, that produces the "competition" for attention among the stimuli, which are, of course, differentially relevant when the subject is asked to learn and recall particular subgroups of stimuli in particular orders, and so forth. These recent studies have thus clarified the ambiguous results of earlier attempts to predict from Embedded Figures Test performances to performances in learning and recall situations (e.g., the study of Gollin and Baron, 1954).

Messick and Fritzky (1963) recently reported results suggesting two correlated dimensions of analytic approach to stimuli. One of these involves the articulation of discrete elements; the other involves the articulation of figural forms. A third aspect of analytical approach, which involves the use of background information, was correlated with the other two. Performance in a group embedded figures test was related to element articulation in learning of designs tests. Performance in the group embedded figures test and scores for element articulation and use of background information were correlated with a group of speed scores for cognitive interference tasks and control tasks.

Among other recent studies of field-dependence, or field-articulation, two by Karp stand out. Karp (1963) showed the independence of field-articulation from the ability to overcome or ignore distraction per se. Karp, Poster, and Goodman (1963) confirmed the earlier findings of Witkin, Karp, and Goodenough (1959) that alcoholic women are less capable of field-articulation than nonalcoholics.

Hustmyer and Karnes (1964) recently reported a relationship between speed of finding embedded figures and the number of spontaneous GSR fluctuations per unit of time in a small group of college students.

Crandall and Sinkeldam (1964) have provided evidence that performance in the Embedded Figures Test is related to achievement motivation and behavior.

It is important to note here that Vandenberg (1962) has recently demonstrated significant hereditary determination of performances in criterion tests of field-articulation. This is not surprising, in view of the fact that the dimension has many of the characteristics of a capacity or ability, and that intellectual abilities have long been known to have significant genetic components. These findings are nevertheless of considerable importance for understanding the origins of this dimension of cognitive control, and they point to the need for further studies to clarify the relationships reported by Witkin *et al.* (1962) between the encouragement of exploration by mothers and the degree of field-articulation by children. A genetic relationship may be involved in the findings reported and could in part account for results attributed to the mother's behavior.

A Neurophysiological Rationale for Performance in Tests of Selective Attention

In field-articulation tests such as the Embedded Figures Test and the Concealed Figures Test (described below), and also Size Estimation Test II, the essential requirement is that the subject attend selectively to one set of stimuli while actively inhibiting attention and response to other stimuli in the field. In the two embedded figures tests, the subject is required to find a simple figure viewed earlier (now remembered) in a complex figure containing irrelevant lines which make it difficult to isolate the simple figure perceptually. The senior author and his associates (e.g., Gardner, 1959; Gardner *et al.*, 1959, 1960; Gardner, 1961a; Gardner and Long, 1961a) have discussed individual differences in the ability to perform such tasks in terms of selective attention. The neurophysiological findings of Hernández-Peón and his associates referred to in Chapter 1, plus the findings of several others (e.g., Lindsley, Bowden, and Magoun, 1949; Moruzzi and Magoun, 1949; Jasper, 1958), make it possible to describe selective attention in such visual tasks in terms of specific neural control mechanisms of facilitation-inhibition only recently delineated. These findings may also provide a model for other forms of selective facilitation-inhibition of attention. It is now known that neural control of visual input occurs by means of a rapid, continuous process of "feedback" involving a hierarchy of neural structures. At the top of the hierarchy are cortically organized intentions, which in this case include the focal intention to isolate perceptually the simple figure from its complex surrounding. At the next level is the ascending reticular formation, which activates receptor structures under the guidance of a close feedback relationship to cortical determinants of selective retinal activation. Sensory input through the visual apparatus can travel more rapidly to the cortex than to the ascending reticular activating system, so that cortical evaluation of the input can be fed back quickly to the reticular activating system for more selective control of subsequent retinal activation. This is an extremely rapid, complex, repetitive process performed by a clearly delineated, hierarchically organized neural control system.

Let us consider in more detail, then, what happens as an individual attends to a complex figure with the conscious intention of perceptually isolating a simple figure contained within it, the remembered image of which he holds in consciousness. On initial viewing, the pattern of retinal activation presumably represents much or all of the complex figure. Then, in a time-consuming process of gradual approximation based on the continuous feedback process described above and supplemented by coordinated orienting movements of the eyes, cortical representations of the pattern of retinal activation are compared with the image of the simple figure, and the pattern of retinal facilitation-inhibition is altered. Repetition of this process progressively modifies the pattern of retinal facilitation-inhibition until a match is achieved between the cortical representation of the retinal pattern and the memory image of the simple figure. Thus, the ascending reticular formation, under cortical control, directs selective facilitation-inhibition of specific retinal cells by means of a continuous feedback process that gradually adjusts *retinal* activations, and hence cortical representation, to correspond to the remembered image of the simple figure. When the process is completed and the pattern of facilitation-inhibition of retinal receptor cells is such that the percept matches the image, a sudden, clear, and easily reportable phenomenal experience ensues: the simple figure "stands out" vividly from the irrelevant material, the latter "fades" in awareness, and a satisfying feeling of goodness of fit provides affective confirmation that the guiding intention has been executed. It is true, of course, and should be noted here, that many additional cognitive variables affect particular facets of the complex matching process. It is not uncommon, for example, that a subject reports satisfaction within an inadequate percept-image match.

It is important to note that *complete* inhibition of activation is not achieved. Although the perceptual simple figure is experienced with new vividness when the matching process is complete, and although the irrelevant stimuli fade noticeably, they are not blotted out. We have here, in fact, an example of the very kind of attentional gradient Freud (e.g., 1900) referred to in his classic descriptions of the differences in intensity of attention to intentionally focal stimuli and to less focal, incidental stimuli that later reappear as day residue in dreams. Barring internal or external distraction, selective attention (i.e., selective facilitation-inhibition) in everyday life occurs under less difficult conditions than in such laboratory tests. Ordinary conscious experience thus seems to involve only concentration upon relevant ideas or objects; incidental stimuli seem to fall naturally into places of lesser vividness in consciousness. Active processes of facilitation-inhibition are nevertheless involved.

It should be pointed out that, once an embedded figure has been isolated by the process of facilitation-inhibition outlined above, its rediscovery requires much less time. That is, the process of selective facilitation-inhibition of sensory input is "learned"; its final stages can be reproduced without recapitulation of all preceding stages. The fact that learning can be demonstrated in this perceptual instance of selective facilitation-inhibition does not gainsay the contribution of hereditary factors to the wide range of individual differences in speed of extraction of embedded figures. The point of view expressed here does, however, suggest some intriguing new hypotheses about the physical structures involved in response to embedded figures tests. The essential physical-structural differences between persons high and low in this type of field-articulation (i.e., persons more and less adept at articulating or differentiating certain aspects of their experience) could, for example, reside in the differentiation and refinement of the ascending reticular formation. That the hereditary component of these individual differences involves relevant cortical structures may be less likely. Individual differences in the clarity of recall of simple figures seems a minor factor in speed of discovery of embedded figures by normal subjects, in part because the subjects appear not to vary as greatly in this aspect of performance as in the speed and efficiency of the feedback process. Cortical structures are obviously involved in many other high-level activities, and there is ample evidence that performance in embedded figures tests is related only to a specific subgroup of such activities. For example, performance in embedded figures tests is correlated with performance in subtests of standard intelligence scales, which obviously require rapid selective facilitation-inhibition of sensory material. Performance in embedded figures tests is not related to a large array of other mental functions, including the differentiation and sophistication of verbal behavior. That individual differences in speed of perceptual isolation of embedded figures are determined by differences in eye structure seems even less likely. Persons whose visual functioning is biased by minor degrees of astigmatism, myopia, and so forth do not show the slowing of performance one would expect if receptor-specific factors were key determinants of speed of performance. In addition, the individual's speed in discovering embedded figures is correlated with performance in a wide variety of other tests, including tests involving auditory input.

This neurophysiological rationale for performance in a test of selective facilitation-inhibition has been offered not only because it is now possible, but also because it exemplifies the kind of continuous feedback process that is required in all secondary-process thinking and that becomes a critical issue in considerations of temporal factors in the activation of mental structures in primary-process and secondary-process thinking.

The essential features of this neurophysiological rationale for performance in embedded figures tests can be applied to other tests of selective attention, including Size Estimation Test II described above.

Embedded Figures Test

The first twelve of the twenty-four items of Witkin's Embedded Figures Test (1950) were administered to the children. A two-minute time limit was used, rather than the original five-minute time limit. Witkin, Lewis, Hertzman, Machover, Meissner, and Wapner (1954) report that these items are an adequate short form of the test. Earlier studies of adults have suggested that satisfactory results are obtained with time limits shorter than five minutes. The score is the mean time in seconds required to find the twelve simple figures. Two additional scores were also obtained: number of requests for simple figures (i.e., requests to see simple figures again) and number of errors (i.e., number of incorrect tracings).

Concealed Figures Test

Thurstone's Concealed Figures Test, used by him as a measure of the intellectual ability, "flexibility of closure," was shown by Gardner *et al.* (1960) to provide a measure of the field-articulation control principle, for which the Embedded Figures Test has served as a criterion test. A paper-and-pencil embedded figures test, it requires the subject to find each of a series of simple figures in adjacent complex figures and to indicate these by making check marks beneath the appropriate complex figures. A five-minute time limit was used. The usual score is the number correct (i.e., the number of correct checks). This traditional score was used in the present study after it was found to be correlated .93 with the more psychometrically justifiable score, number correct minus number incorrect.

Size Estimation Test II

As noted earlier, residual illusion-effect scores for the three illusion-producing figures employed in Size Estimation Test II were considered field-articulation scores in the present study. The hypothesis was that effectiveness of performance in the Embedded Figures and Concealed Figures Tests and the capacity to overcome these particular illusions depends upon the capacity to direct attention selectively to relevant versus irrelevant portions of stimulus fields. This hypothesis is firmly grounded in earlier results that Gardner (1961a) obtained with adults, indicating relationships between adult performance in the Embedded Figures Test and capacity to "solve" illusions of this general type.

Tolerance for Unrealistic Experiences

The first laboratory study of this aspect of ego organization was conceptualized as a study of tolerance for a particular form of instability (Klein and Schlesinger, 1951). A subsequent study was predicated on the assumption that this particular form of instability involves individual differences in willingness to experience, or to produce, organizations of stimuli at variance with what the subject "knows" to be true in a relatively literal and conventional sense. In the second study (Klein, Gardner, and Schlesinger, 1962), individual consistencies were shown to link response to an apparent movement test in which the subject is explicitly made aware that the movement experience is an illusion; mode of approach and responses to the Rorschach Test; response to reversible figures in which the two experienced phases vary in their conformity to conventional reality; and so forth. This study seemed to delineate clearly a dimension of individual consistencies in tolerance for unrealistic experiences. This dimension seems to have implications for defenses and other variables ordinarily inferred from behavior in the clinic. A study by Gardner *et al.* (1959) suggested that this dimension of individual differences may find expression in the Schematizing Test and a kinesthetic time-error test also designed to measure assimilation; the apparent movement test described earlier; productivity and length of verbal units in a free association test; production of vague versus clearly defined forms in the Rorschach Test; and stability versus variability of reading speed within the interference portion (Part III) of the Color-Word Test.

Rating

Since an adequate apparent movement apparatus was not available at the time the preadolescent children were tested, it was possible to obtain only one score for this dimension of cognitive control. This measure consisted of the average rating of the children's sixty Rorschach protocols, which were classified according to a Q-sort by two independent raters who have had extensive experience with the Rorschach Test (Gardner and Schoen, 1962) and who were unaware of the laboratory or other test performances of the children. The protocols were arranged in a random order before each set of ratings. The criteria for these ratings were identical to those employed with adults, which were spelled out in some detail by Klein *et al.* (1962). The Pearson *r* between Q-sorts by the two raters was .97. The average of the Q-sort values for the two raters was used as the score for each subject.

Constricted-Flexible Control

This dimension of cognitive control was originally postulated by Klein (1954), who demonstrated the differential effects of a need (thirst) on the cognitions of subjects differing in this dimension of cognitive control. Related findings have been reported by Lazarus, Baker, Broverman, and Mayer (1957) and Hardison and Purcell (1959). Holt (1960) has presented evidence that constricted-control subjects are characterized by ineffective use of their primary-process thinking and by poor impulse control.

The criterion test of constricted-flexible control has been, and is in the present study, the Color-Word Test, which presents the subject with the difficult task of naming colors printed in incongruous color words (flexible-control subjects are those who can name colors rapidly under these conditions). A version of Stroop's Color-Word Test (see Ligon, 1932; Stroop, 1935a, b; 1938) was used by Thurstone (1944) in his extensive study of individual differences in perception. This test, with the interference score used in the present study, was employed in a number of earlier studies of cognitive control (e.g., Gardner *et al.*, 1959; Gardner *et al.*, 1960; Gardner and Long, 1962b). The rationale for the key interference score centers around the requirement to inhibit irrelevant, overlearned, and highly compelling motoric responses—reading the words—while verbalizing the names of the colors.

The Color-Word Test is unique among the cognitive control measures in that the substructures involved in the individual's prior learning of color names, which under most circumstances is adaptively effective, *disrupt*, rather than facilitate performance. It is presumed that such substructures are "tools of cognition" that are learned to make response more economical and less demanding of the effortful concentration required for performing novel tasks. Whether or not a set of structures is adaptively effective in a particular situation, however, depends upon the particular ecological conditions that obtain. The Color-Word Test conditions are such that the prior learning of color-name associations (i.e., the set of substructures involved) interferes with performance, whereas the more general control structure governing the inhibition of irrelevant motoric responses facilitates performance.

In an ingenious set of experiments that contributes to understanding of the response processes involved in the Color-Word Test, Klein (1964) has shown that the degree of interference is a function of the verbal context (reading times increase progressively when the colors are printed in nonsense syllables, rare words, common words, words related to the colors in the test, color words other than those used in the test, and, finally, the color words themselves). Thus (Klein, 1964, p. 588), "the *attensive* power of a word—i.e., the word's capacity, when the word is present in the color-context, to bring about a rise in activation of the vocal motor-component of the word's structure" is one major determinant of the interference effect. Klein also showed that the interference effect is dissipated when subjects are allowed to read the word, then the color, in each color-word item. In his view, inhibition of word reading in the standard test allows the subject to restimulate himself with the color, "which makes possible the release of the relevant motor-response and its domination of the vocal output-channel."

In terms of individual differences in the standard test, the key variable seems to be the capacity to inhibit the irrelevant motoric response of reading the word, so that the process of restimulation Klein describes can occur. Effective performance also requires not only inhibition of irrelevant motor responses, but also flexible modulation of inhibition as the subject proceeds from one color-word combination to the next.

As pointed out by Spivack, Levine, and Sprigle (1959), Gardner *et al.* (1960), and Gardner and Long (1962b), the Color-Word Test requires one important form of delay. Spivack *et al.* (1959), who used an interference score different from that used in the cognitive control studies, found lack of interference in the Color-Word Test to be correlated with IQ scores, presumably because of the importance of delay to Color-Word Test performances and the development of the skills sampled by intelligence tests. These authors also found lack of interference in the Color-Word Test performances related to delay in time estimation, which apparently represents a further substantiation of the contention that a key aspect of delay is involved in response to the Color-Word Test. It seems likely, however, that the capacity to delay affects the formation of all cognitive structures and that various expressions of delay capacity are more often uncorrelated than correlated. If not, degree of cognitive differentiation would be a single variable. A host of earlier studies, including studies of cognitive controls, clearly indicates that this is not the case (see, e.g., Gardner and Schoen, 1962). Earlier cognitive control studies have shown, for example, that the capacity to inhibit irrelevant motoric responses in the Color-Word Test is uncorrelated with the capacity to inhibit response to irrelevant stimuli in field-articulation tests.

Other studies of the interference effect and other aspects of performance in the Color-Word Test include those of Callaway and Band (1958), Broverman and Lazarus (1958), Broverman (1960a, b), Wapner and Krus (1960), Hörmann (1960), and Lang (1964). Smith has performed extensive studies of the correlates of response to repeated administrations of the test (e.g., Smith and Nyman, 1959). A study by Comalli, Wapner, and Werner (1962) of developmental changes in Color-Word Test performance from ages seven to eighty is especially relevant to the present study. These authors found that (p. 50) "interference is greatest with young children, decreases with increasing age to adulthood and increases again with older age." A subsequent study by Rand, Wapner, Werner, and McFarland (1963) showed that the frequency of five categories of deviant verbal response to the Color-Word Test decrease with age. The frequency of another category increases with age, however, and the frequency of still another decreases with age but increases in the oldest group of children included (aged sixteen to seventeen).

Color-Word Test

This test has been described in some detail by Gardner *et al.* (1959). In the total test, the subject is required to read three pages of one hundred items each (ten lines of ten items). The first page (Part I) consists of the names of colors. The second page (Part II) consists of colored asterisks. The third page (Part III) consists of the color words printed in incongruous colors. In the present study, only the first six lines of each page (sixty of the one hundred items) were used. The interference score for each subject consists of the difference between his actual reading time on Part III and his time predicted on the basis of the regression of reading time for Part III on that for Part II. This type of score is necessitated by the fact that the correlation between reading times for Parts II and III is highly significant in the present study (as it has been in earlier studies of adults).

Conceptual Differentiation

The concept of a dimensional principle of cognitive control relevant to the degree of differentiation persons impose in categorizing arrays of heterogeneous objects, persons, events, and the like has arisen from a series of studies beginning with Gardner's (1953) exploration of relations between the number of groups subjects form in the categorization of objects and performance in a variety of other tests, including constancy procedures. Although the original results suggested that a subject's "equivalence range" (category width) in an object sorting test may be correlated with the degree of "error" he allows when asked to make retinal and object matches in certain constancy tests, subsequent results (Gardner *et al.*, 1959) have suggested that the latter measures are also influenced by individual differences in field-articulation and are therefore not ideal measures of this principle (see also the discussion of this point by Gardner and Schoen, 1962).

Dissertations by Dickman (1954) and Marrs (1955) also contributed to the delineation of the area of generality relevant to this control principle. In particular, the study by Marrs demonstrated that individual differences in conceptual differentiation in the spontaneous sorting of objects in Gardner's Object Sorting Test are related to degrees of conceptual differentiation in the categorizing of statements concerning behavior.

A subsequent study by Gardner *et al.* (1959) suggested that subjects referred to here as high in conceptual differentiation (or, in the original terms, subjects with "narrow" equivalence ranges) give fewer human responses, whole responses, human plus mammalian animal responses, human movement responses, color responses, and extensor (versus flexor) responses to the Rorschach Test. In general, adult subjects low in conceptual differentiation "projected more life and activity into the inkblots" (Gardner *et al.*, 1959, p. 108).

Gardner *et al.* (1959) also found that adults high in conceptual differentiation define groups they form in the Object Sorting Test in terms representing minimal conceptual distance from the physical properties of the objects. This finding seems related to the finding of Gardner and Schoen (1962, discussed below) concerning the tendency of persons high in conceptual differentiation to produce TAT stories that are conceptually close to the physical properties of the pictures. The latter finding is discussed in greater detail in Chapter 5.

A later study by Sloane (1959; see, also, Sloane, Gorlow, and Jackson, 1963) confirmed the original hypothesis that equivalence range, or conceptual differentiation, is a meaningful dimension of individual consistency, and extended the earlier results concerning grouping dispositions to paper-and-pencil forms of the Object Sorting Test and to the categorizing of pictures of people. His results, like those of Gardner *et al.* (1959), failed to show the relations between categorizing and size constancy judgments referred to above.

A study by Gardner *et al.* (1960) showed that individual differences in equivalence range, or conceptual differentiation, are independent of a group of intellectual ability factors isolated by Thurstone and subsequent workers, including the abilities called induction and deduction. It was also shown that the mean level of abstraction represented by the subject's reasons for grouping in the criterion Object Sorting Test is uncorrelated with the number of groups formed (i.e., conceptual differentiation) in the case of female college students.

In a recent study of adult females, Gardner and Schoen (1962) employed the paper-and-pencil form of the Object Sorting Test [1] developed by Clayton and Jackson (1961), a new Behavior Sorting Test, a Photo Sorting Test (pictures of people), and a variety of additional procedures to explore relations between conceptual differentiation and

---

[1] As indicated in this discussion, paper-and-pencil tests have proved useful in providing substitute measures of the total-number-of-groups score for the Object Sorting Test. In other respects, however (e.g., the kinds of definitions used, their conceptual distance from the objects, the numbers of single-item groups versus multiple-item groups, and so forth), pilot work indicates that these tests are not comparable to the original Object Sorting Test. Group administration of paper-and-pencil tests also makes it difficult to insure that items the subject appears to place (or leave) in single-item categories are perceived as such by the subject and do not represent omissions, i.e., items carelessly overlooked.

performance in potentially related concept formation tests employed by a number of other investigators. The results of this study have clarified and extended the demonstrable realm of situational generality of this control principle. The results indicate, for example, that individual differences in conceptual differentiation in the Object Sorting Test are predictably related to conceptual differentiation in the Photo Sorting Test, the Behavior Sorting Test, Pettigrew's Category-Width Test, and a variety of other procedures, including a very simple test in which subjects are asked to draw first a square and then a rectangle. Subjects high in conceptual differentiation (i.e., subjects who categorize objects, persons, statements about behavior, and the like into many small groups) also exemplify their emphasis on difference by drawing squares and rectangles that are relatively different as measured by the ratios of the shorter to the longer sides. The study also showed the independence of conceptual differentiation from the level of abstraction at which the subject prefers to perform in these same sorting tests, his capacity to abstract, and his IQ scores and subtest scores for the Wechsler-Bellevue Intelligence Scale.

It should be noted here, as Gardner and Schoen (1962) have pointed out, that conceptual differentiation and category width per se (e.g., in simpler tests requiring the subject to indicate the breadth of single categories) are related but far from identical concepts. The former refers to spontaneous differentiation in much more complex multiple-category situations and involve a number of additional variables not elicited by category-width tests. The major groups of such variables are discussed in Chapter 5.

An intriguing finding in the study by Gardner and Schoen was the confirmation of the predicted negative relationship between conceptual differentiation in categorizing tests and the degree to which the stories subjects tell in response to Thematic Apperception Test pictures are conceptually distant from the physical properties of these stimuli. Adult subjects high in conceptual differentiation, i.e., those who categorize objects and events into many small groups, produce relatively constricted stories involving considerable amounts of description of the properties of the stimuli and minimal creative thematic material. Subjects low in conceptual differentiation, i.e., subjects who organize objects and events into a few broad categories, produce more original and creative stories. This finding seems to provide a bridge between studies of conceptual differentiation and the work of Barron (1955) on "originality" in response to Thematic Apperception Test pictures. Like the earlier finding that subjects high in conceptual differentiation produce relatively few human responses in the Rorschach inkblots, this result suggests that such categorizing behaviors may be embedded in more general aspects of the individual's orientation that may include traits at least similar to those involved in regression in the service of the ego; the accessibility and effective control of material relatively close to primary-process levels of the conceptual hierarchy; and preferred social distance from other people. These hypotheses and a group of additional hypotheses are being tested in a current study that includes exploration of relations between conceptual differentiation and experienced differences among other persons, social distance, preference for simplicity versus complexity, the organization of discrepant information about individual persons, and the like.

On the basis of these earlier findings, scores presumed to represent conceptual differentiation and related aspects of concept formation were drawn from three procedures in the present study: Gardner's original Object Sorting Test; a special Photo Sorting Test; and the Thematic Apperception Test.

Object Sorting Test

This test has been described in detail by Gardner *et al.* (1959). In brief, the subject is asked to group seventy-three familiar objects in the way that seems "most logical, most natural, and most comfortable." The objects are presented in a random array on a large table. When the subject has completed his grouping, he is required to give the reason for putting the objects in each group together. As pointed out by Gardner and Schoen (1962), these reasons are essential for accurate scoring of number of groups conceptualized by the subject. When, for example, a subject forms a group he conceives of as having two subdivisions (e.g., "tools: these for adults and these for children"), two groups are scored. Also, each object left by itself is scored as an additional group if inquiry reveals that it is conceived of as belonging with none of the other objects. The major scores used in the present study are the total number of groups and the preferred level of abstraction, as employed by Gardner *et al.* (1960) and Gardner and Schoen (1962). Preferred level of abstraction scores of 1, 2, and 3, were assigned to definitions that are concrete, functional, and abstract as defined by Rapaport, Gill, and Schafer (1945). Details of the application of this scoring procedure to the Object Sorting Test are described by Gardner and Schoen (1962). The mean level of abstraction score was obtained for each child by averaging the scores for all definitions (i.e., the reasons given for all groups containing two or more objects).

In the interest of careful delineation of possible differences between the performances of adult subjects in earlier studies and children of the present study, a series of additional scores was also obtained. Although not used in the factor analyses or other major data analyses of the present study, these scores were employed in the special analyses of developmental changes in various aspects of categorizing behavior described in Chapter 5.

The Homogeneity of the Total-Number-of-Groups Score for Sorting Tests

Messick and Kogan (1963) have argued that the single-item categories subjects form in the paper-and-pencil versions of the Object Sorting Test represent a qualitatively different aspect of concept formation than groups of two or more objects. They refer to the former as "compartmentalization." Their argument, which implies that the total-number-of-groups score for such procedures is inhomogeneous, is based upon the observation that the number of single-item categories and the number of groups of two or more objects are negligibly correlated. This argument seems to involve inadequate appreciation of the nature of distributions of group sizes in such tests, plus arbitrary division of the distribution at a point that leads to questionable conclusions. The relevant facts are listed below.

1. Each part-score for number of groups of different sizes is related to any other part-score (a subject who forms many large groups will inevitably form few small groups). Relationships between the numbers of groups of different sizes change systematically as the distribution is divided at different points. Part-whole correlations must therefore be interpreted with unusual caution.

2. If the distribution of group sizes is normal in a particular sample, identical correlations (with opposite signs) will obtain between the total number of groups and (a) the number of single-object categories and (b) the number of large groups equidistant from the mean in the other direction, provided, of course, that the distributions of these extreme scores are also normal and have equal variances.

4. To divide the distribution of group sizes at either extreme, while ignoring the other, makes it *appear* that the total-number-of-groups score is inhomogeneous, whereas it is actually not.

5. It can be demonstrated (even in samples in which the distribution of group sizes is skewed) that highly significant part-whole correlations and correlations with independent scores obtain for *both* the number of extremely large groups and the number of single-item categories. These correlations are automatically opposite in direction. Which set of correlations is higher depends primarily upon the direction of skewness in a particular sample (which tail of the distribution has more variance is a function of the nature of the skewness; correlations are depressed when variance is restricted).

Results demonstrating these points about analyses of group-size distributions are presented in Chapter 5. These results make it clear that both the nature of such distributions and the nature of the distribution for a particular sample must be carefully considered in interpretations of part-scores for such tests.

The reader is reminded, in this connection, that adequate administration of such tests requires the subject to consider each object, or object name, in terms of its relation to the others. If he arrives at single-object categories in a way qualitatively different from that in which he arrives at groups of two, three, four, or larger numbers of objects (e.g., by failing to carry out the instructions or by careless omission of objects), the test has not been administered in the way described by Gardner (1953) and employed in subsequent studies in our laboratories, including the present study.

Tajfel, Richardson, and Everstine (1964) have suggested using the number of items in the first few groups as a measure of categorizing in such tests. Scores similar to those they suggest were included in the detailed analyses of grouping scores described in Chapter 5.

Photo Sorting Test

In this test, which is comparable to the Object Sorting Test in general format and instructions, the subject is required to sort thirty-six pictures of persons into groups. The magazine cutouts used were selected to represent variations in age, race, occupation, activity, and so forth. Pictures of both sexes were included. Ten of the pictures are colored; twenty-six are black and white.

In view of the fact that this test all but requires grouping at an abstract, conceptual level, the only score used was the total number of groups the subject formed, which is comparable to the criterion conceptual differentiation score extracted from the Object Sorting Test. Subjects were required to define each group in a manner similar to that required in the inquiry portion of the Object Sorting Test.

Conceptual Distance of Responses
to Thematic Apperception Test Pictures

Responses to two TAT pictures (Cards 2 and 11) were selected to provide measures of the conceptual distance subject's stories moved from the physical attributes of the pictures. Responses to each of these pictures were rated independently by two raters who have had extensive experience with the TAT.[2] Each of the raters sorted the protocols into twelve classes on a quasi-normal frequency basis, as for a Q-sort. These ratings were done without reference to the names of the subjects, and the protocols were independently randomized before each rating. For rater A, the Pearson r between the Q-sorts of stories to the two pictures was .55, $p < .001$. For rater B, this r was .64, $p < .001$. The r's between the raters' Q-sorts of Card 2 was .90, $p < .001$, of Card 11, .85, $p < .001$. Ratings of the two pictures were averaged for each rater. The r between the two average ratings was .93, $p < .001$. The average ratings of the two raters were averaged to provide an over-all score for conceptual distance in response to the TAT pictures. In view of the highly significant correlations between ratings of responses to the two pictures by each rater and the high correlations between their ratings, it was felt that even this small sample of TAT pictures could provide an index of conceptual distance in response to the test as a whole.

Additional Cognitive Control Scores

Mean reaction time scores for the Rorschach Test and the Thematic Apperception Test were also obtained, because of their possible relations to extensiveness of scanning in the size estimation tests. A study by Gardner and Long (1962a) suggested that adults who are extremely extensive scanners spend more time examining Rorschach inkblots before responding than extremely limited scanners.

[2] Riley W. Gardner and R. A. Schoen.

4 Age and Sex Differences in Five Cognitive Controls

ADMINISTRATION TO the children of the present study of cognitive control procedures given earlier to large samples of adults made it possible to perform detailed analyses of developmental changes in cognitive controls from early to late preadolescence and from preadolescence to adulthood. The adult scores used in this chapter were compiled from earlier studies of cognitive controls and related phenomena in The Menninger Foundation laboratories. The fact that neither sex differences nor age differences in most of the cognitive controls have been found in adults of the ages represented seemed to justify use of various combinations of men and women in amassing all possible prior data on adults in the case of those controls. The age discrepancy between preadolescents and adults is rather large, and it should be kept in mind that the preadolescent-adult comparisons made here leave unexplored the nature of changes during adolescence.

The cognitive controls dealt with in this chapter are leveling-sharpening, scanning, field-articulation, tolerance for unrealistic experiences, and constricted-flexible control. The more extensive results concerning the conceptual differentiation control principle and other major features of performance in categorizing tests (preferred level of abstraction, the meaning bases for grouping objects and pictures of people, and some revealing additional scores) are described in Chapter 5.

The basic procedure selected to measure each control principle was the major means of assessing that group of individual consistencies as defined by the formulator(s) of the control principle concept and as further indicated by results of earlier studies with adults. Additional procedures were drawn from those of proven value in earlier studies. The stability and generality of the field-articulation principle has been so well established that a new procedure was added to provide a further test of the hypothesis that this control implies selectiveness of attention to relevant versus irrelevant aspects of the visual fields involved in certain illusions. The illusions selected were judged to be similar, in attentional terms, to those used earlier by Gardner (1961a), but represented an extension of his work in this area.

Sex Differences in Cognitive Control Scores

Of the cognitive control principles included in this study, adult sex differences have been found consistently only in the case of field-articulation. Men are slightly but reliably more adept than women in such criterion laboratory tests as Witkin's modification of Gottschaldt's Embedded Figures Test (see Witkin *et al.*, 1954, 1962). Boys are comparably more adept at such tests than girls. With the exception of one relatively minor score for the Color-Word Test of constricted-flexible control, such differences have not been found in the case of the other controls, either in studies involving samples of men and women or in comparisons of data for combined samples from studies of the sexes separately.

Since significant differences between cognitive control test scores for boys and girls of the present study were found only in the case of the reading-time score for Part III of the Color-Word Test of constricted-flexible control, results for the sexes separately will be discussed only for this test and for the field-articulation tests.

Leveling-Sharpening

Mean Leveling-Sharpening Scores of Younger and Older Children

The leveling-sharpening scores of the younger and older children (mean ages of 10.5 and 12.1) indicate a progression toward greater accuracy and lesser increment error and lag in this relatively brief period of development. Although it seems logical that assimilation among new percepts and related memories should be greater at younger ages, the specific processes involved in the developmental change are not clearly understood. It could be that older children concentrate more unequivocally on the squares, perceive them more vividly, and hence show less assimilation (cf. Gardner and Lohrenz, 1961). It could also be that the older children have higher levels of activation (Duffy, 1962), leading to greater perceptual vividness. Or, unknown maturational changes specific to the perceptual or memoric apparatuses involved may account for the reduction in assimilation with age.

Mean Leveling-Sharpening Scores of Children and Adults

In view of the gross differences in age between these children, who range from nine to thirteen years, and the adults, who range from twenty to sixty-six years, the similarity of mean ranking-accuracy scores for children and adults is a surprising fact, particularly since increment error and lag clearly decrease from preadolescence to adulthood. It would appear, as suggested in Chapter 3, that the ranking-accuracy score represents a different constellation of response operations, in spite of the correlation of ranking accuracy with the other two scores in adult samples.

Relations Among Leveling-Sharpening Scores

As noted in Chapter 3, the ranking-accuracy score has consistently been correlated to a modest but significant degree with the increment-error score in samples of adults. It is rather startling to find, in view of this, that the correlations of ranking accuracy with increment error and lag ($-.15$ and $-.16$) are in the predicted direction but nonsignificant for the children (the correlation between the related increment-error and lag scores is .79). Apparently, the functions involved in the observed adult consistencies have not yet crystallized into the adult syndrome at preadolescence. These intriguing results may point to the fact that there are at least two main lines in the development of the cognitive structures relevant to this control principle in the case of adults: those contributing to ranking accuracy, and those contributing to lagging behind the trend of size increase. As indicated in the discussion of the factor analysis of major cognitive control scores in Chapter 6, the lack of correlation between these scores in the case of children, as contrasted to adults, seems to derive in part from the fact that, at the age levels represented by the children, the processes determining the ranking-accuracy score are part of a general syndrome in which they seem to be linked to field-articulation.

Extensiveness of Scanning

Mean Scanning Scores of Younger and Older Children

Scanning by the younger and older children was remarkably similar in the two size estimation tests. Of the six scanning scores, the two nearly significant differences did not appear consistently in the three test conditions and may be attributable to chance. If not, they suggest a slight tendency for younger children to make fewer centrations on the standard in the control condition of Test II and to spend less time checking their judgments in the experimental condition of Test II.

Mean Scanning Scores of Children and Adults

For Test I and the control condition of Test II, the results are quite similar and indicate patterned differences between children and adults. The children spend more time making their judgments and stop oftener in adjusting the comparison stimulus. Their average times per centration on the standard stimulus are shorter, however, and their percentages of time on the standard are considerably less than those of adults. The essential finding here seems to be that they spend more time looking at the comparison stimulus. This could mean, also, that children adjust the comparison stimulus more slowly, a possibility that cannot be tested, since rates of adjustment were not recorded.

The fact that children spend more time in making these judgments may be attributable to their experiencing these tests as more difficult than do adults. It is impressive, however, that the inability to delay, which might be expected of children in these procedures, finds expression, if at all, only in their shorter centrations on the standard.

Observations of some of the children suggested that their lesser percentages of time on the standard stimulus may reflect their fascination with the ability to change the comparison stimulus and their interest in watching it change as they turn the adjustment crank. It could also be that they are slower to form adequate anticipations concerning the rate of change in the comparison stimulus brought about by turning the crank and hence spend more time checking the changes in it, as if this new hand-eye coordination were more difficult for them than for adults. Otherwise, they seem even more painstaking than the adults in judging the sizes of the disks and the circles.

Under the more difficult judgment conditions of the experimental condition of Test II, only two of the four child-adult differences in Test I and Test II, control condition, obtain. The children make more stops in adjusting the comparison stimulus and spend less time on the standard, as before. They do not, however, spend less time per centration on the standard or more time in the entire judgment process. Both children and adults are slower in making these more difficult judgments than the control condition judgments and both spend a greater percentage of time on the illusion-producing standard stimulus (as compared to the comparison stimulus). The latter fact may be attributable both to the illusion-producing nature of the stimuli and to practice in adjusting the comparison stimulus. It will be recalled that these illusion-producing stimuli were judged last in the sequence of three size estimation conditions.

The judgment time results seem to indicate a greater increase for adults from the control to the experimental condition. An analysis of covariance showed, however, that the children and adults did not differ significantly in the degree of increase from the easy to the more difficult condition.

Relations Among Scanning Scores

In view of the complexity of the earlier studies that indicated adult individual consistencies linking various facets of response to size estimation tests (Gardner and Long, 1962a, b), comparisons of correlations for children and adults are included in this chapter. Table 4–1 contains correlations between the same scanning scores for the three conditions of size estimation for the children and the one sample of adults appropriate to such an analysis. With the exception of time per centration on the standard (i.e., constant) stimulus, the adults seem to show slightly greater individual consistencies in the three conditions presented in the two tests. All the correlations for the children nevertheless greatly exceed the .001 level. Although the correlations between time per centration on the standard in Size Estimation Test I (gray, black, and heavy gray disks) and the control and experimental conditions of Size Estimation Test II (circles, circles with illusion-producing other circles, and so forth) for the adults are in the predicted direction and one is significant at the .05 level, they are, in fact, much less consistent than the children. In view of the high correlation for adults between time per centration on the standard in the two conditions of Test II, these results indicate that individual adults are differentially responsive to the gross changes in stimuli from Test I to Test II. The children, in contrast, seem not to react differentially to these stimulus differences. A possible interpretation is that children are on the whole less sensitive to such stimulus variations, or that they persist rather rigidly in patterns of response to these related procedures in spite of their awareness of differences in the stimuli judged. In either case, it is clearly apparent that the stimulus differences produce

TABLE 4-1

Pearson Correlations for Children (N = 60) and Adults (N = 34)ª Between
Scanning Scores for Size Estimation Tests I and II

| | Correlations Between Tests | | | | | |
| | I:II-Control | | I:II-Experimental | | II-Control: II-Experimental | |
Mean Score	Children	Adults	Children	Adults	Children	Adults
Judgment Time	.65 ***	.80 ***	.77 ***	.83 ***	.76 ***	.91 ***
Number of Adjustment Stops	.69 ***	.83 ***	.75 ***	.87 ***	.69 ***	.89 ***
Number of Centrations on Standard	.63 ***	.71 ***	.79 ***	.84 ***	.78 ***	.91 ***
Percentage of Time on Standard	.63 ***	.60 ***	.66 ***	.68 ***	.78 ***	.81 ***
Time per Centration on Standard	.75 ***	.33	.79 ***	.38 *	.87 ***	.85 ***
Redundant Scanning Time	.63 ***	.71 ***	.79 ***	.79 ***	.77 ***	.83 ***

* $p < .05$.
*** $p < .001$.
ª Women aged 24 to 46, mean, 34.6.

more child-adult patterning differences in time per centration on the standard than in any of the other aspects of scanning assessed.

Mean Constant Error Scores of Younger and Older Children

The means and sigmas of the Test I constant error scores of the younger and older children are notable in two ways: the mean errors are remarkably small; and the younger children tend to make consistently smaller mean errors than the older children, although these differences do not reach significance. Both of these findings might be considered opposite to common anticipations concerning developmental changes in perceptual accuracy. It will be recalled that the nature of the judgments in this test (in which a circle of light on a ground-glass screen is adjusted to perceived equality of size to solid-colored hand-held disks) makes accuracy a function of the simultaneous resolution of several interacting illusions (see Chapter 3) and the ability effectively to "transport" impressions of relative size from a highly complex to a relatively simple stimulus. One is reminded here of Piaget's "Type II" illusions, which increase with age (Piaget's earlier work on the two types of illusions is summarized in his 1961 monograph, *Les mécanismes perceptifs*). If Type II illusions occur, children as a group should be more accurate than adults in Test I. The confirmation of this hypothesis is discussed in the section below on child-adult differences in constant errors under the three conditions of size estimation.

In the control condition of Test II, the younger children tend to make slightly larger errors of overestimation than the older children, but the mean differences are again nonsignificant. The notable fact here is the reversal of direction of errors: in Test I, younger children overestimate slightly less; in the control condition of Test II, which does not involve the multiple illusions of Test I, they overestimate slightly more. It could be that a Type I illusion is involved here. Presentation of the line-drawn black circles on horizontally rather narrow strips of white cardboard (as compared to the comparison stimulus, which appears in the center of a square field) should tend to produce an illusion of enhanced magnitude of these Test II control stimuli. To overcome this illusion would require that attention be directed selectively to the circle, and withheld from the shape of the background. This is another way of saying that the field-articulation control may be implicated to a minor degree in these control judgments, as well as in the experimental condition of Test II, in which the relevant and compelling irrelevant cues are parts of the line drawings.

This interpretation would seem to correspond to prior findings concerning developmental increases in the capacity to articulate such visual fields, as well as Piaget's general conception of Type I illusions. This interpretation seems to receive support from the fact that the children's constant errors in the control judgments and the experimental judgments (two of three of which involve the Type II Delboeuf illusion, the third, illusion-producing arrows) are all significantly correlated (range, .35 to .61; p range, .01 to .001). It was these significant correlations that led to the computation of residual illusion-effect scores as hypothesized measures of field-articulation in Test II. Since it could not be proved that these correlations were produced by related illusions in the control and experimental conditions, the conservative approach was to "remove" the base level represented by each subject's control judgments from his illusion score. It seems possible, however, that this conservative approach reduced the effectiveness of the residual score by removing some of the illusion variance itself.

Similar results obtain for the experimental condition of Test II. Once again, younger children consistently overestimate somewhat more. Only one of the mean differences, however, is significant. Both younger and older children show the intended illusion effects by judging the embedded circles of the experimental condition larger than the same circles presented alone in the control condition, but these differences are relatively small, except for the potent illusion produced by embedding the 30 mm. standard in a 45 mm. surrounding circle.

Three analyses of covariance were performed to test for differences in the degree of increase by younger and older children in size estimation from the control to the experimental conditions (i.e., degree of illusion effect, with the differences in overestimation in the control condition in effect "partialed out"). A significant increase difference obtains only in the case of the 45 mm. circle containing the arrows.[1] It should be noted, however, that, as in the case of the residual scores discussed above, the reduction from a difference significant at the .01 level for the raw experimental condition score to one significant at the .05 level for the residual score could be attributable to the fact that elimination of differences in

---

[1] Several other investigators (see, e.g., Piaget, Lambercier, Boesch, and Albertini, 1942; Giering, 1905, as referred to by Wohlwill, 1960; Santostefano, 1963) have reported developmental decreases in the positive illusion produced by enclosing a judged circle within an appropriately larger circle.

the control condition may have eliminated some of the very illusion variance the experimental condition was designed to measure.

Mean Constant Error Scores of Children and Adults

The notion that Test I may involve Type II illusions seems to receive support from these intriguing results. Children make consistently *smaller* mean constant errors than adults, and all of the differences are highly significant. This group of results could be anticipated only tentatively at best, and they clearly negate any overgeneralized assumption that perceptual accuracy increases with age under all conditions of perception. The general point made by Piaget in his extensive *Recherches sur de Développement des Perceptions (Archives de Psychologie*, 1942 on, summarized in Piaget, 1961) concerning two types of perceptual change during development is well taken and provides a natural base for exploration of still other types of developmental change.

In Test II, which seems to involve Type I illusions in the control condition, Types I and II in the experimental condition, matters are largely reversed. With the exception of the 45 mm. circle surrounding the 30 mm. circle, children overestimate more than adults. In the control condition, these differences are suggestive but nonsignificant. In the experimental condition, differences with respect to the two more powerful illusion-producing figures are significant. It should be noted here that the apparent reversal of change for the double-circle Delboeuf illusion when the inner and outer circles are judged is not necessarily an incongruity. As noted by Piaget (see Piaget, 1961, for summary statements), the illusion effects for the inner and outer circles vary in complex ways as a function of the relative sizes of the circles. We have here sampled only one point on this continuum. By so doing, we have incompletely represented the parameters involved and, as a result, have achieved a much greater illusion with the inner circle than with the outer circle. It should be added here that these illusions reverse from size increase to size decrease at points along the size-ratio continuum specified by Piaget in his earlier experimental work.

To test for child-adult differences in degree of increase in perceived size from the control to the experimental conditions, three analyses of covariance were performed. As might be expected from the preceding results, the only proportional increase significantly greater for children was with the relatively great illusion produced by enclosing the 30 mm. standard in the 45 mm. circle.

Relationships Among Constant Error Scores

Intercorrelations among Size Estimation Test I constant error scores for the children and six samples of adults are shown in Table 4–2. It is evident that the children's consistencies in judging the magnitude of these stimuli are, at the most, slightly less than those of adult women.

TABLE 4–2

*Pearson Correlations Between Size Estimation Test I
Mean Constant Error Scores for Children and Adults* [a]

| | Correlations for 40 mm. Disks | | |
| | | Gray: | |
Sample	Gray:Black	Heavy Gray	Black:Heavy Gray
Children (N = 60)	.69 ***	.67 ***	.73 ***
Adults 1 (N = 34)	.66 ***	.74 ***	.81 ***
Adults 2 (N = 80)	.73 ***	.74 ***	.85 ***
Adults 3 (N = 68)	.65 ***	.55 ***	.75 ***
Adults 4 (N = 30)	.80 ***	.77 ***	.51 **
Adults 5 (N = 53)	.85 ***	.86 ***	.89 ***
Adults 6 (N = 61)	.76 ***	.74 ***	.86 ***

** p < .01.
*** p < .001.
[a] The adults are women of the following ages tested in other studies: Sample 1, 24 to 46, mean, 34.6; Sample 2, 17 to 22, mean, 19.4; Sample 3, 17 to 30, mean 20.2; Sample 4, 16 to 19, mean, 17.2; Sample 5, 18 to 45, mean, 30.6; Sample 6, 17 to 44, mean, 22.5.

TABLE 4–3

*Pearson Correlations for Children and Adults Between Constant Error Scores for
Size Estimation Tests I and II*

| | Correlations | |
| | Children | Adults [a] |
Constant Error Scores Correlated	(N = 60)	(N = 34)
I:II-Control (30 mm.)	.43 ***	.29
I:II-Control (45 mm.)	.35 **	.44 **
I:II-Experimental (30–45)	.27 *	.33
I:II-Experimental (45-Arrows)	.26 *	.39 *
I:II-Experimental (45–30)	.18	.28
II-Control (30 mm.):II-Experimental (30–45)	.47 ***	.58 ***
II-Control (45 mm.):II-Experimental (45-Arrows)	.61 ***	.65 ***
II-Control (45 mm.):II-Experimental (45–30)	.49 ***	.54 ***

* p < .05.
** p < .01.
*** p < .001.
[a] Women aged 24 to 46, mean, 34.6.

Correlations of the total constant error scores for Tests I and II are shown for children and adults in Table 4–3. These correlations are also remarkably similar for children and adults.

It is apparent from the results shown in these two tables that the children are roughly the same as adults in the consistency of their constant errors in response to different stimuli within the two tests and in the two tests taken as a whole. It is thus demonstrably true that these preadolescent children are not more erratic and unpredictable than adults in these aspects of their test performance.

Relationships Between Scanning and Constant Error Scores

Gardner and Long (1962a, b) found that extensiveness of scanning, defined as the mean number of centrations on the standard, was negatively related to constant error in Size Estimation Test I and in judgments of a 35 mm. circle (otherwise identical to the 30 mm. control circle used in the present study) in the control condition of Size Estimation Test II. The results indicate that no such relationship obtains for children. In fact, the only significant relationships between scanning and constant error scores occur with respect to the 30 mm. circle when it is contained within the illusion-producing 45 mm. circle. This result seems primarily attributable to the relationship of time per centration on the standard stimulus to the apparent size of the 30 mm. circle under these illusion-producing conditions. That is, children who spent more time per look examining the 30 mm. circle under these conditions showed greater illusion effects, which could mean that extended centration increased the illusion, or that children who had the most difficulty overcoming this relatively powerful illusion made longer centrations in an attempt to overcome the distortion. These results are thus in rather striking contrast to those for adults. It is remarkable, in fact, that there is no relationship between extensiveness of scanning of the standard and comparison stimuli under neutral conditions and the experienced magnitudes of the stimuli.

Field-Articulation

Sex Differences in Field-Articulation Scores

Small but significant sex-linked differences have been observed consistently in measures of field-articulation. In the present study, the boy-girl differences in scores for the Embedded Figures and Concealed Figures Tests were in the expected direction, but none reached significance. This is undoubtedly a minor artifact of sampling resulting from the small sizes of the groups of boys and girls in the present study. It is interesting that results for two of the three illusions assumed to involve field-articulation are also in the predicted direction.

The results for adults indicate the expected difference in the Embedded Figures Test score but not in the Concealed Figures Test score. The latter mean difference is, however, in the expected direction.

Mean Field-Articulation Scores of Younger and Older Children

These results support the finding of Witkin (1950) and Witkin *et al.* (1954, 1962) that the capacity to isolate embedded figures increases during childhood. This holds true in the present study for both the short form (first twelve of twenty-four items) of Witkin's Embedded Figures Test and for Thurstone's analogous Concealed Figures Test.

Mean Field-Articulation Scores of Children and Adults

The capacity to articulate experience increases notably from pre-adolescence to adulthood, as reported by Witkin in earlier publications (e.g., Witkin *et al.*, 1954, 1962). These earlier results concerning major field-articulation scores receive further support from the present findings. It is interesting, however, that the older children, taken alone, do not differ from the adults in time per figure on the Embedded Figures Test, whereas they achieve only half as many correct responses in the Concealed Figures Test. This finding should be checked in further studies. As it stands, it seems to suggest that the Concealed Figures Test yields larger developmental differences in the preadolescent-adult age span, in spite of the fact that these tests are correlated and factorially similar in the case of both adults and children (see Gardner *et al.*, 1960, and the results for children in Chapter 6). Perhaps the Concealed Figures Test is relatively more difficult for children because of the requirement to decide whether each simple figure is present in each of four complex figures, which may be confusing to children, and the fact that the subject is under continuous time pressure in this test. In the Embedded Figures Test, the subject is under time pressure in each item, but has a few moments to rest and prepare himself for each subsequent item. However, these are but speculations at this point.

Tolerance for Unrealistic Experiences

Because of the nature of the rating procedures used to evaluate tolerance for unrealistic experiences, no comparison of preadolescents and adults was possible.

Mean Tolerance for Unrealistic Experiences Ratings
of Younger and Older Children

The mean rating of the thirty younger children was 5.82, sigma 2.47. The mean rating of the thirty older children was 6.18, sigma 1.65. This mean difference was not significant. The fact that the younger and older children do not differ in tolerance for unrealistic experiences is intriguing, but may have been dictated in part by the limited age range involved.

As noted by Gardner (1964a), the Rorschach protocols of the children contained greater numbers of specific indicators of intolerance of unrealistic experiences than the protocols of adults. No direct comparison of children and adults seemed possible because of the nature of the assessment procedure and the gross quantitative and qualitative differences between the records of preadolescents and adults. It was the raters' impression, however, that the present group of children was less tolerant of unrealistic experiences in general—as well as in terms of specific, overt indicators—than the groups of Midwestern adults who have participated in earlier studies.

Constricted-Flexible Control

Sex Differences in Color-Word Test Scores

The only unexpected sex difference among all the cognitive control scores was that for reading time in Part III of the Color-Word Test, in which the subject is confronted with the difficult task of naming as fast as possible the colors in which incongruous color words are printed. Although the samples are small, and this finding should be replicated, the superiority of girls in this task is of considerable magnitude. The girls are also faster at reading color alone in Part II of the test.

In the case of adult subjects tested earlier, results are roughly similar for color naming, but the sexes do not differ significantly in reading time for the color-word portion of the test. The available sample of men is rather small in this case, so that this finding must be considered a tentative one in need of further study.

Mean Color-Word Test Scores of Younger and Older Children

The results indicate that the older children read color names more rapidly and tend toward naming the colors more rapidly in the difficult color-word combinations of Part III. These differences are relatively small, however, and suggest only a moderate change toward more effective performance within this age range. The stepwise increase in interindividual variability from Part I to II to III is also notable and is compatible with the three levels of difficulty (and familiarity) of the three tasks.

Mean Color-Word Test Scores of Children and Adults [2]

Here we see gross superiority of adult over preadolescent performance. The magnitude of the increase in speed of naming colors printed in incongruous words, 40.1 seconds, is particularly impressive. This aspect of cognitive control shows rather radical change from preadolescence to adulthood, possibly because of the extended time pressure in this test, which also requires rapid shifting from item to item. In this sense, the Color-Word Test has something in common with the otherwise different Concealed Figures Test discussed earlier. In both, the subject must deal with different sets of stimuli in a rapid sequence that requires fluent set shifting. In both, he is under time pressure throughout. The instructions discourage the subject from allowing himself momentary respite in either test, and to do so reduces the adequacy of performance. It thus seems apparent that, although the specific cognitive operations elicited by these tests are quite different, they make similar demands upon the subject's ability to remain unruffled under temporally extended pressure for speed. Adults are apparently much superior to children in maintaining a consistent focus on a task over such extended periods.

With these considerations in mind, it is not surprising that adults show extreme superiority to children in these two tests.

Adequate scores for the interference of color words in the naming of colors requires that reading time for colors alone (Part II of the test) be controlled. The procedure used for this in the present and earlier studies has been to employ as the individual subject's score the difference between his actual score and his score as predicted on the basis of the regression of reading time for Part III on that for Part II. In order to compare the relative amounts of interference for children and adults, a double classification analysis of covariance of reading time in Part III of the Color-Word Test, with reading time in Part II controlled, was performed. The adjusted means and the significant Sex X Age interaction reveal that girls show proportionately less increment than boys in reading time from Parts II to III (i.e., girls show less interference effect), but that

[2] It will be recalled from the description of this shortened test in Chapter 3 that these results are for the first six of the ten lines in the total test.

the men and women do not differ appreciably in this respect. It is also clear, from the adjusted means and the highly significant F attributable to Ages, that the adults show much less interference than the children. Thus, not only the raw reading time scores, but also the increment in reading time from Part II (colors alone) to Part III (color-word), are much less for adults.

Conclusion

The results presented in this chapter point to several general conclusions concerning sex differences in cognitive structures and the multiplicity of developmental-change patterns apparent even in the limited aspects of cognition represented by the four control principles dealt with. The general paucity of sex differences in these constellations of cognitive behaviors is remarkable. This general finding is also compatible with earlier findings for adults. In addition, an equal lack of sex difference is described in Chapter 5 with respect to the conceptual differentiation control principle and related aspects of concept formation. That sex differences do not appear in most of these variegated aspects of cognitive organization—which follow more than one developmental route from early preadolescence to adulthood—emphasizes the complexity of cognitive development and raises general questions concerning the potential relative importance of heredity, sex-linked roles, and other environmental factors to major classes of personality structures that are discussed in more detail in Chapter 15. Suffice it to say here that boy-girl similarities may be as revealing as boy-girl differences in future explorations of culturally determined roles as determinants of individual personality organization.

The various patterns of developmental change characterizing different aspects of cognitive structuring once again point to the complexity of personality organization. The patterning of cognitive controls in the individual adult is arrived at by a multiplicity of developmental routes. With respect to some constellations of cognitive operations, little, if any, change occurs from preadolescence to adulthood. In the case of others, development moves toward lesser perceptual accuracy, or more effectively rapid response. Or (as will be discussed in Chapter 5), both quantitative and qualitative features of cognition may change while individual consistencies remain highly similar from preadolescence to adulthood. Apparently, personality development, even in the extremely limited area represented by five selected cognitive controls, is more complicated than is ordinarily assumed. This complexity will become even more strikingly apparent in Chapter 11, when the sex differences in individual defense mechanisms and the patterning of defense mechanisms in the present sample are introduced.

5 Age and Sex Differences in Conceptual Differentiation and Other Features of Free Categorizing by Preadolescents and Adults

CATEGORIZATION OF the heterogenous arrays of seventy-three objects in the Object Sorting Test and thirty-six pictures of persons in the Photo Sorting Test invokes responses of extreme complexity. In part, this complexity is elicited by the openness of the instructions, which, in brief, require the subject only to put the items of each test into groups in the way that seems "most natural, most logical, and most comfortable." The present chapter is devoted to exposition of a conceptual scheme that includes not only the key features of response referred to in terms of the cognitive control principle, conceptual differentiation, but also several other aspects of response.

Major Determinants of Free Categorizing

Free categorizing tasks of the kind employed in this study seem to evoke the operation of a cognitive control determining the degree of differentiation imposed upon arrays of stimuli but whose operation is not restricted to performance in such tasks (see Gardner and Schoen, 1962). Operation of this control in categorizing tests implicates several other aspects of cognitive control, as well as elaborate sets of learned substructures. Primary among the latter are learned associations between objects and object characteristics, persons and person characteristics. The nature of the interaction of the control principle with these substructures is one of the most interesting general questions concerning the operation of the control in free categorizing tasks. It might be assumed, for example, that the nature of the individual's prior associational structures dictates the degree of conceptual differentiation he imposes on the stimuli in a categorizing test. It might also be assumed that operation of the regulatory control mechanism has shaped the formation of associative structures in prior development. One of the questions posed in the present study was the relationship of the "conceptual distance" from external objects and persons, represented by the individual's associations, to the degree of conceptual differentiation he imposes. As discussed later in this chapter, the relationship between differentiation and conceptual distance seems to vary with the kind of task performed. The results, therefore, suggest the partial autonomy of the control structure from the associational substructures.

Performance in free categorizing tests is sufficiently complex that it will be profitable to consider in detail the major substructures and other aspects of control involved in performance. Examination of our free categorizing tests from this vantage point suggests that at least five major sets of determinants are involved in response, in addition to the control of spontaneous conceptual differentiation: the types of concepts employed in categorizing (including the nature of previously formed associations among objects and pictures drawn upon by S and the conceptual distance of these associations from the physical properties of the test items); capacity to abstract; preferred level of abstraction; involvement in categorizing; and the nature of the instructions and the items categorized.

The presumed disposition to categorize narrowly or broadly in this type of free categorizing situation (i.e., spontaneous conceptual differentiation) is a dimensional aspect of cognitive control inferred from a series of earlier studies of adults (see Chapter 3). The nature of the specific concepts (verbal or other) employed in the grouping of items is obviously an important determinant of performance, but is more obscure and perhaps more complex in its determination. What dictates, for example, the fact that one subject tends to group objects in terms of their physical properties, whereas another groups in terms of the objects' relevances to particular persons? Capacity to abstract, preferred level of abstraction, and conceptual differentiation can be assumed to account for this facet of performance only in part. Individuals may be as consistent in the types of definitions on which their groupings are based, or in the stance toward reality represented by their definitions, as they are in other aspects of performance. One way of dealing with types of definitions in such tests is in terms of the classes of concepts (e.g., person, use, physical property, location) subjects employ. When performance is viewed in this way, such questions as the following become relevant: Is the use of certain types of definitions associated with broad or narrow grouping? Do men and women, boys and girls, differ in the types of concepts they employ? Do the tests evoke different types of concepts from children and adults? What is the relation of types of concepts to capacity to abstract, preferred level of abstraction, verbal IQ, and so forth?

Another way of dealing with types of definitions is in terms of the degree of conceptual distance the subject adopts toward the items to be categorized. Definition in terms of the physical properties of objects (or pictures) represents a categorizing stance very "close" to the objects. Definition in terms of persons represents a categorizing stance very "distant" from the objects as objects.

Among normal adults, conceptual differentiation is related to the subject's stance toward the objects, as indicated by the conceptual distance from physical properties of the objects represented by their definitions of groups (Gardner *et al.*, 1959). This early finding was extended in a recent pilot study of adults employing the more elaborate scheme for classifying definitions described later in this chapter. In this pilot study, the r between the total number of groups and conceptual distance in the OST was $-.80$. The stance of subjects high in conceptual differentiation (i.e., narrow categorizers) is "close" to these stimuli; their definitions of groups tend to involve physical properties of the objects, functions of the objects, and so forth. The stance of subjects low in conceptual differentiation (i.e., broad categorizers) is "distant" from the stimuli; they tend to categorize objects in terms of extraneous factors, such as location, association with persons, and so forth, and their definitions are thus more personalized and less stimulus bound. In adults, these individual differences in conceptual distance from objects and events in the external world have been shown to express themselves in the conceptual distance of free associations from stimulus words (under relaxed conditions with verbal response, but not in a more highly structured paper-and-pencil test), and in the conceptual distance of TAT stories from the physical properties of the pictures (Gardner *et al.*, 1959; Gardner and Schoen, 1962). The results concerning the conceptual distance represented by TAT stories are shown in Chapter 6 to obtain also for the preadolescents of the present study.

This intriguing group of findings, which suggests that a high degree of conceptual differentiation is associated with closeness to the physical properties of external objects, can, of course, be described in terms of the nature or "level" of previously formed associations *S*s characteristically draw upon in their interactions with external reality. *S*s high in conceptual differentiation seem to draw upon associations concerning the relatively limited and verifiable properties of objects. Their performances seem "constricted" in this sense, and they seem to distrust response in terms of levels of the associative hierarchy representing more distant, and more personalized, reactions to external stimuli. It is as if their "style" of reality contact, at least in these kinds of situations, is rooted in literality and stereotypy in respect to both external and internal events. Because of this, they seem inhibited and unimaginative in these kinds of situations.

Ss low in conceptual differentiation seem freer to draw upon less verifiable associations drawn from levels of the associative hierarchy more distant from the stimulus properties. These findings are in striking agreement with the finding by Gardner *et al.* (1959) that adult *Ss* low in conceptual differentiation (i.e., broad categorizers) give more human, movement, and color responses in the Rorschach Test. That is, their preference for responses based upon levels of the associative hierarchy relatively distant from the concrete properties of stimuli seems apparent in the Rorschach, as well as in the other procedures referred to. These findings are also in keeping with the finding in the present study (see Chapter 12) that broad categorizers are more openly explorative than narrow categorizers.

The relationship of conceptual differentiation to conceptual distance is, however, demonstrably more complex than the above findings would seem to indicate. As shown by Gardner and Schoen (1962), for example, the individual consistencies in conceptual differentiation can be demonstrated by highly significant correlations between grouping scores for the OST, in which gross differences in conceptual distance are apparent, and comparable grouping scores for Photo and Behavior Sorting Tests. Conceptual distance and level of abstraction are both arbitrarily limited in the latter tests. The fact that significant grouping correlations are found even when abstraction and conceptual distance are limited suggests, of course, that conceptual differentiation and these other aspects of response are interrelated, but distinctly different, aspects of cognitive organization. The fact that the conceptual differentiation factor for preadolescents (Chapter 6) is very similar to that for adults, even though the range of individual differences in conceptual distance in the OST is restricted in the case of the children, suggests a similar tentative conclusion. It is obvious, then, that these findings require much further research before the key interpretive issues are resolved. A further study by Gardner and Schoen designed to explore some of these issues in more detail is now in progress. Not only the implied differences in conceptual distance, but also the individual differences in emphasis on difference versus similarity, social distance, person versus object orientedness, preference for simplicity versus complexity, and a series of related possible correlates of conceptual differentiation are being explored in detail.

The origins of individual consistencies in this kind of conceptual differentiation have remained obscure. The search for information concerning developmental changes in conceptual differentiation is made more difficult by the likelihood that capacity to abstract (an aspect of intellectual ability that probably has an important degree of hereditary determination) may be a much more important determinant of free categorizing among children than among adults. Scores representing conceptual differentiation for adults could be contaminated, when applied to children's performances, by individual differences in their generally more limited capacity to group objects in meaningful ways. A major determinant of children's performances may thus be the capacity to abstract. Experience with objects and exposure to verbalized categorizations by adults must also be important determinants of the child's capacity to group objects in meaningful ways that are not unique or autistic but that resonate appropriately with categorizing by other persons and provide the basis for appropriate communication. The degree to which the capacity to abstract is a purely maturational phenomenon and the degree to which it is determined by commerce with objects and persons, plus others' expressed conceptions of relations between objects and persons, is, of course, an unanswered question. It can be said only that the interaction of these two major sets of determinants somehow brings the individual child to a certain potential for grouping that must be one determinant of his performance in a complex free categorizing test.

Two distinct facets of grouping can be distinguished in the free categorizing tests used as criterion measures of conceptual differentiation: the motor acts of grouping and the selection (before, during, or after grouping) of verbal concepts that "define" the associations between items in the groups the subject forms. At first glance, it might seem that verbal concepts are always regnant in the grouping process and that active grouping is subservient to its verbal masters. Since children can often perform more effective acts than they can adequately explain or conceptualize, however, it seems possible that the verbal and performance aspects of grouping may be distinguishable and may be characterized by different degrees and qualities of coordination in the case of children than in the case of adults. A child may, for example, base his grouping to a greater degree upon his earlier perceptions of and motoric interactions with objects. His groupings could thus be based to a greater degree upon visual images of previously experienced objects and object relationships and even more primitive motoric remembrances concerning the functional utility of objects. Adults, on the other hand, usually seem to approach tasks of complex free categorizing by first forming verbal concepts, then "fitting" objects into groups effectively coordinated to these concepts. It therefore seems possible that the causal sequence of behaviors involved in complex categorizing is different in the case of preadolescent children than in the case of adults. The child may also be more likely to "feel" his way toward a group, so that the motor act of grouping may tend to have priority and precedence over the formation of a reportable verbal concept. In other words, the *balance* of verbal and motor components of grouping may be discernibly different in adults, as compared to preadolescents. These issues cannot be resolved by use of these categorizing tests alone. An analysis of relationships between groups and definitions presented later in this chapter seems, however, to provide support for this rather obvious hypothesis.

Results of earlier studies of adults indicate that the preferred level of categorizing in the Object Sorting Test (in which no demand is made for abstraction) cannot be predicted from Wechsler-Bellevue IQ scores or subtest scores, including the Similarities test score often presumed to measure capacity to abstract. The levels of abstraction at which the subject chooses to perform in free categorizing may, nevertheless, be an important determinant of performance. A subject who can allow himself only highly abstract reasons for his groupings may be forced to limit the sizes of some groupings in the interest of effective definition. Or he may draw the most generalized similarities from the items and hence form larger groups. The present study provided an opportunity to explore relations between preferred conceptual level and group size in preadolescents and adults. It should be noted, however, as discussed in more detail in the presentation of these results, that current methods of assessing level of abstraction on the basis of verbalization, including the method employed in the present study, are grossly inadequate in some instances. As pointed out by Goldstein and Scheerer (1941) and others, grouping a number of red objects together and defining the group as "red things" meets the formal requirements for scoring as "abstract," but can in actuality be a profoundly concrete response.

Another determinant of performance in free categorizing tests seems to be the subject's investment in categorizing as a means of organizing his experience. Categorizing seems to be a more natural, and possibly more necessary, means of ordering experience for the narrow categorizer. This possible determinant of performance has not been measured systematically, so that such postulations are highly speculative. It can be noted, however, that great investment in such tasks could lead to expenditure of more time and effort in categorizing, perhaps independent of the number of groups formed but directly relevant—particularly in the case of children—to the adequacy with which a group and its verbalized definition are matched, the occurrence of misidentification of objects, and so forth. It can be noted, also, that a subject impatient with the requirement to categorize may find the quickest exit from the situation by forming a few large groups, possibly with an additional single object or two that did not fit the first large categories that occurred to him.

Further, and more obvious, determinants of response to free categorizing tests are the nature of the instructions and the materials to be categorized. The effects of the permissiveness of instructions on performance has already been commented on. Effects attributable to the kinds of stimuli categorized are gross in some areas of response, but apparently minor in others. In many ways, the categorizing of objects seems very different from the categorizing of pictures of persons, statements about behavior, Chinese characters, and so forth, used in various earlier studies. The possible bases of grouping are inevitably different. In addition, a "person-oriented" individual may approach the categorization of pictures of people in ways different from those in which he approaches the categorization of objects, and vice versa. The *ranges* of item characteristics and combinations of characteristics is also of great importance in studies of individual differences. The Object Sorting Test allows greater freedom of response than the Photo Sorting Test, since the variations in person characteristics that can be represented in photographs are inevitably restricted. The interaction of all the major aspects of response described above are undoubtedly affected by the nature of the items and the interrelationships among item characteristics. As will be noted later in this chapter, such key differences between the two tests employed in the present study did not obscure the individual consistencies in conceptual differentiation, but had notable effects on several other aspects of performance.

Each of the major aspects of response described above is assumed to interact with all the others in the process of categorizing the items of the Object Sorting Test and Photo Sorting Test. The potential number of patterns of interaction is thus very large.

It should be re-emphasized here that the process of free categorizing in these tests is extremely complex at every step. Few, if any, adult subjects appear to group with but one category in mind. Most adult subjects appear, from the onset, to be considering relations among two or more tentative grouping concepts simultaneously. Proceeding from these initial concepts to a more and more complex array of interrelated concepts, they move quite fluently toward a final solution that ordinarily requires little or no regrouping. Subjects who place all the objects of the Object Sorting Test into the three very broad categories of "Mother," "Father," "Child," for example, usually have all these concepts in mind before and during their grouping, and all three categories are often begun before any one is completed. This also seems true, although perhaps to a lesser degree, in the case of preadolescent children. The degree to which multiple categorizing occurs could be a function of the subject's capacity to conceptualize similarities and differences and his capacity to keep several concepts in mind and manipulate them flexibly in integrating workable *clusters* of concepts. It could be that intellectual abilities have their greatest role in this unscored aspect of performance, rather than in the conceptual differentiation represented by the final outcome. On the average, preadolescent children seem to approach these tests in a more step-wise fashion. That is, they more often seem to form a single first group, then to form other groups from the remainder.

The fact that at least the aspects of performance referred to above are involved in a single complex response process makes it difficult, of course, to obtain information concerning causal interdetermination among the major determinants of over-all performance. That adult narrow categorizers are "object-close" in their verbalized bases for grouping in the Object Sorting Test could as easily be interpreted to mean that their propensity for narrow categorizing led to employment of certain types of grouping principles as that their preference for a particular degree of distance from objects (with its effect on the types of principles employed) dictates the formation of narrow groups. These and related questions concerning interactions among these and other determinants must await other types of investigation than those included in the present study. Detailed information concerning multiple grouping, the behavioral sequence involved in grouping, and so forth also await further studies. The present study provided, however, a first opportunity to explore the major facets of response thus far discernible, as well as some of their interrelationships, in the case of preadolescents. Such analyses can yield results that add to our understanding of these complex performances and provide a basis for more refined hypotheses concerning the meaning and developmental emergence of individual consistencies in these aspects of concept formation.

Free Categorization of Objects

As noted in Chapter 3, the Object Sorting Test has been used in a number of studies of individual consistencies in conceptual differentiation. The analyses of Object Sorting Test protocols described below followed the scheme originally proposed by Gardner (1953), but which has been elaborated upon considerably in the present study.

Mean Grouping and Abstraction Scores of Boys and Girls

There were no sex differences in the grouping, abstraction, or time scores for this free categorizing test. These results are thus comparable to earlier findings of no sex differences in the grouping scores with adult samples. The boys and girls differ neither in the total-number-of-groups score used as a criterion of conceptual differentiation, nor in the two major components of this score, the number of single-object groups (i.e., categories) and the number of groups of two or more objects.

Mean Grouping and Abstraction Scores of Younger and Older Children

The younger and older children do not differ significantly in the number of groups of two or more objects, but approach a significant difference in the number of single-object groups, and hence in the total number of groups. This means, of course, that the groups of two or more objects made by younger children contain fewer objects than those of older children. The conclusion is, then, that younger children form smaller groups in this test, a result that may in part be attributable to their lesser ability to conceptualize meaningful relationships among objects. It could also mean, however, that younger children are more difference oriented.

The fact that younger and older children do not differ in level of abstraction may be attributable to the fact that the smaller groups made by the younger children are easier to conceptualize at adequate levels of abstraction. Both groups' average level of abstraction is close to 2.0, the score assigned to functional (i.e., use) definitions.

The relatively small difference in numbers of groups did not produce a difference in sorting time, which is significantly correlated (positively) with the number of groups formed.

Mean Grouping and Abstraction Scores of Children and Adults

Conceptual differentiation is much greater in the children than in the adults. From preadolescence to adulthood, there is an obvious progression from emphasis upon differences in objects to synthesis in terms of similarities. This result is relevant to an important theoretical point: whereas the kind of differentiation represented by response to field-articulation tests increases from preadolescence to adulthood (Chapter 4), spontaneous differentiation in concept formation moves in the opposite direction, i.e., toward less differentiation with increasing age.

The much greater number of groups formed by the children is evident both in the mean size of groups of two or more objects and in the number of objects placed by themselves.

It could be that children form pervasively smaller groups because of their relative inability to conceptualize relationships, which, as indicated earlier in this chapter, is a function of ability to abstract and extensiveness of experience with objects. The apparently paradoxical finding that the childrens' preferred level of abstraction is higher than the adults' is thus not to be taken at face value. The mean size of groups of two or more objects (i.e., groups for which definitions are required) is 2.79 for children, 3.24 for adults, and smaller groups are generally easier to define abstractly than larger groups. The children's definitions scored at the conceptual level (the highest level of abstraction in the scoring scheme used) are also more likely to be pseudo-conceptual definitions that are actually concrete, a deficiency common to methods of scoring abstraction that depend entirely upon the subject's verbalized account. One of the most frequent distortions produced by such scoring schemes involves pseudo abstractions that refer to relatively pervasive physical properties, such as substance and color, and are actually concrete responses.

It is assumed here that one determinant of the greater conceptual differentiation by children, as compared to adults, is their relative inability to make meaningful groups. The relationship of grouping scores to intellectual capacity scores for the group of children is thus of particular interest. In view of the significant correlation between age and number of groups for the children, the appropriate tests of such relationships are semipartial r's with age-corrected WISC Verbal, Performance, and Total

IQ scores and the Similarities score. These partial r's are $-.10$, $-.02$, $-.07$, and $-.02$, indicating no relationship with these intelligence test scores. Ability to abstract, at least as measured by these WISC scores, is not an important determinant of conceptual differentiation at preadolescence. It is thus again obvious that high degrees of this form of conceptual differentiation are not attributable to skill in articulating experience. It seems apparent, however, that this test is more difficult for children than adults. It is also reasonable to assume that at least part of the gross differences in grouping is attributable to their gross differences in ability to conceptualize similarities among large groups of otherwise disparate items.

Additional information concerning the relationship of ability to conceptual differentiation is provided by the correlations of conceptual differentiation factor scores to WISC factor scores in the final analysis described in Chapter 12, where the general independence of these major scores at preadolescence is indicated by different patterns of factor loadings. It is to be noted, however, that a partial association of verbal skills with conceptual differentiation (both being loaded on a factor called "Explorativeness") is also apparent there. Taken together, the results summarized here seem to indicate that these aspects of intellectual ability determine only a small percentage of the variance in children's conceptual differentiation scores.

Longitudinal studies are required to supply more adequate answers for this type of question. The most important implication of the present finding is that the process by which preadolescents and adults perform the same task is discernibly different in one respect. The hypothesis remains viable, however, that children are not only less capable of grouping, but also more oriented toward differences than are adults. The progression is toward synthesis of experience in the form of lesser spontaneous conceptual differentiation with increasing age from preadolescence to adulthood. The progression presumably involves at least an increasing capacity to conceptualize similarities, an increasing experience with objects, and an adaptive decrease in this kind of conceptual differentiation (i.e., a greater emphasis on similarities) in the service of economy of thought.

In the case of the children, the r between sorting time and number of groups is .30, $p < .05$, indicating that greater conceptual differentiation takes more time. The significant difference between the sorting times of children and adults may thus be attributable in part to the difference in numbers of groups.

Interrelations of Grouping and Abstraction Scores for the Object Sorting Test

As noted in Chapter 3, analyses of components of the total-number-of-groups score requires that adequate consideration be given to the nature of the distribution of groups of different sizes. We argued there that dividing the distribution between the single-object groups and two-or-more-object groups yields misleading results concerning the homogeneity of the total-number-of-groups score. Table 5–1 contains results that explicate these points. When compared with the correlation of .42 between the number of groups of two or more objects and the total number of groups, the very high r (.91) between the number of single-object groups and the total number of groups *seems* to show that the major portion of the variance of the total-number-of-groups score is attributable to the number of single-object categories. As noted in Chapter 3, however, this is an unjustifiable interpretation based on an arbitrary division of the distribution of group sizes. In the present study, the broad groups comparable in extremeness of size to single-object categories (i.e., equidistant from the mean in sigma units) are groups of *six or more* objects (not two or more objects). When the skewing in the direction of single-object categories is considered, the correlation of the number of groups of six or more objects with the total number of groups ($-.66$) is predictably high and predictably *opposite* in sign. The correlation between the number of groups of six or more objects and the number of single-object groups is $-.50$, whereas the correlation between the number of groups of two or more objects and the number of single-object groups is .00. It is obvious from these results that such analyses must be based on cutting points determined by the total distribution, rather than on an arbitrary division between single- and multiple-object categories. In keeping with these findings, the correlation between the number of groups of six or more objects and the number of groups of two or more objects is negative ($-.48, p < .001$).[1]

The r's of two additional scores—the numbers of objects in the largest group and the largest three groups—with the total-number-of-groups score further confirm our contention. These r's are $-.61, p < .001$, and $-.74, p < .001$. Both are significant. In spite of the skewing toward single-object groups, not only the number of single ob-

[1] Comparable results were recently obtained in a study of fifty-six adults with one of the paper-and-pencil object sorting tests referred to briefly in Chapter 3.

jects but also the numbers of very large groups are highly correlated with the total score, with the signs predictably opposite. Whether the number of single-item groups or the number of very large groups is more highly correlated with the total number of groups is primarily determined by the distribution of group sizes in a particular sample.

TABLE 5–1

Pearson Correlations Among Children's Grouping and Abstraction
Scores for the Object Sorting Test
$(N = 60)$

Score	1	2	3	4	5
1. Number of Groups					
2. Number of Single Objects	.91 ***				
3. Number of Groups of Two or More Objects	.42 ***	.00			
4. Number of Groups of Six or More Objects	−.66 ***	−.50 ***	−.48 ***		
5. Sorting Time	.30 *	.12	.44 ***	−.34 **	
6. Level of Abstraction	.24	.22	.07	−.24	.38 **

* $p < .05.$
** $p < .01.$
*** $p < .001.$

The correlation of the sorting-time score with the total-number-of-groups score is lower than in pilot analyses of adult data. It is notable that the r is positive (.44) with the number of groups of two or more objects but negative (−.34) with the number of groups of six or more objects, once again indicating that greater time is required to form greater numbers of groups.

It is important to note that the number-of-groups scores are not significantly correlated with preferred level of abstraction. The latter is correlated only with sorting time, a result that lends itself to no single, unambiguous interpretation.

The Attribution of Meaning in Object Sorting by Preadolescents and Adults

Not only formal properties of free categorizing, such as number of groups and level of abstraction of the definitions S chose to employ, but also the nature of the concepts on which categories are based shows important changes from preadolescence to adulthood. The emphasis on capacity to abstract in the literature on concept formation seems to have restricted exploration of developmental changes in the meanings employed in spontaneous categorizing. To use a term employed by Bolles (1937), preadolescents and adults may also differ greatly in the "bases of pertinence" involved in categorizing. It also seemed important to explore relations between the formal properties of grouping dealt with in this chapter and the definitions employed by children in groups of two or more objects.

Analysis of the definitions of groups offered by preadolescents and adults took the form of categorization of definitions in the Object and Photo Sorting Tests in a framework applicable to the performances of both preadolescents and adults. One investigator [2] developed empirical categories for the children's Object Sorting Test definitions, another [3] developed such categories independently for adults. Each developed his category scheme empirically, i.e., on the basis of detailed examination of test protocols and without advance commitment to any method of categorizing types of definitions. In each case, the developer collapsed a larger number of initial categories into a smaller number of final categories that seemed to fit the data in a natural way and that involved a minimum of judgment concerning the categorization of individual definitions. Differences in these empirical schemes for categorizing definitions were reconciled in meetings of the two raters and the senior author. The two raters then independently scored the children's and adults' protocols according to the single scheme adopted. An analogous procedure was followed in the development of empirical categories for types of definitions in the Photo Sorting Test.

Types of Definitions in the Object Sorting Test

Each definition was assigned to one of the categories described below. The first five of these categories were designed to represent five degrees of conceptual distance from the physical properties of the objects.

1. *Identity.* Definitions naming groups of objects that are identical or nearly identical (e.g., the corks, the candles, the candle holders, and so forth) were assigned to this category. Designating the dime and the penny as "Money" was also considered Identity, because this kind of designation seems to be primarily a simple naming operation.

[2] Robert Schoen.
[3] Allen Willner.

2. *Physical Properties.* Definitions specifying size, shape, substance, color, capacity to make a sound, and so forth.

3. *Use.* Definitions specifying the use of objects for certain purposes or by certain persons, and definitions involving such terms as "Instruments" or "Tools."

4. *Location.* Definitions including mention of a specific location, e.g., "Tools used in a workshop," "Kitchen things," "Things on a dresser." Mention of location was given precedence over all the categories except the Person category described below.

5. *Person.* Definitions containing any reference to a person, e.g., "Children's toys" or "Men's things," with the exception of "Carpenter's tools," in which the word "carpenter" is but a descriptive adjective. In an attempt to maximize the range of distance scores, this category was given preference over categories 1–4, i.e., any mention of a person in the definition itself led to assignment of the definition to this category.

6. *Food.* Definitions specifying that the objects are edible, taste good, are candy, and so forth.

7. *Personal Appearance.* Definitions specifying cosmetic properties of objects, e.g., "For good grooming" or "For keeping neat."

8. *Residual.* All other definitions. Many of the definitions assigned to this category were unique, but the common definition "medicine," and related references to health were also placed here.

Conceptual Distance Score

Five of the categories described above lend themselves to the classification of definitions in terms of the psychological distance from the physical properties of the objects they represent. A distance score was therefore employed in which the following weightings were assigned: Identity, 1; Physical Properties, 2; Use, 3; Location, 4; and Person, 5. The mean of these weighted scores was used as the conceptual distance score for each subject.

Mean Numbers of Boys' and Girls' Definitions in Eight Categories

In view of the statistical interdependence of these categories, the t tests used to test boy-girl differences elsewhere in the study are not appropriate here. The relevant findings are results of an analysis of variance of the numbers of definitions of the eight types. The significant Group (boys-girls) X Category interaction shows that boys and girls differ in the patterning of employment of the categories of definitions.

The most obvious differences are that boys use more Personal Appearance and Physical Property definitions, girls more Use and Identity definitions.

Mean Numbers of Younger and Older Children's Definitions in Eight Categories

The Group (younger-older) X Category interaction in this case is nonsignificant, indicating that the younger and older children of the present sample do not differ in the patterning of types of definitions employed.

Mean Numbers of Children's and Adults' Definitions in Eight Categories

In this case, the Group (children-adult) X Category interaction is highly significant, indicating that the patterning of use of the different types of definitions differs for preadolescents and adults. The most apparent differences are the adults' greater use of Person and Location definitions and the children's greater use of Personal Appearance, Physical Property, and Identity definitions. Both groups give more Use definitions than any other type.

The Relation of Group Size to Type and Conceptual Distance of Definition

One of the most intriguing unanswered questions concerning free categorizing is the relation of individual consistencies in conceptual differentiation to the bases of pertinence individuals employ in categorizing. In the subject's grouping performance, these two aspects of categorizing seem impossible to disentangle by ordinary methods. Rather, they appear to be two interacting aspects of a total performance. Examination of the relationship of group size to type of definition and conceptual distance may, however, give new insight into the meaning, as well as a possible correlate, of broad and narrow categorizing. Gardner and Schoen (1962) have shown that the conceptual distance of stories from the physical characteristics of TAT pictures is negatively correlated with conceptual differentiation. Results of the present study (see Chapter 6) indicate that the same kind and general degree of relationship holds for preadolescent children. The distance score for definitions of groups by preadolescent children in the Object Sorting Test is an analogous measure that may provide further insight into developmental changes in categorizing behavior.

It is apparent from the significant Group (children-adults) X Category interaction that the children and adults differ in the relationship of group size to type of definition. A key to the difference is that the largest groups formed by adults are based on definitions involving persons, whereas the children's largest groups are based on definitions involving uses of the objects. Thus, the children's definitions are not only conceptually closer to the physical properties of the objects, as shown earlier, but also their relative group sizes for different definition types are patterned differently from those of adults. The fact that children make many more single-item groups than do adults makes it inevitable that the average size of their groups of two or more objects (i.e., those assigned to definition categories) is smaller. The results show, however, that this reduction in size is not uniform. The children have fewer objects per group in Use, Location, and Person categories, but more objects per group in all the other categories. The most notable differences are in the Person and Location categories.

Another way to summarize these findings is in terms of the relationship between group size and the average distance from the physical properties represented by S's groups. In a pilot study of adults, the r between the total number of groups (equivalent to the mean size of all groups) and conceptual distance was $-.80$, $p < .001$. For the children, this r is $-.56$, $p < .001$. Thus, we seem to find similar patterns of relationship between group size and conceptual distance for preadolescents and adults.

The gross differences between the children and adults in "closeness" to the objects and in the similar relationship between distance and group size is worthy of special note. When one considers that the much greater number of singles produced by the children also represents closeness to objects, the difference in "stance" with respect to the objects is magnified. In this test, placing an object by itself is a deliberate act of categorization (when the test is adequately administered, of course, no items are overlooked or omitted). To place an object by itself is, almost inevitably, the product of an impression of its uniqueness *as an object* such that no abstraction of properties linking it to other objects occurs. When viewed in this light, the performances of even bright normal children are thus dramatically different from those of adults in terms of closeness to the objects. Here, then, is a glimpse into an aspect of the psychological stance of the preadolescent child. In marked contrast to the obvious fact that his coordination to external reality is less firm and effective, and his experiencing of reality more personalized and "autistic" than that of the adult, he is notably "closer" to external reality in this test. In some ways, the present finding is reminiscent of the well-known concreteness or inability to abstract that so clearly distinguishes children from adults. But the results discussed earlier indicate that this difference in stance cannot be explained entirely in this way, at least in terms of some common criteria of capacity to abstract.

Special Features of Children's Definitions of Groups in the Object Sorting Test

Inspection of the children's Object Sorting Test protocols suggested that their performances include instances of qualitative phenomena that are rare or nonexistent in the large number of protocols obtained from normal adults in earlier studies. Like the analysis of definition types, analysis of these features of the children's performance was dictated largely by the data themselves, rather than by any preconceived scoring plan. The scoring schemes described below were developed [4] and applied after detailed study of the protocols. The tentative scoring schemes were then further refined in discussions with the first author. Definitions were scored for presence or absence of the features of performance listed below, which were selected from a larger preliminary group on the basis of frequency of occurrence. In view of the preliminary nature of these new scores and the relative infrequency of occurrence of some of them even in the protocols of preadolescents, no attempt was made to analyze these data in terms of boy-girl or younger-older children differences. The over-all results reported here seem revealing, however, of further differences between preadolescent and adult performances.

Inadequate Definitions

Seven types of definitions were included in this category:

1. *Failure.* Object naming or failure to attempt a definition, e.g., "I don't know why I put them together."

2. *Inaccurate definition.* Definition inappropriate to the objects grouped, without misidentification of objects, e.g., defining the Mercurochrome, pill, and eyedropper as "Medicine."

3. *Unverbalized definition.* Definition in which the grouping clearly implied a perceived relationship, but the verbalization did not; e.g., defining the brush, broom, and comb as "brushes and combs."

[4] By Robert Schoen.

4. *Unspecific definition.* Definition in such terms as "Have the same purpose," "Look alike," "Go together."

5. *Leaving the field.* Definitions such as the following for the pipe, pipestem, cigar, cigarette, two small candles, and large candle: "Well, you both use matches (not among the test items) to light the candles and the cigar."

6. *Definition based on misidentification of objects.* Definition based, in part, on misidentification of one or more objects, e.g., defining the tie, earring, sunglasses, button, and mothball as "all something you can wear"; or defining the whistle and bell as "bells."

7. *Syncretistic definition.* Such overinclusive definitions as "All belong to men," "All manufactured," "All a type of material."

The incidences of these seven forms of inadequate definition are shown in Table 5–2. The results show clearly that several forms of inade-

TABLE 5–2

Numbers of Inadequate Definitions *

Category	Number of Children	Number of Instances
1. Failure	6	8
2. Inaccurate	41	75
3. Unverbalized	26	42
4. Unspecific	31	42
5. Leaving the Field	5	5
6. Misidentification	23	27
7. Syncretistic	11	12
8. Total	56	211

* In a total of 978 definitions by the 60 children.

quate definition that are rare or nonexistent in the protocols of normal adults are common to considerable numbers of the sixty children. The most frequent type, the inaccurate definition, occurs occasionally in adult protocols, but in nothing like the frequency apparent here. Misidentification of an occasional object (particularly the pebble) also occurs, although infrequently, among adults, but again with nothing like the frequency that it appears in the children's protocols. Syncretistic definitions also occur infrequently in the protocols of normal adults. The other categories of inadequate definition—failure, unverbalized, unspecific, and leaving the field—are all but nonexistent in normal adults' protocols.

This analysis of inadequate definitions points up several important differences between free categorizing by preadolescent children and adults. First, the matching of verbalization to grouping (which is generally more adequate than verbalization) is less in the case of the children. The relationship of verbalization to grouping seems to indicate a greater fluidity of group boundaries for the children than for adults. The second generalization that can be drawn from these results is that children form a considerable number of groups without having adequate definitions in mind in verbalizable form. That is, they seem to approach grouping effectively, but with less conscious control and less mediation via verbal concepts than is true of adults. Some of the children's responses are, in fact, of a quality suggesting that groups are based on prelogical, rather than fully logical concepts.

The frequency of misidentification of objects suggests that, in spite of their stimulus-boundness in this test (as discussed earlier in this chapter), the children are in less effective and less accurate perceptual contact with the objects. Their percepts tend to be coordinated more completely to anticipation, at the expense of objective accuracy, than is true of adults. In one sense, they seem to show greater assimilation (i.e., leveling), in that memories of objects common to their experience seem to interact with incoming percepts to a greater degree than is true of adults. A common misidentification among children was based on perception of the (small, gray, irregular) pebble as a wad of gum.

Examination of the incidences of inadequate definitions in Table 5–2 also suggests that a quality of vagueness concerning the relationship of a fully conscious, verbalizable concept to the group formed is frequently apparent in children's protocols. In some instances, it is as if the child formed a group on the basis of earlier motoric and perceptual interaction with objects, rather than on any verbally articulated basis.

These aspects of performance suggest that preadolescent children form groups in ways that are similar, but also notably different, from those of adults. Adults are more likely, it would appear, to form clearly articulated verbal concepts, then to arrange the groups to match them, so that the process of reporting the concept to the experimenter seems easy and natural to them. Children seem to form groups on the basis of lesser verbal mediation and in some instances to experience the demand for a verbalized definition as a new and unexpected task requirement.

The semilogical quality of some of the children's definitions is perhaps most apparent in the unverbalized category. In the case of these definitions, each of the experimenters who examined the protocols felt that there was a clear and effective basis for the child's grouping (e.g., the group was identical to one given frequently and defined clearly and adequately by adults and other children), but that the act of grouping had not involved the verbalized form of the concept.

These findings concerning the matching of verbalization to grouping thus indicate further differences between the performances of preadolescents and adults that illuminate the stage of conceptual development characteristic of the children. In spite of their closeness to the stimuli, their coordination is more autistic, less accurate, and less dictated by verbalizable concepts. In effect, their coordination to reality, in the limited sense appropriate to such a specific categorizing test, is still not fully articulated and not fully verbalizable.

It should be noted here that the protocols of some adults also contain indications of a partial incoordination of grouping and verbalization. This occurs most frequently when the adult must pause to formulate a verbalization when required to define his group. Sometimes this leads to what appears to be an on-the-spot finalization of a half-formed verbal concept employed in grouping. Occasionally, but rather infrequently, the requirement to define a group serves as a reality-testing check for an adult, who discovers a discrepancy between his verbalization and the group, which may lead him to regroup or extract a single discrepant object. The impression the experimenters consistently have of such adult responses, however, is that the lack of coordination between the guiding verbal concept and the grouping is only partial. It is as if the adult either forms his group on the basis of a clearly defined verbal concept or he does this in part and finishes a process already begun when required to give the definition. In the case of some of the children, in contrast, there seems to be no clear verbal concept or the verbal concept employed fits the group inadequately. More often than not, this occurs without the improvement of reality-testing occasioned in some adults by the requirement to define the group. Thus, the children's inadequate definitions range from bafflement at the requirement to define the group verbally to definitions implying minor conceptual or perceptual inadequacies.

Ineffective Elaborations of Definitions

Examination of the children's Object Sorting Test protocols also suggested that their definitional statements contain much larger numbers of ineffective elaborations than do those of adults. Inspection of the protocols led to the formation of three categories of ineffective elaboration:

1. *Unnecessary elaboration.* Definitions assigned to this category included statements that added nothing to the explanation of the grouping but were not vague, e.g., defining the dime and penny as "They're money—*dime and penny together would make 11 cents.*"

2. *Uncertain elaboration.* This category was reserved for explicit statements of uncertainty, e.g., defining the glasses and tie as *"I don't know—for a man?"*; defining the jar and lid as "The lid goes on the jar, *I think*"; and the like.

3. *Vague elaboration.* This category is exemplified by the definition of the six silverware items as "Utensils that you use to eat *and everything,*" addition of such words to definitions as *"and stuff," "something like that,"* and so forth. (It is obvious, of course, that some of the definitions assigned to these categories were also assigned to categories of inadequate definition in the preceding scoring scheme.)

The incidences of ineffective elaborations of definitions by the children is shown in Table 5–3. As in the case of the inadequate definitions, the numbers of responses assignable to these categories is rather low but still much higher than in the case of normal adults. It can also be seen that each of the categories in one way or another reflects the fluidity of coordination of verbalization to grouping that was apparent in the results concerning inadequate definitions. It is also notable that forty-five children (75 per cent of the sample) gave one or more such elaborations.

TABLE 5–3

Numbers of Ineffective Elaborations of Definitions *

Category	Number of Children	Number of Instances
1. Unnecessary	26	57
2. Uncertain	17	19
3. Vague	25	43
4. Total	45	119

* In a total of 978 definitions by the 60 children.

Other Special Features of the Children's Definitions

The children's Object Sorting Test definitions were different from adults' in a number of other ways. Four additional categories of definitions were employed to represent the most common of these differences. In the case of multiple definitions, such responses are given occasionally by adults, but in lesser numbers and with fewer instances of fluctuation from one conceptual level to another.

1. *Multiple definition.* Three subclasses of multiple definition were scored: (a) "spoiled" definitions, in which the second definition is at a lower level of abstraction than the first; (b) those in which the second definition is at the same level of abstraction as the first; and (c) "improved" definitions, in which the second is at a higher level of abstraction than the first.

2. *Emergent definition.* A definition was assigned to this category when it seemed to be formulated in the course of the subject's attempt to define a group, as in the following verbalization about a group consisting of all the silverware (six items), the sucker, whisk broom, and jar rubber: "Well, I think of candy as a food. It goes in the kitchen. Does this go on the top of the jar? One reason for the broom being in the kitchen—all go in the kitchen." Definitions assigned to this category seemed to represent either deliberate groping toward a clear concept or almost "accidental" discovery of a verbal concept in the course of naming objects, describing objects, verbal circumlocutions around the requirement to provide a definition, and so forth.

3. *Implied fabulizing.* This category was limited to definitions in which a linking of objects involving fabulizing was clearly implied by the subject's definitional statement, e.g., "Locks and police go together."

4. *Action-based definition.* A definition was assigned to this category if it involved latent or implied activity as the essential basis for grouping, e.g., defining a group consisting of the Mercurochrome, bottle, and eye-dropper as follows: "Take the lid off and put this in there and it goes up in the tube and that's the way it works"; defining a group as "A washing group," "A dressing group," and the like.

The incidences of these additional special features of children's definitions, which are also infrequent or nonexistent in the protocols of normal adults, is presented in Table 5–4.

More than twice as many multiple definitions involve fluctuations from one conceptual level to another as involve maintenance of the same level. The frequency of "spoiled" multiple definitions is more than three times as great as that of improved definitions. These findings, like those concerning inadequate definitions, suggest looseness in the child's coordination of a verbal concept to groups he has formed. They also reaffirm other suggestions that children are less capable of true abstraction. In addition, these findings suggest that, within the limits of their capacity to abstract, children may be less consistent in the spontaneous levels they adopt in free categorizing.

The incidence of verbal responses apparently masking latent or

TABLE 5–4

*Numbers of Other Special Features of Children's Definitions *

Category	Number of Children	Number of Instances
1. Multiple Definition		
a. Spoiled	16	19
b. Same Conceptual Level	8	9
c. Improved	3	5
d. Total	24	33
2. Emergent Definition	16	21
3. Implied Fabulizing	9	9
4. Action-Based Definition	17	28
5. Total	42	91

* In a total of 978 definitions by the 60 children.

unexpressed tendencies to link objects by fabulizing again suggests a looser coordination of verbal concept to group in the case of the children. It is to be noted, also, that both the implied fabulizing and the verbal expressions that seem to mark such fabulizing are appropriately considered extremely concrete. These attempts at definition also indicate that these children were not aware of the inefficacy of their verbal statements as meaningful communications to the experimenter. Their apparent assumption that what is only half verbalized is understandable implies an inadequate appreciation of the other person's problem in understanding and a vagueness about the distinction between self and other persons. In effect, these children seem to assume that a concrete, image-like verbal representation of an essentially fabulized linkage of objects is sufficient. Although rather infrequent and subtle indicators, these responses clearly imply an inadequacy of reality-testing contingent upon an unarticulated conception of the needs of other persons.

The greater frequency of action-based definitions is in keeping with preadolescent children's generally acknowledged tendency to experience objects in terms of their functions and the actions relevant to those functions. The fact that these definitions are rooted in images of motoric events, rather than verbal concepts per se, is also compatible with this general view of preadolescent cognition, which has been spelled out in greater detail by Piaget, Werner, and others.

Free Categorization of Pictures of Persons

The Photo Sorting Test described in Chapter 3 involves free categorization of thirty-six pictures of persons. As noted there, the instructions are as nearly identical as possible to those for the Object Sorting Test. In the study by Gardner and Schoen (1962) of adults' spontaneous conceptual differentiation, the number of groups formed in a paper-and-pencil version of the Object Sorting Test and in a different Photo Sorting Test were significantly correlated, indicating individual consistencies in conceptual differentiation independent of the materials categorized. The analyses of grouping behavior in the Photo Sorting Test are analogous to those for the Object Sorting Test. Since the Photo Sorting Test all but requires abstract definitions, no abstraction scores were employed.

Mean Grouping Scores of Boys and Girls

As in the case of the Object Sorting Test, no significant differences appear for boys and girls.

Mean Grouping Scores of Younger and Older Children

The differences approaching significance here are again analogous to those in the Object Sorting Test. That is, the younger children tend to form more single-picture categories and hence to have greater total numbers of groups, possibly because they have more difficulty conceptualizing relationships among the items.

Mean Grouping Scores of Children and Adults

Again as in the Object Sorting Test, the children form many more single-item groups and thus have greater total numbers of groups. They also spend more time in grouping the pictures.

Interrelations of Grouping Scores for the Photo Sorting Test

The results shown in Table 5–5 are analogous to those presented earlier for the Object Sorting Test. It is even clearer here that analysis of components of the total-number-of-groups score should be based upon the sample dealt with, rather than on unjustified assumptions about single-item versus multiple-item groups. When the distribution of group sizes is divided at a point on the broad-group end equidistant from the mean with single-item groups at the narrow-group end, the r's with the total score ($-.82, .95$) are almost identical in level. The r between groups of five or more pictures and the number of singles is again much higher than that for groups of two or more pictures.

The relation of the number of pictures in the largest group and the three largest groups to the total number of groups, $-.70$, $p < .001$, and $-.75$, $p < .001$, are also highly significant. Once again, it is apparent that division of the group-size distribution at the single-item versus two-or-more-item point leads to erroneous conclusions concerning the relation of part-scores to total scores in such tests.

Sorting time is correlated somewhat higher with number of groups than in the Object Sorting Test, as is sorting time with the number of groups of five or more pictures.

TABLE 5-5

Pearson Correlations Among Children's Grouping Scores for the Photo Sorting Test
($N = 60$)

Score	1	2	3	4
1. Number of Groups				
2. Number of Single Pictures	.95 ***			
3. Number of Groups of Two or More Pictures	−.18	−.47 ***		
4. Number of Groups of Five or More Pictures	−.82 ***	−.70 ***	−.10	
5. Sorting Time	.47 ***	.38 **	.15	−.52 ***

** $p < .01$.
*** $p < .001$.

Grouping Consistencies in the Object and Photo Sorting Tests

Table 5-6 contains correlations between scores and component part-scores for the Object Sorting Test and Photo Sorting Test. It is interesting that the correlation between the total-number-of-group scores for the Object Sorting Test and the Photo Sorting Test appears, in the case of the children, to be produced by the numbers of single-item groups. The correlation between the numbers of single-item groups formed in the two tests is .57, in effect identical to the correlation (.58) between the total-number-of-groups scores. As noted earlier, this correlation is similar to those obtained between adults' performances in Object and Photo Sorting Tests, although the numbers of single-item groups are negligible for adults. It is notable, however, that the correlation between the numbers of groups equidistant from the mean at the broad-group ends of the two distributions (i.e., groups of six or more objects and five or more pictures) is also highly significant. Once again we see that arbitrary division of these distributions at the single-item versus multiple-item point would be grossly misleading. The numbers of objects in the three largest groups are similarly correlated, although the numbers in the largest groups are not. The latter is predictable from the fact that the distribution for the children, in contrast to adults, is strongly inclined toward small groups, which means that a small amount of the individual difference variance attributable to conceptual differentiation is represented by the single largest group in each test. As expected from the correlation of sorting time with number of groups in each of the two tests, and also from the correlation between the number of groups in the two tests, the two sorting-time scores are also significantly correlated.

TABLE 5–6

*Pearson Correlations Between Children's Grouping Scores for the
Object Sorting Test and Photo Sorting Test*
$(N = 60)$

Score	*r*
1. Number of Groups	.58 ***
2. Number of Single Items	.57 ***
3. Number of Groups of Two or More Items	.22
4. Number of Groups of Six or More Objects and Five or More Pictures	.38 **
5. Number of Objects in Largest Group	.16
6. Number of Objects in Three Largest Groups	.36 **
7. Sorting Time	.47 ***

** $p < .01.$
*** $p < .001.$

The Attribution of Meaning in Photo Sorting
by Preadolescents and Adults

Because of the nature of the materials, response variance in definitions of Photo Sorting Test groupings is limited in several important respects not characteristic of the Object Sorting Test. The great majority of definitions are, for example, directly or indirectly rooted in physical properties of the pictures (age, size, dress, and so forth). Because all the pictures are of persons, nearly all definitions are at the highest conceptual level in the kind of level of abstraction scoring done with Object Sorting

Test definitions. These two limitations on variation in Photo Sorting Test definitions also make it impossible to achieve an ideal score for the conceptual distance of Photo Sorting Test definitions from the physical properties of the items. In spite of these limitations, some apparent differences in the kinds of definitions offered by children and adults led to the use of a four-category scheme for types of definitions in the Photo Sorting Test. These categories were selected by the same kinds of preliminary empirical analyses of types of definitions employed in developing definition-type categories for the Object Sorting Test. Category 1 represents extreme closeness to the physical properties of the pictures, Category 2 somewhat greater distance from the physical properties, and Category 3, still greater distance.

Types of Definitions in the Photo Sorting Test

Definitions were assigned to the following categories:

1. *Objective Characteristics.* This category included definitions based on characteristics of the pictures, rather than the person represented (e.g., "all black-and-white pictures"); age; sex; race; and dress.

2. *Activity.* Definitions based on the activity or the occupation of persons depicted were assigned to this category.

3. *Personal Characteristics.* This category consisted largely of definitions in terms of emotions. A small number of definitions by both children and adults in terms of character traits, status, and the strangeness or ordinariness of persons depicted were also assigned to this category.

4. *Residual.* All other definitions were assigned to this category.

Mean Numbers of Boys' and Girls' Definitions in Four Categories

The relevant Groups X Category interaction approaches, but does not reach, significance (significance would indicate that boys and girls show different relations among the categories). This tendency toward a significant interaction is determined primarily by the boys' relatively greater numbers of Personal Characteristics definitions and the girls' relatively greater numbers of Objective Characteristics definitions.

Mean Numbers of Younger and Older Children's Definitions
in Four Categories

The younger and older children clearly do not show different patterns of definition type employment.

Mean Numbers of Children's and Adults' Definitions in Four Categories

Because of the difficulty of performing this analysis of variance with unequal numbers of subjects in the two groups, thirty-four children were selected at random from the total group of sixty to form a group that could be effectively compared with the thirty-four female adults who have thus far taken this Photo Sorting Test. It is obvious from the results that the preadolescents differ from the adults in their relative employments of the definition types and that they do so principally in defining smaller numbers of groups in terms of objective characteristics and larger numbers of groups in terms of personal characteristics.

The children's definitions are thus less closely tied to objective characteristics of the pictures of persons, hence more saturated with injected meaning and representative of a stance toward persons (or, at least, pictures of persons) that is more distant and more personalized. These results with Photo Sorting Test definitions are in sharp contrast to those for the Object Sorting Test, in which the children's definitions were pitched much closer than adults' to physical properties of the objects. In the Object Sorting Test, in fact, the children appeared notably "stimulus-bound."

The Relation of Group Size
to Type and Conceptual Distance of Definition

The Groups X Category interaction just reaches significance, indicating that the children and adults use these categories in relatively different proportions. Examination of the means indicates that the adults show a greater range of mean group sizes, although the rank order is the same for the two groups. Thus, the adults give considerably more Objective Characteristics definitions and considerably fewer Residual definitions. It is also obvious from these means that the adults' definitions in this test are of lesser conceptual distance.

As in the case of the Object Sorting Test, another way to look at the question of relations between group size and distance is in terms of the r between the total number of groups and the mean distance of S's definitions. Here, the contrast with the Object Sorting Test results is striking. It will be recalled that for adults in a pilot sample the r between number of groups in the Object Sorting Test and the mean distance of definitions (computed in the manner described earlier for Object Sorting Test definitions) was $-.80$. In the Photo Sorting Test, the analogous r's are .28 for thirty-four adults used in these analyses and .36, $p < .05$ for the comparable group of thirty-four children, indicating that those forming many groups give definitions of greater, rather than lesser, mean conceptual distance in this test. It is also interesting that the r between the children's mean conceptual distance scores for the two tests is but .13. The individual consistencies in grouping behavior thus have different relations to the conceptual distance from the stimuli represented by definitions of groups in the two tests. This result suggests that subjects high in conceptual differentiation show conceptual closeness to objects and distance from persons, an intriguing possibility that could be evaluated in further studies. That is, our results seem to suggest that narrow and broad categorizers may be characterized by different "stances" toward objective versus interpersonal aspects of the external environment.

Discussion

The major purpose of the analyses described in this chapter was to sample the behavioral richness of free categorizing performances in a more comprehensive way than had previously been done. Not only the individual consistencies in spontaneous conceptual differentiation, but also the levels of the associative hierarchy involved in the selection of reasons for grouping, the relation of verbal concepts to grouping per se, the adequacy of verbalized reasons for grouping, the "fit" of such reasons to the groups formed, the time spent in grouping, and relations among a number of these and additional aspects of concept formation were explored.

One of the more intriguing sets of new findings concerns the relation of spontaneous conceptual differentiation to conceptual distance from the physical properties of items categorized. These analyses were stimulated by earlier results with adults suggesting that, in the categorizing of objects, subjects high in conceptual differentiation (narrow categorizers) show greater conceptual closeness to the physical characteristics of the stimuli, whereas subjects low in conceptual differentiation (broad categorizers) employ reasons for grouping that represent greater conceptual distance. This relationship is apparent also in the Object Sorting Test results for preadolescents. Related results showing that the TAT stories of adult narrow categorizers are more closely tied to physical properties of the TAT pictures also seem to be replicated for preadolescents in the present study (Chapter 6). In the categorizing of pictures of persons, however, narrow categorizers, if anything, show greater conceptual distance than do broad categorizers, which suggests that differential stances toward objects versus persons may characterize subjects high and low in conceptual differentiation. What is required, of course, is a further test of the conceptual distance hypothesis employing independent procedures in addition to the TAT.

With respect to conceptual differentiation itself, the most impressive finding is the similarity of preadolescent to adult individual consistencies, including the relationships to conceptual distance referred to above. This similarity obtains in spite of the fact that gross changes in grouping behavior and in conceptual closeness-distance occur between preadolescence and adulthood. Children form more groups than adults, use different reasons for grouping, and seem conceptually closer to the specific characteristics of the stimuli. Their conceptual closeness is probably further indicated by their larger numbers of single-item groups, which also seem to indicate closeness to the specific properties of stimuli.

It was also demonstrated in this chapter that arbitrary divisions of grouping-score distributions for sorting tests can be misleading in ways that become evident when adequate consideration is given to the nature of the distribution of such scores.

The multiple indications that preadolescents' approaches to such categorizing tasks involve lesser degrees of verbal concept formation than adults' approaches are among the most interesting new results concerning these tests. The fit of verbalization to grouping is generally less adequate, in a variety of ways, in the case of preadolescents. It appears that preadolescents group relatively more in terms of perceptual and kinesthetic memories of objects and relatively less in terms of initial formations of regnant verbal concepts than do adults.

The general lines of developmental change from preadolescence to adulthood are thus toward lower degrees of spontaneous conceptual differentiation, greater distance from the physical properties of objects categorized, lesser distance from the physical properties of pictures of persons, greater reliance on verbal concepts, and more effective coordination of grouping to verbal concepts. The individual consistencies referred to as conceptual differentiation are independent of these quantitative and qualitative developmental changes. This seems to indicate that the individual consistencies in grouping behavior are referable to relatively autonomous controlling structures that persist in the face of changes in relevant substructures.

6 Dimensions of Cognitive Control at Preadolescence

A MAJOR question posed in the present study was that of the similarity of cognitive control principle factors for preadolescents and adults. The earlier studies of cognitive controls in adults referred to briefly in Chapter 3 indicate that a number of control principles can be distinguished on the basis of work done thus far and suggest that these are but a few of a much larger potential group of such principles. Certain of the principles already defined seem to be differentiable components of aspects or areas of cognitive functioning that have been referred to as if they involved single sets of psychological processes. Field-articulation and conceptual differentiation, for example, are independent control principles, both of which are relevant to different aspects of the "articulation" of experience. Scanning and field-articulation controls have direct implications for strategies of attention deployment in response to certain adaptive requirements and have been shown to account for *different* facets of the same total sequences of response processes (Gardner, 1961a; Gardner and Long, 1962b).

The definitions of the cognitive controls thus far explored allow limited but rather precise differential predictions concerning adult behavior. Whether these dimensions of individual difference in cognitive control are as specialized and distinct from each other at preadolescence as in adulthood is of major importance. One trend of earlier thinking about cognitive development suggests that such specialized patterns of cognitive processes emerge from more undifferentiated earlier constellations. It is often assumed, for example, that children's behavior is more globally organized—i.e., is organized in terms of fewer principles—than that of adults. In the present study a major question relevant to this often held, but perhaps questionable, assumption was that of the *number* of different control factors that would emerge from the matrix of intercorrelations among major cognitive control test scores at preadolescence, as compared to the numbers that have emerged in roughly comparable studies of adults. It seemed possible that control principles that are demonstrably independent in adults would be less independent in preadolescents.

A less often expressed point of view concerning cognitive development is that it moves from a constellation of specific and unintegrated patterns to more simply and generally organized patterns. It thus seemed possible that criterion scores for a single control that are significantly correlated in adults (e.g., the number-of-groups scores for Object Sorting and Photo Sorting Tests that have served as major score criteria of the conceptual differentiation control principle) would not be so correlated in preadolescents.

A third, and perhaps more adequate view of cognitive development has become almost a stereotype: that the development of structured patterns in cognitive behavior involves both differentiation and integration (see, e.g., Werner, 1940; Murphy, 1947). This type of statement, however, leaves a number of important questions unanswered: Does the development of each cognitive control involve such differentiation-integration? Does the development of some controls primarily involve differentiation, whereas others involve synthesis and integration? Do different facets of cognitive structuring develop in different ways? Answers to these and related questions require that cognitive development be viewed from the vantage points provided by at least *two*, and preferably more, qualitatively different aspects of cognitive development. Previous isolation of a number of controls in adults made it possible to pose such questions with respect to relations between the cognitive organizations of preadolescents and adults.

In addition to the above considerations, little is known of the effects of puberty on the individual consistencies from which adult control principles have been inferred. It may be that extensive reorganization of an individual's cognitive controls occurs under the impact of increased instinctual pressures at puberty and that adult patterns of cognitive control are forged in this period. On the other hand, cognitive controls may attain enduring organization early in life and may, if appropriately measured, appear in similar forms in groups of preadolescents and adults.

Partial answers to such questions were obtained by examining relations among clusters of scores with respect to single control principles in Chapters 4 and 5. The results described there suggest that preadolescent individual consistencies in at least some cognitive control test performances are remarkably similar to those of adults, with the major exception of scores for the leveling-sharpening control principle. In the case of the conceptual differentiation control principle, the adult and the preadolescent consistencies appear similar, even though the manner of expression of the principle differs. It was also noted in Chapters 4 and 5 that these similar patterns of individual consistencies for preadolescents and adults are obtained in the face of developmental changes in levels of performance that range from slight to gross.

A full complement of answers to the general questions posed above will require longitudinal studies. The group of preliminary answers discussed in Chapters 4 and 5 is further clarified by the factor analysis of major cognitive control scores described in this chapter.

The selection of cognitive control scores for the present study was based upon results of the adult studies summarized briefly in the descriptions of procedures for obtaining control scores in Chapter 3. The major scores selected were assumed to represent the following control principles: extensiveness of scanning, spontaneous conceptual differentiation, field-articulation, leveling-sharpening, constricted-flexible control, and tolerance for unrealistic experiences. In the case of all but the last two of these, enough criterion scores were employed so that a factor could reasonably be expected to appear. The lack of an adequate apparent movement apparatus made it impossible to obtain the second criterion score for tolerance for unrealistic experiences used in earlier studies of adults.

In addition to providing results that could be compared with earlier findings for adults, the factor analysis reported here served the essential purpose of reducing the matrix of intercorrelations among the twenty-three scores selected to a smaller number of dimensions.

Factor Analysis of Cognitive Control Scores

The matrix of intercorrelations among the twenty-three control scores was factor analyzed by the principal axis method. As in the other factor analyses of this study, the highest correlation was inserted in the diagonal cell as a communality estimate for each score. Six orthogonal factors accounted for all the common variance among the scores. The scores with loadings of .30 or more on each of the six rotated factors are listed and the factors interpreted below.

Factor I
Scanning A

Score	Loading
18. Size Estimation II Exp.: Redundant Scanning Time	86
12. Size Estimation I: Redundant Scanning Time	81
15. Size Estimation II Contr.: Redundant Scanning Time	80
14. Size Estimation II Contr.: Judgment Time	39

It is apparent from examination of this factor and Factor III that the cluster of scanning scores obtained from each of the two size estimation tests is determined by two major orthogonal factors.[1] Factor I primarily represents individual consistencies in redundant scanning time, i.e., the amount of time the children spent scanning the size estimation disks after they had made their final adjustments of the comparison stimuli and before they closed their eyes to indicate completion of their judgments. Although the judgment time score for the control condition of Size Estimation Test II has a defining loading on this factor, it has a much higher loading on Factor III, as do the other judgment time scores.

This factor could thus represent individual consistencies in a particular form of doubtfulness about the judgments, compulsive carefulness, or obsessiveness. It could also, or simultaneously, represent individual consistencies in one form of delay. Children with high factor scores seem particularly careful or doubt-ridden in checking their judgments before closing their eyes. Children with low factor scores spend relatively little time examining the relative sizes of the stimuli once they make their final adjustment.

Factor II
Conceptual Differentiation

Score	Loading
4. Object Sorting: Number of Groups	71
9. Photo Sorting: Number of Groups	61
5. Object Sorting: Abstraction	37
26. TAT: Conceptual Distance	−35
13. Size Estimation I: Constant Error	−35

[1] The comparable scanning scores for adults were not factor analyzed in the original study by Gardner and Long (1962a). Correlations among these scanning scores were sufficiently high and uniform for adults, however, that the appearance of two scanning factors for children was unexpected.

This is the anticipated conceptual differentiation factor. As in the studies of adults referred to earlier in this chapter and discussed in Chapter 5, children show striking individual consistencies in the number of groups they form in categorizing objects and pictures of persons. The loading for the conceptual distance moved from the physical properties of the cards in telling TAT stories is directly parallel to that found for adults by Gardner and Schoen (1962). Children with high factor scores tend to limit their TAT stories to descriptions of the pictures. Children with low factor scores tell more elaborate, original stories, i.e., move relatively far from the physical properties of the pictures. In addition, and unlike adults, children who impose a high degree of conceptual differentiation upon arrays of objects and pictures of persons also make small errors in Size Estimation Test I. It seems possible that these preadolescent *S*s, whose "equivalence ranges" are characteristically narrow, may limit their adjustments of the comparison stimulus in this test to a rather narrow category of equivalence with the standard stimulus.

The positive loading for preferred level of abstraction in the Object Sorting Test was not anticipated. In the case of normal adults (Gardner and Schoen, 1962), preferred level of abstraction and conceptual differentiation are clearly independent. In the case of more difficult sorting tests, which introduce preferred level of abstraction as a determinant of the number of groups, the degree to which preferred level of abstraction determines performance is generally predictable from the difficulty of the test. That is, for adults preferred level of abstraction is a negligible determinant of the number of groups formed in the Object Sorting Test, a more important determinant of this score for the Behavior Sorting Test, and a still more important determinant of this score for a Photo Sorting Test roughly comparable to that used in the present study. The fact that preferred level of abstraction loads on the preadolescents' conceptual differentiation factor could be understood in either or both of two ways: (a) only one preferred level of abstraction score was included in the present study—in contrast to the adult study of differentiation and abstraction (Gardner and Schoen, 1962), in which conceptual differentiation and preferred level of abstraction were separate factors—so that a preferred level of abstraction common factor could not emerge; and (b) the Object Sorting Test is more difficult for preadolescents than adults (see Chapter 5), so that preferred level of abstraction is a more important determinant of the number of groups formed in the case of preadolescents.

Factor III
Scanning B

Score	Loading
17. Size Estimation II Exp.: Judgment Time	−85
11. Size Estimation I: Judgment Time	−80
14. Size Estimation II Contr.: Judgment Time	−74
5. Object Sorting: Abstraction	32
19. Size Estimation II Exp.: Illusion *30–45*	−30

This second scanning factor is highly loaded on judgment time scores for the three size estimation conditions. Judgment time, it will be remembered, is a function of the number of looks and the length of looks at the standard and comparison stimuli in the course of arriving at an *adjustment* of the comparison stimulus satisfactory to S. Judgment time does not include redundant scanning time (i.e., the time S spends checking his judgment *after* his last adjustment of the comparison stimulus).

Ss with high factor scores make their judgments quickly in all three test conditions. To a minor degree, they tend to perform at an abstract level in the Object Sorting Test (another unanticipated loading for this score) and to experience little illusion with one of the figures employed in Size Estimation Test II. The last two of these loadings are much lower than those for the judgment time scores.

As anticipated in the discussion of results concerning extensiveness of scanning in Chapter 4, this factor, like Factor I, closely parallels remarkable adult consistencies in extensiveness of scanning in size estimation tests observed in previous studies (Gardner and Long, 1962a, b). As noted earlier in this chapter, the appearance of two factors for children may suggest that components of the adult scanning syndrome become integrated into a more general pattern of scanning as cognitive development progresses from preadolescence to adulthood.

Factor IV
Field-Articulation

Score	Loading
24. Concealed Figures: Correct Checks	70
21. Embedded Figures: Time	−66
19. Size Estimation II Exp.: Illusion *30–45*	−45
1. Schematizing: Accuracy	39
20. Size Estimation II Exp.: Illusion *45*-Arrows	−30

This is the anticipated field-articulation factor. It is closely comparable to field-articulation factors obtained in earlier studies of adults (e.g., those obtained by Gardner *et al.*, 1959, 1960) and those obtained for children by Goodenough and Karp (1961). The factor thus supports the contention of Gardner *et al.* in a number of earlier studies that, in these situations, the general principle of field-articulation defined and experimentally verified by Witkin and his co-workers and others manifests itself in selective attention to relevant versus irrelevant aspects of stimulation.

Children with high factor scores correctly identify many concealed figures within the time limit, identify the embedded figures in Witkin's test in short times, and experience small illusion effects with the two figures employed in the experimental condition of Size Estimation II, which was specifically designed to test individual differences in the capacity to attend selectively under these conditions. The fact that the loading is higher for the 30 mm. circle enclosed in a 45 mm. circle than that for the 45 mm. circle containing arrows is attributable to the lesser illusion variance obtained with the latter figure. *S*s with high factor scores are also more accurate in the Schematizing Test. This is not surprising. Accuracy in this test requires that the *S*'s size judgments reflect adequate *ranking* of the sequential stimuli. This requires, of course, that each new stimulus be effectively compared with the one that preceded it. As demonstrated by Gardner and Long (1961b) and Long (1962), adult *S*s high in perceptual field-articulation are also adept at selective attention to relevant versus compelling but irrelevant memories. In the Schematizing Test, inability to respond selectively to the relevant memories would automatically reduce the accuracy score.

*S*s with low factor scores identify few concealed figures within the time limit, are slow to identify embedded figures in Witkin's test, experience great illusion effects in Size Estimation Test II, and are inaccurate in the Schematizing Test.

Factor V

Constricted-Flexible Control

	Score	Loading
29. Color-Word: Interference		−47
7. Object Sorting: Inadequate Definitions		46
8. Object Sorting: Elaborations		37
20. Size Estimation II Exp.: Illusion *45*-Arrows		−34

In view of the fact that the Color-Word Test interference score has the highest loading, this factor may represent the dimension of individual consistencies in constricted-flexible control originally described by Klein (1954). The form of the factor is intriguing, however, and was not anticipated. Ss with high factor scores, i.e., "flexible-control" Ss, are capable of the smooth and effective motoric inhibitions required for rapid, low-interference performance in Part III of the Color-Word Test. It is intriguing that these subjects also give relatively many inadequate definitions and elaborations in the Object Sorting Test. It will be recalled that the elaborations made by the children were generally ineffective verbalizations which added little or nothing to their definitions of groups. If anything, this finding seems to make it even clearer that the capacity for motoric inhibition involved in the Color-Word Test is not dependent upon verbal skills per se. This factor may, in fact, exemplify a point made by Klein (1954) in his original discussion of performance in the Color-Word Test: that highly verbal persons often have particular difficulty in this test. (It will be recalled that color-naming time under noninterference conditions is controlled in computation of the interference score itself.) It may also be that children of "flexible" control make many redundant and ineffective verbalizations in the Object Sorting Test because they are free and spontaneous. Ss with high factor scores also seem to show little of the illusion effect induced by the presence of outward-pointing arrows within the 45 mm. circle.

Ss with low factor scores, i.e., "constricted-control" Ss, show little capacity to inhibit the overlearned tendency to read the words in the Color-Word Test, give few inadequate definitions and elaborations in the Object Sorting Test, and show great illusion effect with one of the two figures in the experimental condition of Size Estimation Test II.

Factor VI
Spontaneity

Score	Loading
27. Rorschach: Reaction Time	−67
26. TAT: Conceptual Distance	59
25. TAT: Reaction Time	−56
8. Object Sorting: Elaborations	35
28. Rorschach: Tol. for Unrealistic Experiences	32
3. Schematizing: Lag	−32

This factor seems to represent individual differences in the openness and spontaneity with which the children respond to certain of the testing situations. The factor also seems to have implications for the imaginativeness and creativity of the children. It seems primarily to be an "attitudinal" factor, independent of some of the specific skills involved in other cognitive control tests.

*S*s with high factor scores respond rapidly to the Rorschach inkblots and TAT pictures, show imaginativeness in their story productions, and elaborate their definitions of groups in the Object Sorting Test spontaneously (whether or not these elaborations are effective). One aspect of their spontaneity in these situations seems to be a tolerance for unrealistic experiences. It is apparent, however, that this is but one of a greater number of determinants of this quality of spontaneity and is not primarily a tolerance for unrealistic experiences factor. Children with high factor scores also show little lag in the Schematizing Test. It is conceivable that the quality of alert spontaneity that characterizes their approach to the testing situations leads to relatively vivid experiencing of the squares and is one determinant of reduced assimilation in the Schematizing Test. It could also be speculated that the relationship of lagging to difficulty in shifting sets makes levelers "unspontaneous" in situations permitting rapid or variegated responses to new stimuli or the production of stories that ideally involve integrated sequences of imagined activity on the part of the principal characters.

*S*s with low factor scores are slow to respond to the Rorschach blots and the TAT pictures, are unimaginative in their story productions, verbalize little in addition to their specific definitions of the object groups they form, seem intolerant of unrealistic experiences, and show greater lag in the Schematizing Test.

Selection of Scores for the Final Analysis

Factor scores were computed for each of the factors described here by the method outlined in Chapter 2. These scores were included in the final analysis described in Chapter 12. Because no factor appeared for children comparable to the leveling-sharpening factors in earlier studies of adults, the leveling-sharpening scores were omitted from the computation of factor scores. The lag score was included in the final analysis of interrelationships among variables representing the major blocks of data (Chapter 12). The same procedure was followed for the tolerance for unrealistic experiences score, which was based on qualitative evaluations of the Rorschach. In each case, no factor loading was particularly high for the score and its communality was also low. In addition, the importance of these scores in earlier studies of adults pointed to the value of observing their relationships to other variables in the final analysis of individual consistencies in different aspects of behavior. In the case of the tolerance for unrealistic experiences ratings, it was also felt that no other score in the matrix adequately represented this variable.

Predictions Based on Conceptual Differentiation Factor Scores

The present study provided an opportunity to determine whether the relationships found by Gardner *et al.* (1959) between conceptual differentiation (equivalence range) factor scores and Rorschach scores for adults also obtain for preadolescents. Since the r between the conceptual differentiation factor score and the total number of responses to the Rorschach Test was nonsignificant, zero-order r's were computed between the factor score and each of the relevant Rorschach scores (H, M, FM, Number of Color Responses, A, Mammals, Lower Animals, W, D, Dd). Only the r for W approached significance ($-.22$, p .10). Despite the fact that these tests ignore the distribution assumptions for r (the peculiarities of Rorschach score distributions are well known), it would appear that the relationships found for adults do not hold for preadolescents. In view of the extreme complexity of Rorschach performances and of developmental changes in various aspects of response to the Rorschach, this result is not surprising, although it differs notably from some of the other results reported in this chapter.

Discussion

The most important general point to be made concerning the factors that emerged from the analysis of cognitive control scores and ratings is their general similarity to factors obtained earlier for adults. The absence of a leveling-sharpening factor is the outstanding discrepancy. As noted earlier, the absence in children of a significant correlation between the accuracy and lag scores for the Schematizing Test is of central importance here. For preadolescents, more than for adults, the ranking accuracy of sequential judgments of square sizes in the Schematizing Test implicates the field-articulation control principle. The lag score for this test, which can be considered a more adequate index of assimilation, does not. Maintenance of adequate ranking accuracy requires that each square be judged effectively in spite of the confusing array of sizes judged previously, and that the judgment be independent of the memory schema representing the sizes of these preceding squares. In one sense, this seems to make the accuracy score, like the embedded figures and other field-articulation scores, an index of the subject's capacity to attend selectively to relevant cues while actively withholding attention from irrelevant cues. To the degree that this is true, the aspect of performance represented by the ranking-accuracy score at preadolescence seems analogous to the aspects of learning and recall of highly similar words that Gardner and Long (1961b) and Long (1962) have shown to implicate field-articulation.

The appearance of two scanning factors was also unanticipated and seems to suggest that the adult syndrome is not fully integrated at preadolescence. This interpretation must be qualified, however, in view of the fact that the intercorrelations among scanning scores are similar to those for adults and the fact that the adult studies did not include the kinds of analyses performed here.

With respect to the single rating of tolerance for unrealistic experiences, the important point is the independence of this aspect of cognitive control from the other controls dealt with in this study. The only loading of any consequence for this score was the .32 for Factor VI, Spontaneity. The major portion of the variance of this score is thus not accounted for by the six control factors.

The extension of adult findings concerning the relevance of field-articulation to illusions requiring selective attention to relevant cues and selective inattention to compelling irrelevant cues (Factor IV) is also worthy of note. These individual consistencies occur at both preadolescent and adult age levels in spite of the fact that the developmental curves for performance in the embedded figures tests and illusion tests are strikingly different. The individual consistencies in cognitive control seem to cut across these variations in developmental curves in a way that directly reveals the autonomy of such control structures. A related finding is the clear evidence of individual consistencies in conceptual differentiation in the Object and Photo Sorting Tests, in which the relationship of grouping style to the conceptual distance of the subject's reasons for grouping is reversed. The fact that cognitive controls are relatively autonomous structures is perhaps nowhere more evident than in this type of result.

7 Individuality in the Holtzman Inkblot Test

THE HOLTZMAN INKBLOT TEST, hereafter referred to as the HIT (Holtzman *et al.*, 1961), is a promising new research tool that samples perceptual-cognitive functioning under relatively unstructured conditions in a manner that allows more effective quantification of response dimensions than is true of the Rorschach Test. The inkblots were originally selected by Holtzman and his associates to provide systematic variations of relations between major determinants of scores in the principal Rorschach Test scoring schemes. Final selection of inkblots was focused on maximization of the reliability of the six major scores—Location, Form Definiteness, Form Appropriateness, Color, Shading, and Movement—and of the discrimination between college students and psychotic patients (Holtzman *et al.*, 1961, pp. 22–28).

Because of the improvements it incorporates and because it samples children's response consistencies under conditions in which they can actively structure responses to a great degree, the HIT was considered an ideal addition to the other assessments of structural organization at preadolescence. The HIT—like the Rorschach Test—allows the subject great latitude of choice with respect to the areas and aspects of the blots responded to, the "content" (animal, human, and the like) of responses, and the perceptual organizations of responses. In the present study, it was thought to represent a middle range of self-determination—between the highly structured control and ability tests on the one hand and the largely self-directed over-all aspects of response to the clinical and laboratory testing situations (Chapter 9) on the other. It was also employed because of the opportunity the present study provided of exploring relations between individual consistencies in HIT performance and other aspects of structural organization.

Fifty of the sixty children (twenty-six boys and twenty-four girls) were available for further testing. Form I of the HIT was administered to those 50 children an average of 5.1 months following the laboratory testing. This test was given by an examiner who had not administered the other procedures of the present study.[1] In the HIT, the subject gives one response to each of two sample inkblots, then to each of forty-five test inkblots. The twenty-two major HIT scores included in the standardization studies by Holtzman and associates were obtained for each of fifty children of the present study.[2]

Mean HIT Scores of Boys and Girls

Statistical comparisons of the means and sigmas of the twenty-two scores for the twenty-six boys and twenty-four girls of the present sample who were available for testing with the HIT showed that only the difference in number of space responses is significant (higher for girls). One such difference could be attributed to chance.

Mean HIT Scores of Younger and Older Children

With the exception of the Penetration score, no significant differences appear. Although one significant difference in a group of twenty-two *t* tests could be attributed to chance, it may be that younger children give more responses "symbolic of an individual's feelings that his body exterior is of little protective value and can easily be penetrated . . ." (Holtzman *et al.*, 1961, p. 77).

Comparison of Present Sample with Normative Samples

The standardization samples most comparable to the present sample are 72 Connecticut fourth graders and 197 Texas seventh graders. These groups are roughly equal in mean age to the youngest and oldest children of the present study.

Our sample differs significantly from the Connecticut fourth graders in nine of the twenty-two scored aspects of response. They respond to smaller areas; give fewer Color, Shading, and Movement responses; give fewer responses including Pathognomic Verbalization, fewer responses

[1] Mrs. Rosalie Mayman.

[2] The authors are indebted to Dr. Wayne H. Holtzman, who arranged for scoring of the HIT protocols and a preliminary factor analysis of the twenty-two scores.

scored Barrier, and fewer Popular responses. The present sample differs significantly from the Texas seventh graders in ten scores. They respond more quickly; reject fewer cards; respond to smaller areas; give fewer Space responses; show less Form Appropriateness; give fewer Color and Shading responses; give more Human and Animal responses, and fewer Popular responses. They differ significantly from both the Connecticut fourth graders and Texas seventh graders in five important aspects of performance: they respond to smaller areas and give fewer Space, Color, Shading, and Popular responses. In the case of four of these scores, the difference is gross. The mean Color score for the present sample is less than one third that of the Connecticut fourth graders, and only slightly more than one half that of the Texas seventh graders. Their mean Shading score is less than one fourth and one third those of the normative samples. Their mean Space score is less than one third and only slightly more than one half those of the normative samples. Their mean Location score is much higher than those of the normative samples, indicating response to considerably smaller areas of the inkblots.

It would appear that the generalized constriction and conformity that seems to characterize the present sample (see Chapter 2) finds expression in these HIT scores and indicates rather cautious, unimaginative, conventional responses to restricted areas of the inkblots. These results suggest that employment of the defense of "ego restriction," so aptly described by Anna Freud (1936), may be a prominent characteristic of the present sample taken as a whole. The fact that the form appropriateness of responses by the present sample is significantly lower than that of the Texas seventh graders, and about the same as that of the Connecticut fourth graders, seems to support this assumption. The Form Appropriateness score reflects a key attribute of effective reality testing. Children of the present sample thus seem to show excessive inhibition of affect without the superior differentiation of conscious experience that occurs in some forms of affective inhibition—for example, that commonly observed when isolation and intellectualization are prominent defensive maneuvers. The present sample does not, however, show greater evidence of thought disorder than the two normative groups considered here. The over-all impression is, therefore, one of generalized constriction and inhibition that serves to limit originality, flexibility, and creativity of response to relatively unstructured stimuli and that dampens emotional participation in a profitless way.

Estimated odd-even reliability coefficients were calculated for the present sample and compared to those for the two standardization samples (following Holtzman *et al.*, 1961, p. 107, these coefficients are based on the first twenty-two odd- and twenty-two even-numbered inkblots). Holtzman and associates (1961, p. 108) pointed out several factors limiting certain of these coefficients, e.g., skewness and truncation of distributions. For four of the six scores that yielded accurate reliability estimates in their studies—Reaction Time, Location, Form Definiteness, and Form Appropriateness—the coefficients for the three samples are closely comparable. For the other two—Animal and Popular—coefficients for the present sample are closely comparable to those for the Texas seventh graders. Among the other scores with means greater than zero (i.e., scores for which a meaningful reliability coefficient could be obtained), the only gross discrepancy between coefficients for the present sample and those for the sample of Texas seventh graders are the values for Anatomy (.86 and .54). In view of the limited dispersions of several of the scores, the over-all agreement among reliability coefficients seems quite high.

Holtzman *et al.* (1961, pp. 137–38) were able to show satisfactory test-retest reliabilities for fourteen of the twenty-two scores (all but Integration, Popular, Space, Pathognomic Verbalization, Anatomy, Sex, Abstract, Balance) in a study of Austin, Texas, elementary school children employing Forms B and A over a one-year interval. These forty-two children, second through sixth graders at the time of the initial testing, were considerably younger than those of the present sample, for whom test-retest reliabilities would presumably be at least as high.

Factor Analysis of HIT Scores

The matrix of intercorrelations among nineteen HIT scores was factor analyzed by the principal axis method (means for the three scores eliminated—Sex, Abstract, Balance—were zero or nearly zero). The highest correlation for each score was used as the communality estimate. Factoring was terminated when the common variance was accounted for. The five uncorrelated factors extracted were rotated by the normal varimax method. Scores with loadings of .30 or more on these orthogonal (i.e., uncorrelated) factors are given below, with interpretations of the factors and cross references to the comparable factors obtained by Holtzman and his associates for standardization samples. The latter were obtained from twenty-three scores by the centroid method and were rotated in such a way as to yield "the best-fitting orthogonal factors for the hypothesis that five factors are commonly present" in intercorrelation matrices for the sixteen samples studied (Holtzman *et al.*, 1961, p. 150). The correspondence between factors for the present sample and the factors identified by Holtzman *et al.* is nevertheless great.

Factor I

Score	Loading
17. Anxiety	84
18. Hostility	84
9. Movement	69
10. Pathognomic Verbalization	67
20. Penetration	65
3. Location	−55
11. Integration	54
14. Anatomy	38

This factor is comparable to Factor III in the factor analyses for sixteen samples by Holtzman and associates. The high loadings identifying this factor are those on Anxiety, Hostility, and Pathognomic Verbalization. Holtzman *et al.* state (1961, pp. 159–61): "With rare exception, the significant loadings on Factor III all point to an interpretation of an underlying common core indicative of disordered thought processes, bizarre perception, and fantasy life of an emotionally disturbing nature."

Subjects with high factor scores give relatively many responses scored Anxiety, Hostility, and Pathognomic Verbalization. The high loading for the Movement score indicates that they also tend to give responses in which movement (not necessarily human movement in the HIT scoring scheme) is relatively vigorous or violent. They also give many responses contributing to the Penetration score. Such responses can be construed as symbolic of weakness of ego boundaries and inadequacy of self-nonself distinction. The negative loading on the Location score indicates that children with high factor scores tend to combine "two or more *adequately* perceived blot elements into a larger whole" (Holtzman *et al.*, 1961, p. 64). They also have high Anatomy scores (it should be noted that relatively great weightings are given to crude anatomy responses concerning internal organs in scoring anatomy responses).

Children with low factor scores give fewer responses indicative of anxiety, hostility, thought disorder, and feelings of penetrability. They experience movement less frequently and in relatively controlled forms. They respond to smaller blot areas in and of themselves, with relatively little integration of smaller areas into larger wholes. They have relatively low Anatomy scores.

This factor seems to represent at least one aspect of individual differences in ego strength. Children with high factor scores seem to be in turbulent states of disequilibration leading to generalized instability of control.

Factor II

Score	Loading
6. Form Appropriateness	69
4. Space	64
3. Location	54
13. Animal	−41
19. Barrier	30

This factor is analogous to Factor IV for the normative samples of Holtzman *et al.*, who found that it showed the least comparability across their sixteen samples. The key loadings are those on Form Appropriateness and Location, which indicate that response by children with high factor scores to smaller areas of the blots, including white spaces, is generally associated with high accuracy of form. This is not surprising in a sample of children, for whom adequate response to an entire blot is relatively difficult. The fact that the children with high factor scores give relatively few Animal responses is more difficult to understand. The loading on Barrier (Fisher and Cleveland, 1958) implies that children with high factor scores tend to give responses that refer "to any protective covering, membrane, shell, or skin that might be symbolically related to the perception of body-image boundaries" (Holtzman *et al.*, 1961, p. 74).

Children with low factor scores respond to larger areas or whole blots with lesser form accuracy, give fewer responses to white spaces, give more animal responses, and give fewer responses symbolic of body-image boundaries.

Factor III

Score	Loading
5. Form Definiteness	−79
7. Color	79
8. Shading	63
13. Animal	−62
3. Location	−34
14. Anatomy	32
6. Form Appropriateness	31

This factor corresponds roughly to Factor II for the normative samples, although the negative loading for the Animal score in the present study is exceptionally high. Holtzman and associates (1961, p. 156) suggest that this is essentially a bipolar factor, "with form dominance to the detriment of other stimulus qualities at the low extreme and with over-emphasis upon the rich variety of color and shading, frequently to the detriment of form, at the high end of the dimension." The negative loading on Location also conforms to the pattern found by Holtzman *et al.* (1961, p. 157), whereas the loading on Anatomy does not.

Children with high factor scores show relatively great responsiveness to color and shading. This understandably involves large areas of the inkblot organized with minimal definiteness of form. Children with low factor scores offer more form-definite responses, including frequently clear and "easy" animal percepts, which understandably involve somewhat smaller areas of inkblots. In terms of rationales for emphasis on color versus form in the Rorschach Test (e.g., Rorschach, 1949; Klopfer and Kelley, 1942; Beck, 1949; Rapaport *et al.*, 1946), children with high factor scores may show affective responsiveness, including perceptual reflections of the affect of anxiety, whereas children with low factor scores may show more highly controlled, "reality-bound" approaches to the inkblots.

Factor IV

Score	Loading
22. Popular	79
12. Human	70
11. Integration	61
9. Movement	44

This factor is comparable to Factor I for the normative samples. The key loadings are those on Human, Integration, and Movement. The high loading on Popular conforms to the pattern for most of the normative samples. Holtzman *et al.* (1961, p. 151) suggest that the factor "deals mainly with perceptual maturity, integrated ideational activity, and awareness of conventional percepts."

Children with high factor scores (i.e., those who give many Popular, Human, and Movement responses and who effectively integrate smaller areas of the inkblots into larger units) manifest one obvious component of ego strength, with positive implications for the integrity of their views of themselves and others and for social appropriateness. Children with low factor scores may tend toward unusual constriction or inappropriate responses.

Factor V

Score	Loading
2. Rejection	79
1. Reaction Time	67
19. Barrier	−30

This factor is most similar to Factor V for the samples of Holtzman *et al.*, although the key loadings on Rejection and Reaction Time are accompanied by a fairly high negative loading on Animal in their studies (i.e., long reaction times and many card rejections are associated with few Animal responses).

Children with high factor scores respond slowly, reject relatively many cards, and give relatively few barrier responses, i.e., few responses implying symbolic representations of body-image boundaries.

Children with low factor scores respond quickly and reject relatively few cards. That they also receive high scores in Barrier may suggest that something more than ego strength or affective appropriateness is involved. As such, the loading on Factor V could indicate associations among active, open participation in the test and clarity of the self-nonself distinction. But since all separate articles of clothing are scored Barrier, a high score could also indicate an inhibited, regressive, or moralistically "proper" concern with "covering up" the negatively evaluated body and a generalized constriction of awareness in which affect is held to a minimum.

Discussion

The five factors obtained from the HIT scores are comparable to factors isolated by Holtzman and his associates in their studies of normative groups, in spite of the elimination in the present study of scores with inadequate distributions and differences in the methods of factoring and rotation of factors.

The degree to which these factors represent dimensions of response to the HIT is, however, obscured to some extent by multiple artifactual relations between the twenty-three scores used by Holtzman *et al.* and between the nineteen of these twenty-three scores selected for factor analysis in the present study. R (number of responses), which poses serious impediments to effective analysis of Rorschach Test scores, is controlled in large part in the HIT by permitting the subject only one response to each inkblot. The effect of R on other scores is not entirely eliminated, however, since the subject may reject inkblots.

The number of rejections has some degree of limiting effect on all the other scores. Other kinds of statistical artifacts may link other clusters of scores. The limit on R also dictates that a subject who gives many Animal responses reduces the number of possible Human responses, and so forth. The Location and Integration scores provide another example of the artifactual inter-score relationships involved in the scoring scheme. In this case, integration of parts of the inkblots into organized combinations inevitably decreases the Location score (low scores are assigned to responses to large areas). Similarly, responses determined by Color and Shading are inevitably low in Form Definiteness. Responses scored Popular, on the other hand, will inevitably be scored high on Form Definiteness.

It is obvious, therefore, that interacting artifactual relationships may constitute an error component. The issue is, of course, the degree to which associations among response tendencies presumed to be represented by the scores are distorted by this important source of error. Since it is not known to what degree the various artifactual relationships inherent in the scoring scheme cancel each other out, this is difficult to determine. It may nevertheless be profitable to consider the obtained factors in the light of some of the more obvious artifactual relationships among scores. Although the loadings of each score on each factor could be considered in this way, the discussion here will be limited to scores with major loadings on each factor.

The highest loadings on Factor I are those for Anxiety (+), Hostility (+), Movement (+), Pathognomic Verbalization (+), Penetration (+), Location (−), and Integration (+). In addition to the possible links between Anxiety, Hostility, Penetration, and Pathognomic Verbalization, it is obvious that Movement responses ordinarily occur in relatively large areas, in keeping with the loadings on Location and Integration. The artifactual relationship between Location and Integration, which tends to bring them together in factoring, has already been noted.

The highest loadings on Factor II are those for Form Appropriateness (+), Space (+), and Location (+). The association of Form Appropriateness and Location is predictable: particularly among children, appropriate form is more likely in smaller, more manageable areas; a child who tends to give whole responses should have a reduced Form Appropriateness score. In addition, space responses are ordinarily given only to rather definite forms, and these areas are characteristically small.

Factor III is more obviously determined by artifactual score relationships. The Form Definiteness (−), Color (+), Shading (+), and Animal (−) scores have the highest loadings. Response to Color or Shading inevitably reduces Form Definiteness, also the number of Animal responses.

Factor IV may also involve artifactual score relationships. The Popular, Human, Integration, and Movement scores have the highest loadings. A number of the responses scored Popular and Movement *are* Human responses, and several common Human responses require integration of parts of inkblots into large totalities.

Factor V, which primarily represents the link between Reaction Time and Rejection, seem less artifactually determined.

The above considerations suggested that the HIT factors be dealt with cautiously. These factors do seem, however, to represent meaningful aspects of response, and it would be a serious error to assume that HIT factors are determined solely by the possible score artifacts discussed above. Two recent studies (Moseley, Duffey, and Sherman, 1963; Holtzman, Gorham, and Moran, 1964) have, in fact, provided further evidence of the validity of HIT factors by showing that they are meaningfully related to scores derived from a variety of other tests.

In order to explore the psychological meaningfulness of the HIT factors further, factor scores were obtained for the five HIT factors of the present study. These factor scores were included in the analysis of relations between variables drawn from the major blocks of data described in Chapter 12. The loadings on Reaction Time were not used in the computation of these factor scores. Rather, Reaction Time was used as a separate variable in the analysis of relations between scores and ratings from major blocks of data because the variance this score has in common with other HIT scores (57 per cent) is much less than the square of its estimated reliability (.92). In other words, much of the Reaction Time score variance was not accounted for by the factors obtained.

8 Individuality in Wechsler's Intelligence Scale for Children

THE CLASS of variables commonly referred to as "intellectual abilities" represents controlling structures of undoubted importance to reality testing and the general effectiveness of adaptation. Although high degrees of ability in no sense guarantee effective over-all equilibration in personality organization, sufficiently differentiated ability structures are an essential prerequisite to effective adaptation in this culture and subculture. This may be particularly true of verbal ability, but is also true of the analytical skills involved in effective attentional selectivity, visual-motor skills, and other functions relevant to acting upon the environment.

The earlier studies of adults referred to in Chapters 1 and 3 have indicated patterns of relationship and nonrelationship between various cognitive control and ability variables. As discussed in Chapter 10, it is commonly assumed that certain defense mechanisms facilitate or inhibit the development of certain abilities, and vice versa. In a more general sense, all of the major aspects of controlling structures sampled in the present study could be assumed to have at least some relationship to one or another ability. In fact, such terms as "ability," "cognitive control," and "defense" may have considerably more in common than their separate histories may seem to imply.

In view of the exploratory nature of the present study, it was decided to include two of the best-known and most-studied aspects of intellectual ability—the relatively general verbal and performance abilities that are major determinants of scores for the Wechsler Intelligence Scales. The use of these scales was also dictated by the fact that verbatim protocols (such as those obtained by tape recording in the present study) provide unusually rich qualitative material of value in the assessment of defense mechanisms and other aspects of ego organization (see Chapters 10 and 11). Finally, the Wechsler scales are composed of subtests that provide meaningful quantitative and qualitative information concerning differential response to particular types of intellectual tasks.[1]

All sixty children were given eleven subtests of the Wechsler Intelligence Scale for Children (Wechsler, 1949) as part of a clinical test battery that also included the Rorschach Test and portions of the Thematic Apperception Test. Twenty of the children (ten boys, ten girls) had been given the WISC during latency.

The boys' tendency toward superiority in Verbal IQ, which is attributable primarily to their superiority in Information and Vocabulary, and the girls' superiority in Coding (B) are obviously minor artifacts of sampling.

It is apparent from the mean IQ scores that the average child in the present sample performs at the "bright normal" level in the WISC. The ranges of the IQ scores are: Verbal, 95–140; Performance, 92–143; Total, 94–144.

Factor Analysis of WISC Scores

Although each of the eleven WISC subtest scores has specific variance, previous research has shown that only a few major response dimensions are represented by these scores (e.g., Hagen, 1952; Gault, 1954; Cohen, 1959).[2] Determination of the major dimensions of response to the WISC by a group of sixty children poses several problems, however. The traditional approach to intellectual factors by American investigators, and one supported by considerable empirical evidence, is to assume that correlated factors are involved, to rotate factors to an oblique solution (i.e., a solution yielding correlated factors), and, frequently, to extract a second-order factor representing general intelligence from intercorrelations among the oblique primary factors. Cohen's (1959) detailed study of WISC scores for the standardization samples presented by Wechsler

---

[1] The assessments of qualitative material in the present study are referred to in Chapters 10, 13, and 14.

[2] We shall not deal here with the question of the total numbers of factors that may be sampled by the WISC at different age levels. As Green and Berkowitz (1964) recently pointed out, this is a complex issue and results relevant to it have in part been dictated by the methods of factoring and rotation employed.

(1949) follows this general line of approach. Oblique factors, however, are notoriously unstable, and the differences in the four major factors Cohen identifies at ages 7–6, 10–6, and 13–6 may in part be attributable to this fact. At age 7–6, for example, the highest loading of any of the four oblique factors he extracted on the Vocabulary score was only .26. The inherent instability of oblique factors is, of course, greater in relatively small samples, including that of the present study.

In spite of these inevitable limitations, Cohen's studies seem to provide valuable information concerning relations between the general factor and the more specific primary factors he extracted. He found, for example, that in the case of his ten-and-one-half-year-old standardization group, 40 per cent of the total variance of twelve WISC scores (those used in the present study, plus the Mazes Test) was attributable to G, a general intellectual factor producing some degree of correlation among all the subtests. At this same age, only 18 per cent of the total variance was attributable to subtest specificity.

In the case of adults, G accounted for a still higher percentage of the total variance (52 as against 40 per cent). This finding seems counter to the common assumption that cognitive development moves primarily in the direction of greater *differentiation*. In keeping with the hypothesis offered in Chapter 1, and several groups of results in the present study (see, for example, Chapter 5), some aspects of cognitive development may involve increases in the synthesis of behavior, i.e., may be organized according to progressively fewer principles from childhood to adulthood. As Green and Berkowitz (1964) have indicated, however, this hypothesis has not yet been fully tested in the area of intellectual abilities, and the reverse may actually be true in that area.

Taken together, the earlier findings could lead to at least two approaches to the WISC data obtained in the present study: (1) extraction of primary factors; oblique rotation; and a second-order analysis yielding a general factor; (2) a more conservative approach employing identical methods of factor extraction, but with rotation to an orthogonal solution (i.e., a solution yielding more stable, uncorrelated factors). Since obvious compromises are involved in either approach, it was decided to extract principal axis factors by analytical methods, to rotate them to both oblique and orthogonal solutions, and to base further decisions about analysis of these data on differences in the psychological meaningfulness of the two sets of results.

Because age was included as a variable in the final analysis of relations between variables drawn from the major blocks of data in the present study, which included WISC factor scores, the *raw* WISC scores were reduced to major dimensions by a principal axis factor analysis of the matrix of intercorrelations among scores for the eleven subtests administered. It should be noted here that the intercorrelations are inflated somewhat because the raw scores were used (i.e., age was uncontrolled). The first unrotated principal axis factor is often a general factor representing the maximum communality that can be accounted for by one factor. As such, it is roughly comparable to the second-order general factor extracted by Cohen. It is impressive that this first unrotated factor accounts for 39 per cent of the total variance in the present study, which is closely comparable to the 40 per cent of total variance accounted for by the second-order general factor for age 10–6 in Cohen's analysis of Wechsler's data. The four principal axis factors accounting for all the common variance were first rotated by the oblimax method of Pinzka and Saunders (1954). Examination of these factors suggested only gross correspondence to the four major primary factors extracted by Cohen.

The four principal axis factors were then rotated by the normal varimax method. Of the two major factors, Factor I represents verbal skills and Factor III represents performance skills. Factors II and IV were considered of questionable psychological validity. Plotting Factors I and III against each other suggested that slight adjustment by further hand rotation would better represent the underlying dimensions and increase their psychological validity. Factors I and III from the normal varimax rotation were therefore further rotated orthogonally by hand to achieve the slight but important adjustment indicated.

Orthogonal Factors I and III, so adjusted, seemed both more interpretable and more psychologically meaningful than the oblique factors. It was therefore decided to compute factor scores for these two major WISC factors for inclusion in the analysis of relations between major blocks of data (Chapter 12). Scores that had loadings of .30 or higher on these factors are listed below, with interpretations of the factors.

In considering these orthogonal factors and their interpretation, it should be kept clearly in mind that both are in part determined by G (variance common to all the tests). It is probably for this reason that two performance tests have loadings on the verbal factor and two verbal tests have loadings on the performance factor.

Factor I

Score	Loading
5. Vocabulary	83
1. Information	78
4. Similarities	78
2. Comprehension	65
3. Arithmetic	49
7. Picture Completion	38
9. Block Design	34

This is clearly a verbal factor. Its highest loading is on Vocabulary, its lowest (.13 and .10) on Digit Span and Coding. This factor is roughly comparable, in raw score terms, to the total verbal score the test was designed to yield, but provides more precise weightings for the contributions of all eleven subtests. The factor scores obtained from it could thus be considered improved verbal scores when used, along with age, in the analysis of relations between blocks of data. This factor is comparable to Verbal Comprehension Factor I obtained by Cohen for the standardization samples of children aged 7-6, 10-6, and 13-6, but it also includes features of Verbal Comprehension Factor II in Cohen's study.

Factor III

Score	Loading
10. Object Assembly	58
9. Block Design	54
7. Picture Completion	54
8. Picture Arrangement	40
2. Comprehension	32
5. Vocabulary	32

This is clearly a performance factor. Like its verbal counterpart, Factor I, it provides factor scores representing a refined weighting, in raw score terms, of the contributions of all eleven tests. This factor is comparable to the Perceptual Organization factor obtained by Cohen for the standardization samples.

9 Ratings of Individuality of Response to the Clinical and Laboratory Testing Situations

RATINGS OF multiple characteristics of a child's behavior bring at least the following groups of variables into complex interaction: (1) the actual strength or relative prominence of the rated attributes in the child's behavior; (2) conventional linguistic associations between traits (independent of their association in the individuals rated) ; (3) the rater's personality, leading to selective attention to certain constellations of attributes and selective inattention to others, differential evaluations of attributes or groups of attributes, and imposition of a unique conception of relations between attributes upon the behavior observed; (4) the implicit or explicit theoretical views of the rater, leading to imposition of a preorganized pattern of relations between attributes upon the behavior observed; (5) the training and experience of the rater. Mulaik (1964) has shown that conventional associations between trait words can produce "personality factors" in ratings of persons. There is ample evidence (e.g., Filer, 1952; Schafer, 1954; Steiner, 1954) that the rater's personality affects his evaluations of others. Kelly (1955) has suggested that an individual's personal constructs provide a dimensional framework for evaluations of other persons. Koltuv (1962) has shown that a perceiver assumes correlations among others' traits and that these assumed correlations are higher for personally relevant than nonrelevant traits and for unfamiliar than familiar persons. There is evidence that implicit personality theories (Bruner and Tagiuri, 1954; Cronbach, 1955) affect several aspects of the perception of others (e.g., Secord and Berscheid, 1963). There is also evidence (e.g., Chance, Arnold, and Tyrell, 1962) that the rater's theoretical orientation affects his evaluation of behavior and that, within a single theoretical framework, evaluation varies as a function of training. It seems likely, too, that with training the balance may shift from personal to theoretical orientation as the principal determinant of rating.

Two sets of ratings made in the present study were based upon direct observations of the children. The first set was done by an experienced clinical rater (AM) who had made these and other ratings of twenty-eight of the children during their preschool evaluations. These ratings were based on total performance in the clinical testing situation. The second and smaller set of ratings was done by a less experienced rater [1] on the basis of observations made during the laboratory tests of cognitive controls.

The practical necessity of obtaining evaluations by only one rater in each of the testing situations leaves the question of rater reliability unanswered within the present study. The decision to include these ratings in the study was based in part upon earlier findings concerning the reliability of the clinical ratings when performed at preschool by AM and others and experience with carefully defined ratings in earlier studies and other portions of the present study. In one of the earlier studies (Gardner *et al.*, 1959), for example, correlations between preliminary ratings of two defense mechanisms by the senior author and Philip S. Holzman exceeded .90. These ratings were based on Rorschach protocols and were considered much more difficult than the observational ratings described in this chapter. The reliability of ratings of tolerance for unrealistic experiences, based on a still more complex set of Rorschach criteria, was adequate in the original study in which they were employed (Klein *et al.*, 1962). In the present study, the correlation between these ratings by two raters was .97 (see Chapter 3). In a study of twins and their parents now in progress (see Gardner, 1964a, b, c), the reliability coefficients of ratings similar to those reported here, including some of the same ratings based on similar observations of behavior, have ranged from about .45 to .90. The majority of these coefficients range from .65 to approximately .90 when the values are intraclass r's for three experienced raters or for two other raters, who had no previous rating experience except for intensive briefings on the meaning of the ratings and the behavioral attributes implied, plus practice with a few pilot *S*s.

The conclusion suggested by these rating experiences is that observational ratings of the kind reported here can be performed with relative

---

[1] Mrs. Gail Bishop.

effectiveness if the rating concepts are carefully formulated and are thoroughly understood by the rater, if interpretive discrepancies are reconciled in pilot work before a study is begun, and if the sample of behavior is sufficiently extensive.

It is obvious, of course, that the employment of single raters is not ideal, in that relatively unreliable ratings, ratings on which different raters show significant mean differences, and so forth cannot be eliminated before the data are analyzed. Use of single raters also allows maximal expression of rater idiosyncrasies in assumed relations among traits, "latent personality theories," and the like.

In view of the obvious limitations of such ratings, a final decision concerning their inclusion in the present report was made only after the factor analyses of each set of ratings had been completed. Although no direct test of the validity of the ratings could be made, and although the adequacy of the factors as indexes of actual dimensions of the children's behavior could not be tested, the obtained factors seemed remarkably appropriate to the sample.

Further indirect evidence of the usefulness of the factors accrued as the various data analyses proceeded. The two sets of rating factors seemed, for example, to differentiate superficially similar but theoretically distinct aspects of the children's behavior. The factors also contributed valuable new information concerning the children's behavior. The ratings of performance in the two divergent settings seemed meaningfully related to factors extracted from the other blocks of data and yet distinctive in their contribution to the over-all picture of the children's personality organizations. The reader may, however, wish to evaluate these *impressions* for himself by examining the findings reported in this chapter, the fit of the two sets of rating factors to other material included in the case studies presented in Chapters 13 and 14, the relationships of the factors to defense ratings reported in Chapter 11, and the relationship of these factors to other factors in the over-all analysis reported in Chapter 12.

All the ratings of behavior in the clinical testing situation and nearly all the ratings of behavior in the laboratory testing situation were drawn from a larger group of preschool ratings performed by members of the longitudinal study group with thirty-two of the sixty children. The following criteria were used to select seventy-five ratings from those made in the preschool evaluations: (1) potential relevance to the cognitive control principles and the other variables being studied; (2) feasibility of rating on the basis of WISC and TAT protocols and accompanying behavior on the one hand, laboratory observations on the other; (3) representation of a wide range of theoretically important aspects of the children's behavior.

Definitions of all the ratings employed are given in the appendix. In contrast to the preschool ratings, which were made on a variety of scales, all the present ratings were made on point scales with a range of 0 to 10.

Ratings of Behavior in the Clinical Testing Situation

Following her administration of the WISC and TAT, the examiner (AM) made seventy-five ratings of each child on the basis of test responses and additional observations during administration of these tests. Although the child's test performance per se had some effect on these ratings, they were chosen, and applied, to represent *over-all* aspects of the child's performance in this testing session. Extra-test behavior was at least as important as test responses to these ratings. The rater's earlier report (Moriarty, 1961) demonstrates the usefulness of extra-test, as well as intra-test, observations for assessment of various aspects of the child's personality.

Inspection of intercorrelations among the seventy-five ratings showed that the majority comprised only a few major clusters. In view of the high degree of meaning-overlap among items in these large clusters, the practical difficulties of obtaining factors and factor scores for a matrix of seventy-five ratings, the apparent inadequacy of the observations as a basis for certain ratings, the limited individual differences in certain ratings, and so forth, forty-seven of the seventy-five ratings were selected for inclusion in a factor analysis designed to reveal major cognitive-affective dimensions of the children's behavior represented by the ratings. A deliberate attempt was made to retain a number of ratings from each of the major clusters apparent on inspection of intercorrelations among the seventy-five ratings. Whenever possible, care was exercised to employ ratings that had proved optimally useful and meaningful in the earlier longitudinal studies of some of the children.

Mean Ratings of Boys and Girls

The general lack of significant differences between boys and girls in these variegated aspects of over-all behavior in the clinic is impressive. There are, in fact, fewer differences than would be expected by chance.

The significant and near-significant differences seem to center largely around greater assertiveness and active explorativeness on the part of the boys, and may contain a bit of useful information. The only suggestive difference ($p < .10$) in the factor scores derived from these ratings (see Chapter 12) appeared with respect to a factor described later in this chapter as "Accuracy of Reality Testing," however, so that this interpretation is at best highly speculative.

Mean Ratings of Younger and Older Children

The lack of significant differences between younger and older children is even more striking, in spite of the relatively restricted age range involved. It would appear that in such small samples, at least, individual differences in these highly diverse aspects of behavior are sufficient to override the kinds of developmental changes one would expect to find if a greater mean age difference separated the two groups.

Factor Analysis of Ratings in the Clinical Testing Situation

The matrix of intercorrelations among the forty-seven selected ratings was factor analyzed by the principal axis method. This analysis indicated that six orthogonal factors account for all the common variance among these ratings. These factors were rotated by the normal varimax procedure. The six orthogonal (i.e., uncorrelated) factors resulting from this rotation are interpreted below. In the eyes of the investigators, the value of the ratings and the effectiveness of the final selection of ratings retained receives some support from the fact that each of the rotated factors seems easily interpretable and clinically meaningful.

Factor I
Active Openness to New Experience

Rating	Loading [2]
10. Translation of Ideas into Action	87
62. Action upon the Environment	86
25. Expressive Rigidity	−85
54. Curiosity	84
47. Flexibility	83
53. Openness to New Experience	80
1. Coping I (Activeness of Problem-Solving)	78
73. Spontaneity	77
44. Affective Differentiation	76
29. Social Insightfulness	72
23. Ability to Ask for Help	71

Rating	Loading [2]
3. Cognitive Coping Capacity	71
63. Independence, Self-Reliance	70
8. Mobilization of Resources under Stress	69
65. Drive Toward Mastery	69
22. Range of Areas of Enjoyment	68
6. Ability to Synthesize Thought, Affect, Action	66
35. Energy Level	65
27. Accuracy of Evaluations of Others	62
19. Adequacy of Self-Appraisal	62
15. Speed of Orientation	62
2. Coping II (Internal Equilibration)	57
51. Warmth	54
52. Trust	47
38. Enjoyment	44
66. Determination	43
32. Observable Tension	−43
18. Clarity of Identity	42
71. Freedom from Doubt and Ambivalence	41
34. Task-Involvement	40
68. Stubbornness	35
13. Clarity of Perception	33
70. Attention to Fine Detail	31
14. Accuracy of Perception	31

This general factor (which accounts for 29.9 per cent of the total rating variance) seems primarily to indicate a dimension of individual consistencies in the openness with which children relate themselves to others and engage themselves in a variety of new experiences.

Children with high factor scores show lively, spontaneous involvement in relations with other people, open receptivity to internal or external stimulation, and concomitant effective and flexible mobilization of their resources under a variety of conditions. They are ready to absorb new experiences and to act freely upon a multiplicity of facts, feelings, and ideas. They are curious and show great drive toward mastery. They grasp the subtler interpersonal implications of situations rapidly and are determined and task-involved in responding to demands made by an adult examiner. They are free of inhibition in interpersonal relationships and express themselves flexibly. They seem to experience subtle nuances of feeling and to enjoy multiple interests. These children show warmth, trust, and a minimum of tension in relating to the adult examiner, which is associated with positive self-appraisal. They are self-reliant, but ap-

[2] Loadings of .30 and above are listed for each factor.

propriate in seeking help. They seem clear about their identity and free of doubt and ambivalence. They are also alert, aware of details, and able to use reality effectively in problem-solving situations.

Children with low factor scores appear more passive, shy away from close involvements, and are generally less vigorous and enthusiastic. They seem more constricted, more dependent, and less able to seek help. They seem less clear both about themselves and about the situations they find themselves in.

Active openness to new experience, as conceived here, is not presumed to be primarily a function of high intelligence. Rather, it seems to represent the effectiveness with which the child uses whatever intellectual, affective, and social skills he may have, which is associated with the intensity of his enjoyment of new experiences and the liveliness of his interpersonal exchanges.

The individual consistencies represented by this general factor are apparently similar to those referred to by a number of other authors. Maslow's (1956) distinction between tendencies toward "defense" and "growth" is potentially relevant here. Schachtel's (1959) distinction between the "autocentric" and "allocentric" person also seems relevant. The factor also appears similar to the flexible openness to varieties of experience which Rogers (1959) conceptualizes as one component of "constructive creativity." Other recent work on creativity and related general aspects of behavior may involve similar individual differences. The complexity of the personality characteristics referred to above, plus the consistent finding in the present study that superficially similar aspects of behavior may involve several independent dimensions of individual consistency, rather than one dimension, exemplifies the tentativeness with which such potential relationships must be dealt.

Factor II

Unity of Identity

Rating	Loading
24. Pleasure in Own Body	78
18. Clarity of Identity	75
57. Identification with Own Sex	71
71. Freedom from Doubt and Ambivalence	65
33. Fearfulness	—61
52. Trust	59
32. Observable Tension	—56
19. Adequacy of Self-Appraisal	50
2. Coping II (Internal Equilibration)	49

	Rating	*Loading*
27.	Accuracy of Evaluations of Others	40
46.	Clarity of Fantasy-Reality Distinction	36
73.	Spontaneity	35
63.	Independence, Self-Reliance	35
29.	Social Insightfulness	34
30.	Cooperation with Authority	33
39.	Frustration Tolerance	32
67.	Perseverance	31

This factor seems to indicate individual differences in the consonance and coherence of identity, including sex identification, feelings of personal integrity, and healthy narcissism. The high loadings on trust, absence of tension, spontaneity and self-reliance, lack of fearfulness, and freedom from doubt and ambivalence seem to be components of a clear and unified pattern of identity. Associated with their relative unity of identity, children with high factor scores distinguish clearly between fantasy and reality, are insightful in social situations, realistic in their evaluation of others, and cooperative with the examiner. They also seem relatively able to tolerate frustration and to sustain effort toward completion of tasks.

Children with low factor scores, on the other hand, seem to be relatively unclear about their personal identity, including their sexual identity, and to be relatively confused, disorganized, less realistic, and more tension-ridden. They tend to be dissatisfied with their physical appearance and their capacities. They are relatively uncooperative, and relatively incapable of effective interaction with other persons.

Factor III
Accuracy of Reality Testing

	Rating	*Loading*
13.	Clarity of Perception	78
14.	Accuracy of Perception	73
70.	Attention to Fine Detail	68
55.	Adequacy of Spatial Orientation	64
72.	Capacity to Delay for Appraisal	63
15.	Speed of Orientation	62
3.	Cognitive Coping Capacity	54
6.	Ability to Synthesize Thought, Affect, Action	50
69.	Attention Span	48
67.	Perseverance	43
1.	Coping I (Activeness of Problem-Solving)	42
65.	Drive Toward Mastery	40
22.	Range of Areas of Enjoyment	40
46.	Clarity of Fantasy-Reality Distinction	38
19.	Adequacy of Self-Appraisal	36

Rating	*Loading*
74. Meticulosity	36
30. Cooperation with Authority	33
8. Mobilization of Resources under Stress	33
66. Determination	31
34. Task-Involvement	30

The common thread among the ratings which have high loadings on Factor III appears to be general accuracy of reality testing. The factor thus seems to imply consistent individual differences in the clarity with which incoming stimulation is apprehended and the capacity to check experience effectively against known facts and prior experiences.

Children with high factor scores show clear, accurate perception, considerable attention to details, good spatial organization, capacity to delay in order to appraise situations, long attention span, and sustained effort, all keys to effective reality testing. They show a distinct drive toward mastery, seem to have many interests, distinguish clearly between reality and fantasy, and work in a meticulous, determined, and task-involved fashion. They also seem able to mobilize their resources effectively under stress.

Children with low factor scores seem less effectively coordinated to reality. They show less task-involvement and less drive toward mastery and are less meticulous. Their lesser clarity of apprehension and inadequate attunement to reality are associated with inadequate and unrealistic self-evaluation and uncomfortable and uncooperative relations with authority figures.

Factor IV
Cooperativeness

Rating	*Loading*
34. Task-Involvement	71
39. Frustration Tolerance	71
30. Cooperation with Authority	69
38. Enjoyment	69
51. Warmth	62
67. Perseverance	58
68. Stubbornness	−54
52. Trust	50
33. Fearfulness	−41
53. Openness to New Experience	39
27. Accuracy of Evaluations of Others	35
69. Attention Span	32
71. Freedom from Doubt and Ambivalence	30
23. Ability to Ask for Help	30
2. Coping II (Internal Equilibration)	30

Factor IV seems to indicate consistent individual differences in comfortable cooperativeness in the clinical testing situation. The cooperativeness of children with high factor scores is associated with warmth toward and trust in others, adequate evaluation of others, enjoyment of the testing situation, and comfortable, unfrightened patience in sustaining effort toward the completion of tasks posed by an adult. They involve themselves freely in the testing and are tolerant of the frustrations involved in dealing with difficult items. They also show relatively little stubbornness and fearfulness and seem open to new experience. This, plus the fact that *S*s with high factor scores show adequate internal equilibration, including freedom from doubt and ambivalence, suggests that they cooperate comfortably with the adult examiner, without the compulsive drivenness that characterizes another form of cooperation in such testing situations.

Children with low factor scores seem to avoid intense participation in the testing relationship. They find it difficult to deal with frustration, seem unsure of themselves, and experience subjective discomfort in the testing situation. They lack trust and appear stubborn, fearful, and constricted. Their unwillingness to participate fully in the situation is associated with unrealistic evaluations of others.

Factor V
Compulsive Exactness

Rating	Loading
21. Concern with Goodness and Badness	57
74. Meticulosity	54
66. Determination	49
68. Stubbornness	44
65. Drive Toward Mastery	37
72. Capacity to Delay for Appraisal	30
67. Perseverance	30

This factor seems to indicate individual differences in the kind of compulsive exactness that is associated with a relatively high degree of superego pressure and that is assumed by psychoanalytic theorists to be referable to anal fixations and conflicts.

Children with high factor scores are determined, stubborn, and meticulous, with an associated "moralistic" concern over the "rightness of things." [3] The factor thus seems to represent aspects of obsessive-

---

[3] It should be noted here that the children of this sample in general choose to abide rather carefully by the moral standards of the community. This general observation is confirmed by their responses to the Comprehension subtest of the WISC,

compulsive behavior, with overtones of denial and projection. The constellation of loadings suggests that children with high factor scores achieve meticulous exactness at a considerable cost of flexibility and enjoyment.

Children with low factor scores show less meticulosity, stubbornness, determination, and drive toward mastery, as well as less of the moralistic concern with rightness that seems to typify children with high factor scores. Their capacity to use delay for appraisal is lower, as is their capacity to sustain effort toward completion of tasks under the conditions in which these observations were made. In view of the fact that the factors interpreted here are orthogonal to each other, low factor scores on Factor V do not, however, imply generalized inadequacy in this aspect of delay. A child may have a low score on Factor V, yet be high, for example, on Factor IV, which seems to represent a dimension of effective delay without the implication of moralistic concern with the correctness of behavior.

Factor VI
Sporadic Disruption of Control

Rating	Loading
40. Variability	59
33. Fearfulness	47
32. Observable Tension	40
66. Determination	−34

In this factor, variability is associated with fearfulness, overt or observable tension, and lack of determination, apparently indicating consistent individual differences in sporadic disruption of performance, rather than variability in the form of effective flexibility. Children with high factor scores seem to show a specific inadequacy of over-all control that manifests itself in sporadic disruption of reality contact, at least in the kind of child-adult testing relationship that served as the basis for the ratings. A high factor score therefore seems to indicate a special form of partial ego weakness associated with ineffective, anxious constriction.[4]

---

and by their TAT protocols. Most of the children in this sample seem not in conflict about moral precepts, but rather to have incorporated strong moral standards. In this sample, children with high factor scores may thus be quite outstanding in the degree to which meticulous exactness is associated with moralistic concerns.

[4] It is the investigators' impression that nearly all the children in this sample are to some degree anxious and fearful in such testing situations. For some of the children, such apprehensiveness leads to alert readiness (cf., Moriarty, 1961, pp. 75–76; Duffy, 1941, p. 182). In others, apparently those with high scores on Factor VI, the anxiety occasionally disrupts test performance and contact with the examiner.

Children with low factor scores perform more smoothly, maintain contact with the examiner and the testing procedures more effectively, and do so with less tension and fearfulness and greater determination.

This factor seems to have much in common with what George Klein (1954) has described as "constricted and flexible control" on the basis of performances in the Color-Word Test. In his view, long reading times in the difficult portion of this test (in which S is required to inhibit the overlearned tendency to read words while naming incongruous colors in which the words are printed) are the product of the sort of constricted, sporadically disrupted control apparently represented by this factor. The inclusion of the Color-Word Test among the cognitive control measures made it possible to test the relationship of Factor VI to a factor including Color-Word Test performances in the final analysis of factor relationships described in Chapter 12.

Discussion of Rating Factors for Behavior in the Clinical Testing Situation

Five of the six clinical rating factors seem to have implications for the over-all adaptive effectiveness of the children's behavior. Factor I, for example, which we termed "Active Openness to New Experience," includes the active, flexible pursuit of experiences often assumed to be a key to creativity. It should be remembered, however, that knowledge of a child's score on this factor leaves unanswered many other critical questions concerning his consistent behavioral patterns. It is obviously possible to be open to new experience in a differentiated or undifferentiated way, to be relatively closed to new experience for a number of qualitatively different reasons, or the like.

In contrast, assessment of over-all ego strength implies that relationships among a wide variety of such behavioral attributes be considered for the specific purpose of evaluating the place of each component variable in the totality of personality organization. And, as noted repeatedly in this study, personality organization is far more complex than has often been assumed. In spite of these limitations on the interpretation of single dimensions of personality organization, Factor II seems relevant to a limited aspect of ego strength, the unity of identity. Factor III, which seems to represent accuracy of reality testing, seems even more relevant to the mental health of these children, as does Factor VI, which seems to represent a particular kind of gross disruption of control. Factor IV, representing Cooperativeness, seems referable to a general aspect of response. Factor V, Compulsive Exactness, seems primarily relevant to the strength of superego pressures in the context of obsessive-compulsive defenses.

It is noteworthy, although not surprising, that several of the clinical rating factors have implications for the quality and effectiveness of delay, the degree of trust in others, and several other presumably basic aspects of personality organization. Since these are orthogonal (i.e., uncorrelated) factors, the obvious conclusion is that the individual factors represent distinguishable aspects of these fundamental attributes of personality organization as these appear in varied contexts of other traits. Delay, for example, is presumably involved in the formation and employment of all cognitive structures. Since it involves defenses and other control structures, delay can appear in a variety of forms, each with unique implications for the pattern of equilibration represented by the child's total array of motivational and cognitive structures.

Ratings of Behavior in the Laboratory Testing Situation

Twenty-three ratings were made independently on the basis of observations made during the laboratory tests of cognitive controls. Twenty-two of these were drawn from the total group of seventy-five made on the basis of WISC and TAT responses and observations, but only sixteen overlapped with the forty-seven clinical ratings included in the data analyses (see Appendix). One additional laboratory rating, 78. Gross Scanning, was made only in the laboratory and dealt with the extent to which the child spontaneously scanned the laboratory before, during, and after the cognitive control tests.

In addition to the uniqueness of the laboratory setting and the unfamiliarity of the tasks, the following conditions obtained in the laboratory that did not obtain in the WISC and TAT session: (1) the examiner was a man;[5] (2) a woman observer was present; (3) the children had met neither examiner nor observer prior to the testing sessions and had not been tested in a laboratory setting earlier; (4) the tests were generally brief and varied in nature; (5) one of the procedures (the Schematizing Test) was given in a dark room; (6) the observer was positioned so that she could see as little as possible of the child's actual test performance in each of the procedures. She was instructed to base her ratings only on other features of the child's behavior.

[5] Robert Long.

Prior to the study, the clinical and laboratory raters met to clarify the meaning of the twenty-two overlapping ratings. Subsequently, they resolved discrepancies in the interpretation of ratings that became apparent in practice ratings of other children. The clinical and laboratory ratings employed in the data analyses were done in complete independence, and neither rater was aware of the child's performance in any of the other procedures included in the study.

Mean Ratings of Boys and Girls

It is worthy of note that more differences between boys and girls appear in the ratings of behavior in the novel laboratory testing situation, in which the examiner was a man whom the children had not met previously and in which the tasks were unfamiliar, than in the clinical testing situation. As a group, the laboratory tests also provide greater freedom of motoric activity that may have allowed some of the gross boy-girl differences to appear in observable forms. The boys were rated higher in energy level, curiosity, action upon the environment, drive toward mastery, spontaneity, and gross scanning of the laboratory. In view of the nature of the situation, these differences are not surprising and seem to fit anticipations concerning greater overt activity, overt expressions of curiosity, and assertiveness on the part of the boys. The near-significant differences in talkativeness, openness to new experience (in this situation), and acting out seem compatible with the other differences (the higher mean for girls on the last of these indicates greater overcontrol).

Mean Ratings of Younger and Older Children

The general lack of differences between the younger and older children is nearly as impressive here as in the ratings of behavior in the clinical testing situation. The older children did, however, seem more in command of the situation and less fearful than the younger children.

Correlations Between Ratings of Behavior in the Two Settings

Correlations between the sixteen pairs of ratings of the child's behavior in the clinical and laboratory testing situations appear in Table 9–1. Although most of these correlations are significant, which attests indirectly to the reliability of the independent raters, they are low enough to suggest that these two very different situations may have had considerable differential effect on individual children. The lack of correlation between ratings of trust, warmth, fearfulness, and variability could be attributable to differential reactions to male and female examiners and (in the case of about half the children) a familiar versus an unfamiliar situation.

TABLE 9–1

Pearson Correlations Between Ratings of Behavior in the Clinical and Laboratory Testing Situations
(N = 60)

Rating	r
32. Observable Tension	.47 ***
33. Fearfulness	.14
34. Task-Involvement	.44 ***
35. Energy Level	.33 **
38. Enjoyment	.35 **
39. Frustration Tolerance	.27 *
40. Variability	.06
51. Warmth	.15
52. Trust	.25
53. Openness to New Experience	.55 ***
54. Curiosity	.33 **
62. Action upon the Environment	.40 **
63. Independence, Self-Reliance	.47 ***
65. Drive Toward Mastery	.45 ***
73. Spontaneity	.55 ***
74. Meticulosity	.27 *

* $p < .05$.
** $p < .01$.
*** $p < .001$.

Factor Analysis of Ratings in the Laboratory Testing Situation

The matrix of intercorrelations of the twenty-three ratings was factor analyzed by the principal axis method. This analysis indicated that four orthogonal factors account for the common variance among these ratings. The four factors were rotated by the normal varimax method. The resulting orthogonal factors are interpreted below.

Factor I
Impulsive Spontaneity

Rating	Loading
51. Warmth	85
36. Friendliness	81
37. Talkativeness	77

Rating	Loading
73. Spontaneity	75
77. Acting Out–Overcontrol	−63
35. Energy Level	62
62. Action upon the Environment	59
65. Drive Toward Mastery	50
40. Variability	48
53. Openness to New Experience	43
54. Curiosity	42
52. Trust	40
38. Enjoyment	33

This factor seems to indicate a dimension of individual differences in laboratory behavior, in relation to a male examiner, that ranges from impulsive spontaneity to constricted inhibition.

Children with high factor scores are energetically warm, friendly, trusting, and talkative, but with overtones of difficulty in impulse control and excessive variability of behavior. Their curiosity, openness to new experiences, and pleasure in this testing situation seem generally positive but lacking in subtlety and organization.

Children with low factor scores are less variable, but seem inhibited, constricted, distant, unfriendly,[6] and lacking in trust.

Factor II
Anxious Dependence

Rating	Loading
31. Confidence in Abilities	−89
63. Independence, Self-Reliance	−89
32. Observable Tension	73
34. Task-Involvement	−65
39. Frustration Tolerance	−64
33. Fearfulness	56
52. Trust	−53
38. Enjoyment	−52
64. Grasp of the Situation	−47
73. Spontaneity	−40
53. Openness to New Experience	−39

This factor seems to indicate a dimension of individual differences in the children's laboratory behavior ranging from anxious dependence to nonanxious independence. The discomfort associated with the dependent extreme of this dimension suggests that something more than simple dependence-independence is represented by the factor, particularly at the dependent end of the dimension.

[6] None of the sixty children was actively hostile.

Children with high factor scores are unusually dependent in a context of low confidence in their abilities. In the laboratory, they show anxious, fearful distrust associated with inhibition and constriction, low confidence in their abilities, relatively poor grasp of the situation, low task-involvement, and low frustration tolerance.

Children with low factor scores show confident independence associated with an effective, comfortable grasp of the situation, a high degree of task-involvement and frustration tolerance, and compatible openness and spontaneity in relation to the examiner.

Factor III
Explorativeness

Rating	Loading
78. Gross Scanning	75
54. Curiosity	71
65. Drive Toward Mastery	66
53. Openness to New Experience	48
64. Grasp of the Situation	46
62. Action upon the Environment	42
76. Avoidance	−34
35. Energy Level	33

This factor seems to indicate that the children's laboratory performances can be arranged along a dimension of individual differences in explorativeness.

Children with high factor scores show lively curiosity about the laboratory and active eagerness to understand the situation. That their scanning ranges far beyond the actual tasks presented them implies coming to terms with the situation by active efforts to master it, rather than distractibility.

Children with low factor scores appear passively inhibited and avoidant in this completely new situation. They perform the required tasks, but show little or no active curiosity about the room, the experimenter, the rater, and so forth.

This factor seems to have rather obvious implications for differences in the children's defense mechanisms. Nunberg (1961, p. 78) has pointed out that "Curiosity and the need for causality are boundless." He also states (pp. 73–74) that he "cannot but agree with Freud that one of its functions is to help in mastering the external world, the reality." These remarks seem particularly appropriate to this factor and to the authors' impression that apparent lack of curiosity by a child in a new and potentially intriguing situation implies powerful defensive maneuvers. Repression, for example, could be a relatively important defense for children with low factor scores. The analysis in Chapter 11 of relations between defense ratings and other scores, including factor scores for the laboratory ratings, provided an opportunity to test such hypotheses.

Of potential relevance to the individual consistencies indicated by this factor is the work representing a revival of interest in the problems of curiosity and explorativeness (see, e.g., Berlyne, 1960). In Berlyne's terms, the ultimate question might be stated as that of the causes of individual differences in the "arousal potential" of certain stimulus attributes, the ranges of discrepancy between the familiar and the novel that different individuals deal with, and so forth. Motivational variables, as well as defensive and other cognitive variables, are obviously of vital importance to these questions. Berlyne (1962) has, in fact, defined curiosity as a motivational state. Other recent investigations (e.g., Glanzer, 1958; Houston and Mednick, 1963) have shown that curiosity is related to exploratory drive, novelty, and a need for novelty. Cantor and Cantor (1964) have demonstrated that kindergarten children in general spend more time observing novel than familiar visual stimuli. Maw and Maw (1962) have shown that curious children prefer unfamiliar designs, which again indicates the motivational components of curiosity.

McNamara, Murphy, and Harrell (1964, p. 976) recently reported a relationship between active curiosity and effectiveness of reality contact. These authors emphasize that, in addition to its motivational features, curiosity involves "a system of responses, which when elicited have self-reinforcing properties. . . ." They point to the attentional nature of this system of responses, a view with which we would concur, adding only the reminder that cognitive controls, defenses, and other structures relevant to attention deployment must be included as a third major class of components in any comprehensive consideration of curiosity.

In a stimulating discussion of the contrasting ideological positions commonly called "left-wing" and "right-wing," Tomkins (1964) has noted both the stimulus-hunger and the tendency to sustain and enjoy tension states characteristic of the "left-wing" orientation. In part, at least, his description seems relevant to Ss with high scores on the explorativeness factor, with its implications of emphasis on change, high valuation and active pursuit of novelty, and potential for creative reorganizations of experience.

Factor IV
Acting upon the Environment

Rating	Loading
74. Meticulosity	−59
35. Energy Level	59
62. Action upon the Environment	54
77. Acting Out–Overcontrol	−48
34. Task-Involvement	−43
37. Talkativeness	41
38. Enjoyment	−39
52. Trust	−34
39. Frustration Tolerance	−32

This factor seems to indicate a dimension of individual differences in laboratory behavior ranging from acting upon the environment to excessive control of overt behavior. In the present sample, in which gross acting out was a rarity, Rating 77, Acting Out–Overcontrol, which has the fourth highest loading, may primarily represent a tendency toward active, motoric behavior, rather than acting out per se.

Children with high factor scores show a tendency toward acting upon the environment in a context of high energy level. These children are careless, talkative, involve themselves to a minimal degree and with a minimum of pleasure in the highly structured, delay-demanding laboratory tests, and are relatively distrustful of the examiner.

Children with low factor scores seem to have obsessive-compulsive traits in a context of generalized overcontrol, high task-involvement and frustration tolerance in the laboratory tests, pleasure in the new and rather challenging tests, and trust in the examiner. In view of the nature of this factor, the low ratings assigned to these children on energy level, action upon the environment, and talkativeness probably indicate moderate levels of these variables in keeping with overcontrol, rather than truly low energy, unusual passivity, or exceptional verbal inhibition.

Discussion of Rating Factors for Behavior in the Laboratory Testing Situation

Although there are apparent similarities between some of these rating factors and some of the clinical rating factors, the differences are more impressive than the similarities. Obvious reasons for the apparent uniqueness of these laboratory rating factors are the different ratings and numbers of ratings used in the two situations. Even more impressive, perhaps, are the gross differences in the two situations, including the sex difference of the examiners. The fact that three of the four factors (I—Impulsive Spontaneity, III—Explorativeness, and IV—Acting upon the Environment) relate to the children's control over motoric behavior is particularly impressive and may be referable to the increased opportunities for expression of motoric styles in the laboratory. The tests given there generally involved greater degrees of motor activity, and the child could explore this new situation as freely as he dared in the pauses between the tests. The appearance of a factor called Anxious Dependence may be attributable, at least in part, to the lack of familiar supports in this novel situation.

The apparent differences between these ratings and the clinical ratings are also referable, of course, to the different kinds of observations made by the two raters. The clinical rater was both administering tests and observing the child's extra-test behavior. The laboratory rater could not observe the child's test performance proper and relied more completely upon his facial expressions, exchanges with the experimenter, locomotion, and overt or covert exploration of the unusual setting.

In general, the uniqueness of these ratings seems advantageous in that new aspects of the children's complex behavioral repertories were apparently sampled.

Relationships Between Rating Factors for Behavior in the Clinical and Laboratory Testing Situations

The fact that sixteen ratings (of the forty-seven used by the clinical rater and the twenty-three used by the laboratory rater) were employed in both the clinical and laboratory testing situations raises the obvious question of overlap in the two sets of factors. The important findings here are that only four of the twenty-four correlations between the six clinical rating factors and the four laboratory rating factors are significant and that all four barely exceed significance at the .05 level. General clinical rating Factor I, Active Openness to New Experience, is correlated .28 and −.26 with laboratory rating Factors I and II, indicating that such active openness is to a minor degree associated with impulsive spontaneity and a lack of anxious dependence in the laboratory. Clinical rating Factor III, Accuracy of Reality Testing, is correlated .28 with laboratory rating Factor III, Explorativeness. Clinical rating Factor V, Compulsive Exactness, is correlated −.27 with laboratory rating Factor IV, Acting upon the Environment, indicating that children who are compulsively exact in the clinical testing interaction are low in acting upon the environment in the laboratory. All four of these correlations seem to represent obvious relationships that pose no interpretive difficulty. The surprising fact is that correlations between the two sets of ratings are not higher and more numerous.

It also seems possible that differences in the personalities of the raters and their levels of training led to selective focusing on different constellations of behavior in the children. The fact that the two groups of factors seem more different than similar may also mean, of course, that individual differences in the children's behavior in the two testing situations can be understood in terms of at least ten dimensions that overlap to only a minor degree. The final analysis of relations between factor scores for the clinical and laboratory ratings and other major scores (Chapter 12) provided a partial test of this hypothesis.

10 The Assessment of Defense Mechanisms and General Characteristics of Ego Organization

A MAJOR purpose of the present investigation was to extend earlier explorations of the relations of cognitive controls and intellectual abilities to the defense mechanisms and general attributes of cognitive structuring postulated by Freud and later psychoanalytic theorists. Studies of cognitive controls were initiated in part under the impetus of Hartmann's (1939) emphasis on relatively conflict-free aspects of the apparatuses employed in various cognitive functions, so that relations between cognitive controls, the constellations of cognitive functions Freud discussed as defenses, and general characteristics of cognitive functioning was considered a critically important issue. This chapter is devoted to presentations of the defense and general concepts employed and the methods of assessing individual differences in these aspects of cognitive organization. Chapter 11 contains descriptions of some of the empirical results obtained with these variables in the present study.

As noted in Chapter 3, earlier studies of relations between cognitive controls and defenses have suggested that extreme repression is related to leveling (Gardner *et al.*, 1959; Holzman and Gardner, 1959) and that projection and isolation are related to extensiveness of scanning (Gardner and Long, 1962a; Silverman, 1964b) in female adults. Work summarized by Witkin *et al.* (1962) suggests that denial and other defenses referred to by those authors as "unstructured" are related in children to inadequate articulation of experience, whereas defenses they refer to as "structured" (e.g., isolation) seem to be associated with greater degrees of articulation. The assessment of "structured" and "unstructured" defenses reported by Witkin and his associates was more global, the assessment of the single defense of denial more specific than the evaluations of defenses made in the present study (denial was there evaluated on the basis of but four indicators applied to TAT responses). The interpretation of groups of defenses as "structured" and "unstructured" also involves different assumptions about defenses than those employed here.

The present study provided an opportunity to determine whether relationships between controls and defenses are similar for adults and children and whether comparable results are obtained for children when defenses are assessed individually and when they are assessed in the aggregate. The study also provided an opportunity to deal with a more comprehensive array of defenses and general characteristics of cognitive organization than has previously been evaluated in a single study.

In view of the importance of defense constructs to psychoanalytic explanations of behavior, detailed exploration of relationships between a number of defenses and other aspects of individual consistency, such as dimensions of cognitive control, could provide unique information concerning the complexity of cognitive structuring. The results may also provide a more comprehensive view of relations between structural aspects of personality organization that are assumed to arise out of conflict resolution and structures that represent relatively conflict-free aspects of individuality. When compared with earlier studies of defense-control relations in adults, exploration of relations between defenses and controls at preadolescence may also provide evidence concerning developmental changes in the integration of defense structures and in the course of automatization of defenses. In advance of the study, it seemed likely that the "change of function" described by Hartmann (1939)—in which a set of cognitive operations originally used for strictly defensive purposes is later used for such purely adaptive purposes as adjustment and organization (Hartmann, 1950)—is more complete in adults than in preadolescents. If so, *particular* defenses, assessed as separate entities, could be related to cognitive control variables to a lesser degree at preadolescence. The gradual automatization of isolation could, for example, lead to a relationship between generalized use of isolation and extensiveness of scanning in adults that is not yet present at preadolescence.

Assessment of defense mechanisms and such over-all aspects of cognitive organization as the relative autonomy of the ego as defined by Rapaport (1951a, 1958), over-all ego autonomy as defined by Gill and Brenman (1959), and ego strength presents a series of special methodological problems and involves as yet unanswered questions concerning the conceptualization of developmental changes in such structural aspects of cognition. The method employed for the assessment of specific defenses and certain over-all aspects of ego organization is therefore discussed in detail in subsequent sections of this chapter. The questions concerning cognitive structuring at preadolescence revolve primarily around the issue of the degrees of change that occur in various defenses and general aspects of cognitive structuring from preadolescence to adulthood. It may be that an individual's preadolescent defenses change radically under the increased drive pressures contingent upon adolescence and that it is this newly reorganized array that stabilizes in young adulthood. The emphasis in psychoanalytic theorizing upon the importance of early childhood, including the several stages of early development, for ultimate ego organization could, on the other hand, lead to the assumption that the *general* pattern of adult character structure, including predominant defenses, crystallizes before puberty, and that subsequent changes in ego organization occur within rather strict limits provided by the previously formed structures. The fact that hereditary characteristics of the apparatuses employed in cognitive functions probably are important determinants of defense patterning (see Freud, 1937) may also suggest that the general outlines of adult defense organization are formed at preadolescence, or even earlier. It is also possible that individuals differ in the longitudinal consistency of their defense organizations.

Of course, no defense is ever employed alone in any bit of behavior and no bit of behavior is purely defensive. The ratings of specific defenses, which in the present study were based on three sets of clinical test protocols, are therefore abstractions of a simpler and more static nature than the actual behaviors from which they are inferred. They represent the rater's judgment, based on careful consideration of these test performances, of the child's tendency to employ particular defenses to a greater or lesser degree, as compared to the degree characterizing other children in the sample. Each child's defense ratings also indicate the rater's evaluation of the relative importance of particular mechanisms in the child's defensive hierarchy.

The Concept of Defense

The general concept of defense and the place of defense in personality organization that served as a background for the present ratings was provided by Freud. His works on defense have been supplemented by the writings of Anna Freud, particularly her classic book, *The Ego and the Mechanisms of Defense* (1936); the excellent collative statements and original contributions of Fenichel (1945a, b); and the contributions of a considerable number of other psychoanalysts.

Freud introduced the concept of defense early (Freud, 1894) but varied in his use of the term "defense" and in his conception of relations among defenses in his subsequent writings. Repression (the definition of which also changed during the years of Freud's work) is a cornerstone of the general theory. In Freud's early writings, in fact, repression was equated with defense. Freud then dropped the concept of defense as such until much later (1926), when he elaborated upon earlier suggestions that repression is one of a number of distinct defense mechanisms. At various points, he spoke of several other defenses as "repressive" defenses because of their intricate relationships to repression or their inclusion of repression in a larger constellation of defensive operations. Freud and others (e.g., Anna Freud, 1936; Fenichel, 1945a; Madison, 1961) have classified the major defenses and types of defense, the major motives for defense, the major functions of defenses, and the relationships of defenses to symptom formation.

The current point of view concerning the pivotal place of repression among the defenses has perhaps been best stated by Anna Freud (1936, pp. 53–54):

Theoretically, repression may be subsumed under the general concept of defence and placed side by side with the other specific methods. Nevertheless, from the point of view of efficacy it occupies a unique position in comparison with the rest. In terms of quantity it accomplishes more than they, that is to say, it is capable of mastering powerful instinctual impulses, in face of which the other defensive measures are quite ineffective. It acts once only, though the anticathexis, effected to secure the repression, is a permanent institution demanding a constant expenditure of energy. The other mechanisms, on the contrary, have to be brought into operation again whenever there is an accession of instinctual energy. But repression is not only the most efficacious, it is also the most dangerous, mechanism. The dissociation from the ego entailed by the withdrawal of consciousness from whole tracts of instinctual and affective life may destroy the integrity of the personality for good and all. Thus repression becomes the basis of compromise-formation and neurosis. The consequences of the other defensive methods are not less serious but, even when they assume an acute form, they remain more within the limits of the normal. They manifest themselves in innumerable transformations, distortions and deformities of the ego, which are in part the accompaniment of and in part substitutes for neurosis.

Defenses assessed in the present study include both "repressive" defenses (repression, isolation, reaction formation, projection) and certain defenses (or pre-stages of defense) involved in ego restriction (avoidance and denial). In one way or another, both groups of defenses have traditionally been assumed to have as their primary function the prevention of potentially painful or threatening conscious experiences. They are assumed here to be major features of the child's personality organization that give order and consistency to his behavior at preadolescence. It seems likely, in fact, that the most general purpose of defense mechanisms is the preservation of effective order in consciousness. Disorder, in this formulation, may be unpleasant not only because the failure of defense allows frightening or unpleasant impulse derivatives, memories, affects, and percepts to enter consciousness, but also because the adaptive necessity of optimal equilibration of the total personality requires that the characteristic nature of the individual's consciousness be preserved, both in terms of types of ideas, memories, affects, and percepts and in terms of the quality of consciousness itself. Whatever the effectiveness of the individual's total pattern of equilibration, disordered consciousness is inherently maladaptive and, apparently as a consequence, is associated with intense negative affects, including anxiety.

In normal functioning of a defense, neither the cognitive operations involved nor the anxiety that instigates its employment are represented in consciousness (see Freud, 1926). Under these circumstances, anxiety is assumed to serve only as a "signal" leading to activation of a particular constellation of cognitive operations. Only when a defense is weak or in danger of collapse (i.e., when the forbidden drive representations threaten imminent entry into consciousness) does the threat of disorder, self-punishment, or retaliation from the external world manifest itself in conscious anxiety. Conscious anxiety can also be activated nondefensively, by danger in external reality.

Method of Assessment

Six major defense mechanisms (repression, isolation, reaction formation, projection, avoidance, and denial) were assessed by the first author. The six mechanisms were selected from the larger number of mechanisms postulated in the psychoanalytic literature because of their signal importance to the psychoanalytic theory of personality organization and because it seemed clearly feasible to assess individual differences in these constellations of cognitive operations on the basis of the clinical test protocols available.

The ratings were made on the basis of detailed blind analyses of typed protocols of tape-recorded WISC, TAT, and Rorschach Tests. The

WISC and Rorschach protocols also contained scoring by the original examiner.[1] In addition, the rater used brief notes by each examiner on major qualitative features of the child's test performance, including any unusual features of the interpersonal relationship.

The rater assessed the defense mechanisms (as well as the four general characteristics of ego organization discussed later in this chapter) without knowledge of the child's performance in any other situation and without reference to his age. He first read the three test protocols for one child carefully, with the defense and general rating concepts in mind. During this initial reading, he made detailed notes of tentative inferences concerning the defense operations apparent in the child's responses, test scores, and test-taking attitudes. He then compiled his notes and listed major differential decisions required in the case of test behaviors potentially attributable to the operation of two or more defenses. At this point, he reconsidered all the test productions and scores in terms of these differential decisions. The general method described here was patterned closely after that exemplified in the works of Rapaport *et al.* (1945, 1946) and Schafer (1948), except that the emphasis was on defenses, rather than diagnostic syndromes. The approach to the Rorschach was modeled after that of Schafer (1954), who has provided a detailed exposition of the assessment of certain defenses on the basis of Rorschach performance.

Three important points about this type of defense rating should be stated clearly and unequivocally. First, the method of evaluating clinical test performances developed by Rapaport, Gill, and Schafer requires detailed knowledge of the psychoanalytic literature sampled briefly in this chapter, as well as related contributions too numerous to mention here. Second, this type of assessment requires extensive training in the application of these defense constructs to performance in psychological tests. Third, training in dealing with the kinds of differential analyses referred to above is of critical importance in the assessment of individual defenses, as well as patterns of defense. To assess any defense without simultaneous evaluation of the other defensive and nondefensive interpretive possibilities and without careful attention to the uses of such defenses as repression in conjunction with other defenses (see Siegal and Ehrenreich, 1962, on this important point) is to evaluate aspects of cognitive organization more global than the specific defense mechanisms, to introduce gross error into defense assessment, and to produce ratings or scores

[1] The WISC and TAT were administered by the second author, the Rorschach by Mrs. Pitsa Hartocollis.

that are *artifactually* similar to scores representing other aspects of cognitive organization. To assess defenses in a general way, or without careful consideration of the differential interpretations possible, could, for example, produce spurious correlations between defenses and cognitive controls or defenses and intellectual abilities. "Cookbook" approaches, use of checklists of indicators, and so forth, which are inadequate for any evaluation of complex test responses, are, if anything, more inadequate when differential interpretive decisions are made concerning variables as specific in their behavioral implications and as intricately related as the defense mechanisms. The same statements apply to the ratings of general characteristics of ego organization described later in this chapter, which involved equally complex assessment processes that included the prior assessments of the defense mechanisms.

Following detailed evaluation of a child's test protocols, the rater assigned tentative values for each defense on a scale ranging from 0 to 10. He then re-evaluated the *pattern* of relationships to insure an adequate fit to his conception of both the relative and absolute values appropriate to the child's performance.

The entire process outlined above required a minimum of two and one half to three hours per subject. Evaluation of the protocols of a few subjects who posed particularly difficult problems of differential defense rating required as much as four or five hours. When the ratings were completed for all sixty children, ratings of the first children assessed were reconsidered, in sequential order, to insure that scores for these children were as comparable as possible to those of children rated later (it was correctly assumed that the rater's initial normative anticipations would be modified as he proceeded through the sample). The rater continued this process of reconsideration of protocols and minor adjustments of ratings to conform to norms for the total sample until there were no more discrepancies from the over-all norms developed by the rater. Early assessments of one or a few defenses were altered slightly in the case of about fifteen children.

The reliability of such ratings is an important matter which could not be dealt with in the present study. No qualified rater was available who could spend the 160 or more hours required. Past experience with such ratings has indicated, however, that, given comparable levels of training and experience, defense ratings as conceptualized here can be made independently with surprisingly high inter-rater reliabilities. In the study by Gardner *et al.* (1959), in which independent ratings were discussed and pooled into a consensus rating, the original intercorrelations between two judges' ratings of isolation and repression exceeded .90.

The Defenses Assessed

The concepts employed in the assessment of particular defenses are outlined below. The sources of inferences concerning each defense are also indicated, with references to relevant literature.

Repression

Freud assumed that what he termed "repression proper" involves two principal sets of cognitive operations (Freud, 1911b, 1915a): (a) assimilation of a new experience to that which is already repressed, in which the concept of "primal repression" (Freud, e.g., 1915a, 1926) is of critical importance; and (b) an active expulsion and subsequent holding of ideational or perceptual elements from consciousness by means of countercathexis, the continued expenditure of which he assumed to be involved in the subsequent unavailability of the relevant memories or ideas from consciousness (see also Freud, 1937). Repression was thus conceived by Freud as a dual set of operations whose principal effects are upon the contents and scope of consciousness. In his formulation, adequate, but not excessive, repression is a *sine qua non* of adaptation; without it, ideational representatives of primary-process thinking would pervade consciousness in chaotic fashion. Excessive repression, however, is assumed to restrict awareness, hence intellectual articulation of experience, to a maladaptive degree. Pervasive repression has also been conceptualized as a key to several related classes of symptoms which will not be dealt with here.

Although most other defenses in some way involve repression, in that they operate in conjunction with repression or serve to reinforce or maintain it, repression is also assumed to operate independently (cf. Siegal and Ehrenreich, 1962; Holzman, 1960).

In the case of the WISC, the entire protocol was read carefully for qualitative signs of the limiting effects of repression on performance, lack of verbal articulation and sophistication, suggestions of phobic tendencies, and the like. The scatter of subtest performances was also examined for indications of repression (cf. Rapaport *et al.*, 1945; Schafer, 1948). TAT protocols were read carefully for such indications of repression as ideational paucity, naïveté, and phobic tendencies. Some specific features of Rorschach protocols used to assess the strength and pervasiveness of repression were spelled out earlier by Gardner and his associates (1959). Schafer (1954) has dealt with Rorschach evidence of repression in greater detail. Indications of repression in the three tests were reviewed and considered in relation to each other. Relations to other defenses were also considered before a tentative rating was assigned.

The complexity of the rating process can be exemplified here. To take one common example of the decisions involved in assessing repression, a set of protocols containing impoverished productions could indicate that any one of several defenses is excessively employed, or that certain extraneous conditions obtain, either as individual or combined determinants of performance. Effective assessment of repression requires that the available test materials be considered with each of the relevant possibilities in mind. The type of performance referred to could, for example, indicate massive repression, generalized constriction of overt expressions, acting out, avoidance, unwillingness to respond based on paranoid distrust, depression, limited ability, brain damage. Delineation of such arrays of initial possibilities in terms of relative likelihoods requires careful analysis of all the relevant possibilities and careful re-examination of the protocols with such differential questions in mind. In the case of the present sample, judgments concerning repression, although complex, were for the most part not unusually difficult. The most difficult decisions were ordinarily those in which a child's generalized constriction led to a paucity of material with which to make the kinds of differential judgment indicated above.

Isolation

The defense of isolation involves the splitting of affect from idea (by repression of affect) and the splitting of idea from idea in consciousness (by repression of the connecting meaning-links). After describing the relevant traits of orderliness, parsimony, and obstinacy in relation to anal erotism in his 1908 paper on "Character and Anal Erotism," Freud articulated the concept of isolation in his report on the "rat-man" (Freud, 1909). Comparing hysterical amnesia to isolation (pp. 195–96), he stated that:

In this amnesia we see the evidence of the repression which has taken place. The case is different in obsessional neuroses. The infantile preconditions of the neurosis may be overtaken by amnesia, though this is often an incomplete one; but the immediate occasions of the illness are, on the contrary, retained in the memory. . . . The trauma, instead of being forgotten, is deprived of its affective cathexis; so that what remains in consciousness is nothing but its ideational content, which is perfectly colorless and is judged to be unimportant.

Freud continued his articulation of the defense of isolation and its causes in several of his subsequent works (e.g., 1913, 1918). In one of these elaborations, he described a major effect of isolation upon the nature of consciousness (Freud, 1926, p. 120):

When something unpleasant has happened to the subject or when he himself has done something which has a significance for his neurosis, he interpolates an interval during which nothing further must happen—during which he must perceive nothing and do nothing. This behavior, which seems strange at first sight, is soon seen to have a relation to repression. We know that in hysteria it is possible to cause a traumatic experience to be overtaken by amnesia. In obsessional neurosis this can often not be achieved: the experience is not forgotten, but, instead, it is deprived of its affect, and its associative connections are suppressed or interrupted so that it remains as though isolated and is not reproduced in the ordinary processes of thought.

Whereas repression constricts awareness, isolation extends it, at least with respect to the availability of ideas. The typical extreme isolator is highly verbal, somewhat overideational, given to intellectualizing, and more likely than other persons to employ reaction formation rather extensively. In the clinic, the person who overuses isolation may recite his major conflicts and their developmental evolution with startling clarity but be unable to experience the associated affects. He is in many ways the antithesis of the hysterical person, who represses ideas but may experience the related affects.

The linkage of isolation and reaction formation has been discussed at length by Shapiro (1962). Anna Freud (1936, p. 51) has noted the manner in which reaction formation follows the initial repression of affect and serves to prevent its return to consciousness in cases of obsessional neurosis.

Isolation can have at least two major consequences. The first is compulsivity, represented by an emphasis on neatness and orderliness that, in extreme cases, leads to an over-all impression of rigid, affectively sterile externalizing (i.e., ordering the outer world is used as a substitute for ordering the inner world, a key component of which is largely unavailable to consciousness), repetition, exaggerated "rituals," and the like. The second consequence, which is related to the first but qualitatively different, is a tendency toward doubt-riddenness, indecision, and obsessive vacillation. Although these two consequences are presumed to be related expressions of the operation of a single defense mechanism, their overt manifestations often appear quite different. In the present study, an unusual degree of either or both led to a high rating.

Isolation is obviously associated with unusual delay of expression of relevant impulses (primarily aggressive) and hence is generally antithetical to acting out, as well as generalized repression. It is ordinarily associated most closely with intellectualizing and reaction formation. Isolation is also quite frequently associated with denial or projection, or both.

The major indicators of isolation in clinical psychological tests have been spelled out by Rapaport *et al.* (1945, 1946) and Schafer (1948, 1954). Some specific indicators have also been described by Gardner *et al.* (1959) for performance in the Rorschach Test. A key set of manifestations, particularly in the WISC and TAT, appears in the quality of verbalizations. It is here that the major aspects of isolation are often most apparent.

Reaction Formation

The term, "reaction formation" (Freud, 1905a, 1926), has been used to describe a group of "secondary opposite attitudes" (Fenichel, 1945a, p. 151) that can be considered forms of negation. Reaction formations are usually conceptualized as character traits, in that they involve a relatively permanent alteration of the personality structure. One of the most common forms of reaction formation and the one dealt with in the present study, is the transformation of aggressive impulses into rigid attitudes of kindness and solicitude that often seem incongruous because of the trained observer's simultaneous impression that the subject is expressing anger. Such cloying sweetness is often experienced as irritating in its own right, presumably because the thinly masked aggressive intention is also experienced. Persons who use this defense excessively are thus given to "speaking in opposites." This form of reaction formation must therefore be distinguished from the simpler type of negation involved in the defense of denial per se, which is associated with reaction formation in some individuals but not in others. A key to the distinction between this type of reaction formation and denial lies in the transformation of internal aggressive impulses in reaction formation, which can be contrasted with the primitive, unarticulated negation of internal or external realities involved in denial. In keeping with this formulation, denial seems primarily to keep painful realities out of consciousness and thereby restricts consciousness by a kind of rudimentary analogue of turning away. Reaction formation, in contrast, allows ideational representations of unacceptable impulses into consciousness, albeit in the form of opposites.

Reaction formation is one of the more difficult defenses to evaluate on the basis of the test protocols employed in the present study. Although in extreme cases the "sweet biting" quality of the aggressiveness involved may show itself clearly in one or more TAT stories, or in the verbalization of test responses themselves, the rating must in some cases be based on more tangential hints in the test protocols or on the absence of positive indications.

Projection

Freud's first statements about projection appeared in his original discussion of the "defense neuro-psychoses" (Freud, 1894). Subsequently, he spoke of projection as a means of protecting consciousness from an unbearable idea by "the defensive symptom of *distrust of other people*" (1896, p. 184). In so doing, he indicated clearly the intimate relationship of projection to repression. Later, Freud (1911b) developed the notion that Schreber's delusions of persecution were the outcome of the failure of defenses against unconscious homosexuality occurring in a person with a narcissistic fixation. Following this (Freud, 1915b), he described a woman in whom homosexual impulses appeared to be less important to feelings of persecution and to be embedded in a different dynamic constellation from that described earlier. Other psychoanalysts have expressed a variety of points of view concerning the relationship of unconscious homosexual impulses to projection and, in fact, the relevance of such impulses to projection (see, for example, the discussion by Hesselbach, 1962). The ratings of projection made in the present study were based on the general model provided by Freud but were not restricted by assumptions concerning the specific nature of the "forbidden" repressed, except that (whether aggressive, sexual, or both) it be dissonant with respect to the subject's conscious view of himself and therefore intolerable in awareness. The concept of projection was thus closely tied to Freud's (e.g., 1937) notion concerning the externalization of motives and feelings unconsciously conceptualized as "bad." Projection of positive aspects of the self was thus excluded from consideration in the assessment of projection.

Anna Freud, who notes the pervasiveness with which projection is used by normal children in early childhood, has also pointed out the great similarity of projection to repression (1936, p. 132):

The effect of the mechanism of projection is to break the connection between the ideational representatives of dangerous instinctual impulses and the ego. In this it resembles most closely the process of repression. Other defensive processes, such as displacement, reversal or turning round upon the self, affect the instinctual process itself: repression and projection merely prevent its being perceived. In repression the objectionable idea is thrust back into the id, while in projection it is displaced into the outside world. Another point in which projection resembles repression is that it is not associated with any particular anxiety-situation but may be motivated equally by objective anxiety, super-ego anxiety and instinctual anxiety.

Miss Freud (1936, p. 133) has also described a "normal and less conspicuous form of projection" combined with reaction formation, for which Bibring coined the term "altruistic surrender" (A. Freud, 1936, p. 133). Although this special form of projection leads to positive relations to other people, extensive use of the usual form of projection characteristically has severely disruptive effects on interpersonal relations.

Rapaport *et al.* (1945, 1946) and Schafer (1948, 1954) have described in detail expressions of projection in clinical psychological tests. A number of the most frequent sources of inferences concerning projection in clinical psychological tests can be organized in terms of three major themes: distrust, including suspiciousness and certain forms of fearfulness; hyperalertness; and arbitrariness with peculiar overtones.

Projective distrust can be expressed in a variety of ways. Common examples drawn from the subject's interpersonal behavior include the imputation of aggressive motives to the examiner, e.g., in statements that the examiner is trying to trick the subject, that the test stimuli are designed to embarrass or mislead the subject, or that failure of an item was caused by the examiner. In test responses, children may manifest projective distrust by perceiving dangerous, attacking animals or persons in the Rorschach inkblots, running streams of "wild" and frightening ideas in the TAT, and the like. Such projective fearfulness must, of course, be differentiated from anxiety about achievement, phobic tendencies, and so forth. Suspiciousness itself may also be projected onto figures included in TAT stories or certain figures in the WISC Picture Arrangement subtest.

Hyperalertness can be expressed either directly toward the examiner, as when the child watches the examiner more closely than is appropriate and in a fearful way, or in test responses. In the latter case, response to minute details of test stimuli (which must be differentiated from obsessive inclusiveness) may be a prominent feature of performance.

The arbitrariness involved in projection must, of course, be distinguished from such other forms of arbitrariness as narcissistic "willfulness" and compulsive rigidity. Projective arbitrariness, e.g., in the form of peculiar word usage, or word creation, or in rigid adherence to deviant responses, must also be distinguished from pathological looseness per se. Projective arbitrariness may also be apparent in the general test-taking stance of the subject, who may seem fearful of being dominated or controlled by the experimenter. Ancillary interpretive themes of potential relevance to projection include, of course, direct or indirect expression of, or denial of, guilt feelings. In such instances, the differential problem is often one of depressive tendencies versus depression with paranoid tendencies, depression versus paranoid tendencies per se, and the like.

Denial

The denial of unpleasant aspects of internal and external reality is among the earliest and most primitive defenses (Freud, 1894). Anna Freud (1936), in fact, discusses denial as a "preliminary stage of defense" involving ego restriction (cf. Freud, 1926). Freud (1925) noted that certain repressed ideas or images are represented in consciousness, but only as direct negations. He described such denial as a surmounting of repression without conscious acceptance of the repressed. As he (1911a) observed, use of such primitive maneuvers (which he early conceptualized as a direct manifestation of the pleasure principle) is automatically restricted, and the forms of its expression altered, as the reality principle becomes progressively more dominant in early childhood. Fenichel (1945a) has made the related point that the tendency to deny is inevitably opposed by both perception and memory.

Anna Freud (1936) has noted that denial is ordinarily directed toward events outside the self. Hartmann (1956b) has added that denial may also be directed to inner reality.

A valuable brief description of denial and its relation to avoidance and repression has been provided by Bibring, Dwyer, Huntington, and Valenstein (1961, pp. 65–66):

Denial accomplishes the negation of awareness in conscious terms of existing perceptions of inner or outer stimuli. Literally seeing but refusing to acknowledge what one sees or hearing and negating what is actually heard are expressions of denial and exemplify the close relationship of denial to sensory experience. It is to be distinguished from avoidance which is manifested, for example, by the actual closing of the eyes or the refusal to look. Denial plays its part as an important defense with respect to experience in the spheres of action, affects, and thought. In contrast to repression, which is immediately concerned with drive discharge, denial is closer to the perceptual system, whether it operates with regard to the external world, the environment, or the internal world, the self. Denial may be made more effective through exaggeration, negation, fantasy formation, or displacement.

"Screen memories" (Freud, 1901), play, daydreams, and *deja vu* (Freud, 1913) are among the behaviors in which denial (i.e., reversal) of unpleasant realities is commonly apparent.

Anna Freud (1936) has provided an excellent discussion of the reversal (e.g., the changing of "bad" to "good") involved in denial by means of fantasy, word, and act. She points out that the pervasive denial of early childhood does not impair the child's budding powers of reality testing. Only as reality testing becomes more dominant and more effective does denial provide serious impediments to the development of an adequate ego organization. Although extreme forms of denial are a hallmark of the psychoses, minor forms of denial and partial denial are apparent in the behavior of normal children and adults. Tendencies toward extensive use of denial are also found in persons who are not psychotic but whose egos are rather primitively differentiated. In such cases, denial is often associated with avoidance, another relatively primitive method of "turning away" from unpleasant experiences. Among the other constellations in which denial may be particularly evident are those in which extreme compulsivity (i.e., excessive isolation) appears in a context of generalized constriction, and the various patternings of defense in which projection is outstanding. Fenichel (1945a) has discussed the relationship of denial to other defenses. Grinberg (1961) has suggested that denial is involved in all mechanisms of defense. Since all defenses involve some form of negation of drives and drive representations, this general statement seems tenable. It seems equally clear, however, that very different constellations of cognitive functions are involved in the different defense mechanisms and that denial can be considered a separate entity amenable to assessment in its own right.

Expressions of denial in the Rorschach have been spelled out by Schafer (1954). In the WISC, denial may be apparent in the subject's test-taking attitudes, in negation of anxiety or discomfort, denial of failures, overt negation of negative attitudes toward the examiner, and so forth. As in the Rorschach, denial may show itself in both the WISC and TAT in what Schafer (1954) has termed "Pollyannaish" responses involving reversal or, more indirectly, in hypomanic activity (see Schafer, 1954). In the TAT (as in certain items of the WISC Comprehension, Picture Arrangement, or Picture Completion subtests), denial may take either a "Pollyannaish" form or a related form in which anxiety-arousing features of questions or stimuli having aggressive, sexual, or other connotations are "overlooked" in response. In relatively extreme cases, gross perceptual distortion by omission or direct expressions of denial (e.g., "he looks angry but he really isn't") may occur.

Avoidance

The defense of avoidance also falls in the general class of defenses involving inhibition or ego restriction (Freud, 1926), rather than repression per se. In this case, the inhibition is usually overt (see Madison, 1961). Anna Freud (1936, pp. 100–101) has described avoidance, like denial, as a "preliminary stage of defense." Her classic statements concerning this mechanism also articulate its relationship to denial:

The method of denial, upon which is based the phantasy of the reversal of the real facts into their opposite, is employed in situations in which it is impossible to escape some painful external impression. When a child is somewhat older, his greater freedom of physical movement and his increased powers of psychic activity enable his ego to evade such stimuli and there is no need for him to perform so complicated a psychic operation as that of denial. Instead of perceiving the painful impression and subsequently cancelling it by withdrawing its cathexis, it is open to the ego to refuse to encounter the dangerous external situation at all. It can take to flight and so, in the truest sense of the word, "avoid" the occasions of "pain." The mechanism of avoidance is so primitive and natural and moreover so inseparably associated with the normal development of the ego that it is not easy, for purposes of theoretical discussion, to detach it from its usual context and to view it in isolation.

Anna Freud delineates a normal form, which she terms "ego restriction," and an abnormal form stemming from true neurotic inhibition. All children avoid one or another type of situation at various points in development in order to prevent the activation of memories of earlier experiences for which the new situations serve as anxiety-arousing symbolic substitutes. Ego restriction of this kind (directed toward external reality) can be relaxed if the external conditions are changed. Often, too, ego restriction in one area may lead to an acceleration of activity in another. In cases of avoidance attributable to neurotic inhibition, however, the defense is more unequivocally employed to control internal drive pressures and is thus more autonomous with respect to conditions in external reality, more rigidly used, and more damaging to ego development.

Ratings of avoidance based on clinical test protocols may involve both kinds of avoidance. Indications of pervasive use of avoidance are assumed, however, to suggest a generalized pattern of warding off internal impulses (i.e., maladaptive use of avoidance) and to imply rather severe ego weakness. Lower ratings were assigned to children in whom avoidance was apparent, if at all, in relatively innocuous forms. Avoidance attributable to normal ego restriction may, in fact, find greater expression in the patterning of abilities and interests apparent in a child's test productions than in the kinds of avoidant statements or actions used as primary evidence in rating of this defense.

Perhaps because it often involves action, avoidance is not infrequently associated with such other simple and relatively primitive means of warding off unpleasant experiences as denial and acting out. Avoidance due to neurotic inhibition, however, may appear in a variety of contexts.

The aspects of test performance used to evaluate avoidance are relatively obvious and specific (see Schafer, 1948). In the present study, a common differential question occurred in the case of relatively impoverished test protocols (e.g., when WISC and TAT verbalizations were limited, failures occurred on the Rorschach). In such cases, the possibility that acting out, repression, generalized constriction, and so forth, were responsible for the child's minimal productions required simultaneous evaluation. In many instances, however, indications of avoidance took clearly identifiable forms, such as attempts to interrupt the testing, other forms of evasion, or unwillingness to respond followed by adequate response on inquiry.

Assessment of Four General Characteristics of Ego Organization

Four general aspects of ego organization—acting out–overcontrol, the relative autonomy of the ego, the over-all autonomy of the ego, and ego strength—have sufficient bases in the literature to be useful to a study of preadolescence and are clearly applicable to the children of the present sample. Although limited in range, individual differences in these aspects of behavior were great enough to make assessment in terms of the four general variables a complex but relatively easy matter.

Each child was assigned ratings on the general variables immediately following completion of the defense ratings. All the raw test material and all the defense ratings were considered in arriving at these judgments. Although the relationships of each general variable to one or more defenses is in part dictated by theory, each general variable was assumed to be superordinate to the defenses in terms of the hierarchy of personality organization and to include attributes not reducible to defense patterning alone.

Acting Out–Overcontrol

This general variable has not been discussed as such in the psychoanalytic literature. One portion of the relevant literature deals with acting in the transference (i.e., in psychoanalytic treatment) and acting out as a syndrome, way of life, defense, or—we would suggest—pre-stage of defense. The other portion of the relevant literature deals with generalized inhibition and ego restriction. The decision to rate the children on a continuum from acting out to overcontrol, rather than on acting out alone was dictated in part by the over-all balance of acting out–overcontrol in the sample. Since there were no extreme cases of habitual acting out, rating of acting out alone would have produced a limited range of individual differences. In addition, the acting out–overcontrol continuum represents a more general aspect of ego organization than acting out alone. In this sense, the dimension selected may best represent current views of generalized acting out tendencies as "a way of life," rather than a specific defense mechanism. Had the range of acting out been greater in the present sample, however, acting out alone might have been rated.

Freud first commented on acting out in *The Psychopathology of Everyday Life* (1901) and provided clinical examples in his report on the case of Dora (1905a). Greenacre (1963, p. 158) notes that Freud later (1911a) presented a concept of "the different stages in the development of communication which furnishes the fundamental background for understanding the acting out by the individual." Still later, he spelled out the core concept—compulsive repetition of the past in action, instead of remembering the past—in his paper, "Remembering, Repeating and Working-Through" (1914). Subsequent to these early works, rather extensive literatures deal with acting out in the transference (following Freud's early emphasis on action in the treatment process) and acting out as a more general feature of personality organization. Although these two forms of acting out are in some ways related, several writers have emphasized the differences between "habitual acting out" (Greenacre, 1950) or the "acting on impulse" Michaels (1958) refers to as "primary acting out" and the type of neurotic acting out to forestall painful remembering that occurs under the special conditions of the transference.[2]

Major contributors to current conceptions of the preconditions of acting out have emphasized the following: alloplastic readiness, fixation on orality, intense narcissistic needs, inadequate tension tolerance, and early traumata (Fenichel, 1945b); early separation from the mother (e.g., Bowlby, 1944; Kaufman, 1955); and hereditary predispositions related to body types (Glueck and Glueck, 1950, 1962). Greenacre (1950, p. 458) has added the following points to Fenichel's formulation of preconditions: "a bent for dramatization" and "a largely unconscious belief in the magic of action." She also suggested (*ibid.*) that "the common genetic situation" involved in the various manifestations of acting out may be "a distortion in the relation of action to speech and verbalized thought. . . ."

In discussing the evolution of habitual acting out, Fenichel (1945b) emphasized early disturbances of the mother-child relationship and pointed to discoordination in the development of motor and verbal behavior. Several other authors have also emphasized the importance of the early mother-child interaction to acting out. Altman (1957), for example, has discussed excessive symbiosis as a key to the incomplete development involved. Greenacre (1963, p. 147) has noted that multiplicity of authoritative figures in childhood may contribute to later acting out, especially if there is tension among these "parents."

In addition to early disturbances in the mother-child relationship, several authors (e.g., Szurek, Johnson, and Falstein, 1942; Johnson, 1949; Johnson and Szurek, 1952; Giffin, Johnson, and Litin, 1954; Rexford and Van Amerongen, 1957; Van Amerongen, 1963; Malone, 1963) have pointed to (a) emotional problems of the mother which make it impossible for her to set effective limits on drive gratification or (b) unconscious parental sanctioning of impulsive action as key determinants of acting out.

In addition to Fenichel (1945b), Greenacre (1950) and a number of others have emphasized the inhibition of speech and general verbal development in favor of motor development which becomes a hallmark of acting out in the test productions of some adults (see Rapaport *et al.*, 1945; Schafer, 1948). Greenacre also points out that, in keeping with the

---

[2] The concept of acting out was dealt with at some length by a 1956 panel of the American Psychoanalytic Association (see Kanzer, 1957a) and was the subject of a recent issue of the *Journal of the American Academy of Child Psychiatry* (1963, Vol. 2).

tendency to externalize and the narcissistic manipulation of others in acting out, use of language tends to be exhibitionistic rather than communicative.

In a discussion of adolescent acting out, Ekstein and Friedman (1957) have suggested that the syndrome may represent efforts at conflict resolution, as well as repetition of conflict-laden past experiences in actions.

At the present time, the following points concerning acting out seem generally agreed upon: the identifications of persons given to extreme acting out are primitive; their ego organizations involve a general lack of differentiation and synthesis, in part because of the primitivity of verbal development, without which reality must be dealt with in relatively crude and unmodulated fashion (cf. Lidz, 1963); "the sense of reality is disturbed," since it "has never been relinquished as the source of direct satisfaction on the level of need fulfillment" (Blos, 1963, p. 123); visual imagery and fantasy are excessive and overly real (cf. Carroll, 1954); a profound distortion of object relations is involved so that the outer world is used as a "tension relieving object" (Blos, 1963); the inevitable sexualization of action in such an undifferentiated context makes later acting out of feelings in part a derivative of phallic masturbatory influences (A. Freud, 1949); persons given to extreme acting out express basic disorders of identity in imitation and role playing; certain kinds of parental emotional problems and certain other anomalies of authority figures contribute to acting out; impulsive motor behavior, low frustration tolerance, unreliability of controls, concreteness of thinking, lack of intellectual differentiation (except in motor and visual-motor areas), primitivity of play and work habits, and absence of refined creativity are key aspects of the behavioral syndrome.

It is obvious from this brief (and incomplete) reference to the literature on acting out, which is designed only to indicate its major features, that a critical aspect of the syndrome is generalized inadequacy of delay of impulse expression. This deficiency of delay is assumed to make fully articulated verbal development impossible.

Jacobson (1957) has developed the point of view that acting out is directly linked to denial. Although this seems true in many instances, it is recognized here that denial may be used extensively when acting out is a relatively minor defense. Kanzer (1957b) and Blos (1963) have noted that projection is often associated with acting out.

The overcontrol extreme of the continuum represents excessive behavioral inhibition. Anna Freud (1936, p. 109) has described one form of excessive overcontrol—neurotic inhibition—with particular effectiveness: "A person suffering from a neurotic inhibition is defending himself against the translation into action of some prohibited instinctual impulse, i.e. against the liberation of 'pain' through some internal danger. Even when . . . the anxiety and the defence seem to relate to the outside world, he is really afraid of his own inner processes." Although she applied it to specific neurotic inhibition, her formulation is also applicable to children characterized by generalized overcontrol. In such children, severe defensive struggles with self-prohibited impulses and their derivatives lead to maladaptive overuse of defenses employing behavioral inhibition. When used excessively, a number of defenses can contribute to such generalized inhibition, e.g., excessive repression, excessive isolation (to the point of obsessive immobilization or extreme compulsive rigidity), projective suspiciousness or fearfulness, or massive denial. The degree of generalized inhibition characterizing a child is also assumed to be partially independent of defenses and may reflect the values placed by the family and its socioeconomic group on certain general aspects of behavior. Generalized inhibition can itself have the characteristics of a defense. It is a means of controlling drive expression that serves to preserve a constant, if maladaptive, equilibration by preventing consciousness of large groups of forbidden impulses and their derivatives. This postulated independence is incomplete, however, because of the intricate relation of specific defenses to behavioral inhibition.

The normal forms of ego restriction discussed by Anna Freud (1936) involve more specific forms of overcontrol which are also more situationally variable. A distinction should also be made here between avoidance (which often implies impulsive action, rather than true overcontrol) and other forms of ego restriction.

As a group, the children of the present study tended toward overcontrol, rather than acting out. Their test productions nevertheless suggested a wide range of individual differences in this general aspect of ego organization. It should be noted here that any such general scale has the advantage of providing for assessment of individual differences in an aspect of behavior that is rather pervasively apparent. It has the disadvantage, however, of placing qualitatively different syndromes at similar points. Excessive acting out, for example, can be a relatively constant feature of a child's behavior throughout his development. In this form, it can appear to be a habitual aspect of behavior with heavy overtones of defense or preliminary state of defense. Excessive acting out can also, however, be a major symptom of unstable equilibrations, such as those often referred to as borderline conditions between severe neurotic disturbance and overt psychosis. The latter conditions, and the early phases of acute psychosis, seem to exemplify with particular vividness Freud's major point about acting out as a means of preventing the recall of painful memories (and also, apparently, painful impulses, self-images, and the like). In such conditions, acting out may be a less permanent feature of personality organization that is also qualitatively different from habitual acting out. The disturbed individual may, for example, be aghast at his impulses to act out, whereas habitual acting out is characteristically egosyntonic.

The relative emphasis upon motoric versus verbal activities and skills associated with acting out (e.g., in the syndromes described as narcissistic character disorder or psychopathic character disorder) finds direct representation in relations among subtests of the WISC, as well as predictable manifestations in the TAT and Rorschach (see Rapaport *et al.*, 1945, 1946; Schafer, 1948, 1954). Primitivity of thought, impulsivity, and related manifestations of acting out are, in general, indicated by overt actions or qualitative and quantitative features of test performance that are easily identified. Assessment of the degree of overcontrol requires careful differentiation between inhibition and highly controlled but more flexible attempts at precision; between inhibition leading to impoverishment of test performances and inhibition in the form of ideational rigidity, and so forth.

The optimally adjusted child of the present study would probably be assessed as falling slightly above the middle of the acting out–overcontrol scale. This would mean that he tends toward control, rather than lack of control, but remains capable of flexibility in his approach to different situations.

The Relative Autonomy of the Ego

Hartmann has spelled out the concepts of primary and secondary autonomy of the ego from the id (Hartmann, 1939, pp. 25–26). According to him, primary autonomy is provided by the evolutionarily given apparatuses of the ego (the apparatuses involved in perception, memory, motor behavior, and thresholds). Secondary autonomy primarily involves defenses that, having undergone a "change of function," become independent structures serving the functions of adaptation, synthesis, and the like. These two forms of autonomy—the one given by evolution, the other developing with experience—guarantee the partial independence of the ego as a whole from the id (Rapaport, 1958, p. 17). Rapaport added a conception of the means by which partial autonomy from the environment is insured. As he summarized his formulation (1958, p. 18): "Man's constitutionally given drive equipment appears to be the *ultimate* (primary) *guarantee* of the ego's autonomy from the environment, that is, its safeguard against stimulus-response slavery. But this autonomy too has *proximal* (secondary) *guarantees;* namely, higher-order superego and ego structures as well as the motivations pertaining to them." Rapaport (1951a, 1958) at the same time developed the notion that the ego can be characterized in terms of its *relative* autonomy from the id on the one hand and the environment on the other.

Ratings of the relative autonomy of the ego of children in the present study were intended to conform as exactly as possible to Rapaport's definition. The raw data and scores for the WISC, TAT, and Rorschach Test, plus the defense ratings, were used in making these ratings, which were also made on scales ranging from 0 to 10. A low rating indicates low autonomy from the id; a high rating indicates low autonomy from the environment.

Each of the defense ratings has its own implications for the relative autonomy of the ego. Rapaport (1958, p. 23) has pointed out, for example, that "Obsessive-compulsive defense . . . maximizes the ego's autonomy from the id, but it does so at the cost of an ever-increasing impairment of the ego's autonomy from the environment: the suppression of affective and ideational cues of drive origin renders the ego's judgments and decisions increasingly dependent on external cues."

Rapaport also pointed out, however, that excessive use of the defenses of isolation and intellectualization in this syndrome leads also to a lack of autonomy from drives and their representations. Thus, he stated that "only autonomy within the optimal range—is compatible with a relative—that is, optimal—autonomy of the ego from the environment, and vice versa" (Rapaport, 1958, p. 24). Implications of this fact for a conception of the autonomy of the ego from *both* id and environment are discussed in the following section.

Over-all Ego Autonomy

Gill and Brenman (1959) have pointed out that the relative autonomies from the id and the environment may be asymmetrical. If so, our ratings of relative autonomy as defined by Rapaport may be less accurate than if true reciprocity obtained between autonomy from the id and autonomy from the environment. Gill and Brenman have developed a concept of autonomy that is of particular value for studies of ego development and that may define more accurately the nature of over-all ego autonomy. In their formulation (1959, p. 176), "Autonomy is the name for that relative independence which the growing and maturing ego attains from the id on the one hand and the environment on the other." Here, then, is a concept of ego autonomy that involves a key facet of ego strength, in that it refers to the effective independence of the ego from both the id and external conditions. As we see it, a child in whom this over-all autonomy is maximal is characterized by adequately differentiated ego structures that he can employ with considerable flexibility. It is important to note here that autonomy in this sense does not imply that id forces or environmental conditions are ignored or blocked out. To be characterized as having optimal over-all ego autonomy, a child should be attuned both to drives and their representations and to external reality, but his behavior should be dominated by neither. As Gill and Brenman (1959, pp. 175–76) stated it: ". . . we shall speak of increased autonomy only when we mean increased autonomy in an ego which both has access to input and is not oblivious to this input."

In the terms of this constructive articulation of the concept, a child whose behavior is excessively dictated by id forces *or* external reality is low in ego autonomy. Children whose autonomy from the id is insufficient (e.g., those given to excessive acting out of impulses or those whose consciousness is distorted by primary-process thinking) and children whose autonomy from the environment is insufficient (e.g., extremely obsessive-compulsive children, whose overuse of the defense of isolation blocks out affect to a maladaptive degree and whose attention to external reality is excessive) may be equally lacking in over-all autonomy. As Rapaport (1958) and Gill and Brenman (1959) have emphasized, lack of autonomy from the id to some degree implies lack of autonomy from the environment, and vice versa. This is clearly apparent, to take but one example, in the case of children given to acting out. Their undifferentiated cognitive structures lead to acting upon impulses, rather than to effective cognitive manipulation of impulse derivatives followed by controlled action. Their tendency toward action is obviously id-close. At the same time, however, such children are extremely dependent upon momentary conditions in the external world. Their lack of cognitive differentiation puts them at the mercy of conditions in external reality that can trigger their tendency to act impulsively. Action is triggered easily both from within and without by virtue of the lack of differentiation of mediating control structures.

Although the concept of over-all ego autonomy developed by Gill and Brenman served as a model for the assessment described below, no claim can be made that the rating values assigned the children represent this concept with more than moderate precision. It is all but impossible at this point, for example, to resolve the issue of symmetry-asymmetry of autonomy from id and environment.

In considering means of assessing over-all ego autonomy, it became apparent that a rough approximation would be made in the course of rating relative autonomy as described by Rapaport. That is, it seemed likely that the ratings of relative autonomy, if "folded" at the appropriate scale point, would provide as effective a measure of over-all autonomy as could be made with data from the three tests used. It will be recalled from our earlier discussion of relative autonomy that ideal over-all autonomy in the present sample was probably indicated by a point slightly above the middle of the relative autonomy scale. Records of subjects assigned values in this range were thus examined from the point of view of over-all autonomy. On the basis of this examination, optimal over-all autonomy was established as points 6 and 7 (on the 0 to 10 scale used). The ratings of relative autonomy were transformed into a five-point scale representing over-all autonomy as follows: relative autonomy ratings of 6 and 7 were assigned the maximum over-all autonomy value, 6; the adjacent ratings, 5 and 8, were assigned the value, 5; ratings of 4 and 9 were assigned the value, 4; ratings of 3 and 10 were assigned the value, 3; and ratings of 2 were assigned the value, 2 (there were no relative autonomy ratings of 1 or 0).

In view of the partial asymmetry of autonomy from the id and the environment, this transformation of the relative autonomy scale into an over-all ego autonomy scale perhaps introduces additional error. However, to adjust the transformation would have required questionable decisions concerning differential weights for different points on the relative autonomy scale, and it was, therefore, not attempted. Thus, the new ego autonomy scale involves no assumptions concerning differential implications of points equal distances above and below the optimal points on the relative autonomy scale. Although this could be considered a limitation of the ego autonomy scale, it may also be an advantage, in view of the unsubstantiated assumptions that would be involved in an attempt at differential weighting.

From a statistical point of view, the over-all ego autonomy scale should bear a linear relationship to ego strength, whereas the relative autonomy scale should be related in curvilinear fashion.

Ego Strength

In addition to a number of contributions focused specifically on the problem of ego strength, a considerable portion of the general psychoanalytic literature has direct or indirect implications for the over-all integrity and adaptive effectiveness of ego organization.

Anna Freud (1936, p. 193) defined ego strength in terms of defense. She stated that

. . . the ego is victorious when its defensive measures effect their purpose, i.e. when they enable it to restrict the development of anxiety and "pain" and so to transform the instincts that, even in difficult circumstances, some measure of gratification is secured, thereby establishing the most harmonious relations possible between the id, the super-ego and the forces of the outside world.

Glover (1943) has emphasized that ego strength is most effectively conceptualized in terms of adaptation to the external environment. Hartmann (1950, p. 94) has added that "the autonomous aspect of the ego has to be considered." He has also pointed to the value of considering ego strength in terms of "the interrelations between the different areas of ego functions, like defense, organization, and the area of autonomy." As he has noted, excessive use of defenses, as well as weak or ineffective defenses, including those that tend to regress under stress to their developmental antecedents, can be understood as components of ego weakness. The "secondary autonomy" (i.e., resistance to regression) of ego functions is, according to Hartmann, a key aspect of over-all ego strength.

Karush, Easser, Cooper, and Swerdloff (1964) recently summarized the difficulties involved in achieving an unequivocal definition of ego strength that would allow effective quantification. They point out the variations in concepts of ego strength formulated by different psychoanalytic theorists who have dealt at length with the subject (e.g., Glover, 1943, 1958; Fenichel, 1945a, 1954; Nunberg, 1942; and Hartmann, 1939, 1950). They note, however (p. 335), that "despite these differences, everyone agrees that ego strength and the ego's adaptive capacity are one and the same." Taking as their point of departure Glover's emphasis on ego strength in terms of the balance of adaptation, these authors have developed an elaborate assessment technique for interview data that produces an "adaptive balance curve" representing nine distinct facets of adaptive balance.

The concept of ego strength employed in the present study—which is focused on the adaptive effectiveness, flexibility, and cohesiveness of ego organization—was more limited in scope but was designed to include such relevant emphases in recent psychoanalytic theorizing. In contrast to some earlier views of ego strength, and in keeping with our remarks in Chapter 1 concerning the ineffectiveness of earlier psychoanalytic concepts of relations between energy and structure, the assessment of ego strength was not based on the assumption that the core problem is the strength of the instincts and the "counterforces" pitted against them. In the present assessments, ego strength was viewed in more unequivocally structural terms. Our orientation toward the problem of ego strength also reflects the recent emphasis on the ego and the id as evolving out of a common matrix, rather than the ego as evolving out of the id itself (see Hartmann *et al.*, 1946). This view, supplemented by the contributions of Hartmann (1939), Rapaport (1951a, 1958), and others, implies an ego more autonomous, both in terms of evolutionary givens and structure formation contingent upon experience, than the id-locked ego of the earlier psychoanalytic literature, in which the force-counterforce model was used rather pervasively in explanations of ego development.

An effective concept of ego strength inevitably implicates the concept of the synthetic functions of the ego (Freud, 1926). Rapaport (1960a, p. 240) has stated that Freud's crystallization of the concept of an "autonomous synthetic function of the secondary process" (i.e., an autonomous tendency toward connection, unification, integration, and rationalization of experience) represented a significant advance over his earlier discussions of the secondary processes in terms of their drive-restraining function alone. Rapaport pointed out, in this context (p. 240), that Freud (1937) subsequently extended his view still further, to include "innate ego factors in general, not limiting them to the restraining and integrating factors." Nunberg's (1931, p. 125) statements about "the ego's influence as an intermediary and binding force," i.e., what he termed "its synthetic capacity," are also relevant here. As he described it, "the synthetic capacity of the ego manifests itself . . . as follows: it assimilates alien elements (both from within and from without), and it mediates between opposing elements and even reconciles opposites and sets mental productivity in train."

Hartmann (1939, p. 40) has discussed Nunberg's concept as "a special case of the broader biological concept of fitting together." He further articulated ego synthesis in terms of the four kinds of equilibria he believes to be involved (between individual and environment; between intrinsic drives; between mental institutions, i.e., "structural" equilibrium; and between the synthetic function and other aspects of the ego).

The innate synthesizing tendency referred to here has a variety of manifestations ranging from symptom formation to adaptively effective organization of experience. The nature of synthesis varies, also, with states of consciousness (Rapaport, 1957). The implications of different forms of synthesis for ego strength are therefore presumed to depend upon the specific manifestations of the synthetic function in the individual child. It is the child's characteristic mode of synthesizing experience, therefore, rather than the degree of synthesis, that is relevant to his over-all ego strength. A child who employs projection excessively to integrate the logic of his conscious experience is synthesizing important groups of experiences in a generally maladaptive manner. A concept of the synthetic functions of the ego thus provides a framework in which to assess the over-all organization of one important aspect of ego functioning, rather than a measuring instrument per se.

Erikson (1950) discusses adult ego strength, which he terms "ego integrity," as the product of successful resolution of nuclear conflicts at seven earlier stages of development. His description of ego integrity is unusually lucid (pp. 231–32):

Only he who in some way has taken care of things and people and has adapted himself to the triumphs and disappointments adherent to being, by necessity, the originator of others and the generator of things and ideas—only he may gradually grow the fruit of these seven stages. I know no better word for it than ego integrity. Lacking a clear definition, I shall point to a few constituents of this state of mind. It is the ego's accrued assurance of its proclivity for order and meaning. It is a post-narcissistic love of the human ego—not of the self—as an experience which conveys some world order and spiritual sense, no matter how dearly paid for. It is the acceptance of one's one and only life cycle as something that had to be and that, by necessity, permitted of no substitutions: it thus means a new, a different love of one's parents. It is a comradeship with the ordering ways of distant times and different pursuits, as expressed in the simple products and sayings of such times and pursuits. Although aware of the relativity of all the various life styles which have given meaning to human striving, the possessor of integrity is ready to defend the dignity of his own life style against all physical and economic threats. For he knows that an individual life is the accidental coincidence of but one life cycle with but one segment of history; and that for him all human integrity stands or falls with the one style of integrity of which he partakes. The style of integrity developed by his culture or civilization thus becomes the "patrimony of his soul," the seal of his moral paternity of himself. . . .

Erikson recently summarized his contributions (e.g., 1950, 1956) to a concept of ego strength in terms of the interaction of the individual and the social group at various stages of development. In his words (1962, p. 463): "Mutual activation is the crux of the matter; for human ego strength while employing all means of testing reality depends, from stage to stage, upon a network of mutual influences within which the person actuates others even as he is actuated, and within which the person is 'inspired with active properties,' even as he so inspires others."

Objecting to the common view that the infant ego is "weak" as compared to the adult ego, and employing his distinction between "reality" and "actuality," Erikson continues (p. 466):

Why burden babyhood with the prototype of a weak ego and adulthood with the utopia of a strong one? It is here where our habitual concept of reality fails to account for the fundamental fact that the infant, while weak in our reality, is competent in his actuality. Nobody is ever stronger; for actuality at all stages rests on the complementarity of inner and outer structure. Ego strength at any level is relative to a number of necessities: previous stages must not have left a paralyzing deficit; the stage itself must occur under conditions favorable to its potential; and maturing capacities must evoke in others cooperative responses necessary for joint (ego) survival. This, then, is *developmental actuality;* it depends at every stage on the active, the selective ego being in charge, and being enabled to be in charge by an Umwelt which grants a human being the conditions it needs—and thus includes the condition of being needed.

A basic premise guiding assessment of ego strength in the present study was that evaluation of the adaptive effectiveness, flexibility, and cohesiveness (i.e., resistance to regression and disintegration) characteristic of this large array of cognitive structures must be based on consideration of a large sample of behaviors. It was assumed here that neither a single test score nor performance in a single test could provide adequate information concerning over-all ego strength. It was also assumed that prior evaluations of major defense mechanisms, major intellectual abilities, and key features of the child's organization of spontaneous, self-organized productions, such as those required in the TAT, were necessary prerequisites of an attempt to assess ego strength in the limited context provided by the study. In order to explore relationships to other blocks of data in the study, the attempt to assess ego strength as defined above was limited to a detailed blind analysis of performance in the WISC, TAT, and Rorschach, plus the evaluations made earlier of major defenses, acting out–overcontrol, and the two aspects of ego autonomy. The specific test productions, test scores, and prior assessments incorporated into this general rating were considered minimal requirements for the assessment of ego strength. Fully adequate evaluation would require knowledge of the child's performance in many other situations and detailed knowledge of a number of additional aspects of his behavior.

The definition of ego strength offered above implies that, within limits, children with different constellations of defenses could receive equal ratings. Provided that ego functioning as a whole seemed adaptively effective, suitably flexible, and without significant potential for disintegration—i.e., without excessive over- or undercontrol, aberrant maladaptive thinking, excessive rigidity, impulsive motor behavior—no special value judgment was placed on the specific nature of the constellation. Provided his level of verbal development was adequate, a subject whose orientation was more motoric than verbal, but who seemed to be effectively and stably organized, was rated as high as a child whose orientation seemed equally effective and stable but was, say, more obsessive-compulsive, more verbal, and less motorically adroit. The emphasis was thus upon adaptive effectiveness, flexibility, and cohesiveness per se. Excessive use of any defense was, because of its maladaptive implications, considered an indication of ego weakness. Over-all ego autonomy was obviously more directly related to over-all ego strength than any individual defense, but was not considered identical to ego strength.

In terms of this definition, children of the present study appeared to range in ego strength from the upper limits of "borderline states" (Knight, 1953) to effective, stable, flexible organizations leading to general appropriateness of behavior, interpersonal sensitivity, and creative spontaneity. Test productions of two or three children assigned ratings at the low end of the scale contained such overt evidences of gross disturbance as the following: extreme anxiety, arbitrary and peculiar ideation, perceptual distortion, and incapacitating constriction. Records indicating this degree of disturbance were few, however. Most of the children's test performances fell within the limits of a broadly conceived "normal" range. Among the latter children, individual differences in ego strength were often inferred from the presence or absence of indications that individual defenses are used excessively, and so forth, rather than from the grossly pathological responses or the indications of unusually effective organizations available in extreme cases.

11 Findings Concerning Defense Mechanisms and General Characteristics of Ego Organization

THIS CHAPTER is devoted to results concerning changes in defense mechanisms and general characteristics of ego organization from early to late preadolescence, interrelations among these variables for the entire sample and the sexes separately, and relations between these variables and major variables in the other five blocks of data.

Preliminary Comments on the Empirical Results

The unavailability of validating information and the fact that the assessments of major defense mechanisms and general characteristics of cognitive organization were made by a single rater should forewarn the reader that the results discussed in the section below are tentative at best. The apparent predictability of some of the relationships found between these assessments and other blocks of data may enhance the apparent validity of these assessments but cannot, of course, substitute for assessment by multiple raters of equal levels of training in such analyses, validation against independent criteria, replication, and similar procedures. These results are presented because of the theoretical importance of the variables involved, because of their seeming meaningfulness, and because of our belief that empirical attempts to explore the relationship of defenses and general characteristics of ego organization to other aspects of personality organization are necessary to ultimate understanding of the major outlines of personality organization.

Sex Differences in Defense and General Ratings

The results indicate that boys of the present sample tend toward greater use of isolation, reaction formation, and denial, whereas girls tend toward greater use of repression. Although the absolute differences between boys and girls are small, these findings are in keeping with what might be anticipated on the basis of the literature on defense. It is generally agreed that repression is more often used pervasively by females (e.g., in "hysterical" syndromes), whereas the syndrome of isolation, reaction formation, and projection is more common in males.

It should be noted that the partial nonindependence of these variables (e.g., the negative relationship of isolation to repression) dictated by theory makes the use of independent *t* tests of mean differences an approximate method that may artificially inflate the number of statistical dimensions on which boys and girls appear to differ. With this qualification in mind, these results seem most clearly to indicate an over-all difference between use of repression and use of the antithetical isolation–reaction formation syndrome.

The common anticipation that boys use acting out more extensively is not supported in the present sample, possibly because of the inhibition characterizing the entire sample and the resultant limitation of the range of acting out. Whether the relationship observed here would obtain in children of lower socioeconomic status is open to question. This result is in keeping, however, with our impression of gross similarity between the test performances of boys and girls of this sample.

In general, the similarities and differences between the boys and girls in defense employment and in over-all characteristics of ego organization seem to conform to theoretical anticipations concerning the use of defense mechanisms by children of this age level, subculture, and range of socioeconomic levels.

Defense and General Rating Values of Younger and Older Children

The rater ignored age in making his evaluations of defenses and general characteristics of ego organization, and no subsequent attempt was made to adjust these ratings according to hypotheses concerning relationships to age. There were no significant differences between younger and older children of the present sample in mean ratings on the six defenses, acting out–overcontrol, relative autonomy of the ego, or ego strength. It is also notable that in this sample these characteristics of ego organization seem as clearly apparent in the clinical test performances of the younger children as in those of the older children. This fact seems to provide indirect evidence of similarity of defense employment through the age range, 9.6 to 13.4 years. In view of the ambiguity referred to earlier surrounding the evolution of defense mechanisms and the ages at which defense employment crystallizes, this finding could be of general importance, although it must be considered tentative because only one rater is involved.

It is intriguing that the older children may be characterized by greater over-all ego autonomy (i.e., from both the id and the environment). This finding suggests that over-all ego autonomy may continue to increase during the latency-preadolescent period even though the main outlines of defensive patterning have been established. An adequate test of this hypothesis requires a longitudinal study of relations among these aspects of ego organization. The present results do seem to indicate, however, that defense organization at preadolescence is more fully and clearly articulated (i.e., less global and diffuse) than has often been assumed, whatever the extent of subsequent reorganizations contingent upon puberty and adolescence.

Relations Among the Defense and General Ratings

Psychoanalytic theory implies a pattern of relationships among defenses that should emerge in analysis of group data in spite of gross variations in individual patterning. Isolation and reaction formation, for example, involve related, although not identical, sets of cognitive processes that are largely mutually exclusive with repression.

No deliberate attempt was made to reproduce theoretical assumptions about relationships among defense and general ratings in the rating process. The rater attempted to assess each of the ten variables as a unique entity, a necessary precaution since relations among these variables could presumably differ greatly from child to child and could vary with age and sample characteristics. The intercorrelations among the ten ratings shown in Table 11–1 nevertheless bear the stamp of the theoretical framework employed and fit theoretical anticipations reasonably well. The fact that this occurred is not seen as a deficiency of the ratings but as a more or less automatic consequence of the concepts employed. Defense ratings in which isolation is not correlated with acting out or repression would obviously reflect the application of defense concepts other than those derived from psychoanalytic observations. To take another example, theory suggests that extensive use of isolation is also related (as it is here) to high scores on the scale based on Rapaport's conception of relative autonomy.

As noted in Chapter 2, significant differences between boys and girls in patterns of intercorrelation among variables within the major blocks of data appeared only in the case of the defense and general ratings. Intercorrelations are therefore presented below for the total sample and for boys and girls separately.

Relations Among Defense and General Ratings of the Total Sample

It is obvious, of course, that the intercorrelations among ratings presented in Table 11–1 involve not only a general patterning dictated in part by theory, but also defensive and general characteristics of cognitive functioning in this particular sample of preadolescent children and any idiosyncratic features of the rater's employment of the concepts. Application of the same rating scheme by the same rater to clinical test protocols of other samples of preadolescent subjects should result in roughly similar, but not identical, results.

It is notable that application of the conceptual framework described earlier in this chapter to the clinical test protocols of preadolescents yields a pattern of intercorrelations similar to that which might be anticipated for adults. This finding suggests that the major defense structures are apparent in behavior prior to adolescence, in spite of the qualitative differences in defense employment with increasing age that are attributable to continued maturation and articulation of a number of the component cognitive structures involved in particular defensive operations.

The two major groups of defenses indicated by the patterning of intercorrelations for the total sample are: (1) projection and denial; and (2) isolation, reaction formation, and repression (negatively related to the other two). Ego strength is significantly related to all the variables except reaction formation. Avoidance is apparently associated with both clusters. In the present sample, the defenses of repression, projection, avoidance, and denial are negatively related to ego strength, whereas isolation is positively related. These results apparently indicate that children in the present study who use isolation to a greater than average degree were seen as more effectively integrated than subjects who used the other defenses referred to. Whether this would be true in other samples may be open to question. It was assumed that a variety of rating patterns could represent high or low degrees of ego strength, here defined in terms of the adaptive integrity and capacity to withstand various kinds of stress indicated by the total pattern of cognitive functions represented in the clinical tests. It is to be expected, however, that extensive employment

TABLE 11-1

Intercorrelations Among Defense and General Ratings
(N = 60)

Rating	1	2	3	4	5	6	7	8	9
1. Repression									
2. Isolation	-66 ***								
3. Reaction Formation	-41 **	76 ***							
4. Projection	03	-03	07						
5. Avoidance	48 ***	-53 ***	-50 ***	39 **					
6. Denial	14	-23	-03	48 ***	51 ***				
7. Acting Out–Overcontrol	-22	55 ***	60 ***	03	-50 ***	-24			
8. Relative Autonomy	-20	41 **	35 **	-14	-37 **	-18	69 ***		
9. Over-all Ego Autonomy	-22	32 *	21	-21	-32 *	-22	20	48 ***	
10. Ego Strength	-38 **	31 *	25	-48 ***	-62 ***	-47 ***	24	36 **	43 ***

* $p < .05.$
** $p < .01.$
*** $p < .001.$

of projection, denial, repression, and so forth occurs only when ego strength is less than maximal.

It is notable that ego strength is most highly correlated (negatively) with avoidance in the present sample. The fact that the optimal point on the acting out–overcontrol scale is probably near the midpoint undoubtedly reduces the correlation of this scale with ego strength. The restricted range of acting out and the even balance of under- and overcontrol in the present sample may also contribute to the emergence of avoidance, rather than acting out, as a key indicator of pathology. In another sample, excessive use of projection, or some other defense with strongly maladaptive implications, might be most highly related to over-all ego strength. It is also apparent that the over-all autonomy of the ego is, at least as assessed in the present study, only one of the determinants of ego strength. Although significant, the correlation of .43 between over-all ego autonomy and ego strength is only moderately high.[1]

Relative autonomy of the ego is predictably related to acting out–overcontrol, as well as to isolation and reaction formation, both of which imply one form of overcontrol. The negative correlation of relative autonomy with avoidance is also predictable. The correlation of relative autonomy with over-all ego autonomy is artifactual, since it is determined by the point at which the former scale was "folded" to create the latter. The significant correlation of relative autonomy with ego strength is attributable to the fact that optimal relative autonomy is somewhat above the midpoint of this scale.

Relations Among Defense and General Ratings of Boys and Girls

In spite of the increased unreliability contingent upon reduction of the sample size, the significant number of significant differences in correlations for boys and girls makes it important to consider the nature of the observed differences in detail. The two correlation matrices are presented in Table 11–2. The six correlations that are significantly different for boys and girls are indicated in this table.

It should be noted that the number of significantly different correlations is quite small. It is notable, also, that all of the six pairs of significantly different correlations involve either acting out–overcontrol or over-all ego autonomy. Three of the four correlations higher for boys

---

[1] This finding is in keeping with Hartmann's (1955, p. 12) statement that "If we take an overall picture of an individual ego, the degree of autonomy is correlated with what we call ego strength, though it is not its only source."

TABLE 11-2

Intercorrelations of Defense and General Ratings for Boys and Girls

Boys (N = 29)

Rating	1	2	3	4	5	6	7	8	9	10
1. Repression		−.68 ***	−.51 **	−.07	.63 ***	.24	−.68 ****†	−.52 **	−.17	−.38 *
2. Isolation	−.64 ***		.68 ***	−.04	−.57 **	−.28	.79 ****†	.59 ***	.35	.17
3. Reaction Formation	−.30	.80 ***		.03	.64 ***	−.07	.74 ***	.48 **	.20	.35
4. Projection	.18	−.19	.01		.23	.44 *	.01	−.09	.13 †	−.29
5. Avoidance	.48 **	−.64 ***	−.43 *	.51 **		.53 **	−.68 ****†	−.50 **	−.17	−.50 **
6. Denial	.19	−.37 *	−.11	.47 **	.49 **		−.35	−.27	.05 †	−.35
7. Acting Out–Overcontrol	.07 †	.35 †	.47 **	.06	−.26 †	−.14		.76 ***	.42 *	.44 *
8. Relative Autonomy	−.04	.33	.28	−.17	−.23	−.09	.60 ***		.72 ****†	.54 **
9. Over-all Ego Autonomy	−.32	.39 *	.27	−.54 **†	−.48 **	−.46 **†	−.08	.20 †		.27
10. Ego Strength	−.47 **	.58 ***	.27	−.60 ***	−.73 ***	−.52 **	.04	.18	.58 ***	

Girls (N = 31)

* p < .05.
** p < .01.
*** p < .001.
† Correlations significantly different for boys and girls.

involve acting out–overcontrol; the fourth involves over-all ego autonomy. The last of these also involves the artifactually related relative
autonomy score and is of dubious interpretive value. The two correlations
higher for girls involve over-all ego autonomy. The sigma (i.e., a measure
of the variability of these scores among individuals) of the acting
out–overcontrol score is considerably greater for boys, and the sigma of
the over-all ego autonomy score is considerably greater for girls, which
suggests that the lower correlations in each case are attributable in part
to restricted score ranges. It seems clear, however, that these sigma
differences cannot account for all of the observed differences. In boys,
overcontrol is more closely associated with isolation and more antithetical
to repression and avoidance. In girls, projection and denial are more
antithetical to over-all ego autonomy. These seem to be genuine sex-
linked differences in relations among these variables, at least in the
present sample.

Selection of Ratings for the Analysis of Relations Among Major Blocks of Data

Because of the theoretical assumptions concerning relations among
defense mechanisms and the general aspects of ego organization assessed,
factor analysis was not appropriate as a means of reducing these variables to major dimensions to be included in the analysis described in
Chapter 12. Neither, however, is it logically defensible to assume that
correlations among these variables imply communality of response processes. Since it would be indefensible on statistical grounds to include all
the correlated variables in the final analysis described in Chapter 12, a
method of cluster analysis was employed to select five relatively independent variables to represent the total group of ten. In view of the
relative unreliability of correlations based on smaller samples, this clustering was based on the patterning of intercorrelations for the total
sample. The rating most highly correlated with the others in a cluster,
most similar to others in the cluster in correlations with ratings outside
the cluster, and most different in these respects from key ratings in other
clusters was the one selected to represent each cluster. As indicated
earlier, the six defense ratings were divisible into two groups consisting of
(1) isolation, reaction formation, and repression and (2) denial and
projection. Repression was chosen to represent the first group, projection
to represent the second. Acting out–overcontrol, over-all ego autonomy,
and ego strength were also selected. Although ego autonomy and ego

strength are significantly correlated, their patterns of correlation with the other three variables are quite different.

Relations of Defense and General Ratings to Cognitive Control Scores

General Findings

The impressive fact about the results presented in Table 11–3 is the paucity of significant correlations between the defense mechanisms and general characteristics of ego organization assessed and the cognitive controls. None of the factor scores representing cognitive control dimensions is related to ego strength. The negative correlation of Field-Articulation and repression is low but in keeping with results reported by Witkin *et al.* (1962). The other defenses included in the groups of "structured" and "unstructured" defenses in the analysis by Witkin and associates are not, however, related to Field-Articulation. This result may exemplify the interpretive ambiguities contingent upon dealing with defenses in the aggregate. At least in the present study, repression is the only defense related to Field-Articulation, and the correlation is quite low.

The relationship of Field-Articulation to over-all ego autonomy is intriguing. Although low, this significant correlation suggests that the capacity to articulate experience is more common when the ego is not excessively dependent on either momentary drive or reality conditions. This result also implies that an "active" versus a "passive" ego stance is associated with effective articulation, a finding in keeping with earlier observations by Witkin *et al.*

Of greater significance are the higher relationships between Constricted-Flexible Control and projection, denial, and over-all ego autonomy. It will be recalled that *S*s whose scores fall in the flexible-control half of this dimension are those most capable of moment-to-moment inhibition of irrelevant motoric responses in the Color-Word Test. In the present study, these children are characterized by relatively great over-all ego autonomy and less than average use of denial and projection. Apparently, an ego relatively unfettered by impulse demands or particular stimulus conditions is most effective for rapid performance in the difficult color-word portion of the Color-Word Test, which requires maintenance of a subtle, consistent balance between inhibition of irrelevant responses and fluent scanning of the incongruous colors in which the color words are printed. Apparently neither the hyperalertness associated

TABLE 11-3

Pearson Correlations of Defense and General Ratings with Cognitive Control Factor Scores
($N = 60$)

			Factor			
Rating	I Scanning A	II Conceptual Differentiation	III Scanning B	IV Field-Articulation	V Constricted-Flexible Control	VI Spontaneity
1. Repression	.07	.12	.04	−.27 *	−.01	−.29 *
2. Isolation	.06	−.08	−.16	.16	.00	.23
3. Reaction Formation	.18	−.00	−.08	.10	−.12	.24
4. Projection	−.13	−.06	.02	−.05	−.36 **	−.05
5. Avoidance	−.11	.03	−.04	−.17	−.20	−.23
6. Denial	.00	−.16	.14	−.04	−.43 ***	−.02
7. Acting out–Overcontrol	.01	.10	−.09	.15	−.05	.00
8. Relative Autonomy	−.06	.06	−.09	.18	−.00	−.27 *
9. Over-all Ego Autonomy	−.06	−.13	.03	.30 *	.42 ***	−.01
10. Ego Strength	.08	.05	−.08	.22	.21	.16

* $p < .05$.
** $p < .01$.
*** $p < .001$.

with projection nor the primitive negation of reality involved in denial is anything but maladaptive in tasks demanding flexible control. It is impressive, also, that isolation, which is associated with verbal acquisition and verbal fluency, and repression, which is associated with the unavailability of ideas to consciousness, as well as the other aspects of ego organization assessed, are unrelated to this control principle.

The negative correlation of Spontaneity with repression is predictable. "Spontaneity," of course, has not been conceptualized as a formal cognitive control principle and may be most appropriately considered here as an intriguing aspect of response to the control test situations that has important implications for over-all control.

The negative correlation of the Spontaneity factor scores with the relative autonomy ratings indicates that children of the present sample who are high in spontaneity tend to be relatively low in autonomy from the id. This result, too, was to be anticipated.

The Relationship of Scanning to Projection and Isolation in Boys and Girls

The fact that relationships found earlier for female adults between scanning and both projection and isolation do not obtain for the combined sample of boys and girls at preadolescence led to analysis of relations between these variables for the sexes separately. Correlations were performed for both scanning factors (A and B), since these factors seem to represent two aspects of a more homogeneous scanning syndrome found in the study of female adults (Gardner and Long, 1962a). It will be recalled that Scanning A factor scores represent individual consistencies in the time Ss spend checking judgments after final adjustment of the comparison stimulus in the size estimation tests. The correlation of these factor scores with isolation were .05 for boys and .02 for girls, clearly indicating no relationship. Scanning B factor scores represent the major group of individual consistencies in female adult responses to the size estimation tests—those in judgment time (composed of number of looks and time per look). These factor scores are thus more important indicators of extensiveness of scanning and are more closely linked to the major findings of the adult scanning studies. Correlations of these factor scores with isolation were −.14 and −.22. Although not significant, both these correlations are in the predicted direction, i.e., extensive scanners tend toward isolation. The correlations of the Scanning A and B factor scores with projection were −.06 and .12 for girls and −.25 and −.02 for boys. Taken together, these results seem to indicate that the relationships found for adult females do not obtain for preadolescent boys or girls, with the possible exception of the suggestive results concerning scanning and isolation.

The lack of relationship between extensiveness of scanning and the defenses of isolation and projection at preadolescence suggests that constellations of behaviors that appear to be relatively integrated entities in adult females are independent of each other at preadolescence. Although these results are strictly tentative, a complex process of integration of independent but potentially related cognitive dispositions into correlated clusters of dispositions may occur between preadolescence and adulthood. Further exploration of these and related hypotheses are obviously required for elucidation of developmental changes in functional relations among such cognitive structures.

The Relationship of Leveling to Repression in Boys and Girls

Since no Leveling-Sharpening factor appeared in the analysis of intercorrelations among cognitive control scores—which in itself differs from earlier results with several samples of adults—the relationship of leveling to repression found for female adults in earlier studies was tentatively explored at preadolescence by correlating the Schematizing Test scores with the ratings of repression for the sexes separately. It will be recalled from Chapter 4 that the two major scores derived from this test—ranking accuracy and lag—have been moderately but significantly correlated in earlier studies of adults, but are uncorrelated in the present sample of preadolescent children. As in the case of scanning, a relatively homogeneous adult factor seems to be two independent components of cognitive organization at preadolescence. Although this fact raises questions concerning the meaning of Schematizing Test scores at preadolescence (i.e., concerning the constellations of response processes involved in Schematizing Test performance at preadolescence), the correlation of each score with repression at preadolescence could be illuminating. As noted in Chapter 3, for both adults and children the lag score may be a more effective indicator of leveling than the more complex accuracy score.

As expected, the correlations with repression of the accuracy and lag scores for the Schematizing Test are essentially zero for boys (.03 and −.02). For girls, however, these correlations are −.25 and .39, $p < .05$. Both correlations are in the direction predicted on the basis of earlier results with adult females. The former approaches significance and the latter is significant. Like their adult counterparts, preadolescent girls who use repression in a relatively powerful and pervasive manner tend to be levelers in the Schematizing Test. That is, they show relatively great assimilation (a form of contamination) among new percepts and related memories recorded earlier.

Relations of Defense and General Ratings to HIT Factor Scores

Apparently, the ten defense and general aspects of ego organization assessed are not correlated with the five HIT factor scores. The one significant correlation obtained is low (.32) and could have occurred by chance in a matrix of this size.

This result is not particularly surprising, since the HIT factors are based on constellations of *scores* representing complex responses to a particular set of stimuli and since the ways in which defenses, ego autonomy, and so forth manifest themselves in the Rorschach, and undoubtedly in the HIT, are themselves complex and qualitative, as well as quantitative. In addition, a number of other variables must be involved in response to the HIT, including intellectual abilities. The HIT may thus be analogous to the Rorschach, in the sense that assessment of the operation of defense mechanisms requires qualitative, as well as quantitative, evaluation. The appearance of a correlation between employment of a particular defense and a score factor would presumably be a rather fortuitous occurrence dependent upon the particular scores employed.

Relations of Defense and General Ratings to Clinical Rating Factor Scores

It will be recalled that the defense and general ratings and the clinical ratings were made by independent investigators using different groups of rating variables. Relationships between these two groups of variables are presented in Table 11–4.

The general rating factor called "Active Openness to New Experience" is positively related to isolation–reaction formation and negatively to repression. These results suggest an obvious and meaningful association between defense employment and behavior in the clinical testing situation. The isolator is typically intellectually curious, the repressor is typically inhibited in such activity. The positive correlation with denial is puzzling, however, and difficult to explain.

It is rather surprising that Unity of Identity is associated only with ego strength, and that very moderately, in this sample in which ego strength was assessed as slightly higher among children who emphasize

TABLE 11-4

Pearson Correlations of Defense and General Ratings with Clinical Rating Factor Scores
($N = 60$)

Rating	I Active Openness to New Experience	II Unity of Identity	III Accuracy of Reality Testing	IV Cooperativeness	V Compulsive Exactness	VI Sporadic Disruption of Control
1. Repression	−.41 **	−.11	−.21	−.04	.01	.09
2. Isolation	.32 *	.08	.25	.19	.02	.02
3. Reaction Formation	.33 **	.09	.27 *	.14	.21	−.01
4. Projection	.13	−.25	−.02	−.03	−.12	.25
5. Avoidance	−.08	−.18	−.29 *	−.18	−.09	.33 **
6. Denial	.29 *	−.08	−.17	−.04	.09	.16
7. Acting Out–Overcontrol	−.09	.02	.38 **	−.01	−.01	−.16
8. Relative Autonomy	−.13	−.01	.28 *	.08	−.13	−.01
9. Over-all Ego Autonomy	.17	−.05	.04	.19	−.09	.09
10. Ego Strength	.02	.31 *	.40 **	−.02	−.04	−.33 **

* $p < .05$.
** $p < .01$.

isolation, reaction formation, and generalized overcontrol. It would appear (see Chapter 9) that "Unity of Identity" may be an adequate descriptive label for this clinical rating factor, but that the factor nevertheless is based on a composite of observations indirectly relevant to the problem of homogeneity of identity. It is true, of course, that unity of identity may vary considerably at any level of over-all ego strength— from overly narrow to overly diffuse organizations with respect to essential life role. One would expect, however, a moderate positive relationship between ego strength and Unity of Identity assessed as such, rather than inferred from associations among disparate rating variables as in the present study.

In general, the Accuracy of Reality Testing factor is predictably associated with the defense and general ratings, including ego strength. The implication of this group of correlations is the obvious one that adequate reality testing implies at least a moderate tendency toward delay in the form of isolation–reaction formation and an associated moderate tendency toward overcontrol, rather than acting out. It is surprising, however, that over-all ego autonomy is not more highly associated with this clinical rating factor. Perhaps the accuracy component of this factor in part accounts for the lack of relationship. Accuracy per se has rather ambiguous implications for ego organization. Not only effectively clear and articulated perception of reality, but also certain pathological tendencies may enhance the accuracy of reality testing in the sense implied by this factor, e.g., when mild hyperalertness sharpens a child's awareness of his surroundings, albeit for inherently maladaptive reasons. As in the other analyses reported in this chapter, avoidance in this sample seems a key indicator of over-all ego weakness, including inadequacy of the aspect of reality testing represented by this factor.

It is intriguing that the Cooperativeness factor is independent of all the defense and general ratings. The limited instances of uncooperativeness in this generally docile and conformant group of children is undoubtedly important here.

Perhaps the most unexpected result of the entire group is the lack of significant correlations between the clinical rating factor called "Compulsive Exactness" and any of these ratings. This is particularly surprising in the case of isolation, reaction formation, and acting out–overcontrol. Apparently, we are confronted here with the discrepancy between isolation–reaction formation expressed in the form of intellectualizing, affective inhibition, verbal differentiation, and so forth, and isolation in the form of ritualistic ordering of a broader variety of behaviors. Evaluation of isolation and reaction formation on the basis of clinical test performances may limit the judge's assessments primarily to expressions of isolation and reaction formation in highly complex cognitive operations. Ratings based on observations of behavior could reflect compulsivity per se in motoric, as well as verbal, behavior to a much greater degree. We may have returned here to a logical problem posed in the discussion (Chapter 10) of the concept of isolation and its expression. That is, we may be confronted with the theoretical problem of the predictive equivalence of the several classes of behaviors traditionally attributed to the defense of isolation. Does compulsivity in the form of rigidly patterned motoric behavior, for example, have implications so different from those of the intellectualized forms of isolation as to require further articulation of the concept of isolation itself? As noted earlier, the various manifestations of obsessive-compulsive tendencies have been spelled out in numerous contributions to the psychoanalytic literature. The problem of conceptual articulation of this defensive syndrome may nevertheless require further development.

The positive association of the factor called "Sporadic Disruption of Control" with avoidance and its negative association with ego strength conform to anticipation, but the lack of relationship to overcontrol, over-all ego autonomy, isolation, and the others, does not. With the exception of avoidance and ego strength, abortive disruptions of the flow of interpersonal behavior in the clinical testing situation would seem to occur in a variety of ego organizations. The relative independence of this dimension of individual differences is intriguing and invites further exploration, for example, of its relations to activation level, drive level, achievement motivation, and other potentially relevant variables that could not be included in the present study. It would be valuable to know, for example, whether children with unusually high activation levels are less capable of sustaining effective contact with others in task situations and, if so, to what degree this incapacity is independent of the general patterning of personality organization.

Relations of Defense and General Ratings to Laboratory Rating Factor Scores

The laboratory ratings were even more independent of the defense and general ratings than the clinical ratings. Anxious Dependence, the factor most consistently related to the defense and general ratings, seems to add a unique and interesting dimension of response to those identified in the other blocks of data. This factor also elucidates a second major aspect of individual differences in ego strength in the present sample. It will be recalled from Chapter 9 that, in a context of high tension, low frustration tolerance and task-involvement, fearful discomfort, and low trust, children high in anxious dependence are lacking in confident self-reliance. The results shown in Table 11–5 suggest that this syndrome is

TABLE 11–5

Pearson Correlations of Defense and General Ratings with
Laboratory Rating Factor Scores
$(N = 60)$

	I	II	III	IV
				Acting upon the Environ-
Rating	*Impulsive Spontaneity*	*Anxious Dependence*	*Explorativeness*	*ment*
1. Repression	.10	.29 *	−.28 *	−.16
2. Isolation	.05	−.29 *	.17	−.00
3. Reaction Formation	.20	−.22	.11	−.05
4. Projection	.17	.17	.16	−.06
5. Avoidance	−.00	.40 **	.08	.11
6. Denial	.25	.30 *	.20	.24
7. Acting Out–Overcontrol	−.02	−.21	−.03	−.16
8. Relative Autonomy	−.25	−.20	.03	−.12
9. Over-all Ego Autonomy	−.06	−.50 ***	−.15	.17
10. Ego Strength	−.22	−.47 ***	.03	.13

* $p < .05.$
** $p < .01.$
*** $p < .001.$

indicative of ego weakness, low ego autonomy, high denial, avoidance, and repression, and low isolation. The link to avoidance again suggests that, in this particular sample of children, ego weakness manifests itself principally in the child's withholding himself from full spontaneous participation in the laboratory procedures. These procedures were unique in their novelty for the children and may have been the most anxiety-arousing situations in the study for children in whom inhibition is associated with frightened distrust.

That Impulsive Spontaneity and Acting upon the Environment are not significantly correlated with any of the defense and general ratings is rather surprising, particularly in the case of acting out–overcontrol. The limited range of acting out may again be a determinant here. It is also intriguing that the factor called "Explorativeness" is related (negatively) only to repression, and that to a very limited degree.

Discussion

Perhaps the major observation that can be made concerning the results reported in this chapter concern the articulation and complexity of personality organization at preadolescence. The assessment of major defenses and general characteristics of ego organization by means of blind analysis of responses to these clinical tests was a novel attempt, and the results must be considered tentative. As in the case of the other blocks of data, the major dimensions of defense and over-all ego organization seemed evident in the children's performances, however, in articulated, *nonglobal* patterns of organization. The amount of test material employed in the analyses and the general fit of these assessments to independent blocks of test scores and ratings suggest the value of such an assessment, in spite of its obvious limitations.

The fact that the defense and general ratings are all but independent of the cognitive control factors and the HIT factors and are related in only partial and differentiated ways to the other major blocks of data seems to point up the extreme complexity of personality organization. These results, which are generally analogous to results obtained earlier for adult samples, seem to match our anticipation that even defense mechanisms and such general variables as ego strength allow prediction only with respect to limited realms of behavior. The indications of organizational complexity referred to here are further accentuated by recognition of the limited realms of behavior included in the study. Although relatively extensive in terms of the aspects of personality organization sampled, the present study does not include additional groups of motivational, physiological, interpersonal, motoric, and other variables that could well be included in a more comprehensive approach to personality organization at preadolescence.

The factor analysis of relations between blocks of data reported in Chapter 12 was designed to provide the most general view possible in the present study of major lines of organization linking several major aspects of personality organization. The more detailed analyses presented in the present chapter make it clear, however, that as much is obscured as is revealed in such an over-all analysis and that it can at best provide glimpses of personality organization at a more holistic level. It must be remembered that each major block of data also contains only a limited number of a potentially much larger group of relevant variables. The relative independence of the defense and general ratings with respect to the other blocks of data included made it clear in advance of the over-all analysis, however, that complexity, rather than simplicity, is the guiding rule, in spite of the known predictive generality of such variables as ego strength, repression, isolation, field-articulation, and the intellectual abilities assessed in the study.

The questions raised earlier in this chapter concerning the possibility that progressive integration of certain aspects of behavior into hierarchically organized clusters of correlated behaviors occurs between preadolescence and adulthood raise issues that require further investigation. A study that may help to answer these and related questions about the development of personality organization is described in Chapter 15.

12 Structure Formation on a Broader Scale: Individual Consistencies Linking Six Aspects of Preadolescent Behavior

THE STUDIES of individual consistencies in six general aspects of behavior that were described in Chapters 4 through 11 provided materials for an exploratory investigation of broad-scale associations among these variegated facets of individual consistency. In view of the tentative nature of these analyses, the unreliability of results for small samples, and the "distance" from the raw data involved in factoring scores from prior factor analyses, the final analysis reported in this chapter was performed with the entire group of sixty children as one sample. The fact that sex differences appeared in the patterning of intercorrelations among defense ratings (although such differences were surprisingly absent in the other five major blocks of data) suggests that some information may have been lost in pooling boys and girls for this analysis. That is, slightly different factors might have been obtained for boys and girls.

The exploratory nature of this final analysis should be emphasized particularly because of the fact that partial overlap obtains between some of the blocks of data from which factor scores or other summary scores were drawn. This is true of the relationship between the defense and general ratings and the WISC factor scores, in spite of the fact that the observed relationships between these two sets of variables seem to fit theoretical expectations reasonably well. This is also true of the relationships of the defense and general ratings to the ratings of behavior in the clinical testing situation. The latter alone involved observations of the child's behavior in the total situation. They were based in part, however, on the test performances themselves, which were used as the basis for the defense and general ratings. In spite of the fact that different rating variables were used by the two raters, it is possible that relationships between the summary scores selected for the final analysis are to some degree artifacts of partial overlap with respect to both material and concepts. The additional problem posed by correlations among factor scores drawn from the same block of data is discussed later in this chapter. In spite of these several limitations, it seemed worthwhile to explore relations between the blocks of data in detail.

Variables Drawn from the Six Blocks of Data

Criteria for the selection of variables from the six major blocks of data (cognitive control principle factor scores, plus additional scores; WISC factor scores; HIT factor scores, plus reaction time; ratings of defenses and general ego characteristics; ratings of behavior in the clinical testing situation; and ratings of behavior in the laboratory testing situation) were described in the preceding chapters. A total of twenty-nine variables was selected by these methods. Factor scores for the two scanning factors described in Chapter 6 were eliminated because they did not correlate significantly with any of the twenty-nine scores. The four additional variables described below were added to make a total of thirty-three variables for the final analysis.

Additional Variables

Age

It will be recalled that age was not controlled in the analyses of the six major blocks of data reported in preceding chapters. Rather, age changes were explored in each area of personality organization by evaluating mean differences between younger and older children and between children and samples of adults. Age was therefore included in the analysis of relations between scores and ratings drawn from six blocks of data that is described in this chapter.

Sex

Scores of 0 were assigned to girls, 1 to boys. Thus, a positive correlation between the "Sex" score and another variable means that boys have larger values on the second variable, and so forth.

Social Status

The weighted social status index employed was based on dwelling area, father's occupation, and source of income in the manner described by McGuire and White (1955). The use of these largely economic variables as components of this social status index ignores the possibility that social and economic status may to some degree, at least, be independent in this subculture. Support for the use of such variables as indexes of social status in the present study is provided by Kaltenbach and McClelland (1958), who found that occupation, income, and the like are highly correlated with social status only in fairly stable communities. Topeka, Kansas, in which most of the children lived at the time of the study and in which all of the children spent their early years, is an unusually stable community in terms of social class structure, size, and occupational opportunities. Community service, which is of great relevance to social status in less stable communities, is relevant but less important to social status in the stable, relatively conservative, and tradition-oriented setting of the present study.

The evaluations of dwelling area involved in the index were based on census tract information concerning property value and type of house. Only points 2 through 5 of McGuire and White's dwelling area scale were considered relevant. Although the values of the children's homes and surrounding areas differed considerably, no child lived in the unusually exclusive areas warranting a value of 1, or in a deteriorated or slum area that would lead to a rating of 6 or 7.

In the case of two children who had moved to a smaller city nearby and two children of the infancy study who lived in Iowa and Texas at the time of the present study, estimates were based on detailed knowledge of the present home and dwelling area. Since no correction of McGuire and White's weighting for dwelling area was attempted as a control for the attenuated scales used in the present study, dwelling area contributed slightly less to individual differences in the Social Status score than in McGuire and White's studies.

The fact that different child-rearing strategies characterize different social classes has been effectively documented by a number of authors. A recent study by Walters, Connor, and Zunich (1964) typifies the unequivocal findings that have been obtained in laboratory observations. In a study directly comparable to that of Zunich (1961), and in some ways similar to those of Merrill (1946), Bishop (1951), and Schalock (1956), they found dramatic evidence that middle-class mothers, observed in the laboratory, show more (often many times more) instances of active involvement in their children's behavior than do lower-class mothers. As they put it (p. 439), "If any conclusion is warranted from the studies which have employed direct observation, it is that the middle-class child in contrast to the lower-class child lives in a parent-dominated world." Although Schalock (1956) found gross differences in some aspects of mothers' behavior toward their children in the laboratory and at home, the general conclusions drawn from these studies seem valid. The ultimate consequences of greater parental involvement in the behavior of middle-class children are, of course, more difficult to assess. To the degree that this type of involvement in the child's behavior is rooted in middle-class parental anxieties about their child's adequacy, acceptability to others, effectiveness in competing with other children (and his parents' competing with other adults by means of their child), and the like, this degree of parental involvement may be a mixed blessing.

Other differences in family structure related to social class and relevant to the child's personality development include the size and stability of the family; general attitudes toward the child, including his importance as a means of continuing family status and traditions; whole-family versus the mother-centered child-rearing of the lower classes, in which family stability is lesser; emphasis on the child as someone to be tolerated or used to perform service; and so forth (see, e.g., the recent summary by Bossard and Boll, 1960).

Although the present sample gave limited representation to the lowest and highest classes, the families differed widely in their physical settings, educational attainments, occupations, and incomes. In the poorest settings, fathers were full- or part-time laborers; in the richest settings, fathers were professional men, including university professors. The fact that the children were drawn from a larger group of children whose mothers brought them to a well-baby clinic in their infancy may have attenuated the presumed class differences in interest and active involvement in their children's development. The fact that about half the children have participated in longitudinal studies since infancy and that the other half of the sample was willing to return for further study after periods ranging from eight to twelve years may indicate still further attenuation of their class differences in the present sample. Observations in the longitudinal study have nevertheless suggested wide-ranging differences in child-rearing strategies, attitudes toward children, and the like, not out of keeping with the results of other studies.

In investigations spanning the entire range of social class differences (e.g., Havighurst, Bowman, Liddle, Matthews, and Pierce, 1962), social status has proven of great predictive value with respect to major segments of child behavior, including performance in school. The restricted range of social status in the present sample may have limited its observable relationships to the personality variables in the analysis described here.

The nature of the rating scales contributing to the index of social status (termed "Social Status" in relevant tables) is such that a low score indicates high social status.

Religion

The relationship of familial religious affiliation to the child's personality development has been discussed by many psychologists and sociologists.

Children of the present study were divisible into groups of Catholic or Protestant affiliation. Twelve of the sixty children (six boys, six girls) were of Catholic families, forty-eight of Protestant families. In view of the small size of the sample, no division into types of Protestant affiliation was attempted.

The implications of Catholic versus Protestant affiliation for the child have been spelled out by various authors. The consensus is that humility, conformity to the demands and beliefs of authority-figures, acceptance of one's "fate" in the world, and the like are more characteristic of the Catholic orientation and of Catholic children, although several writers (e.g., Lenski, 1961) have pointed out that class status, which is ordinarily correlated with religious affiliation, may be even more important to the ingraining of these characteristics in children. Lenski reports, however, that more Protestant than Catholic children at every class level value thinking for oneself, as opposed to passive acceptance of others' views. Analogous differences in autonomy have been described by Spaeth (1961). Strodtbeck (1958) finds that Protestant and Jewish mothers expect their children to show independence at earlier ages than do Catholic mothers. Here again, social, economic, and ethnic factors correlated with religious affiliation are also involved in the observed differences.

Chapman (1945) is among those who have pointed out that Catholic children tend to come from the lower and lower-middle classes. Warner and Srole (1945) have noted that the Catholic orientation, as expressed in the parochial school, tends to preserve this difference in class status.

These typical findings, drawn from the larger literature on the relation of religious affiliation to personality development, suggest that, in general, Protestant children may be expected to show greater autonomy and independence, greater freedom to explore, question, and challenge, and probably less employment of certain forms of inhibition, conformance, and docility, as well as less repression, in coming to terms with reality. Whether the greater behavioral freedom anticipated for Protestant children is associated with greater over-all ego strength, greater comfort and stability in coping with reality is, however, open to question. What we know of individual differences—including the growing knowledge of hereditary determinants of individual differences—suggests the obvious hypothesis that the greater control provided by a relatively authoritarian surround may be helpful to one Catholic child and unhelpful to another, and that the stress on independence in the Protestant milieu may be stimulating and growth-inducing for one child, anxiety-arousing and destructive to another. Adding to this the fact that individual parents of either persuasion must vary greatly in their personalized ways of experiencing and transmitting the child-rearing correlates of such belief systems leads to the general hypothesis that no pre-established parental orientation—whether dictated primarily by religious affiliation, ethnic background, social and economic status, or other general factors—has in itself the flexibility required for optimal attunement of the developmental surround to the unique control problems and potentialities of the individual child.

Although the number of Catholic children in the study was quite small, qualitative differences in the test protocols of the Catholic and Protestant children were impressive enough to impel inclusion of religious affiliation in the analysis of relations between the six major blocks of data, independent of the theoretical considerations discussed above.

A religious affiliation score (identified as "Religion" in relevant tables) was constructed by assigning values of 0 to Catholic children and 1 to Protestant children. Thus, a positive correlation between Religion and another variable means that Protestant children have larger values on the second variable.

Factor Analysis of Relations Between the Six Types of Variables, Age, Sex, Religion, and Social Status

Means and sigmas of the thirty-three variables were calculated for the total sample, boys, and girls. The superiority of boys over girls in the Verbal factor score for the WISC is analogous to the tendency toward a difference in Verbal IQ ($p < .10$) reported in Chapter 2 and may appear more impressively here because of the slightly, although nonsignificantly, greater age of the boys. This is, of course, an artifact of sampling.

The greater explorativeness shown by boys in the laboratory testing situation is compatible with the results concerning the individual laboratory ratings discussed in Chapter 9. This difference in active, motoric exploration of a novel situation with a male examiner is apparently not an artifact of sampling. This interpretation is supported by the factor analytic results reported in this chapter.

Although suggestive, four differences at $p < .10$ are of lesser importance. It would have been ideal, however, if the means for boys and girls had been exactly equal with respect to the social status index.

Six factors accounted for the common variance among the thirty-three scores and ratings. Scores with loadings of .30 or more are listed and the six rotated factors interpreted below.

A special problem in interpreting factors based in part on factor scores is that of artifactual correlations among factor scores from a single block of data. Whereas the *factors* drawn from one block of data are uncorrelated, the factor scores *would be* uncorrelated only if 1.00 had been inserted in the diagonal cells of the correlation matrix (see Overall, 1962). Correlations among factor scores from a single block of data are pure artifacts. To the degree that they are high enough to distort the factor structure, they impose interpretive limitations. Examination of the intercorrelations among factor scores within single blocks of data in relation to the six factors described below suggested that these artifacts may have had important effects on the HIT loadings on Factor I and, possibly, on the clinical rating loadings on Factor IV. In the case of the other four factors, artifactual correlations among factor scores from single blocks of data seemed of little consequence.

Factor I
Field-Articulation

Score	Loading	Meaning of High Factor Score
HIT II	–70	Form inappropriateness; few space responses; large percepts; etc.
HIT V	69	Many rejections; few barrier responses.
CP IV (Field-Articulation)	47	Great articulation.
HIT III	40	Form indefiniteness; much color, shading; etc.
Repression (Isolation, Reaction Formation)	–38	Little repression (much isolation, reaction formation).
WISC I (Verbal)	34	High Verbal score.
Sex	31	Boy.

Factor I is a sex-linked factor apparently showing *one* constellation in which individual differences in the capacity to articulate experience can occur. Interpretation of this factor primarily in terms of field-articulation, rather than HIT performance, is based on the fact that the loadings for the three HIT factor scores (II, III, V) are inflated by relatively high artifactual correlations among these factor scores. The independent Field-Articulation factor scores are correlated with these HIT factor scores and the other scores with defining loadings in directions compatible with the factor shown above. The factor itself does not, therefore, seem to be an artifact.

In children (more often boys than girls) with high factor scores, excellence in articulating fields (e.g., in the Embedded Figures Test) is associated with a tendency toward indefinite and inappropriate use of form in the Holtzman Inkblot Test (at least in part attributable to relatively great reactivity to color and shading and the use of large areas of the inkblots) and an avoidant approach to this inkblot test. The capacity to articulate fields is also linked to relatively limited repression and relatively high scores on the WISC Verbal factor.

Children with low factor scores (more often girls than boys) respond more quickly and willingly to the inkblots and give responses to smaller areas characterized by a greater emphasis on form that leads to the definiteness and appropriateness of the reported percepts. These children are more repressive and of lesser verbal skill.

The link between field-articulation and repression apparent here corresponds to findings reported by Witkin *et al.* (1962), as does the superiority of boys over girls in the cognitive control tasks specifically requiring articulation under relatively difficult conditions. The relationships to high degrees of form indefiniteness and inappropriateness, and high numbers of card rejections in the HIT, was not anticipated, however, on the basis of earlier findings. Witkin *et al.* (1954) showed that adults high in field-articulation (i.e., adult "field-independent" *S*s) are more effective in articulating whole responses to the Rorschach inkblots, as well as in a variety of related aspects of performance in that test. Their results were confirmed, in some detail, by Gardner *et al.* (1959). It would appear that performance in the HIT produces a rather sharply contrasting set of findings, at least at preadolescence. It should be pointed out, however, that the analysis reported here is different from the earlier Rorschach analyses in several ways. For example, all responses to the HIT are included in the present analysis, so that the artifactual relations among scores described in Chapter 7 are brought into play. Because of the limit on R, responses to large areas may almost automatically increase the Form Indefiniteness and Form Inappropriateness scores. Responses to color and shading (more characteristic of high field-articulators in the present study) also increase the Form Inappropriateness and Indefiniteness scores, again because only one response is allowed per card. The apparently incongruous finding here is thus not directly comparable to the earlier Rorschach studies in which, for example, the degree of articulation of whole responses alone was used as a score, and in which artifactual relations among scores were introduced by correlations with R, rather than by limiting R to 45.

The loading on the WISC Verbal factor was also unanticipated and could be a sampling artifact. Other studies of adults and children (e.g., Gardner *et al.*, 1959; Goodenough and Karp, 1961) have clearly shown that field-articulation is associated with performance in such tests as Block Designs and Object Assembly, Spatial Relations and Orientation tests involving the articulation of relevant versus irrelevant stimuli, and so forth and is not associated with verbal ability as measured in a variety of ways.

Factor II

Spontaneity

Score	Loading	Meaning of High Factor Score
CP VI (Spontaneity)	–74	Unspontaneous.
HIT Reaction Time	66	Long reaction time.
CR I (Active Openness to New Experience)	–53	Closed.
CR IV (Cooperativeness)	–35	Uncooperative.
LR I (Impulsive Spontaneity)	–35	Unspontaneous.
Religion	–33	Catholic.
Repression (Isolation, Reaction Formation)	30	Repressive (little isolation, reaction formation).

This factor seems best interpreted in terms of openness and spontaneity of participation in the clinical and laboratory testing and in the HIT, which was administered subsequently.

Children with high factor scores are relatively unspontaneous in the clinical and laboratory testing situations (as indicated by test performance and independent observations). In the HIT, their lack of spontaneity takes the form of slowness in responding to the inkblots. These children tend to be uncooperative, apparently by virtue of constriction rather than active resistance to participation. The loading for repression is consistent with the impression that these children are generally constricted and inhibited. In this sample at least, this general pattern of behavior is also more apparent in Catholic than in Protestant children.

Children with low factor scores, who are relatively open, uninhibited, and cooperative, and who employ generalized repression to a lesser degree, are more often Protestant than Catholic.

Factor III

Maturity

Score	*Loading*	*Meaning of High Factor Score*
Over-all Ego Autonomy	69	High autonomy.
LR II (Anxious Dependence)	–64	Comfortable independence.
Ego Strength	60	Ego strength.
Age	54	Older child.
WISC I (Verbal)	47	High Verbal score.
CP V (Constricted-Flexible Control)	43	Flexible control.
Repression (Isolation, Reaction Formation)	–38	Little repression (much isolation, reaction formation).
HIT IV	37	Many Popular and Human responses; high integration; etc.
Projection (Denial)	–33	Little projection (little denial).
Social Status	–32	High status.

This factor seems referable primarily to individual consistencies associated with maturity. Although age has a rather high loading on this factor, the factor cannot be defined in terms of age alone. Children with high factor scores, who are more often older children, maintain rather effective balance between drive and reality in the determination of their behavior (over-all ego autonomy), are low in anxious dependence, show over-all ego strength and stability, produce relatively large numbers of Popular, Human, and highly integrated responses to the Holtzman Inkblot Test, and are high in flexible control. These children are low in repression and projection. They have high scores on the WISC Verbal factor and tend to be high in social status.

Children with low factor scores, who are more often the younger children in the sample, are lower in ego strength, ego autonomy, and verbal ability, show more anxious dependence, repression, and projection, tend toward constricted control, and give fewer Popular, Human, and highly integrated responses to the HIT. They also tend to be of lower social status.

Factor IV
Adequacy of Reality Testing

Score	Loading	Meaning of High Factor Score
CP (Schematizing, Lag)	55	Great lag (leveling).
CR VI (Sporadic Disruption of Control)	52	Sporadic disruption.
CR III (Accuracy of Reality Testing)	–50	Inaccurate reality testing.
WISC III (Performance)	49	High Performance score.
CR IV (Cooperativeness)	49	Cooperative.
Ego Strength	–41	Ego weakness.
CP V (Constricted-Flexible Control)	33	Flexible control.

This factor appears to indicate individual consistencies in the adequacy of reality testing that are a key facet of ego strength and that are closely related to the capacity to maintain smooth over-all control over extended periods of time.

Children with high factor scores are levelers who show inaccuracy of reality testing in the Schematizing Test (i.e., they lag behind the progressive increase in stimulus sizes) and are rated inaccurate in a more general sense on the basis of their performance in the clinic. They also show relatively high degrees of sporadic disruption of control in the clinical testing situation. Their inadequate reality testing is associated with general ego weakness, relatively high scores on the WISC Performance factor (indicating great articulation of motor and visual-motor skills), and generalized crudity of reality testing. That these children show a slight tendency toward flexible control (implying, among other things, relatively effective control of irrelevant motoric impulses in the Color-Word Test) suggests that their impulse control problem concerns the maintenance of reality-attuned orientations over considerable periods of time, rather than effectiveness of inhibition for extremely short periods. The appearance of this unique pattern of strength and weakness in impulse control thus appears to support our contention that such concepts as "delay," "inhibition," and so forth implicate variegated substructures of control and are of dubious, if any, value when used as global terms. These children's relatively high cooperativeness ratings further indicate that their generally poor reality testing and sporadic losses of control occur in a context of specific ego weaknesses and are not attributable to the kinds of ego primitivity and undifferentiation attributable to chronic acting out, avoidance, or other gross and generalized inadequacies of impulse control.

Children with low factor scores are sharpeners whose over-all control is smooth and whose reality testing is generally adequate. They are less docile, show lesser articulation of motoric skills, and are characterized by greater ego strength.

Factor V
Explorativeness

Score	Loading	Meaning of High Factor Score
LR III (Explorativeness)	54	Explorative.
CP II (Conceptual Differentiation)	−52	Low differentiation (broad categorizing).
HIT I	51	Much anxiety, hostility, movement, etc.
Sex	50	Boy.
Projection (Denial)	46	Much projection (much denial).
WISC I (Verbal)	44	High Verbal score.
CR I (Active Openness to New Experience)	38	Open.
CR II (Unity of Identity)	−35	Low in unity.
CP V (Constricted-Flexible Control)	−33	Constricted control.
CR III (Accuracy of Reality Testing)	32	Accurate reality testing.
HIT Reaction Time	−32	Short reaction time.

Explorativeness seems the best general descriptive term for this complex factor. The specific form of explorativeness indicated seems to be one associated with generalized openness to new experience and with a restlessness and quick reactivity that is more characteristic of boys than girls. The loading of the Conceptual Differentiation factor score on this factor is particularly interesting. As noted in Chapter 6, both adults and children who are broad categorizers produce TAT stories that indicate great freedom to move away from the physical characteristics of the pictures and to express personalized ideas of minimal stereotypy. This associative distance from the objective characteristics of stimuli is apparently part of a generalized stance toward reality in children as well as adults. That the expressive freedom the broad categorizer's stance implies is associated with greater openness and explorativeness in preadolescents confirms and extends the evidence already available concerning key general characteristics of broad and narrow categorizers. Also, as noted in Chapter 5, the definitions adult broad categorizers give for the groups they form in the Object Sorting Test also represent relatively great "distance" from the physical properties of the objects. The sex-linked nature of this factor suggests that the associative distance, the expressive freedom, and the tendency toward *personalized* experiencing of external stimuli characteristic of adult broad categorizers is, at preadolescence, more apparent in the case of boys than girls.

Children with high factor scores are relatively open and explorative in both clinic and laboratory. As discussed above, they are low in spontaneous conceptual differentiation (i.e., they are broad categorizers), give more responses attributable to active restlessness in the Holtzman Inkblot Test, and are verbally skillful. They are prone to projection, but accurate in reality testing (possibly in part an expression of mild hyperalertness). These children, who are more often boys than girls, seem also to have complex, rather than unified, personal identities. That they tend toward constricted control (e.g., have difficulty inhibiting irrelevant vocalizations in the criterion Color-Word Test) may be attributable to the restless, anxious, highly active nature of their conscious thinking, with its implication of free, but uncomfortable, penetration of consciousness by highly personalized thoughts and feelings.

Children with low factor scores, more often girls than boys, are less explorative narrow categorizers who are apparently more placid, less open to new experience, less projective, and less verbally skilled. In spite of their more unified identities and lesser projection, they are relatively inaccurate in reality testing, a finding which suggests (as in the case of adults) that their "unity" tends toward stereotypy, narrowness and shallowness of consciousness, and rigidity of approach to new situations.

It is interesting that Catholic children, who appear more inhibited with respect to Factor II, Spontaneity, and Factor VI, Acting Out, are not less exploratory in the sense represented by this factor.

Like "delay," such terms as "constriction" and "inhibition" obviously require further articulation and specification in order to be effective behavioral designations. The meaningful questions are obviously "Constricted concerning *what?*" or "Inhibited concerning what aspects of control?" Like delay, these terms, when used globally, appear to mask more than they reveal.

Factor VI
Acting Out

Score	Loading	Meaning of High Factor Score
Religion	57	Protestant.
Acting Out–Overcontrol	−49	Acting out.
LR IV (Acting upon the Environment)	38	Active toward the environment.
HIT IV	37	Many Popular, Human; high integration; etc.
CR V (Compulsive Exactness)	−37	Noncompulsive, inexact.
HIT III	−32	Form definiteness; few Color and Shading responses; many Animal responses; etc.
Social Status	−32	High status.

Although the name, "Acting Out," seems appropriate to this factor, it should be remembered that this sample of preadolescent children is notable for its mild constriction, inhibition, and conformant cooperativeness. None of the sixty children acted out to an extreme degree in any of the situations. The only child who superficially seemed to approach an extreme level was clearly agitated because of gross and frightening ego weakness and was not primarily expressing a characterological tendency toward acting out.

In the context of this qualification, children with high factor scores are given to relatively great acting out in both the clinic and the laboratory. Their tendency to give overt motoric expression to the conflicts and tensions surrounding the clinical testing session also manifests itself in relative carelessness and imprecision. These children also tend to be from Protestant families of high socioeconomic status. Their responses to the Holtzman Inkblot Test are notable for the high number of clear, definite percepts, the numbers of Popular, Human, and Animal responses, the low numbers of Color and Shading responses, and the high degree of integration of parts of the inkblots. These features of their performance are also compatible with the limited degree of acting out characterizing these children.

Children with low factor scores tend to be unusually inhibited and given to compulsive exactness. In the HIT, they give more form-indefinite responses, are more responsive to color and shading, and give fewer conventional responses. Possibly as a result, they achieve less effective integration of parts of inkblots. These children tend to be from Catholic families and to be relatively low in socioeconomic status.

This factor, in combination with Factor II, seems to indicate that the Catholic children are more inhibited and constricted than the Protestant children in at least two specifiable ways. It is also notable that the two aspects of inhibition characterizing the Catholic children have not led to their being rated as low in general ego strength. From the standpoint of the durability and integrity of the ego, their loss in openness, expressive freedom, and the like may be balanced by a conventionality, placidity, and stability that imply one form of ego integrity and suggest a pattern (although somewhat conformant and externalized) of over-all control that may be a stabilizing factor against the onslaught of instinctual forces in adolescence.

Discussion

We noted earlier the evidences that individual personality organization is extremely complex in preadolescence, as in adulthood, and the additional evidences that developmental changes in ego structures follow variegated courses. We noted also the partial autonomy of controlling structures from the substructures whose operation they involve in particular situations and the persistence of controlling structures in the face of variegated changes in specific response processes to which they are relevant. With respect to these observations, it is notable that no single set of variables—including ego strength, the other general characteristics of ego organization, and the defense mechanisms—dominated the final analysis of relations between major blocks of data collected at preadolescence. The extensive interweaving of data from the different blocks in the defining factor loadings of this analysis is notable. The number of over-all patternings characterizing individual subjects is, of course, much greater than the number of factors. The general implication is obvious: the organized complexity of structural arrangements at preadolescence is greater than is often assumed and greater than the present limited results indicate.

It is also obvious that the factors described in this chapter are not "entities" in themselves, but rather represent *some* of the general patternings in which these dimensions of individual consistency can appear. As noted earlier, this is clearly true of the field-articulation factor. It is also true, in all likelihood, of Adequacy of Reality Testing and at least some of the other factors described here. The results presented in this chapter seem to provide valuable new insights into the over-all organization of the dimensions of individuality sampled and suggest further hypotheses concerning possible correlates of some of the cognitive controls and other single dimensions. No claim can be made, however, that all the possible over-all patterns of structural organization have been sampled in a study of this size. Only the addition of other aspects of individuality and the employment of larger and more variegated samples of subjects can provide answers to questions concerning the total realm of over-all structural arrangements.

The fact that six meaningful factors appeared in this final analysis is intriguing and apparently indicates that higher-order principles of personality organization—which could be called principles of cognitive style or principles of reality contact—affect performance even in the very limited and specific samplings of behavior obtained with each of the methods employed.

Although limited in kind by the types of data included, the factors represent considerably more general features of behavior than the individual blocks of data. Only two, the Field-Articulation and Adequacy of Reality Testing factors, seem to involve predominantly cognitive aspects of behavior, and even these are referable to other aspects of behavior as well. The factors identified as representing consistent individual differences in Spontaneity, Maturity, and Explorativeness clearly represent the interrelationship of primarily cognitive with other determinants and as such also represent a higher order of structural arrangement. The Acting Out factor is perhaps more limited with respect to the kinds of variables primarily determining it, but is nevertheless referable to important aspects of responses to the clinical and laboratory testing situations, the clinical tests themselves, and the HIT, as well as to social status and religious affiliation.

In view of the purely exploratory purposes for which the HIT factors were included in this final analysis, note should be made here of the high degree of meaningfulness with which these factors are related to the other aspects of behavior included in the final analysis. This result seems to add further confirmation to the other evidences of the validity of HIT factors discussed in Chapter 7.

In addition to the points made above, it should be remembered that three dimensions of cognitive control appear to be largely independent of all the other aspects of individuality explored in the study. The ratings used to represent the cognitive control principle, tolerance for unrealistic experiences, had but one small loading on a single factor in the factor analysis of cognitive control scores. In the analysis of over-all structural organization, this important control principle rating was related to none of the over-all factors to more than a negligible degree. It was, in fact, the only variable in the final analysis which did not have a defining loading on any of the six factors. This does not mean that tolerance for unrealistic experiences is of no consequence in preadolescent behavior. Rather, it seems to imply that the aspects of total personality organization with which it is associated were not sampled in the present study. The two scanning factors, whose internal consistencies are particularly impressive, are even more independent of the variables included in the final analysis. It will be recalled that they were not included in this analysis because neither set of factor scores was significantly correlated with any of the thirty-three variables.

Although the relative lack of spontaneity characterizing the Catholic children does not appear to signify ego weakness, their exceptional degree of generalized constriction in what appears to be a somewhat constricted total group of children may be worthy of note here. We are inclined to speculate concerning this result that the more authoritarian and conformity-demanding belief systems surrounding these children during development does not disrupt ego organization or render it unstable, but rather serves as a general inhibiting agent that may limit self-expression and active exploration of the environment. If so, the major consequences may be intellectual and affective constriction of a kind that could limit differentiation in these vital areas and hinder the unfolding of potential expressive talents. The more intense and openly spontaneous action upon the environment that seems to characterize the Protestant children is, however, no more associated with ego strength. The potential impediment to adequate development here, of course, is that acting out and acting upon may, in extreme cases, abort the kinds of delay that are presumably essential to structural differentiation.

The complexity of individual personality organizations and the widely different over-all patterns evident in these results suggest that optimal development may be contingent upon recognition by parental figures of the *individual* child's unique pattern of hereditary and learned characteristics. Optimal development thus seems to imply parental figures who are capable, or potentially capable, of an armamentarium of approaches to child-rearing, as well as unusual sensitivity to individuality. This is probably more than most adults are capable of, for the very reason that their behavior involves previously formed autonomous structures. The results do suggest, however, the inefficacy for many children of any stereotypic approach to child-rearing. The multiple evidences of individuality make it clear that the patterns of structural organization, talents, and special problems of individual children require more effectively flexible approaches than those currently associated with the various levels of socioeconomic status or with popular belief systems that include assumptions about the treatment of *all* children.

13 Case Studies of Selected Children—
A Boy and Girl
High in Ego Strength

Introduction

THE AVAILABILITY of extensive samples of observations and test results from infancy to latency on about half the sample made it possible to perform intensive case studies of longitudinal data in relation to performance at preadolescence. The four children (two boys, two girls) discussed in this and the following chapter were selected because they typify certain clusters of boys and girls high and low in general ego strength and because they most vividly exemplify several prominent features of the sample as a whole. Case histories of a boy and a girl rated high in ego strength (as defined in Chapter 10) are presented in this chapter. Comparable case histories of a boy and a girl rated low in ego strength are presented in Chapter 14. In each instance, a summary of material on the child's environment and major features of his development from birth to preadolescence is followed by a discussion of his ratings and test performances in the present study. This approach provides not only for a fairly comprehensive view of major features of development from birth to preadolescence, but also for consideration of the effectiveness of the preadolescent tests and ratings in the light of the rather voluminous material on earlier development. For the reader, the discussions of factor scores for these individual children may further exemplify the meanings of the factor dimensions extracted from the larger numbers of scores or ratings included in the major blocks of data. Some general observations concerning the case study material, including the fit of the preadolescent assessments to the longitudinal data, are presented at the end of Chapter 14.

Ego Strength in a Context of Inhibition—The Case of Harold F.

Harold was selected for case study because he typified a form of generalized ego strength common to a number of children in the sample. His infancy behavior, including the unusual capacity for control he displayed at that early age, bespoke an excellent hereditary endowment. Unlike the children of low ego strength described in Chapter 14, his cognitive development was not impeded by severe physical problems. By preadolescence, his adaptive pattern was effective for many purposes, but he, like many of the children, was rather inhibited. His preadolescent behavior also seemed to imply a mild flatness of affect; although in no obvious way inappropriate, his relations to project members (and apparently others) lacked warmth, vividness, and spontaneity.

Harold's Environment

Harold spent his early years in a modest forty-year-old frame house which was clean and in better repair than others in the neighborhood, but spare of decoration. The worn but comfortable furnishings were drab and utilitarian, except for a large cabinet-style television set and some bright religious pictures on the walls of the small living room. The living room opened into a multipurpose play, work, and dining room, beyond which was a sparkling kitchen conveniently equipped with cabinets made by the father, a skilled workman.

Harold and his oldest brother shared a double bed upstairs. The parents slept in an adjoining bedroom furnished with a chest, a double bed, and a baby crib, which was sometimes available to the youngest child. The mother remarked that she preferred to have the baby sleep in the dining room, since infant sounds during the night tended to disturb the parents. A brother intermediate in age between Harold and his oldest brother slept by himself, since he was a bed wetter. This sleeping arrangement gave the boys considerable independence, as well as separation from the parents. For example, Harold was said to wander about at night, but the mother was not certain how often this happened because she was unable to hear him. The mother read to the children before nap time in their preschool years. Other than this, she went upstairs infrequently.

A small front porch and a tiny front yard hemmed in by neighbors' property allowed less space for play than was available to most of the children in the sample. A larger backyard and a cluttered garage included some play space and access to neighboring yards.

When Harold was seven, the family moved to a small farm just outside the city limits. The farmhouse, set well back from the road in the shadow of several commercial buildings, was in good repair and gave an impression of airiness. Neighbors were not close, but within sight. The move entailed the purchase of a second car to enable Harold's mother to take the children to school. The family also acquired bicycles, and the father set up a basketball goal and swings for the children. Inside, the house was fresh, neat, and furnished with necessary equipment; there were also a few books. The four boys shared upstairs bedrooms. Theoretically, the oldest son had his own room. Actually, there were two beds in each room and a good deal of shifting back and forth as the boys bargained for the best beds. A baby girl was moved about downstairs to keep her from disturbing the parents.

The move provided greatly increased opportunities for outdoor play, but reduced the number of playmates outside the family. It had the advantage of providing a second source of income in gardening. Each spring and summer, the boys and their mother worked hard raising vegetables for their own use and for sale.

Both parents are Catholic. They were married when the mother was nineteen, the father twenty. The father was born in another state, where most of his family still lived. Many of the mother's numerous relatives, including a favorite brother who was very fond of the boys, lived nearby. In the early years of the marriage, the parents spent much time visiting these relatives and friends. As the family's size increased, the inconvenience of transporting the children decreased this visiting. Recreation was then centered on family picnics and games, attendance at and participation in a number of sports events, and church activities. None of the children attended kindergarten. All attended parochial schools. Both parents prided themselves on self-reliance and encouraged independence in their children. They owned their own home and carefully budgeted their income. They bought only according to plan and on a cash basis. They sought no special privileges and prided themselves on having earned the advantages they had obtained. Neither parent had finished high school, but they valued education for their children. In the early years, the parents had little time for reading, but encouraged their children to borrow library books. After the youngest child entered school, the mother taught a popular adult education course.

Thus, both parents were strong in respect to stability and self-esteem, which they seemed to have passed on to their children. They were prone to be "sensible," and perhaps less concerned with nuances in interpersonal relationships than many parents. Family plans were made in accordance with the welfare of the total group, but specific details, such as the sleeping arrangements and the move to the farm, were dictated primarily by parental convenience, and secondarily by the children's feelings or needs.

Compliance with the standards and practices of the Catholic church and school provided consistent, clearly structured patterns of behavior. Even in Harold's infancy, the mother's emphasis was upon the development of independence. The larger family group offered a sense of belonging without demanding closeness. Harold's environment thus provided stability and security in a definite knowledge of expected and acceptable behavior. It also limited the range of his experience, especially insofar as it may have offered little of the more intense or warmer emotional experiences a child of his perceptiveness might have enjoyed in another setting. On the other hand, inhibition was not characteristic of the other children in the family.

During Harold's infancy, his mother was described as an energetic, plain, somewhat masculine-appearing woman who handled her inferiority feelings by jocular verbal aggression or avoidance, often followed by relevant information. An observer remarked of this early period that she characteristically responded to questions by

"I don't know" . . . as though she protected herself against being found in error, and in a way against being held responsible for the content of her statement, by disclaiming definite information or opinion. She appears to be a rather well-organized person who, in social situations of this kind, is not likely to make herself vulnerable and hence is not very self-revealing.

She was capable of flexibility with respect to child-rearing and noted the individual needs of her children with some sensitivity. For the infant Harold, however, her vigorous, direct handling may have been overly rough and excessively stimulating. She was assertive, forceful, and definite, yet warmly proud of her children. She disciplined them primarily by teasing, shaming, cajoling, and "screaming." She met the physical and social needs of her children as the situation demanded, but she admitted during the latency interview that Harold was "a deep thinker" and "a cover-upper," whom "I don't really know much about."

It seems likely that Mrs. F. regarded Harold's passivity as weakness and secretly admired the mischievousness of her older son, who led Harold into such exploits as tree-climbing, breaking windows, and spilling paint. Perhaps she resented Harold's impenetrable self-containment, which, while it approached the self-reliance she so valued, also shut her out.

There were no formal sessions with Mr. F. Except for casual meetings, we knew him only through the eyes of the mother and children. He was described as a shy, reserved man who was physically neat and quite good-looking, and who, as a skilled workman, prided himself on his competence and independence. When the children were little, he often allowed them to watch him at his workbench and took them with him on errands and to sporting events. He left child-rearing to his wife, but was capable of "wielding a mighty blow" (in contrast to his wife's verbal barrages) when his wife sought disciplinary support. Like his wife, he took time to do things with his children, but these contacts were adult-instituted, rather than child-centered, and perhaps failed to provide much opportunity for the expression of differentiated feelings. In any event, interviews with the mother and children, as well as projective test responses, repeatedly indicated that father and son did not know each other very well and that Harold's relationship to his father became one of surface obedience with underlying resentment.

Harold's Physical, Cognitive, and Emotional Development from Infancy to Preadolescence

The Early Years

At twenty-eight weeks, Harold was described as a tall, slender, well-developed infant, definitely masculine in appearance. His complexion was fair, perhaps somewhat pale. He showed varying degrees of shyness with strangers, and was said to smile rarely and only when the observers were at a distance. Yet his face was quite expressive. There was evidence of special sensitivity to sound and touch, but he was also capable of shutting out by turning away. He was soothed best by being held closely or carried. The mother considered him more affectionate than her other boys. She said that he needed more sleep than her other children and was less active and more fatigable. The most remarkable aspects of the infancy tests were Harold's skilled coordination at a slow, deliberate pace and his unusual capacity to explore the potentialities of objects through visual observation. Test demands were often satisfied by his inclusion of correct responses among less common ways of dealing with objects.

Harold was considered a healthy baby, although vegetative processes were not entirely smooth. He suffered colic in the first few weeks, had a severe chest cold, an eye infection, and occasional mild constipation. He had no allergies or illnesses in the first year except colds, which the mother described as "mild," although infancy observers felt the severity of his coughing to be extreme. He was also said to be "choosey" about semisolids, to fight sleep, and to wake frequently during the night. At one year, he was quite ill with enlarged cervical glands.

Harold was described by one observer as "a modulated, inhibited, controlled baby with sensory thresholds apparently high," although he showed an acute awareness of strange places and people. Differentiation in his behavior was high, although drive seemed low. He used avoidance and rejection to handle stress from overstimulation by the mother or others. Fatigue increased sensory sensitivity. Angry crying or squirming to the point of struggling to get his breath were observed only occasionally. Usually, he avoided these extreme moods by turning away or by responding to his mother's facial expression or words of restraint. He showed less mouthing behavior than most babies and nursed for a shorter period than most babies. He rarely protested verbally, but sometimes stiffened his limbs or resisted motor restraint, as when being dressed. When his hunger was satiated, he was said to make "delightful cooing noises" and to carry on a "gurgling conversation" with his mother. Especially outstanding was his ability to inhibit crying when his mother said, "Shh!"

Despite a high degree of competence in observing and handling objects at twenty-eight weeks, he seemed to be less pleasurably involved than many babies, did not resist giving up objects, and was not particularly active, although manipulation of objects was skillful, varied, and deliberate when it was elicited.

The Preschool Years

When examined at four years, eleven months, Harold was a handsome boy, somewhat above average in height and weight. Aside from dental caries, for which he was receiving attention, his physical health was excellent. The pediatrician described him as average in activity and sensitivity, with greatest sensitivity in the muscular and vascular systems. Although a functional heart murmur was reported as having been noted at two or three years of age, there was no evidence of a murmur or irregularity at the time of the preschool examination.

At this time, Harold was described by observers as "unresponsive, laconic, unspontaneous"; "unable to integrate or imagine beyond the barest level of perceptual intake"; and "suspicious, contained and passively hostile." It was observed that he showed strong tendencies toward denial, avoidance, and contact severance, that he limited his perception of environmental stimuli, and that he was affectively "controlled and muffled." It was felt that his unusual withdrawal masked mild phobias and compulsions. His reticence and inhibition even suggested to one examiner that he might be of limited mental ability. These negative evaluations were tempered by momentary glimpses of "more complex integration of perceptual, apperceptive and projective processes," "subdued gratification in extremely competent intellectual functioning," "resourcefulness," "tenacity," "pride," and "emotional availability and capacity for enjoyment of mutual interaction with the environment."

In his preschool psychiatric examination, Harold was guardedly serious at first, but gradually became able to engage in activities suggested by the psychiatrist, although the adult was excluded from the play. Following indirect attacks, he asked the psychiatrist to be his "cowboy partner." In these maneuvers, Harold reflected his initial caution in approaching people, yet also revealed his potential warmth, after slowly sounding out the situation. It became clear that aggressive activity was pleasurable, but that even when he was most enthusiastic, it was somewhat muffled.

Despite the apparent masculine sturdiness of his body, Harold's relatively low energy supply seemed taxed by his slightly exaggerated orientation toward motoric activity. Another important aspect of Harold's behavior was the notable contrast between tension and serenity. The tightness of his posture in a new situation, as well as his reluctance to communicate verbally, were correctly recognized as symptomatic of the inhibition so prominent in his projective test performance. Equally apparent in outdoor situations allowing freedom of movement were his impressive motor skills, which most observers identified as tension-relieving. Harold also seemed, however, to express pride and confidence through his superior motor functioning.

The Latency Years

At seven and a half years, a similar picture of Harold was obtained in a psychiatric interview. Still reserved, Harold conveyed an impression of dignity and self-assurance. Although slow to get under way, he accepted suggestion and help, after which he continued independently. Although partly a function of reserve, his independence had a quality of healthy self-reliance. The psychiatrist also described "a kind of pleasure derived from socially appropriate compulsive ordering and organizing things." Harold engaged in aggressive activity quite forcefully, without bluster, by deliberate, well-coordinated, graceful handling of his body. He spoke in a soft, gentle voice, frequently mumbling as though unsure of what he should say, or perhaps fearful of being contradicted. At first, he communicated largely by nonverbal means. As he became more comfortable, he spoke more clearly, asked questions, and volunteered information. As his spontaneity increased, he described his interest in sports, indirectly suggested concern with mastery and aggressive feelings, expressed wishes to have things definite and final, and showed an unusually mature ability to evaluate reality. Over the course of three hours, he became less inhibited, although it was apparent that he consistently avoided expressing strong feelings. He seemed to prefer "prepared and organized" activity, which he could master cheerfully with little show of irritability. This allowed him to face defeat without loss of face and minimized frustration, but at the price of spontaneity and creativity. In general, he seemed quite capable of dealing actively with objects, but was notably passive in relating himself to other people.

Repeated testings between preschool and preadolescence showed consistently superior intellectual potential (IQ's varied from 129 to 137), with motoric skills considerably more comfortably used than language skills. This discrepancy, which had been apparent in infancy, was more noticeable in preschool years because Harold expressed himself in laconic terms and with marked embarrassment. Despite his impoverished projective test protocols, Harold was subsequently able to use his cognitive resources to the extent that he did moderately well in school. He handled the demands of formal tests of intelligence accurately, but without personal satisfaction or warmth toward the examiners. He understood number concepts, and his memory was potentially good, although selective. He could remember many details of sports activities, for example, but seemed to recall little of his early family life. Excellent motor coordination at a slow, even pace appeared in all performance tests, but the full grace and flexibility with which he could handle his body seemed reserved for outdoor climbing and jumping which he accomplished with considerable purposeful vigor. Reserve and refusal to give much of himself pervaded all his test performances. His silent shrugging or avoidance of the examiner's gaze was not unlike his turning away from the infancy tests at twenty-eight weeks. His frequent "I don't know" responses seemed to offer protection against intrusion or self-commitment in a way strikingly like that of his mother when she was first interviewed by the infancy observers. Harold thus seemed to restrict himself as a self-protective device, rather than from lack of capacity to observe or evaluate his surround. He seemed cautious lest he communicate too much, particularly to women. Although these maneuvers made him seem passively hostile at times, he was never observed to lose control of a situation or his reactions to it. He used his cognitive superiority with moderate effectiveness, but without the vividness or originality implied by his repeatedly superior IQ scores.

By latency, his overt withdrawal from the structured test situation was striking. His motoric behavior continued to be remarkably smooth, and his capacity to handle numbers remained impressive. Communicative inhibitions were still apparent and may have been associated with his difficulties in learning to read. His thinking appeared to be rigid and concrete, especially when he was required to categorize at an abstract level. He was more willing to involve himself in the test situation and was closer to the examiner, as demonstrated by his permitting her to direct his thinking and to share the pleasure he felt in mastering difficult concepts. The rigidity he showed was perhaps partly dictated by a strong need to assess objects and ideas from the point of view of their usefulness and to offer immediate solutions somewhat perseveratively without pushing for refinements. There was in this behavior a kind of intellectual laziness, muting of curiosity, or narrowness in concept formation which ordinarily fell short of the rich potential suggested by a few of his responses. During latency, the rigidity and constraint noted in his earlier motor, affective, and social behavior were more apparent in his thinking. At earlier ages, his affective and social inhibitions had seemed to limit communication of his thoughts. At preschool, "I don't know" seemed to imply, "I don't want to commit myself." At latency, "I don't know" seemed to mean, "I am anxious because I cannot organize my thinking." Prominent themes in his projective test responses and in Comprehension items of the WISC were wishes to be physically strong; to control feelings; to avoid physical injury, darkness, and unknown places; to escape verbal punishment from his mother; and to understand a firm, somewhat inscrutable father.

Several warm, direct contacts with male examiners at this time indicated increasing willingness to relate to men with the limited techniques he could summon for initiating or enjoying these contacts. In some ways, Harold's social behavior resembled that of the preschool child who plays "alongside" rather than "with" another individual. Harold's difficulties in expressing warmth may have stemmed both from his natural restraint and caution and from his idiosyncratic reaction to long-standing family patterns of engaging in mutual activities, such as sports, without accompanying closeness. Years of brusque teasing by his mother probably reduced his capacity for interaction with women. His ability to use help and to share pleasure in successful test responses with a woman examiner suggested, however, that he experienced personal integrity from the stability of his mother's genuine, but perhaps unmodulated, expression of affection for him. He seemed to prefer concrete, reality-bound thinking. He was also able to be abstract primarily when emotion was not involved, as in solving arithmetical problems or dealing with geographical or historical facts.

Summary of Findings Through Latency

This brief review of Harold's first ten years indicates some remarkable behavioral consistencies. The imbalance between reserved use of good verbal skills and freer access to superior performance skills seemed to mesh into a lifelong tendency to turn away from stimulation considered excessive and to terminate social contacts which were uncomfortable.

His generally low drive level perhaps contributed to what seemed almost an innate tendency toward delay. His laconic unspontaneity, his literal approach to reality, and his very limited capacity for creative imaginativeness have been evident from the time each could be clearly observed.

His preference for independence, his distance from his parents, siblings, and others, and his slow, deliberate focus on the functional utility of things, with the accompanying superiority of motor over verbal skills, were also relatively permanent features of his behavior. He thus seemed to maintain a generally effective equilibrium by remaining aloof and matter of fact, and by conforming passively to the rules for behavior provided by his parents.

In contrast to Sharon J. (Chapter 14), whose greater constriction was associated with grossly ineffective employment of defense mechanisms and other coping devices, Harold was an individual of unusual integrity and internal cohesiveness. The stable, effective picture he presented at the threshold of preadolescence was dimmed only by his inability to actualize the full range of his potential talents, particularly those that flower best in the context of greater freedom to explore, to express highly personalized reactions to events and people, and to reorganize experience creatively. He was also denied some of the pleasure in experience as such that can appear in a less inhibited and conformant stance toward reality.

Harold at Preadolescence

By age eleven, Harold seemed better able to mobilize his intellectual resources and much less socially inept. His school grades were improved. He was popular with girls. He was also successful in sports. In keeping with these changes, he no longer viewed the structured tests as a grueling ordeal, but saw them as an intellectual challenge and occasionally as an opportunity to exchange humor or to share the pleasure of a broadened range of knowledge. He communicated more freely and could accept uncertainty or gaps in his knowledge with greater aplomb. His responses were generally brief, but were neither lacking in detail nor submerged in compulsive attention to detail. Especially in performance tests, but also in verbal tests, he was able to suggest alternate solutions to problems and to look ahead effectively. He could integrate a great deal of factual information. Although he never chose to show off his knowledge, he showed confident pleasure in relating what he had learned. By preference a child who appeared to value independence, he was equally able to accept help and confirmation. His thinking was characterized by some originality of approach, but he was least skillful in the free use of imagination. Although this had been most true of him in the preschool period, the psychiatrist who saw him at preadolescence found his content "rather uncreative, conventional, and even a little empty."

Defense Mechanisms and General Characteristics of Ego Functioning

The ratings of Harold's defense mechanisms and general ego characteristics are presented below. These ratings were based on blind analysis of his preadolescent clinical test performances.

Rating Variable	Rating
Ego Strength	6
Over-all Ego Autonomy	4
Repression	2
Isolation	8
Reaction Formation	6
Projection	7
Avoidance	1

Denial	2
Acting Out–Overcontrol	9

Although some of the most general consistencies inferred from the longitudinal material were mirrored here (e.g., the relatively high, but not extreme, ego strength and the high overcontrol), there were several apparent discrepancies. The turning away from excessive stimulation noted repeatedly in the longitudinal study was not so apparent in his test performances and suggested that what was described as a defensive tendency toward avoidance may have been specific to certain types of situations or intensities of stress, rather than a pervasively apparent aspect of Harold's character organization. The kinds of avoidance ordinarily associated with inadequacy of impulse delay and expressed in various forms of acting out were conspicuously absent in his test performances. Denial also seemed less apparent than in the longitudinal material.

In contrast, the preadolescent test picture was one of inhibition associated with isolation (largely compulsivity, rather than intellectualized obsessiveness) and projection, so that Harold was clearly more like the classical compulsive-projective character model than the acting out, avoidant, denying model. The implication of these ratings was that he achieved distance not so much by turning away as by organizing experience in literal, compulsive ways. The apparent strength of reaction formation further reinforced this view. Perhaps these ratings provide a clue to the impression of all the observers that the integrity and stability of Harold's ego mechanisms were greater than those of the average child in this sample, but were associated with excessive inhibition and distance from other persons. The ratings of his behavior in the clinical testing situation suggested that his lack of flexible imaginativeness, his literality, and his steady focus on things outside himself were, in part, products of an isolation–reaction formation–projection syndrome. The latter view may be most compatible with the effectiveness of most of his preadolescent behavior and the unusual self-control he maintained in all situations.

Intellectual Abilities

Harold's age-corrected WISC scores, presented below, very clearly reflected the over-all balance in favor of motor versus verbal skills.

Information	12
Comprehension	16
Arithmetic	14
Similarities	13

Vocabulary	12
Digit Span	10
Picture Completion	13
Picture Arrangement	18
Block Design	13
Object Assembly	16
Coding (B)	13
Verbal IQ	118
Performance IQ	132
Full Scale IQ	127

It is thus clear that the relatively high rating on isolation implied an emphasis on compulsivity, rather than obsessiveness and intellectualizing. One does not see this pattern of skills in typical cases of the obsessive-intellectualizing character make-up. Taken together, the partial views of Harold gained from the defense and general ratings and his intelligence test performances suggested what might be called a mixed picture of compulsivity and action-orientation, without extreme obsessiveness or acting out. In a more intellectually stimulating and supportive environment, Harold might have emerged more like the usual obsessive-compulsive person. Perhaps Harold demonstrated with particular clarity the shaping effect of a particular type of environment on a particular set of inherited potentials.

Harold's relatively low scores on the major verbal tests, Vocabulary and Information, reflected his generalized preference for doing things, rather than thinking or introspecting, as a way of dealing with situations. These scores also reflected the relative impoverishment of his home environment with respect to his use of language and his acquisition of knowledge as such. His remarkably high score on the Picture Arrangement subtest indicated a notably sharp, if not hyperalert, awareness of interactions among people, and a considerable capacity for sensitive anticipations concerning such interactions. Perhaps this score was another reflection of the careful, rather passive observing and scanning that seemed a part of his distance from other people. Perhaps, too, it reflected a potential warmth and sensitivity to others that was often masked by his cautious avoidance of relationships in which he might suffer the kind of belittling criticism to which his mother subjected him. In his case, this unusual sensitivity, mirrored in a related way in his excellent responses to the Comprehension subtest, did not seem to stem—as it sometimes does—from a proclivity to manipulate persons and situations.

Cognitive Controls

Harold's scores on the cognitive control factors are listed below.

Factor	Score	Meaning
I Scanning A	− .65	Slightly less than average post-judgment checking in the size estimation tests.
II Conceptual Differentiation	2.73	Extremely narrow categorizing (high spontaneous differentiation), with associated literality and closeness to physical features of the TAT pictures.
III Scanning B	−1.70	Extensive scanning of size estimation stimuli during judgments; a careful, compulsive approach to this test.
IV Field-Articulation	1.82	High articulation of complex fields; highly differentiated, selective attention under difficult conditions.
V Constricted-Flexible Control	− .14	Average inhibition of irrelevant motoric responses, etc.
VI Spontaneity	− .92	Low in spontaneity; slow responses to inkblots and TAT pictures; literal, unimaginative TAT stories.

Harold's cautious compulsivity, his extreme literality and object-closeness, his lack of spontaneity, and his highly differentiated skill when required to attend selectively under difficult conditions were all apparent in these factor scores. The capacity to articulate fields is known (see Chapter 3) to be inherited (i.e., to be constitutional) to an important degree. His excellence in this area was compatible with his very good performance in the related subtests of the WISC (Picture Completion, Block Design, Object Assembly).

In combination, this arrangement of cognitive controls suggested that Harold as a preadolescent was an externalizer. He allowed little overt expression to his private thoughts and feelings. Rather, he focused intently on the world about him, in a way implying exaggerated carefulness, closeness to objects, and distance from persons. The general picture was one of inhibited, reality-bound caution, effective for practical purposes but lacking in freedom, spontaneity, and pleasure in the use of his cognitive skills. It seemed obvious, once again, that his limitations were products of the excessive use of defenses and controls that kept him closely attuned to events outside himself, but at the price of denying him access to his own unique reactions to his world, rigidifying his use of his intellectual assets, and bleaching his experience of enjoyment for its own sake. All in all, he seemed too serious, too careful, and too distrustful to be optimally comfortable, in spite of his valuable skills and his success in dealing with problems involving the objective features of external reality.

Behavior in the Clinical Testing Situation

The factor scores representing Harold's behavior in the clinical testing situation are presented below.

	Factor	*Score*	*Meaning*
I	Active Openness to New Experience	−2.16	Extreme closedness (withdrawal, lack of curiosity, rigidity, limited range of enjoyment, dependence, etc.).
II	Unity of Identity	.14	Average clarity of identity, identification with own sex, etc.
III	Accuracy of Reality Testing	.58	About average accuracy and clarity of perception, attention to fine details, adequacy of spatial orientation, etc.
IV	Cooperativeness	− .72	A bit low in task-involvement, frustration tolerance, cooperation with authority, enjoyment, warmth, etc.
V	Compulsive Exactness	−1.08	Low concern with goodness and badness, meticulosity, determination, stubbornness, etc.
VI	Sporadic Disruption of Control	−1.89	Low variability, fearfulness, observable tension, etc.

The limits imposed on Harold's curiosity, flexibility, and enjoyment by his generalized inhibitedness were most apparent at preadolescence in his score on Factor I. Although a steady, reliable performer (Factor VI), and although not greatly burdened by moralistic concerns, he was clearly unable to participate fully in the interpersonal relationship or to allow himself pleasure in the situation. With his good intellectual endowment, he might, if more flexibly organized, have actively enjoyed expressing the kinds of curiosity, explorativeness, and pleasure from which he is alienated.

Behavior in the Laboratory Testing Situation

Harold's scores on the four factors derived from ratings of the children's behavior during the laboratory tests are shown below.

	Factor	Score	Meaning
I	Impulsive Spontaneity	−1.66	Quite low in warmth, friendliness, talkativeness, spontaneity, etc.
II	Anxious Dependence	.06	Average.
III	Explorativeness	1.25	High in gross scanning, curiosity, drive toward mastery, openness to new experience, etc.
IV	Acting upon the Environment	−1.33	Generalized overcontrol.

Harold's generalized overcontrol, distance, and reserve were as apparent in these ratings as in the other blocks of data. Their reappearance in these laboratory ratings reinforced the impression that these traits, so evident in all the longitudinal material as well, were among those most firmly established and most pervasive in his preadolescent behavior.

His score on Factor III, Explorativeness, was in rather sharp contrast to other observations of him. Apparently, he appeared more curious and openly involved in the laboratory tests, which are more objective and which involve more motoric activity than the clinical tests. It may be, too, that he was less inhibited in respect to curiosity in the laboratory because the examiner was a man. In either case, there appeared to be notable situational variability in his capacity to express curiosity, and this variability seemed compatible, at least, with his emphasis on motor skills and on objective aspects of reality. He was freest when judging the sizes of objects, categorizing objects and persons (which he does in a notably objective way), employing his considerable skill at selective attention, and the like. He was much less comfortable when confronted with verbal tests and tests inviting him to express his own unique thoughts, feelings, and perceptual organizations in response to more ambiguous stimuli. He was quite clearly most comfortable in highly structured situations that allowed him to pursue undisturbed his bent toward the literal, verifiable, objective aspects of things outside himself.

Cognitive Style—Aspects of Over-all Ego Organization

Harold's factor scores on the six general factors extracted in the final analysis are shown below.

	Factor	Score	Meaning
I	Field-Articulation	2.22	High in field-articulation.
II	Spontaneity	1.63	Unspontaneous.
III	Maturity	− .31	About average.
IV	Adequacy of Reality Testing	−1.20	Sharpening, smooth over-all control over relatively long periods, accurate reality testing, etc.
V	Explorativeness	− .54	Tendency toward unexplorativeness, narrow categorizing, etc.
VI	Acting Out	−1.43	Catholic; low in acting out, etc.

Harold's score on the Field-Articulation factor was the third highest in the sample, indicating his unusual keenness at cognitive articulation of his experience. He was also relatively skillful, although less so, at preserving distinctions between sequential experiences. Adding to these two general characteristics of his over-all cognitive style the relatively literal, unimaginative, unexplorative, stimulus-bound stance reflected in his tendency toward narrow categorizing, one is impressed, from consideration of these three variables alone, with the rather cold, distant, "objective" orientation of this child toward the people and events around him. The other indications of overcontrol—his notable lack of spontaneity, and his notable inhibition of even acceptable forms of acting out or acting upon—could presumably be predicted from his narrow categorizing, high field-articulation, and sharpening tendencies. The other factor scores thus seemed to confirm the expected correlates of this constellation of cognitive controls. Harold is, in fact, one of those children who show most dramatically the relationship of a particular *constellation* of cognitive controls to other aspects of behavior. Harold's array of factor scores thus seemed to typify some of the predictable correlates of what Gardner *et al.* (1959) referred to as a "cognitive style." Gardner and his associates reserved this concept for combinations of cognitive variables, and assumed, as seems apparent here, that these combinations may have predictive value beyond that attributable to the nature of individual cognitive structures.

Summary of Preadolescent Findings

The affective and ideational inhibitions that have characterized Harold from his early years seemed at preadolescence to be more effectively integrated than before. Although he appeared notably freer and more differentiated in motoric than in verbal expressions, his somewhat distant stance was effectively organized as an "analytical" orientation toward verifiable aspects of reality outside himself. He was more confident of his adaptive skills and even readier to share his emotional reactions with others. A core of his effective and coherent, if somewhat inhibited and situationally restricted, integration at preadolescence was the strength of his compulsivity. His compulsive tendencies seemed essential to his effectiveness in solving certain kinds of adaptive problems and his limitations with respect to others.

Harold's history is particularly useful in that it exemplifies the combinations of adaptive strengths and limitations that characterize many children rated above average in over-all ego integrity. All, or nearly all, the structural characteristics that lend stability and coherence to ego organization also have limiting effects on other aspects of behavior. In the case of Harold, the strengths were evident, particularly at preadolescence, but the limitations on his potential self-actualization were also impressive. It should be kept in mind here that he was not judged highest in ego strength, even among the boys of the study, but was judged to be above average in this respect.

Harold's history points up several important questions that can be answered only by extensive studies of other kinds. Some of these concern the importance of a possible hereditary limitation of verbal and verbal-intellectual skills (in relation to his motoric excellence) and the nature of his interaction with his parents as determinants of the imbalance in his skills. On the one hand, the remarkable consistencies in his history could indicate some inbuilt limit on his verbal prowess. On the other hand, his parents' emphasis on action may have been a major determinant of Harold's development, both as a model for imitation and as a key variable in his interactions with them. The fact that his limitations have consistently impressed observers as linked to "self-protective" maneuvers suggests the potential importance of his mother's harsh and undifferentiated verbal directness and his father's affective distance and emphasis on motoric skills. If so, the most adaptively effective resolution for Harold, and one supported by what appeared to be an innate capacity for delaying motoric response, would seem to have been an over-all equilibration involving a relatively distant, outer-directed stance, with emphasis on analytic skills coupled with smoothly controlled motoric activity. Further understanding of the differential inheritance of skills could, however, refine such tentative formulations at some future time.

Ego Strength in a Complex Setting—The Case of Jane K.

Endowed with glowing physical health, high intelligence and beauty, and growing up in a gracious, comfortable environment without excessive pressures or conflicts, Jane K. probably experienced less pain and distress than most children. By preadolescence, she emerged as a poised, socially charming, and alert girl, who met life resourcefully and happily but with some reserve and mild underproductivity.

Jane's Environment

Jane is the younger of two girls born to intelligent, college educated, well-to-do parents who differed in several respects from most families in our sample. They were more aware of the scientific value of child study and willing to cooperate as a social responsibility. At the same time, they were unusually reserved about personal matters, so that relatively little was learned about their values and ideological backgrounds, or their personality structures. On the one hand, Mrs. K. thoughtfully and deliberately answered factual questions about Jane's development and showed considerable capacity to observe behavioral differences in her two children. However, she did not look below the surface for dynamic relationships or show the "intellectual curiosity that (in one observer's words) makes so many of our mothers stimulating people to talk to." She anticipated college training for her children not so much for the intellectual growth it would promote as for its social values. She wanted her children to learn to behave in socially appropriate ways and was concerned lest Jane become too willful, tempestuous, or spirited. She inculcated feelings of social obligation, with definite codes of correct, refined, mannerly, and controlled behavior which she evidently thought would coincide with high standards of good breeding.

At the time of the infancy observations, when Jane was twenty-four weeks old, Mrs. K. was an attractive, well-groomed woman in her late twenties. An air of "expensive simplicity and smart suitability" in her dress was matched by a gracious but deliberately reserved demeanor, which allowed her to say pleasantly but firmly of matters she considered too personal to share (such as her feelings about pregnancy and delivery), "I can't see that it has any bearing on this." Her composure was threatened only when she seemed to regret having been mildly derogatory in describing her older daughter, Caroline, as one prone to whine and fuss about minimal distress, in contrast to Jane's generally more placid behavior, marred only by occasional gross outbursts. She carefully reworded her statement about Caroline to account for her irritability in terms of an early asthmatic condition and to conform to the mother's apparent wish to see the older child as a model of perfect behavior. She took pains to phrase her subsequent comments more cautiously. The observers felt that note taking and prolonged silences made her vaguely self-conscious. One observer inferred that Mrs. K. was subject to "severe and often conscious feelings of anxiety and concern," which were only rarely exposed to view.

Mrs. K. was gentle and warm with Jane. She adapted her own tempo to that of the infant. "She did not engage in much bodily contact but she talked to her a great deal" and often whispered or gestured in ways which fostered closeness and provided reassurance. When she held the baby, she provided adequate support without hampering the infant's free movements. She did not force or rush the baby, but quietly stimulated her by offering numerous toys and by giving verbal approval. She obviously wanted to be relaxed, controlled, sweet, and patient, and behaved in this way so much of the time that it seemed to be her natural way with the infant.

We know less of the father, since he was very busy in an executive position and by choice remained in the background. He was described, on the few occasions when he was seen, as "ultra-polite and reserved," handsome, but "a little adolescent or perhaps not altogether masculine." Although economically comfortable, Mr. K. chose to advance himself by personal responsibility and hard work. He found time for daily play with his daughter and was appreciative of our interest in her. His play involved talking and laughing with Jane, entertaining her by whistling, and making a variety of noises which seemed to delight her thoroughly. He never took care of the child, perhaps because his wife was always available and free from the usual household chores.

The four-year-old sister often joined her father in playing with Jane. She enjoyed showering Jane with toys or holding her, a special privilege reserved for the regularly scheduled afternoon play periods. The mother was surprised and pleased to see no overt evidence of sibling rivalry and therefore comfortably assumed that there were no hidden feelings of jealousy. Apparently, she did not consider Caroline's mildly demanding, slightly rebellious behavior during the home interview as related to her feelings about the attention given the baby. However, she rebuked Caroline mildly, and firmly set a limit to the amount of disobedience she would tolerate.

The three homes in which the family lived were increasingly luxurious, although unpretentious and modest for people of their means. When Jane was almost three, the family moved from a new middle-class residential area on the outskirts of town to a slightly larger home on a quiet street in a settled neighborhood. When Jane was eleven, the family designed and built a large, beautiful home in a spacious residential area. Each home was very comfortable and furnished in exquisite taste by the sophisticated use of muted colors and handsomely finished woods. Each was spotlessly clean but had a lived-in appearance. Bookshelves were filled with popular and classical fiction, and current magazines were available on a coffee table. In each home, Jane had her own room and enjoyed considerable outdoor play space, where she was allowed to climb trees, to explore physically, and to raise numerous pets.

By the time Jane was four, her father had already become a successful businessman in his own right and her mother was stylishly slim and appeared to be more mature and comfortable than she had seemed earlier. She was also more casual in manner. As before, she carefully considered answers to questions, but was able to withhold personal information without any sign of tension. The family attended a large Protestant church quite regularly, but there was no great urgency or pressure on the children for piety. Piano, dancing, French, and riding lessons were given to both children, and Jane took special courses in art for several years.

Jane's Physical, Cognitive, and Emotional Development from Infancy to Preadolescence

The Early Years

At twenty-four weeks, Jane was a healthy, feminine-looking baby, who, despite very mobile facial features, was less active in general bodily movement than many babies and unusually pliant during the manipulations involved in caring for or examining her. Although vigorous and loud, her vocalizations were "relatively undifferentiated, consisting predominantly of rather throaty vowel sounds." She was capable of expressing feeling tones through changes in inflection and tempo. She was described by her mother as "just plain mad" when she could not get at her thumb or when a prolonged nap made her hungrier than usual and therefore less willing to wait for the preparation of food. On the other hand, Jane was content to sit for long periods in her teeter-babe, and did not protest when feeding was delayed in order to set up photographic equipment or fuss when toys dropped out of her hand. Thus, she was capable of protest, but was not irritable for extended periods. In other words, she was on the whole a placid baby, but one whose frustration-tolerance ranged from high in most situations to quite low on occasion. Her general placidity was seen as a product of low drive, of her mother's remarkable capacity to anticipate her bodily needs, and of minimal physical stress. We know, for example, that pregnancy was uncomplicated, that labor lasted only two hours, and that up to four years of age Jane had no serious illness or health problems. Colic was minimal. There were no gastrointestinal disturbances, and the baby accepted new foods readily. There were no problems with bowel or bladder training. Despite the mother's serious illness following a postpartum infection, Jane was breast fed for five and one-half months and was never separated from her mother except for numerous parental social activities during the child's later infancy and early childhood. A capable older woman employed as a sitter in the parents' absence was apparently entirely acceptable to Jane.

Psychological tests at twenty-four weeks showed that postural adjustments and fine motor coordination were advanced for her age, as were language and social responses. Her relatively low (for her) adaptive skills were seen by an observer as reflecting "a lack of interest in activities enjoyed by most children rather than a lack of capacity to perform. . . ." Other relevant comments by this observer were:

The most conspicuous aspect of her test behavior was the unusual delay between clear perception of a stimulus and response to it. . . . If one waited, however, she eventually reached, always with one hand, and in a very slow motion would grasp the object in question with impressive skill. . . . Thumb-sucking acted as a sort of screen against outside stimulation in that, while sucking, her eyes might be in the direction of another object but except for mildly regarding it, no response would be made. If the thumb were playfully removed or if one waited until she had herself ceased sucking, the same object would be responded to in the expected manner.

Jane was seen as "a rather sensitive yet placid baby" who possessed a "peculiar kind of self-sufficiency" so that she could be content with whatever objects were available without exerting a great deal of effort.

The Preschool Years

At about four years, Jane suffered from headaches and had recurrent temperatures of 102 to 103 degrees. Loss of appetite, facial pallor, and lack of energy were observed. These symptoms disappeared after her tonsils and adenoids were removed. Having been especially well prepared for the operation, Jane met the experience calmly.

In the examination with a pediatrician the following year, she was friendly, but somewhat self-conscious. She spoke in a staccato, sing-songy tone and laughed nervously. Although small for her age, she was well developed physically and in good general health. She adjusted well to nursery school and kindergarten, but seemed to prefer to play with boys and enjoyed vigorous outdoor games.

At four years, eleven months, Jane was viewed by a psychologist as a child of softly feminine beauty and good manners. Her movements were graceful. Her voice, although usually gentle and well modulated, like that of her mother, was at times raucous and gutteral, with a tomboy quality, suggesting some embarrassment in being observed, or conflict in expression of the aggression she appeared to avoid so carefully in projective tests and play sessions.

The projective tests further suggested conflict or lack of clarity about her role in her family or society. She enjoyed being the cute, charming baby of the family but felt pressures to conform that dimmed her capacity to enjoy her own lively and whimsical fantasies. She was cognitively alert and assured, but at the same time moderately socially remote and emotionally unspontaneous. Her smoothly effortless motor performance, her verbal fluency, her skill in counting and handling numbers, and her perceptual differentiation were impressive. One sensed that her performance was dampened slightly by her own efforts to meet her family's high standards of correct behavior. As another observer stated, "She feels free to be child-like only when the situation is structured clearly and recognizably—when she knows 'what is done' or what is expected, and whether her responses will be acceptable. . . . This difficulty increases the more emotionally stimulating situations are and the more unstructured they are."

Her preschool Rorschach responses demonstrated "precise reality testing" and an "effective capacity for distinction of fantasy from reality," but also suggested generalized "repression as a characteristic coping mode with a likelihood of impulsive break through," probably appearing in the form of minor naughtiness, teasing or occasional temper outbursts. Although limited in spontaneity, she appeared to be "normal, sound, and undisturbed." She was a deliberate child who carefully controlled her movement into new situations. Her feelings appeared appropriate but controlled, a fact which contributed to her outward poise.

CAT stories of the same period implied mild discomfort in relating to her parents. She sometimes did not understand her mother or felt slightly misunderstood by her in the sense that standards of behavior were experienced as somewhat arbitrary and personally discriminatory.

She engaged in teasing interactions with her father and enjoyed the role of the playful, attractive, admired little child. She recognized that he could be stern and punitive, but without lingering hostility. The immaturity of this relationship suggested avoidance of Oedipal problems.

With her peers in a party situation, she was initially slow to interact, apparently needing time to appraise the situation. She rarely initiated an activity but enriched the activities of others in an especially effective way, as though she, after absorbing the emotional climate, was able to follow the leaders in a manner which gave her pleasure and provided support to others. Although not completely at ease, she was never completely immobilized.

The Latency Years

As at preschool, her test scores at seven and a half years reflected superior cognitive resources. She mobilized motor skills with effortless grace. The WISC performance IQ of 129 appeared consistent with the preschool Stanford Binet IQ of 132 and the latency Stanford Binet IQ of 130. Verbally, she was fluent, precise, and capable of using language in a differentiated fashion. She was less adequate with arithmetic and rote memory for digits, and it was largely her deficit in these areas that gave her a verbal IQ of 116 and brought full-scale WISC IQ down to 125. She looked ahead to plan what she would do and say in responding to the tests. Her information and interest, although broad, were not outstanding for one of her superior intellectual level. She learned readily and was capable of taking in and integrating numerous cues in her environment. She did so at a leisurely pace, without pressure or a strong desire to achieve.

A notable change occurred in Jane's performance on verbal subtests of the WISC from preschool to latency. Her WISC Verbal IQ, which was 103 at age 4–11, jumped to 116 at age 7–5. Her performance IQ remained at 129. This increase in verbal subtest scores in latency is made more intriguing by the return of Jane's Verbal IQ to the preschool level (103) in the preadolescent testing at age 11–8.

Jane's casual, ladylike poise appeared to be a more integrated, comfortable part of her personality than in her preschool years. Latent aggression was less obvious and her earlier nervous speech mannerisms appeared only in occasional tenseness of the voice or in somewhat inappropriate, self-conscious giggles. She was moderately enthusiastic about structured tests and definitely resourceful and self-assured in handling test demands. Her polite social distance seemed to imply the expectation that most experiences would be "right and convenient" for her.

The psychiatrist who saw her at about the same time noted that she took her time in getting acquainted with the situation and then worked systematically, staying alert to her environment, but not unduly so. Although she was capable of imaginative play, she was more likely to remain concrete in her thinking. She grumbled mildly about her mother and sister, but appeared "to have no difficulty in doing what was expected of her even though she resented it somewhat. At the same time, she seemed to have the capacity to enjoy herself fairly adequately." There were "some remnants of hostility towards her mother and feelings of deprivation from her, which probably carry over from unresolved aspects of the Oedipal conflicts, which, however, seems to be not unusually marked in degree." She reported turning to her mother when others teased her, but also enjoyed rebelling mildly, e.g., by wearing nail polish, of which her mother disapproved. She apparently experienced her father as more generous and kind, yet she was not much interested in his work or other activities. The psychiatrist felt that she was "pretty well balanced in all spheres." She was outgoing and friendly, yet somewhat cautious. She was not really inhibited, but lacked the sparkle of some children. There seemed to be no evidence of overly severe training, or excessive reaction formation. Usually, she could handle the mild difficulty she experienced in family relationships by talking it out, by mild denial, or by occasional projection or substitution.

Summary of Findings Through Latency

Reviewing the findings on Jane from infancy through latency, we are impressed with the general balance and stability of her behavior. As an infant, she was considered to be alert and sensitive, yet placid and with mild drive. She was capable of vigorous protest, but she was not irritable. At preschool and latency, she was seen as a capable, effective child, but one without strong achievement drive. Her unusually smooth motor functioning and her verbal fluency (which seemed to persist in spite of the shifts in Verbal IQ) contributed to an impression of an unhurried, logical, systematic, and practical child. Mild problems in family relationships were handled with resilience and resourcefulness. The raucous soundeffects of her preschool years diminished in latency, although her voice was at times tense and punctuated by giggles. Her poise and selfconfidence in dealing with tests were presumably related to her high intelligence and the minimal amount of stress she had experienced. Her strain in relating to people was of less obvious origin, although it resembled the slight self-consciousness and reserve observed in her mother and perhaps reflected mild internal tension around the mother's pressures to be ladylike. It was not severe enough to produce any major disintegrative reactions.

Jane at Preadolescence

At preadolescence (11-8), Jane's observed behavior was generally compatible with that seen at age 7-5, although there were signs of moderately increased tension. By this time, she was an unusually lovely child with radiant good health and a casual friendly manner which was entirely ladylike, although characteristically reserved. She volunteered little information about herself but willingly answered factual questions in considerable detail. She reported that school was relatively pleasant, particularly physical education and art. Her limited achievement drive was reflected in consistently average grades in most subjects, in contrast to her superior ability on tests. She did poorly in arithmetic. She spoke fondly of square dancing, swimming, and riding, as well as walks in the wooded area around her home, where she could watch squirrels and birds, catch frogs, and swing on the wild grapevines.

Defense Mechanisms and General Characteristics of Ego Functioning

The ratings of Jane's defense mechanisms and general ego characteristics at preadolescence are presented below.

Rating Variable	Rating
Ego Strength	7
Over-all Ego Autonomy	5

Repression	5
Isolation	3
Reaction Formation	3
Projection	3
Avoidance	4
Denial	4
Acting Out–Overcontrol	8

On the basis of her performance in the Rorschach, TAT, and WISC, Jane's employment of the specific defenses rated was judged average or less with respect to the entire sample. Her rather low ratings on isolation and reaction formation reflected her relatively limited verbal performance, her lack of obsessive-compulsive tendencies, and the absence of intellectualizing in her responses. Her approximately average rating on repression and her below-average ratings on avoidance and denial, plus her very high rating on overcontrol, thus represented a rather striking paradox in the light of the gross discrepancy between her prepuberty Verbal IQ (103) and her Performance IQ (131) on the WISC. In the absence of particular types of brain damage, a discrepancy of this magnitude is ordinarily associated with (a) remarkably strong and pervasive repression or (b) unusually strong tendencies toward acting out. In view of the stability of Jane's Performance IQ (129 at preschool, 129 at latency, 131 at preadolescence) and the unusual variability of her Verbal IQ (103 at preschool, 116 at latency, 103 at preadolescence), this apparent inconsistency in her test performances (and in the ratings themselves) is worthy of special consideration. It is this sort of contrast that is often most revealing of a unique pattern of personality organization.

The rater, who carefully considered the gross Verbal-Performance discrepancy in assessing these variables, felt that the predominantly motoric orientation indicated by her much higher scores on Performance tests was latently present but was actively overcontrolled in her responses to the Rorschach and TAT. The overcontrol was of a kind suggesting diametric opposition between the more basic patterning of her behavior and the more superficial, learned role of the dignified, self-controlled, feminine, and ladylike child. It could be speculated that pursuance of this role was at its height in latency, and that an all but determined attempt to fulfill this role (which has direct counterparts in the mother's behavior) was one of the determinants of her greater carefulness with verbal expression, including response to the Verbal subtests of the WISC. Detailed examination of the preadolescent WISC protocol suggested that she was both less involved and less painstaking in responding to the Verbal subtests at that time. Although her erratic errors in the Information and Vocabulary subtests at preadolescence could have been attributed to a heightening of repression, it seemed equally likely that her basic verbal capacity had changed less than her IQ scores themselves. The paradox in Jane's personality organization seemed, then, to reside in the contrast between her considerable interest and skill in motoric behavior (with its suggestions of a tomboyish orientation, its reverberations of her earlier interest in animals, her dream of becoming a veterinarian, her expressed pleasure in outdoor activities, and so forth) and her effortfully overcontrolled, self-consciously proper appearance when relating herself to adults. The impressive fact was (and this fact has relevance for overly stereotyped conceptions of necessary conditions for ego strength) that this paradox led to no apparent disruption of her behavior, no crippling anxieties, no confusion or unclarity of conscious thought. Her rating on over-all ego autonomy, like the independent observations of her in the clinic and laboratory, was intended to represent the general balance of autonomy she maintains. Her low rating on projection and her excellent rating on ego strength (although exceeded by a small number of other children) were intended to represent the pervasive picture of cognitive, affective, and interpersonal integrity, flexibility, fluency, and adaptive effectiveness of her test performances, in spite of the indications of generalized overcontrol.

Intellectual Abilities

Jane's subtest and IQ scores for the WISC are presented below. The subtest scores are corrected for age.

Information	10
Comprehension	13
Arithmetic	9
Similarities	15
Vocabulary	10
Digit Span	5
Picture Completion	17
Picture Arrangement	17
Block Design	14
Object Assembly	11
Coding (B)	13
Verbal IQ	103
Performance IQ	131
Full Scale IQ	117

As noted above, the most impressive feature of Jane's performance in the WISC was the great discrepancy between her average-level Verbal IQ (103) and her superior-level Performance IQ (131). Yet, these IQ scores were essentially identical with her WISC scores at the preschool age (4–11). The fluctuation in Verbal IQ from preschool to latency to preadolescence (103 to 116 to 103) was an intriguing fact of direct relevance to understanding of the gross Verbal-Performance disparity at preadolescence. Examination of her scaled subtest scores (i.e., her scores corrected for age) at ages 7–5 and 11–8 revealed that her Vocabulary score dropped a dramatic six points. Her Comprehension and Digit Span scores dropped four and three points, her Information score two points. Her relatively low score on Arithmetic was equal in the two testings. Her Similarities score was one point higher at preadolescence.

Here, then, is a child who has shown notable variability in verbal subtests, particularly Vocabulary, which is often thought to sample the most stable area of intellectual functioning. As indicated earlier, these fluctuations in test scores appeared, at least, to be dramatic evidences of shifts in the balance of motoric versus more ladylike orientation during her development from preschool age to preadolescence, rather than profound changes in defense employment or basic changes in verbal ability.

Cognitive Controls

The notable contrasts in Jane's behavior seemed apparent, in less dramatic form, in the cognitive control measures. Her highest factor scores suggested (a) that she was given to a rather high degree of spontaneous conceptual differentiation, with the associated stimulus-boundness, literality in storytelling, and so forth, and (b) that she responded to the Rorschach and TAT stimuli quickly and fluently (and, as noted earlier, without indications of uncontrolled impulsivity). She was also more capable than the average child of inhibiting irrelevant motoric responses in the Color-Word Test.

Jane's other factor scores were close to the average of the total sample, indicating adequate, conventional responses to the various procedures involved.

	Factor	Score	Meaning
I	Scanning A	.07	Average checking of judgments in size estimation tests.
II	Conceptual Differentiation	1.40	Rather high spontaneous differ-

entiation (many small groups in the sorting tests; literal "stimulus-bound" approach to the TAT, etc.).

III	Scanning B	— .64	Slight tendency toward relatively great scanning of size estimation stimuli during judgments.
IV	Field-Articulation	— .42	Slightly less than average articulation of complex fields.
V	Constricted-Flexible Control	— .85	More than average difficulty in inhibiting irrelevant vocalizations in the Color-Word Test, etc.
VI	Spontaneity	1.19	Rather high in spontaneity in the form of relatively short Rorschach and TAT reaction times, etc.

Behavior in the Clinical Testing Situation

Jane's cognitive clarity, both with respect to her own identity and her over-all perception of the world about her, was reminiscent of the rather high ego strength rating discussed earlier. Her low score on the Cooperativeness factor, which sharpens our view of her behavior toward the female clinical tester, seemed to reflect her generalized reserve and her overcontrol, which apparently also limited her openness and curiosity to a level below what might be expected on the basis of her total IQ of 117.

	Factor	*Score*	*Meaning*
I	Active Openness to New Experience	— .05	Average.
II	Unity of Identity	1.61	Rather high in clarity of identity, identification with own sex, pleasure in own body, trust, etc.
III	Accuracy of Reality Testing	.70	Somewhat higher than average in clarity and accuracy of perception, attention to fine detail, adequacy of spatial orientation, etc.
IV	Cooperativeness	−1.35	Rather low in task-involvement, frustration tolerance, cooperation with authority, enjoyment, warmth, etc.
V	Compulsive Exactness	— .37	Slightly lower than average in

concern with goodness and badness and in meticulosity, determination, stubbornness, etc.

VI Sporadic Disruption of   .10   Average.
     Control

In the light of her response to the WISC Verbal and Performance
subtests, her lack of morally toned compulsivity and the absence of gross
disruptions of control during the clinical tests were important additions to
the other observations presented earlier.

Behavior in the Laboratory Testing Situation

Although only average, Jane's score on the Spontaneity factor indicated that she was experienced as more open and spontaneous in the
laboratory, with a male examiner, than in the clinical testing session.
Perhaps this fact was in part attributable to the acceptable outlet the
laboratory tests provide for the bent toward motoric activity we have
assumed to be an essential part of Jane's personality organization. The
novelty, brevity, and variety of the laboratory tests may also have
contributed to this apparent difference in her behavior. Her unusual
degree of generalized overcontrol also seemed reduced to an average level
in the laboratory, as indicated by her average score on the Acting upon
the Environment factor.

Jane's higher than average confidence and personal autonomy and
her limited expressions of curiosity and achievement drive were more
highly compatible with the other observations discussed earlier.

	Factor	Score	Meaning
I	Impulsive Spontaneity	.47	Slightly higher than average in warmth, friendliness, talkativeness, spontaneity, etc.
II	Anxious Dependence	−.90	Rather high in confidence in own abilities, independence, etc.
III	Explorativeness	−.95	Rather low in scanning, curiosity, drive toward mastery, openness to new experience, etc.
IV	Acting upon the Environment	.22	Average.

Cognitive Style—Aspects of Over-all Ego Organization

Jane's factor scores for the six general factors representing over-all
characteristics of the children's ego organizations showed again her gen-

eral adequacy of functioning, her cognitive clarity and generally excellent reality testing, and the contrast between her action-orientation and her superficial overcontrol.

	Factor	Score	Meaning
I	Field-Articulation	— .08	Average.
II	Spontaneity	— .45	Tendency toward spontaneity, openness, cooperativeness.
III	Maturity	.98	Somewhat high in age, comfortable independence, ego strength and autonomy, etc.
IV	Adequacy of Reality Testing	—1.07	Sharpening, smooth over-all control over relatively long periods, accurate reality testing, etc.
V	Explorativeness	— .99	Somewhat low in explorativeness; tendency toward narrow categorizing, etc.
VI	Acting Out	.82	Protestant; tendency toward action-orientation, etc.

It is impressive that Jane's considerable strengths did not depend upon unusual excellence in the capacity to articulate experience or in unusual differentiation in other areas of intellectual functioning. Except for the clarity with which she preserved distinctions between sequential experiences (i.e., her sharpening tendency) and her general adequacy of reality testing and gross control, she was in no way unusual with respect to these general dimensions of ego organization. With the exception of her score on the Leveling-Sharpening factor, her scores were, in fact, clustered rather closely around the averages for the sixty children.

Her score on Factor III, which involves age, ego strength and autonomy, and the like, was perhaps slightly more attributable to her ego strength and autonomy than to her age per se. She was less than half a year older than the average of the sixty children at the time she was tested.

Summary of Preadolescent Findings

In spite of the notable contrast between her enduring interests and articulated skills in motoric behavior versus thoughts and words, and her somewhat strained efforts to behave in a proper and ladylike manner, Jane at preadolescence seemed clear-headed, effectively independent, confident, and generally well adjusted. Although apparently an "externalizer" (i.e., relatively unobsessive and unintrospective), she was given neither to excessive projection nor to inappropriate acting out.

Such a mixture of over-all behavioral patternings obviously raises the question of possible discrepancies between her responses to adult examiners in testing situations and her behavior in other settings. Perhaps the presumed interest in motor activity found expression in the quality of her play activities, her orientation toward boys, or the tree-climbing and related outdoor activities she refers to. Perhaps the overcontrolled role of the "proper young lady" was most apparent in her interactions with those adults she perceived as expecting her to play this role. Perhaps, as the differences between the clinical and laboratory ratings suggest, this learned role, which the mother represented in a variety of ways, was more apparent in relationships with female than male adults, or was most evident in situations such as the Rorschach and Thematic Apperception Tests, in which verbal expressions are the only acceptable interpersonal currency.

One wonders, too, about the balance between the internalized models of father and mother as a determinant of the paradox that seems woven into her personality organization at preadolescence.

Jane's basic confidence in her capabilities and the apparent flexibility with which she expressed the two major aspects of her life-orientation were consistent with the high ratings of ego strength, as assessed on the basis of structured and projective tests given in the preadolescent years. The potentiality for increased conflict with the usual adolescent pressures was present, but not of serious proportions at that time.

Jane's history is one that points up most sharply the potential value of simultaneous comprehensive studies of the personality organizations of mother, father, and child, plus major features of their interaction. Detailed knowledge of the parents as imitative models, their similarities and differences, could be especially valuable in such instances. Thoroughgoing consideration of hereditary factors may also be uniquely important in such cases. It is quite possible, for example, that Jane's hereditary potential in the area of verbal skills was less than her innate potential for excellence in motor and visual-motor activities. One current study that provides for simultaneous assessment of parental personality organizations, familial characteristics, hereditary factors, and related variables as determinants of children's personality organizations is described in Chapter 15. Jane typifies one group of children whose performances in the present study reinforced the impression that more comprehensive studies of parents and children should be performed.

14 Case Studies of Selected Children— A Boy and Girl Low in Ego Strength

THE CHILDREN whose histories are described in this chapter exemplify two of the ways in which notable ego weaknesses evolved in the development of some of the children included in the study. In both cases, physical difficulties added significantly to the normal stresses of development and were undoubtedly important contributors to these children's apparent ego weakness at preadolescence.

Ego Weakness with Sensory Deficit—The Case of Gene A.

A child with some marked congenital and acquired sensory deficits which led to numerous difficulties and frustrations in learning, as well as accentuation of dependency and identification problems, Gene A. showed both unusual strengths and weaknesses in coping with a highly supporting, but at times peculiarly stressful, environment.

Gene's Environment

Gene was much wanted and loved by both parents. Yet, his mother's affection and pride, along with high aspirations, were mixed with doubts and anxieties, apparent even when Gene was first seen at four weeks of age. Prizing his neonatal health and sturdiness, contrasting him with less well-developed children she had seen, she was already planning to set aside funds to send the child to college. Nor would she be satisfied with the modest vocational aspirations of the father if Gene could be "something better." When Gene was five months old, she instigated a move from an inconvenient and cramped home to a bright, modern, two-bedroom home.

For some, Gene's early infancy home might have been quite desirable, since it was located close to relatives who were available for advice and help. But both Mrs. A. and her husband tried, in a variety of ways, to be independent of their families. For example, they never relied on the available and willing relatives as baby sitters, rarely allowed Gene to stay overnight alone with the grandparents, and were more likely to consult a doctor for advice than a family member. The mother's independence was also apparent in her selectivity in the use of child-care reading. She rejected breast feeding, avowedly because of difficulties she had with her first child and because she felt bottle feeding was more convenient and less time-consuming, but she did not rigidly schedule Gene's feedings as she had done with her daughter. Her independence was partly a function of some strong feelings, such as her fears of the use of sleeping bags for the children or the practice of tossing children in the air, or her anxieties over possible thumb-sucking, or left-handedness. Her independence probably also stemmed from her image of her mother's strengths in overcoming poverty, as well as her own success at self-improvement.

At the time of the infancy contact and later, Gene's mother showed considerable taste in her selection of simple clothing with good lines and color well adapted to her trim figure and her dark blond complexion. Despite a somewhat stressful and insecure childhood, she had acquired a little specialized education which she proposed to use to promote the economic security of her family. Following the birth of her first child, Mrs. A. worked as secretary to a surgeon. She was proud of her work and hoped to acquire further training to implement her opinion that "every woman should be able to support herself."

Mr. A. shared his wife's pride in his son and her view that his family should be independent of Gene's grandparents. He was, however, less overtly anxious and less concerned than his wife about bettering his own vocational status. A tall, good-looking man, strongly masculine in appearance and manner, Mr. A. was naturally outgoing and friendly with people of all ages and stations. He was also said to be less likely than his wife to plan ahead for current or future activities.

Mrs. A. was gentle, warm, unhurried, and skillful with the baby. She appeared to have a good deal of empathy for his moods and feelings and was alert to his minor discomforts, which she often alleviated by patting or holding him. She attempted to be flexible about his schedule, but emphasized that everything should be "regular and normal." She seemed to encourage independence (such as managing a propped bottle at the 6:00 A.M. feeding), yet she expected that as he grew older he would "mind" and be well behaved, as she also expected her daughter to be. Usually, Mrs. A. felt that she was able to control both children's behavior by a simple word or gesture, but she could tolerate the idea of spanking to terminate behavior she considered inappropriate.

Like his wife, Mr. A. gave baby Gene a good deal of love and attention and was extremely proud of his son's sturdiness and apparent independence. Both parents were pleased that the infant showed some signs of the paternal family temper and was able to express a preference for being held in upright positions in which he could look about. His mother commented, "But of course nobody could get away with holding Gene in any other way than as he liked."

Gene's sister, four years his senior, was a large, sturdy child who was friendly with observers and probably would have engaged in considerable conversation had the mother not silenced her. She was said to like to hold the baby, but was seen on several occasions to observe him with an air of indifference when observers primarily concerned with the baby were present. Mrs. A. felt that Gene's birth had been difficult for her daughter since so much attention, particularly by the paternal grandparents, was given their first grandson, and since the girl and her parents had lived with these grandparents in her own early infancy. Mrs. A. felt that the sister had been more demanding since Gene's birth and that her capacity to play alone was seriously diminished.

Gene's larger family included a maternal aunt and her family, as well as the two sets of grandparents. In spite of his parents' wish to be independent, Gene's paternal grandparents played an unusually important role in his early life. They were devoted to him, visited nearly every day, and, to Mrs. A.'s regret, showered both children with gum and candy. Like his son, the elder Mr. A. appeared to be a jovial, friendly man, who was later said to be the most effective of Gene's disciplinarians. Gene so admired his grandfather that he wanted to be just like him. Although exceedingly fond of the baby, the paternal grandmother was somewhat stiff and anxious with Gene. A nature lover, she taught Gene to love and feel close to plants and animals.

Relatively little information is available in early records concerning the maternal grandparents, except that they lived on the outskirts of the city, where they kept a few animals, such as a pig, chickens, and a saddle pony. The children visited the farm quite frequently with their parents, but they were not in daily contact with these grandparents.

In accord with her Protestant background, Mrs. A. enrolled the older sister in Sunday School and frequently went to church with her. After Gene's birth, attendance was irregular, but Mrs. A. expressed the wish to renew regular church habits when Gene was older, implying that church-going was helpful and natural, rather than mandatory. Apparently, her husband felt less strongly about church attendance, but sometimes joined the family.

More attractive and convenient, the new home, to which Gene's family moved when he was five months, also offered more but not always agreeable play opportunities for the children. As they grew older, a bedroom shared by brother and sister was furnished with a trundle bed, giving a small play area during the day and separate shelves for each child's toys and books. However, Gene tended to show little respect for his sister's toys and was quite proprietary about his own toys. He rarely wanted to play alone. He preferred to be outdoors where he could run or climb, play in a sandbox, or ride his tractor. Playmates were not entirely compatible, since Gene was overbearing with a younger child in the neighborhood and not very successful in handling the aggressive displays of several older children. At one point, he was kept apart from neighborhood children following an explosive altercation during which he was mildly injured.

Though always loving and loved, Gene's mischievous experimenting (such as running off to explore or trying out the hose on the living room rug) and his mother's difficulties in "convincing" him of the necessity of certain prohibitions kept his interaction with his mother at a high pitch a good deal of the time. He was more responsive to discipline from his father and more likely to obey his adored paternal grandfather.

Though the irregularity of Mr. A.'s working hours limited family activities to some extent, the A. family shared a number of recreational pleasures and each parent engaged in some individual activities. As a group, the family enjoyed short trips in their car, along with boating, picnicking, and visiting. Mr. A. liked to fish and hunt and Mrs. A. enjoyed reading, but neither found time to do as much as they liked. Both parents enjoyed being outdoors and attending sports events, which activities they planned to share with the children as soon as they were old enough. In a gregarious family, numerous friends and acquaintances were in and out of the home.

Gene's Physical, Cognitive, and Emotional Development from Infancy to Preadolescence

The Early Years

At four weeks, Gene was a healthy, well-nourished baby who ate greedily and noisily and whose lower jaw quivered in anticipation of the bottle. His well developed, sturdy body and large hands gave him a decidedly masculine appearance. He slept a good deal during the observation period, but when he was awake, his hands and feet were always moving and at times he seemed to quiver all over. Though he seemed interested in looking at and seeing everything, he appeared to be more interested in people than things. Like many babies of this age, he did not yet follow people visually. He smiled broadly in response to observers' smiles, but did not vocalize as he did when his mother held him. He began to cry twice when observers were holding him. He seemed especially sensitive to touch, which was apparently experienced both pleasurably and unpleasurably. For example, he could be soothed by his mother's holding, patting, or gently rubbing him. On the other hand, he flushed deeply when crying, was subject to mild heat rash, and showed a tendency toward slow-healing skin irritations.

Although the observers were not aware of it in his infancy, Gene was born with a loss of central vision in the left eye. Psychological tests at that time suggested better than average development.

In retrospect, the infancy data told us much about Gene's vulnerabilities and strengths. Although he was alert and sturdy, it seemed possible that he would experience learning difficulties and frustrations because of his poor vision; that he might be overwhelmed by excessive contact or affective stimulation; that he could easily have inherited or learned some impulsive behavior patterns from his father and certain anxieties and tendencies toward denial and avoidance from his mother. Furthermore, a child apparently as sensitive to people as Gene must have been aware of parental conflict in relation to plans for economic security. On the positive side, we saw the basis for a good deal of self-respect and security in the love and expressive warmth of both parents.

As a footnote to the infancy picture, we should point out that Gene's first year of life, as reported by the mother, was not complicated by ill health and that his motor development was normal. He was reported to have sat alone at seven months, crawled at eight months, and walked alone at eleven months. At nine months he was said to be tongue-tied and his tongue was clipped.

In several areas, Gene's development appeared to be within an average range but was slow in some respects. Bowel control was established at fourteen months, but he was not dry during the day until eighteen to twenty-four months. Nocturnal control was not established until he was three years old. Verbalization was indistinct and delayed. Single words were not comprehensible until two and a half years, and he did not use sentences until three years.

Beginning in his second year, Gene experienced considerable stress from repeated illnesses and his mother's absence on a full-time job. Following an accident, he had repeated ear infections requiring many penicillin shots and several courses of antibiotics. The left eardrum was lanced twice, the right eardrum once. Temporary hearing impairment was severe, but there was no permanent hearing loss. During his preschool years, Gene was particularly susceptible to colds, which were accompanied by hoarseness and spasmodic croup. Systemic infections also affected the left eye, leaving permanent scar tissue. At two years, he had German measles and at two and a half, a particularly severe case of chicken pox. With each illness, he had high temperatures but recovered quite rapidly.

Despite Gene's physical difficulties, his mother worked during most of Gene's second and early third years. Then, on the advice of her physician, she quit work following a period of the baby's demanding, clinging behavior, in which speech was developing very slowly.

The Preschool Years

When seen at age three and a half, Gene was a chubby, sturdily built child who initially reacted to new people and things with some hesitation and caution but soon became direct, assertive, energetic, and outgoing. There was a quality of bumbling impatience in his manner and holistic vagueness in his visual focusing. His verbal articulation was infantile, his grammatical constructions primitive, and his vocabulary limited. He was impulsive and awkward. His movements came in bursts, alternating with limp relaxation. His balance was steady at times, but at other times he tripped and stumbled. Clumsiness was most noticeable in his immature palmar grasp and his inability to control his fingers effectively for paper-cutting, drawing, or eating. His impulsiveness appeared in his rough handling of toys, in his careless trial and error with puzzles, and in his cursory survey of situations and objects.

There was a quality of intensity or urgency about pleasurable experiencing which sometimes led to emotional flooding and interfered with sustained effort. He seemed to be struggling to overcome the discrepancy between his eagerness to communicate and his infantile speech, and between his need to explore and understand and his motoric clumsiness and limited perceptual skills. In response to these frustrations, his play was often monotonous or repetitive, and he became periodically exhausted.

As might be expected, both Gene's general behavior and his performance in highly structured test procedures mirrored these struggles and conflicts. Not really interested in the intellectual challenge of the tests, Gene responded to the examiner's requests with such erratic attention and effort that his low average IQ (93) was obviously an underestimate of his potential ability. Occasional persistence was short-lived. He was impulsive and easily frustrated if not immediately successful. Verbal tests were especially frustrating to him because of the motoric inactivity involved, as well as because of his verbal inadequacy. His remark, "I can't . . . because I don't want to," seemed to express his mood and a certain defensiveness about recognizing the degree of his handicaps. Still, he was alert and curious and could be intensely interested for short periods.

Initially, he delayed leaving his mother by a series of potentially acceptable requests for reassurance, followed by tearfulness and falling. Once he maneuvered her into accompanying him, however, he became increasingly independent of her and made it clear that he resented her intrusion on his autonomy. Once, when his mother brought him bodily back to the testing table, he flushed, talked loudly, and swung his limbs.

These observations were consistent with his mother's reports of his behavior at home during this period. She described him as a strong-willed, determined child for whom "fences and cupboards and high shelves seem only a challenge." He wanted to find out things for himself and was not satisfied with superficial reasons for prohibitions. After running off to a nearby school yard, for example, he told her, "I just got to." She described him as a child who was not deliberately naughty, but whose activity and curiosity led him into running off to explore, into explosive contacts with other children, and property destruction when his excitement overrode his usual care with things. He could not be quieted in church and was asked to stay out of Sunday School for a time. All of this led to some emotional turmoil for both mother and child.

Gene slept long hours and ate ravenously. His mother sometimes felt at her wits end when he bickered constantly with his sister and could not be trusted when alone. Yet he was a lovable and affectionate little boy who was gregariously involved in everything that happened in his neighborhood. He liked people of all ages and expected respect and consideration in return for his own thoughtfulness of their wishes or preferences. He was sometimes quite generous. His mother felt, however, that sharing, particularly with his sister, was difficult for him.

For Gene, life was exciting, but also very threatening, since it was so easy to be hurt or to let his impulses run away with him. It appeared particularly frustrating for him to want so much to see and do while handicapped by illnesses, poor vision, and motor awkwardness, determined in part by his visual handicap.

Five months later, at the age of four, Gene was seen by several of the longitudinal study staff. At that time, his puppy-like ebullience was less prominent. He was not defeated, but seemed less confident, perhaps a partial result of multiple family mishaps, including his mother's miscarriage, his own renewed eye infection, and several minor accidents (one involving temporary unconsciousness and another requiring stitches).

A CAT examination with a male psychologist seemed particularly distasteful. It was clear, for example, that he was attracted to the microphone, but he insisted that it be held at some distance from his mouth. He repeatedly verbalized a wish to terminate the session and was distinctly aware of his own expressive difficulties. He may have experienced the examiner's failure to understand him as a form of criticism, since he was quite aware of his parents' concern about the immaturity of his speech. His tensions were expressed in his limp, loose-jointed gait, erratic pouncing movements with his hands tensely outspread, a frequent need for urination, and rapid, shallow breathing. Misidentification of the animal pictures apparently was related to poverty of vocabulary and to lack of conceptual skill, leading to gross concretization.

In the face of his considerable difficulties, Gene's efforts were at times ingenious and serviceable. For example, he sometimes sought to identify and differentiate form and essence in terms of color and movement. When he was not understood, he often forced the observer to choose the appropriate meanings from several offered alternate possibilities. Definiteness in stating requests and wishes gave him a feeling of status and integrity, but he could as easily allow himself to be delayed, almost as though he welcomed external control and invited help to clarify his own confusion. Avoidance, though present, was not so much a function of unwillingness as of inability to respond when he was confused.

He responded at a relatively concrete, descriptive level, with limited integration of what he perceived in terms of feelings and behavioral consequences. His short attention span and lack of deep involvement were more marked than average for his age, even when his expressive difficulties were taken into consideration.

Shortly before Gene's fourth birthday, the family moved to another community. This move may have been dictated by the mother's pressure on the father to obtain a higher-paying job with regular hours. Apparently, the father found his new job monotonous, and there was a period when family plans were very indefinite. Mr. A. kept exploring possibilities for different vocations, and Mrs. A. was determined that the father stay with the job, or at least not return to his preferred work, with its lower salary and more irregular hours. During this time, Mrs. A. expressed exasperation with Gene's inability to "conform" to her standards of neatness and his constant activity and destructiveness. Along with this, she experienced considerable anxiety about Gene's continued infections and his resistance to going to kindergarten.

In addition to the numerous body stresses, Gene experienced both love and exasperation from his mother, a number of rebuffs from peers, and some unpleasant altercations with his sister during his preschool years. Nonetheless, his occasional aggressive outbursts were often balanced by such warmth and empathy concerning other people that he never was entirely without friends or affection. Along with his own conflicts and struggles, he was apparently quite aware of parental friction about how best to deal with his problems (the parents disagreed, for example, as to whether Gene should be temporarily removed from kindergarten) and about the father's occupational choice. These pressures apparently continued for some time after the move.

About a year after the first structured tests, a retest (at age four years, seven months) showed a constant IQ (95), but suggested considerable social and emotional growth despite a series of physical traumata. In this retest, Gene was far more businesslike. He was steadily attentive, interested, even eager to participate. Random exploration was diminished, and he was far more ready to seek and use assistance. He was also gayer than he had been immediately before the family move. For example, he showed off a number of "magic" tricks with a good deal of dramatic flair. Vocabulary and verbal concepts were closer to age adequacy, but it was apparent that he perceived more than he could easily report. Coordination was somewhat improved, but he was still awkward.

Entering kindergarten posed special learning problems, since Gene could not see or hear well enough to keep up with his class. He was frequently frustrated and unhappy, as was indicated by his returning home from school several times each week. On these occasions, his mother had to return him to school and force him to stay. These experiences were clearly fraught with impatience and irritability on the part of both mother and son.

At age 5–7, a third examination showed an improvement in total intellectual functioning. His Stanford Binet mental age was 6–8, his IQ 119, 24 points higher than at 4–7. He was as friendly and responsive as ever, but was under more pressure to see and hear everything. He had developed more tolerance for laborious explanations when he could not be understood. His speech was more complex but was still marred by numerous articulatory errors. He printed awkwardly and tended to reverse letters. His progress reflected prodigious efforts to move slowly and carefully, at the expense of a good deal of spontaneous pleasure.

Gene's difficulties at school were further complicated by several illnesses, including another eye infection, measles (with a high temperature and a fifteen-pound weight loss), and an unusually hard fall. Other stresses for the family at that time included the father's acute illness and Gene's acquisition of glasses when it was finally determined that central vision of his left eye was nearly absent. Then, in his sixth year, he experienced the additional stress of beginning speech correction classes, of suffering intensive and painful radium treatment in both ears, and of acquiring a baby sister. Toward the end of the first school year, however, Gene seemed happier and began to respond to his teachers' efforts to involve him in class activities.

The Latency Years

When Gene was seen at age 7–1, it was clear that Mrs. A.'s concern about his progress was well founded. Gene's work continued to be poor in the second grade, and his relationship with his older sister worsened. His competitiveness increased as the discrepancy between his limited accomplishments and those of his bright, well-behaved sister became greater.

He also seemed troubled by feelings of being displaced as the younger child by the birth of the new sister, who occupied the mother's attention a good part of the time and whose well-being required some new prohibitions. On the other hand, there were definite signs of increasing maturity in Gene at this period. His lengthened figure, his glasses, and his engaging earnestness made him appear considerably more serious and sober. There were also signs of improved gross coordination, more refined visual-motor skills, greater resourcefulness in using these skills, lessened distractibility, and more adequate speech. His logic, however, was occasionally poor and his sentence construction awkward. His ideas were often concretely expressed in terms of action, and word-finding problems were obvious.

At times, however, he handled gaps in his vocabulary or expressive capacity with an ingeniousness and qualitative richness suggesting deep empathy for other human beings and an almost poetic enjoyment of nature. Considerable reflectiveness, realistic but also self-protective, appeared in his thinking, as when he did not anticipate getting a train for Christmas because it was too expensive. He was also more open than before in recognizing his limitations. Although not always successful or capable of following through, Gene was more likely to make an honest effort through persistent step-by-step procedures. He was most frustrated and least adequate with school subjects such as spelling, reading, writing, and arithmetic. His learning was most limited in areas demanding accurate and continuous focus on small visual details, a capacity limited by his visual deficit, as well as by his difficulties in concentration and in delaying action. Several other difficulties were observed which could be expected to have a deleterious effect on school progress. These included marked directional confusion in reading and spelling, both in left-right orientation and in the formation of similar letters such as b and d or n and m. He showed negligible knowledge of phonics, little conception of number relations beyond simple addition, and motoric difficulties in forming letters and designs. Holding his face close to the paper, he wrote very slowly in a large primitive scrawl without clearly separating letters. In an effort to explore the possibility of remedial work with him, the examiner found that Gene could apply himself with great persistence and unusual efforts at control, provided the examiner sat very close to him and slowly and patiently offered physical and mental support. It was also obvious that he was greatly interested in mechanical devices, such as the typewriter and dictaphone, which he handled with remarkable skill.

His Stanford Binet IQ (106) was in the average range. He was most effective with easy motoric tasks, which he performed with considerable care. When such tasks became more difficult, however, he was prone to act impulsively, with little planning or organization. His scores on the WISC were higher but still in the average range. Subtest performance varied largely as one might anticipate on the basis of the previous knowledge concerning his development. We can illustrate this by quoting a portion of the structured test summary:

The Wechsler scatter suggested his superiority in perceiving and evaluating the world around him, particularly when human relationships are involved. It further suggested high capacity to work out mechanical relationships, when an available pattern or concrete example is given him. Good capacity to learn new things was evidenced in the rapidity and accuracy with which he learned the coding items. On the other hand, rote memory of an essentially meaningless type, such as in digit span, fell below average. He better remembered a meaningful Stanford Binet sentence than unrelated numbers. His performance was inadequate when he was asked to organize parts into a whole (as in the Object Assembly Test), to abstract, to generalize, or to integrate without specific given cues. These features of his performance, plus immature primitivization and concretization and difficulties in motor execution, both in speech and in written work, raise the possibility of brain damage.

Along with numerous examples of affective warmth toward examiners and social adequacy in meeting people generally, there were evidences of inadequate emotional control. This control difficulty, plus his primitive perception (as seen in his drawings, which lacked perspective and appropriate proportion) also suggested brain damage. A neurological examination suggested "developmental aphasia, predominantly motor type," but yielded no indication of acquired brain damage.

In the third grade, with improved health, fewer absences, and encouragement from an interested and capable teacher, his school work improved. Interest increased and grades were average. Learning was still a laborious process, however, and was often quite frustrating. His mother tried to help him at home, but his teacher discouraged this special help. The teacher felt that the mother put too much pressure on him and was too involved in minor ups and downs to teach him objectively.

During latency, Gene's interactions with his family and his role in his neighborhood and school were not grossly different from those of the late preschool period. However, there was some intensification of feelings between mother and son and an increase in the intensity of her focus on his problems, which perhaps heightened the stress he experienced from sensory deficits, physical pain, and academic frustration. At one point, his mother remarked that sometimes, just when she was most discouraged or irritated, he could change these feelings by being especially lovable and considerate. She was aware of potential problems arising from Gene's "determined" nature, his "roughshod" approach to children, his argumentativeness, and his tendency to provoke other children into fights. She also saw him, however, as kindly and protective of younger children. She was likely to blame his altercations on hostilities arising from neighboring children's poor training and family problems. And at the same time, she felt a deep sense of guilt for her own temporary irritation with him.

At this point Gene's mother was the predominant force in his life, although he had an "us men" attitude toward going off for outings with his father. Mr. A. was a loving father, who was as sincerely concerned about his child's welfare as the mother, but he was less overwhelmed by Gene's intensity and less discouraged by his failures.

Meanwhile, the father took special job training, which made his work more satisfying and gave him more time with his family, who were then able to enjoy camping together. Gradually, the family became more settled in their new home. Parental relationships improved when they were able to discuss their difficulties with the minister of the mother's church. This minister also became a great favorite of Gene's.

At the mother's instigation, an additional series of tests and observations was made when Gene was nine years, eight months old. This was partly a matter of convenience, since Gene's parents were preoccupied with details of the paternal grandparents' pending divorce. It was also clear that the family regarded these evaluations as an opportunity to discuss Gene's assets and problems with interested observers.

Gene was as appealing, friendly, earnest and responsive as earlier, but more restrained than he had been as a younger child. With a female psychologist whom he appeared to regard as "a special old friend," he exhibited mild enthusiasm, courtesy, close attention, and a kind of controlled relaxation. There was an undercurrent of tension, reflected in almost continuous fine movements of the hands and a partially suppressed impulse to hurry through the structured tests, with a superimposed conscious effort to look ahead and plan. He was distinctly proud that his articulation had improved but quite aware that there were still times when appropriate words were not easily available to him or when pronunciation was slurred or distorted.

Both toward his own capacities and toward the family pressures, he verbalized fairly mature acceptance of facts as they were and semirealistic hopes that things might improve. For example, when it was clear that he was not doing very well on the Digit Span Test, he verbalized recognition of failure and temporary disappointment, partially allayed by increased effort. In the same way, he told of being very unhappy when it was necessary to give up his dog because of neighborhood pressures, but then he added a comment to the effect that "time heals all things." He seemed to regard the grandparents' divorce as a private matter, but he indicated strong sympathy and protectiveness toward the grandmother and the wistful hope that he might still see his beloved grandfather. He reported that he liked school except for an art teacher who had publicly ridiculed him for his ineptness in drawing, but even his feelings toward her were qualified as he remarked that she was "not so bad." Apparently he was trying to maintain a positive attitude and to control his own behavior so that he would stay in the good graces of the adults he encountered.

Although his WISC IQ was in the average range, there was considerable variability in this test performance. It was clear that he had an increased fund of general knowledge, and that he was particularly proud of his scientific information, since he admired his male science teacher. There were definite gaps and confusions in his knowledge, however, along with conceptual vagueness suggesting primitive integrations of facts and difficulty in expressing ideas.

Seeing him for the first time, one observer found him friendly and pleasant but slightly "soft," "feminine," and "inhibited." This observer noted some guardedness in relating to adults and in engaging in gross motor activities with peers, perhaps partly related to his visual difficulties. Along with this, there was in Gene's play some hesitation in initiating activity without first asking permission. Nonetheless, he conveyed "a feeling that he is of average popularity and is content" with his peer relationships. Toward his older sister, he expressed some hostility, which he dealt with by avoiding her as much as possible. He resented his mother's demanding control of him, but he had a positive sense of closeness to her. He was reticent to speak of his father, but said nothing negative, implying that his father was too busy to play as large a role in his life as his mother, who was always available when he needed help in practical situations.

About a year later, when Gene was ten years, seven months old, a repeat WISC yielded a full-scale IQ of 120. This was his most effective and least variable test performance since early infancy. Both information and comprehension were more detailed and better organized, although some looseness and confusion in thinking was still present. His vocabulary was good and word-finding problems were reduced, although occasionally still observable. There was an increased tendency to project blame for failure on the materials or on the environment. He was still gracious and friendly, but less effusive. One sensed that he was trying to act with grown-up casualness. He consciously tried to be persistent and careful, but difficulties still resulted in discouragement and frustration, following which he was usually irritable and careless for a brief period.

A physical examination showed that he was both tall and heavy for his age. Throughout the examination, he talked continuously and quite indistinctly. It was also noted that his blood pressure was elevated during the examination and that he was exceedingly ticklish. The pediatrician described him as endomesomorphic in physique and especially sensitive in the upper respiratory tract, probably with allergic diathesis.

A psychiatric evaluation made a year later, when he was eleven and a half, emphasized richness of experiencing coupled with a degree of obsessiveness that sometimes made him uncomfortable or confused. His thinking was so burdened with detail that it was hard for the examiner to follow the thread of his reasoning, although Gene himself appeared to be able to keep a direction without getting bogged down or blocked. There was "a sparkle of eagerness and spontaneity, which mitigates the impression of obsessiveness and continues to motivate one to listen to him very carefully." The psychiatrist also noted intensity of feeling and vigorous abandonment to activity, which contributed to his enjoyment in living. In the psychiatric interview, Gene expressed considerable warmth toward all members of his family, as well as toward peers and adults, apparently being able to see weaknesses in a relatively noncritical fashion and without loss of his basically positive relationship toward all human beings. With this orientation, he seemed able to trust others and to view his handicaps as something to overcome. Following concerted and often quite efficient efforts, he was able to adopt the viewpoint that he could never fail completely, nor was he defeated when he recognized his accomplishments as less than perfect. Thus, his sense of self-worth was maintained and reinforced by support from others, particularly his parents. Although he was not without feelings of insecurity about himself, these feelings never predominated because they were always dealt with resourcefully.

In Gene's eleventh year, his maternal grandparents were divorced. Gene appeared to react strongly, but his concern was as much for his mother as for himself. Although this divorce was stressful, as was the paternal grandparents' earlier divorce, there was some indication that the insecurity of the larger family group increased the cohesiveness of the immediate family. It was as if the parents cut their own family ties and focused on the immediate family.

Summary of Findings Through Latency

All the observers who saw Gene during his early years were impressed with the mingling of strengths and weaknesses in his behavior. They did not always agree, however, on the balance between resources and vulnerabilities. In part, such differences of opinion arose from the special orientations of observers evaluating different aspects of his development. That is, evaluation of the over-all level of Gene's adjustment or integration was a function of whether an observer was primarily concerned with deviant performance in relation to age norms or with the fairly consistent trend toward improved integration and control in relation to probable expectations for this particular child. For example, his speech was so infantile in the preschool years that nearly any observer would have regarded it as substandard. Speech was still poor in the latency years, although it may have seemed worse to one who had not observed the improvement. This was equally true of gross and fine motor skills, of learning capacity, of perceptual functioning, and of affect control. Over time, Gene became more adequate in each of these areas. His improvement was particularly impressive when one considered the restrictions imposed through the intensity, continuity, and variety of bodily and family stresses faced by a child who was judged in infancy to be especially vigorous, alert, and sensitive. In other words, Gene's sensory handicaps and family pressures might have imposed greater hardships on a more passive, less responsive child than he. Another child (that is, a less actively struggling, trustful, and well-supported child) might have shown continued loss instead of gain. They seemed more disturbing to this vigorous young child as he tried to learn to talk, coordinate his muscles, and express and control his feelings. These pressures on Gene were increased by discrepancies between his skills and his mother's demands and aspirations.

Gene at Preadolescence

At the time of the preadolescent testing and observation, Gene was nine years, eight months. The ratings of his defense mechanisms and general ego characteristics are presented below.

Defense Mechanisms and General Characteristics of Ego Functioning

Rating Variable	Rating
Ego Strength	2
Over-all Ego Autonomy	3
Repression	5
Isolation	6
Reaction Formation	3
Projection	6
Avoidance	10
Denial	6
Acting Out–Overcontrol	3

The outstanding feature of the ratings assigned to Gene on the basis of his performance in the WISC, TAT, and Rorschach was the low value on ego strength. Only six other children were rated as low in the over-all integrity or cohesiveness of ego organization. Aside from his maximal rating on avoidance (the highest rating assigned to any child), the reasons for his low ego strength rating were not captured by the other ratings shown here, with the exception of the discrepancy between his tendency toward obsessiveness (isolation) and his marked tendency toward acting out. This type of discrepancy is ordinarily found in individuals whose control problems are associated with ineffective overideational tendencies. The moderate discrepancy between his relatively high rating on isolation and his low rating on reaction formation was also notable in this connection. He was not the typical obsessive-compulsive child. Neither was he the typical child who acts out his conflicts.

His ratings on projection, denial, and repression were approximately average, again indicating that the gross over-all ego weakness apparent in his test performances was not adequately represented by his employment of the defense mechanisms included in this analysis. Other aspects of his performance, including his verbal difficulties and tendencies toward confusion, some of which are described below, contributed heavily to the total picture of ego weakness at this time and in relation to average expectations for a child of his age.

Intellectual Abilities

Gene's age-corrected WISC subtest scores and his IQ scores are presented below.

Information	8
Comprehension	9

Arithmetic	11
Similarities	15
Vocabulary	12
Digit Span	8
Picture Completion	10
Picture Arrangement	15
Block Design	12
Object Assembly	10
Coding (B)	10
Verbal IQ	104
Performance IQ	110
Full Scale IQ	107

In view of the gross discrepancies between Gene's earlier performances in individual subtests of the WISC, his preadolescent scatter was notably homogeneous. His adequacy in Vocabulary and Similarities was impressive. His relatively limited fund of general knowledge, his limited ability to reason appropriately (Information, Comprehension), and his limited capacity to repeat digits appeared to be important reflections of his ideational and attentional limitations, but his scores were not strikingly low. His responses to the performance subtests were generally slightly more adequate. The relatively low scores on Picture Completion, Object Assembly, and Coding seemed to reflect his attentional-perceptual difficulties, his inability to synthesize objects into a pattern guided by an internalized image of the whole, and his immediate sensory and control difficulties. These, too, were not strikingly low scores, however.

With respect to the question of possible brain damage, the scatter alone was negative. There were none of the very low or zero scores that may appear when a child must learn means of coping with defects present at or occasioned by birth in order to develop. Neither was there any gross verbal-performance discrepancy of a kind suggesting damage to either hemisphere of the brain. Although not conclusive, this lack of gross signs of brain damage was impressive in a boy whose behavior has repeatedly raised the question of brain damage.

Cognitive Controls

Factor	Score	Meaning
I Scanning A	− .95	Less than average checking of judgments in the size estimation tests.
II Conceptual Differentiation	− .04	Average conceptual differentiation.

III	Scanning B	−2.34	Very long judgment times in the size estimation tests.
IV	Field-Articulation	−1.63	Very low articulation.
V	Constricted-Flexible Control	.18	Average.
VI	Spontaneity	1.15	Rather high spontaneity; short Rorschach and TAT reaction times; high in conceptual distance in TAT, etc.

Gene's very long judgment times in the size estimation tests may in part have been attributable to his visual defect. It also suggested a painstaking attempt to be accurate. It was impressive that in a context of gross control problems he was able to be so painstaking in this task. Perhaps the fact that his tendency toward action was allowed expression in the size estimation tasks made it easier for him to delay here than in a verbal task. Many children, particularly boys, turn the crank (to adjust the size of the comparison stimulus) with alacrity and pleasure. Boys even more motorically uncontrolled than Gene have been observed to begin cranking vigorously as soon as the apparatus is explained to them, with obvious enjoyment of the motor activity involved. Once he made his judgments, however, he spent less than average amounts of time checking them. His weak field-articulation in tests requiring selective attention to relevant stimuli and inattention to compelling irrelevant stimuli may also have been due in part to his visual defect. It seemed likely, however, that his difficulties in impulse control, his strong avoidant tendencies, distractibility, and so forth may also have interfered with these subtler aspects of attentional control. One was reminded here of his relatively low (for him) score on the Picture Completion subtest of the WISC, which seemed to involve some, but not all, of the same response processes.

The rather high score on the spontaneity factor was more difficult to interpret. In Gene's case, short reaction times in the TAT and the Rorschach Test could have implied impulsivity, as well as quick, spontaneous involvement in these tasks. Although his TAT stories were not particularly dramatic and although inquiry was often required to elicit continuations of the themes he began to develop, some of his productions were quite freely and unhaltingly given. His past experience with these tests could, of course, have reduced his reaction times and increased his responsiveness. It appeared that some of the genuine spontaneity noted repeatedly in his history was also reflected by his factor score. He was less constricted in these aspects of his performance than more than half the total sample of children, an impressive fact in view of his severe difficulties at each stage of his earlier development.

Behavior in the Clinical Testing Situation

Gene's factor scores on the six factors derived from the ratings of behavior during the WISC and TAT are presented below.

	Factor	*Score*	*Meaning*
I	Active Openness to New Experience	.82	Somewhat above average in openness to new experience.
II	Unity of Identity	1.26	Rather high in pleasure in own body, clarity of identity, identification with own sex, etc.
III	Accuracy of Reality Testing	−2.39	Very low in clarity and accuracy of perception, attention to fine detail, adequacy of spatial orientation, capacity to delay for appraisal, etc.
IV	Cooperativeness	2.12	High in task-involvement, frustration tolerance, cooperation with authority, enjoyment, warmth, etc.
V	Compulsive Exactness	.79	Somewhat higher than average in concern with goodness and badness, meticulosity, determination, stubbornness, etc.
VI	Sporadic Disruption of Control	.98	Somewhat high in variability, fearfulness, observable tension, etc.

These factor scores seemed to bring out some of Gene's key strengths in a way not adequately reflected by the other measures discussed thus far. In spite of his great difficulties in adequately perceiving and coordinating himself to external reality, for example, he was high in cooperativeness and impressed the examiner as being adequately anchored in an effective total conception of himself that did not include the confusion over sexual identity that characterized some of the other children. Here we seemed to see the fruits of the positive features of his parents' interest in and concern for him, and his attachment to them. We seemed to see, also, that his identification with his father (and grandfathers) was more adequate than might have been guessed from the characteristic intensity of his interactions with his mother. Here, then, was evidence of identity-anchoring that might account for his valiant attempts to cope with his handicaps, his illnesses, and his often difficult life circumstances. A child less adequate in the unity and clarity of his identity might have appeared more disturbed than Gene and might not have shown the increased degree of adequacy he displayed at preadolescence. Although understandably average in openness to new experience and more prone than the average child to sporadic disruptions of control, his basic stance was active, positive, and problem-oriented. He had not withdrawn into autism; his occasional confusion was not heavily tinged with arbitrary or peculiar thinking; and his orientation toward others was trusting, despite his inadequacies and his many failure experiences.

Behavior in the Laboratory Testing Situation

Gene's scores on the four factors derived from the ratings of behavior in the laboratory are presented below. They seemed to suggest that his behavior in the novel laboratory situation, where he was tested by a male examiner whom he had not previously met, was quite different from his behavior in the familiar clinical testing situation, in which the examiner was an "old friend."

	Factor	Score	Meaning
I	Impulsive Spontaneity	− .97	Somewhat less than average warmth, friendliness, talkativeness, etc.
II	Anxious Dependence	.06	Average.
III	Explorativeness	1.25	High in gross scanning, curiosity, drive toward mastery, etc.
IV	Acting upon the Environment	−1.74	High in compulsive-appearing overcontrol, task-involvement, etc.

It appeared that Gene was more distant and more carefully controlled in this situation than in the familiar clinical testing situation. Perhaps both the newness of the situation and the difficult nature of some of the tasks (e.g., timed tests requiring refined selectiveness of attention) for a child of his limitations contributed to his appearing somewhat more reserved and compulsively task-oriented.

It was impressive that his active stance toward his world found expression even here, however, in his curiosity about the room and the apparatuses, and his determined efforts to master the situation. Here again, we saw cognitive inadequacies bolstered and made the most of by an active, positive stance toward reality. One is reminded of the repeated observation in the longitudinal study of his determined forthrightness in coping with tasks that are at times insurmountable for him.

Cognitive Style—Aspects of Over-all Ego Organization

Gene's scores on the general factors derived from the matrix of intercorrelations among factor scores and selected additional variables are presented below.

	Factor	Score	Meaning
I	Field-Articulation	.30	Average. (It should be noted that, as stated in Chapter 12, this is a somewhat atypical factor representing one of several constellations in which field-articulation skills can appear.)
II	Spontaneity	−1.81	Relative openness, uninhibitedness, cooperativeness.
III	Maturity	−1.48	Low autonomy, low comfortable independence, low ego strength, younger child, etc.
IV	Adequacy of Reality Testing	1.18	High in leveling, with associated sporadic disruption of control, inaccurate reality testing, etc.
V	Explorativeness	− .05	Average.
VI	Acting Out	− .69	Somewhat overcontrolled.

Gene's score on the Field-Articulation factor was about average. This score did not belie his severe difficulties in articulating perceptual fields via attentional selectivity, but was, rather, attributable to the other variables which had major loadings on this factor (especially certain aspects of response to the HIT).

The contrast between Gene's openness and cooperativeness and his somewhat inhibited appearance in certain situations was again notable. His low autonomy, low independence, and low ego strength were evidenced by his score on Factor III, in which these variables were associated with age. Age was probably no more important in Gene's case, however, than the cognitive defects noted earlier. The general inadequacy of his reality testing was also apparent in his score on Factor IV.

Summary of Preadolescent Findings

Gene's development has been a valiant uphill fight against impressive organic handicaps. His preadolescent organization was probably better in some ways than if he were a passive child who gave in to his limitations. In other ways, his preadolescent behavior was probably more disturbed than if his drive to succeed and his efforts to meet family aspirations were less intense and his impulse control more adequate. His performance in the WISC suggested that the ego weaknesses apparent in his unstable control, his distractibility, his specific cognitive disabilities, his gross overuse of avoidance, and his ineffective obsessiveness, often bordering on confusion, occurred in a context of potentially greater intellectual strength. It was the contrast between his potential and his specific limitations, perhaps, that gave a disjointed appearance to his sequences of adequate and inadequate performances. That is, his behavioral disturbances seemed to lack the thematic consistency that often characterizes a more purely dynamically based group of ego weaknesses.

In view of Gene's limitations, it was impressive that his use of denial and projection was not excessive. His stubborn persistence in the face of difficulties found surcease in avoidance, which obviated excessive use of defenses that could grossly distort reality. His general inadequacy in reality testing seemed linked to his limitations, rather than to pathological defense employment per se.

In some ways, these limitations made it more difficult to assess the importance of emotional disturbance, as such, to Gene's adaptation. His ineffective obsessiveness, for example, could have been occasioned as much by a desperate attempt to avoid further failures as by internal conflict per se.

Whatever the actual balance of organic and emotional factors determining his ego weaknesses, Gene's behavior at preadolescence, as assessed from a wide array of psychological tests and experimental procedures, showed marked vulnerabilities, including some conflict about impulse control and specific visual and cognitive deficits. Equally impressive were his strengths from his positive ties to his parents, his dogged persistence, his basic confidence in himself, and his apparent resilience following temporary disintegration. Though below age expectancies in some respects, he was not without resources, nor grossly deficient in meeting the expectations of a boy of his individual make-up and family background.

Ego Weakness in a Setting of Vulnerability and Constriction— The Case of Sharon J.

The Midwestern children of the study were, on the average, somewhat unspontaneous and uncommunicative at preadolescence, a fact perhaps understandable as a function both of age-related conflicts and of the particular demands and expectations of the subculture in which they developed. Added to these causes of constriction, there were, in Sharon's case, multiple developmental and interpersonal factors which made her story a chronicle of unusual vulnerability, frustration, anger, and severe constriction. Nonetheless, a careful review of her sequences of behavior will present to the reader a picture of some, though unduly slow and often inadequate, efforts to achieve a modicum of independence in her own small world. Her developmental career exemplifies certain longitudinal consistencies with unusual vividness and outlines one route to an uncomfortable and, in many respects, ineffective pattern of preadolescent behavior. The limited effectiveness of her resolutions of earlier developmental crises raises doubts that she will more adequately solve the new problems posed by puberty and adolescence.

Sharon's Environment

Sharon spent her first six years in a tiny house that was a model of neatness, cleanliness, and housekeeping efficiency. The compact, two-bedroom home in one of the newer sections of the city was comfortable and attractively furnished in a sophisticated style. In one sense, these physical surroundings were an extension of her mother's personality, although they contrasted strikingly with her mother's more humble background. One observer described the home as an elaborate set in which two children played house with a new doll. The parents' concern with the physical development of their premature baby was less prominent than their interest in manipulating, handling, and elaborately dressing her.

The twenty-year-old mother was mildly pretentious as she mentioned the family's country club associations. She welcomed the opportunity to display her pretty, feminine-looking baby, as well as her own newly acquired status as a financially comfortable young matron married to the only son of well-to-do parents. That she had not fully assimilated her improved socioeconomic status was suggested by her overly dressy clothes, her tinted and elaborately styled coiffure, and her exaggerated application of brilliant make-up, which led observers to describe her as "a little common," and as displaying "wholly likable vulgarity" and "provocative femininity."

Mrs. J., the older of two sisters, was brought up on a farm by relatives following the loss of her own parents when she was quite young. In some respects, her latency and adolescent years were happy, yet she seemed filled with resentment and disappointment concerning her parents.

She enjoyed a good deal of warmth from her guardians and was proud of her physical strength and sturdiness, which was doubtlessly increased by the vigorous life she led on the farm. Following graduation from high school, and prior to her marriage at age nineteen, Mrs. J. did office work for a year. Although her own family was nominally Protestant, she turned to the Catholic faith, attributing her "conversion" to the fact that she found the religion of several Catholic girl friends "very nice." After her marriage, she was more devout than her husband and encouraged her children to participate in religious services and practices.

Although likable, Mr. J. was a poor and disinterested high school student and a passive young adult with no special skills or vocational interests. Following a period of relative inactivity after graduation from high school, he associated himself with his father's loan-shark activities for several years, despite the disapproval of his mother and his wife. The paternal grandmother urged her husband to engage in more socially commendable business ventures because she feared their son might follow in his footsteps. By Sharon's fifth year, her father was working in real estate, presumably still in association with his father. By 1956, he planned and carried through a new business venture.

Although not unfriendly, the father seemed less willing than his wife to offer observations or opinions to the longitudinal study staff. Whereas the mother appeared to be unself-conscious and to enjoy the interaction with the interviewers, the father impressed them as "a person with a very poor opinion of himself and his abilities, resigned to taking a back seat even in his home, but entirely ready to be liked and appreciated." This impression was enhanced by infancy contacts with the paternal grandmother, whose readiness to offer unsolicited advice and brisk behavior with the baby stood in striking contrast to the sluggish reticence of her son. Yet, it was clear that the father was interested in and pleased with his daughter. Unlike most fathers of the longitudinal study subjects, he arranged to be present for the home visit and several times reminded his wife of the need to interrupt the interview to tend to the baby's bodily needs. It was reported that he regularly left work in the late afternoon in order to play with and feed the baby.

The paternal grandparents lived next door during Sharon's first six years. The J. children were as likely to eat or nap at the grandparents' home as at their own. From the mother's point of view, this interchange was a convenient arrangement, since she preferred not to use baby sitters. The paternal grandmother saw herself and her husband as "wrapped up in the children," but felt the proximity of the two homes somewhat "too convenient." As she summarized it, "I get left with them." While there were differences in the attitudes and disciplinary measures of the parents and the paternal grandparents, the mother felt that all of the adults were "pretty easy on the children." Difficulties arose only from conflicts in authority when the children were in contact with the two generations at once. The mother felt that the father "would like to be strict," but never really was. The mother sometimes tried to be strict, but felt that the children usually managed to get their own way. However, she tried to use differentiated punishment to fit the seriousness of the misbehavior. In contrast to the paternal grandparents, who disciplined the children primarily by verbal means, the mother ignored minor misbehaviors, interfered when she thought the children were too rough, and used threats of spanking or isolation as a last resort. Commenting on Sharon's reaction to isolation, she remarked, "This just kills her soul. She is afraid of the dark, anyway, and to be in a room by herself is the worst thing that could happen to her."

In addition to the paternal grandparents, Sharon's larger family included an unmarried aunt and numerous more distant relatives. Of these relatives, the aunt probably played the largest part in Sharon's early life. Although she moved frequently, the aunt managed to see a good deal of Sharon, who was recognized by other family members as her favorite. Since Sharon often confided in her aunt, Mrs. J. felt that she enjoyed this special position. Reasoning that Sharon needed more time and attention than most children, the mother did not overtly resent Sharon's relationship with her aunt. When Sharon was about ten years old, the aunt acquired a dress shop, the responsibilities of which kept her too busy for frequent contacts with Sharon. Like the senior Mrs. J., the aunt offered considerable advice, especially during Sharon's infancy. The mother apparently felt free to accept or reject such advice. According to Mrs. J., the aunt had a façade of strictness, but was, in reality, quite lenient.

Thus, from the mother's point of view, discipline was never overly severe or unreasonable. There were, however, definite standards of appropriate behavior. These standards were determined by the dictates of the Catholic Church, the school the children attended, and the mother's view that her girls should be "helpless and feminine," as well as obedient, respectful, reverent, soft-spoken, and gentle.

Three siblings arrived before Sharon was five. According to the mother, Sharon expressed delight each time at the prospect of a new baby, but she was so impatient for the first sibling that the mother refrained from telling her about the other new babies until shortly before their birth. In contrast to her eagerness to get the baby, Sharon cried excessively, suffered severe nausea, and was unwilling to leave home for any reason each time the mother was hospitalized. Sharon liked to show off the new baby to neighboring children during the first few days at home. As the baby grew older, she tended to ignore it until it became a self-propelling, talking individual capable of being a nuisance. With the first sister, Carol, slightly less than sixteen months her junior, Sharon formed a symbiotic closeness with both protective and aggressive overtones. She often stood close to Carol, fondling or patting her, sometimes roughly. She struck out at anyone she regarded as too affectionate or as potentially harmful to Carol. She once refused to go to nursery school until a classmate was discouraged from holding Carol's hand. The birth of the second sibling, a boy, when Sharon was 3-9, changed this relationship to some extent. The two younger children often excluded Sharon from their play, presumably because she was too bossy and was given to hitting or shoving the boy and taking things away from him. Whereas the more easygoing Carol permitted or enjoyed the vigorous roughness of the active little brother, the more irritable Sharon would not tolerate even mild threats to her own person. At two years of age, the brother was said to be "scared to death of Sharon," whereas he showed a good deal of physical affection toward Carol and shared both his pleasures and discomforts with her. Probably partly in response to feelings of displacement, Sharon, at 4-11, when a second sister was born, chose to play with her in preference to the other two siblings.

All this time, the family lived in a small, two-bedroom house. Sleeping arrangements were unusual and variable. After Sharon's birth, the mother shared a bedroom with the baby, while the father used a second bedroom. This arrangement was presumably dictated by the mother's concern about Sharon's physical vulnerability following her premature birth and also by Mr. J.'s late hours.

During the preschool evaluation, when Sharon was about four and a half, living arrangements were as described above except that there were some deviations from the strict standards of neatness, at least to the extent of permitting accumulation of children's toys, which were cleared away only once a week or for special occasions. The most notable change in the family, however, was in the mother's appearance and manner.

Whereas Mrs. J. obviously still spent a good deal of time grooming herself and her children, she looked more youthful and informal and her make-up and dress were less ostentatiously elaborate. Household decorations were more subdued in color. Social life, rare at the time of the infancy contact, was practically nonexistent by the preschool period. This turn of events may have been dictated by the fact that Mr. J. worked until late at night and was rarely home for the evening meal. It was notable, however, that Mrs. J. made no effort to associate herself with women's groups or with girl friends for the social outings or morning coffees so common among mothers of her social status. She seemed satisfied with her role as a mother and busied herself with caring for and supervising the children. She consciously wanted her children to experience the pleasures of a close involvement with a mother who was always available, in contrast to the deprivation she experienced in her own childhood. At the same time, she genuinely enjoyed her activities with the children.

Mrs. J. also busily involved herself in plans for building and moving into a new home, next door to one owned by the paternal grandparents. These plans were almost entirely of her own making.

By this time, Mrs. J. impressed the interviewer as a thoughtful young woman who clearly recognized a range of problems in relating herself to her sensitive and often quite difficult first child. She tried to handle these problems differentially and welcomed the help she might gain from professionally trained observers. When we remember that this mother was caring for three other children, moving, and handling household chores almost singlehandedly at a time when her husband was rarely home, it is not surprising that her behavior did not always match her hopes in her relationship to Sharon. Her efforts to be sympathetic and understanding must have been pushed to the limits of endurance by Sharon's whining tearfulness and aggressive outbursts toward the intrusive little brother. In addition, Mrs. J. was frequently awakened at night by one or more children's running into her bedroom with requests for attention, reassurance, or mediation of disputes. The helpful but often critical mother-in-law continued to support, but at times to sabotage, her daughter-in-law's efforts.

When Sharon was eight, about a month after the birth of the fifth child (fourth daughter), the family moved into more spacious living quarters close to the school the children attended. A moderate-sized front yard and a larger enclosed back yard increased the usable outdoor play space and permitted more privacy. Aside from these obvious advantages, the new home was the first which was not next door to the paternal grandparents', a fact which both Mrs. J. and the children felt made everyday life simpler. As the mother put it, "There were just too many bosses too close." Yet, frequent visits were a source of friction, since the paternal grandfather (over his wife's protest) still brought expensive presents, especially for his grandson. Mrs. J. tried to allay the girls' jealousy by equating the number of possessions, so that each child occasionally had something new of his own.

The father worked long hours and rarely saw the children during the day. He ate supper with the family, however, and was usually at home on Sundays. He was willing to help Sharon with homework and was much more patient with her than the mother was able to be. Although he was generally passive about questions of child-rearing, he was, according to his wife, very firm in demanding respect and obedience.

Sometime before the birth of the sixth child, when Sharon was ten, Mrs. J. acquired full-time household help. She was then able to spend much more time with the children. As conflicts about her husband's parents were less pressing, and her financial and social status more secure, she was better able to use the support of her religion and to find fulfillment in her role as a mother.

Over the years, three major constant factors were noted in Sharon's background: the relative dominance of the mother; the help and interference of the extended family; and the importance of Catholic ideology. The major changes were the moves to new homes and the growth of the mother from a somewhat pretentious, artificial person to a child-centered woman with considerable insight into her child's problems.

The father's growth was reflected in his movement from a passive man with no definite interests or opinions to a man deeply involved in the establishment of a prosperous business. This greater responsibility improved the family's financial status but decreased the time the father spent with the children.

Increasing family size (with resulting limitations of individual attention and privacy and shifting patterns of alliance within the child group) was the other major environmental change during Sharon's development.

Sharon's Physical, Cognitive, and Emotional Development from Infancy to Preadolescence

The Early Years

Onset of labor occurred approximately seven weeks before term and labor lasted two days and a night, although hard labor lasted only six hours. At birth, Sharon weighed five pounds, necessitating incubator care for several days. Sharon's first few months of life were highly stressful for her, and for her parents and extended family. She cried a great deal and the numerous relatives hovered over her anxiously, probably experiencing considerable helplessness in their excessive handling or manipulating of the tiny baby. With the exception of her mother, everyone who came into contact with Sharon during the first two months of her life wore a facial mask. For the first ten days, she was fed only at the breast. Bottle supplements were then given for one month, after which she was bottle fed every one and one-half to two hours.

At two months of age, Sharon had a severe cold and required hospitalization. She continued to be highly susceptible to throat infections. She was also constipated. Her rectum was dilated at an early age. Suppositories were given daily for a time following cessation of breast feeding, then weekly for at least six months. While the mother was anxious about the baby's frailty, she was most concerned about bowel movements. She used suppositories more often than necessary because she felt that they "improved the baby's mood." Other discomforts included almost constant diaper rash and a navel infection.

Despite the multiplicity of physical problems and the great amount of anxious attention she received, Sharon took solid food well until about the time of the birth of her first sibling. At this time, she developed food allergies and mild eczema on both hands. Between two and four years, she was said to be a "fussy eater." Even at prepuberty, she disliked many foods, was very particular about the way food was prepared and served, would not eat when the dog was in the house, and was very sensitive to unusual odors.

When she was observed at twenty-four weeks, Sharon was an attractive baby with well-defined features. She was as elaborately and expensively dressed as the mother, as though her outfit were an extension of the mother's costume. A small but compactly built, well-nourished infant, Sharon seemed to have caught up with normal levels of functioning in most respects. Immaturity was most noticeable in her motor development (she could not support her own weight on extended arms, was unable to roll from the supine to prone position, and could not bring her legs into high extension). With fatigue or delay on the part of adults in providing something she wanted, her posture stiffened, her hand control decreased, and her face became contorted.

She vocalized considerably, but there was little contented cooing or babbling. Characteristically, she made a sound her mother called "grunting" and related to early efforts to indicate bowel movements. "Grunting" was intermittent, arrhythmic, and vaguely fussy in quality. Although she was heard to laugh several times in response to social stimulation, she rarely smiled spontaneously.

At twenty-four weeks, her performance on the infancy tests was slightly below age norms, with language and motor functioning evaluated as less adequate than adaptive or personal-social functioning. She was able to handle single objects vigorously and purposefully but was less skilled in handling several objects at one time. She seemed to prefer parts of her own body to toys and sucked more vigorously on her own fingers than on objects. The only object which seemed particularly exciting to her was a mirror, the presentation of which elicited squealing and both manual and oral approach. She did not seem to be particularly sensitive to intense auditory or visual stimulation, with the possible exception of bright colors. There were some indications of greater sensitivity to touch, taste, and temperature.

The infancy observers described Sharon as a baby who rejected what she disliked in the environment by spitting out, frowning, and fretting, or who took what the environment offered but did little to structure the situation in positive ways. She especially liked "to look and look." While she had obvious likes, dislikes, and special sensitivities, these "may have had more to do with the defense of her own life space than with threshold per se." She was "irritable and easily fatigued," had "a mother who showed little sensitivity to her needs," and exhibited "a rather narrow range of resources in handling her difficulties."

The Preschool Years

In contrast to Sharon's stressful infancy, the pace of her physical and cognitive development during her preschool years was not markedly unusual, although motor development continued to lag in some respects. In retrospect, it seems likely that part of her stiffness may have been a residue of her prematurity, yet her inadequacy in this area may have been increased by her "reluctance" (her mother's word) to interact with new people in the preschool period.

At four and a half, Sharon was seen by a male psychologist, who administered projective tests. En route to the examining center, Sharon sat wordlessly beside her mother and younger sister. Upon arrival, both children remained silent but moved freely, gracefully, and with apparent pleasure. When Sharon was separated from her sister for an individual examination, her movements became stiffer. Her posture was uncomfortably erect throughout the session. Communication was at first restricted to nodding. Later, Sharon spoke very softly and used as few words as possible. Most of her CAT responses were exclusively enumerative, with rare flashes of appropriate feeling tone, which resulted in a meager test protocol showing only that she was a sad, lonely, and apparently angry little girl with limited outlets for expressing her feelings.

A week later, with a female psychologist, Sharon behaved like a mannequin from a fashionable children's store. Her expensive, well-fitting clothes accentuated her feminine delicacy, but aside from her beauty, she was not charming or appealing. While one could empathize with the apprehension and confusion she felt in a new situation, as reflected by her sobbing, tremulousness, and inability to communicate verbally, she radiated such an undercurrent of coldness, resistance, and hostility that even her misery seemed calculated to control or to defy adults and to express impatience as much as shyness. On two occasions, she managed to keep the familiar adult who accompanied her (once her mother and once her paternal grandmother) within her view, rather than to allow her frightened younger sister their comforting presence. In each instance, she expressed slyly sadistic pleasure that it was the sister who must be "all alone with two strange people." Having won out over her sister, she was able to handle structured tests with considerable efficiency and occasionally a modicum of pleasure.

She used only one-word sentences and sometimes refused test items with a shrug of her shoulders or inexpressive silence; when she spoke, however, her words were clear, of normal intensity, and without articulatory errors. She visually explored everything within range, curiously peeking under and behind test materials and quietly ignoring instructions not to her liking.

She worked rapidly and vigorously at nonverbal tasks involving puzzles, blocks, or toys. At times, there was a breathless hurry, with the accompanying tension most clearly visible in her rigid and unrelaxed postures or the tightness of her fingers. She frequently delayed responding for several minutes or reacted with a facial expression implying that she would do what she wanted when she wanted.

When the mother was present, Sharon made no demands on her. With the grandmother, who offered numerous critical suggestions, Sharon moved physically closer to the examiner. She whispered or turned away to talk directly to the examiner or cast a conspiratorial smile in the examiner's direction as she continued an activity the grandmother had protested. Sharon was quick to understand verbal instructions and had a fairly good vocabulary despite her frequent failure to communicate. It seemed clear that she had at least average capacity to recall and to reason, but her capacity to solve number problems was very limited. Finger coordination was average, although speed and impatience with minor difficulties sometimes led to errors. Her over-all intelligence, as tested, was of high average quality (IQ, 113).

Five months later, when examined by a female pediatrician with the mother and younger sister present, Sharon played intermittently with toys while the mother and doctor talked. She allowed herself to be undressed and submitted to the examination with moderate interest and cooperation. She spoke clearly, but often with a whining quality. She directed most of her comments to her mother, whom she teased occasionally, or to her sister, whom she addressed sharply, as though temporarily assuming the role of a critical mother.

Although short and of delicate bone structure, Sharon was considered relatively healthy at five. There were, however, indications of physical vulnerability in several bodily systems. For example, she continued to be more susceptible to colds than most children. A systolic cardiac murmur, of low intensity and probably functional in origin, was found, as were flattening of the arches and toeing in. It was also reported that Sharon had been hospitalized for four days at the age three with complaints of inability to urinate and a bloody discharge from the genital area. Her white blood count had indicated infection, but the source of bleeding was not determined. According to Mrs. J., Sharon reported scratching herself, but no evidence of this was found. A urinalysis at that time was negative, although during the preceding year two series of terramycin had been given for urinary tract infection. The mother felt that Sharon had not been sick enough to warrant the intensive medical work-up. Comparing Sharon to her siblings, Mrs. J. felt that the child was "alert in her mind, but physically weaker than the others."

A month later, with a male psychiatrist and in the presence of her sister, Sharon seemed more upset. In the psychiatrist's words,

All Sharon's positions are stiff, uncomfortable, angular, always correct, but never free or adapted. Similarly, her movements are rigid, jerky, and lack grace. Her constant tension interferes with her coordination so that she only barely is up to her age level, be it in finger or in gross coordination. One soon understands the source of this rigidity. Her frequent caresses of her sister much more resemble the caresses of a chimpanzee than of a human being. They frequently looked like aggressive approaches which were stopped in the last minute and converted into their apparent opposite. It was noticeable that Sharon carried out tasks which did not have aggressive implications far better than tasks which were, or could be, aggressive. While coloring, for example, she managed to stay inside the line surprisingly well, while her handling of the peg board was just as remarkably awkward. She held the hammer by the head and never produced one honest stroke.

The gross difference in her motor coordination observed by the female psychologist and a male psychiatrist suggest several speculations. It is possible that Sharon could express her motor skills more freely in the presence of a woman. Or, she may have found the structured tests less threatening, or at least less emotionally toned, than the psychiatric play sessions. Or, the presence of her sister, which she demanded to enable her to come to the session, may have raised competitive issues, especially since Carol was much more skilled motorically for her age than was Sharon (Sharon had exhibited considerable jealousy toward more motorically skillful children in nursery school).

Summarizing the findings of these sessions with respect to Sharon's physical health and cognitive resources at the preschool period, we note improved general health over the years, although there were constitutional weaknesses in the respiratory and urogenital systems and some deformities of the feet. There were also indications of moderate lag in motor development, associated with vulnerability and deterioration under stress, as observed in the psychiatric session. Cognitive resources, both as reflected by test scores and performance in the psychiatric play session, were essentially average, but cognitive functioning was rarely comfortable or fully effective. Her general knowledge and her memory, although age-adequate, were in no way spectacular. Her functioning was so often dimmed by overwhelming feelings that the content of her thinking was unclear. Her massive verbal inhibitions and her motoric variability were particularly outstanding.

The Latency Years

When Sharon was next seen, at seven, these impressions were on the whole reinforced, although all the observers found her constricted, aloof, and only superficially interested. As earlier, her clothing was expensive and somewhat oversophisticated for her age and the subculture in which she lived. Her postures were stiff, almost stylized, as though they came from a manual of ballet poses (she had been taking ballet lessons).

Although she no longer tearfully protested against coming to the sessions, her defiant passivity was increased, and her interaction with the female structured test examiner was lifeless and distant. Her speech was toneless and flat. A few quick verbal replies had the quality of automatic blurting out, after which she appeared annoyed, as though she had been tricked into responding. Her constriction was so great that it was impossible to complete an intelligence test, and the projective tests were omitted altogether. When verbal items were presented, Sharon sat motionless, except for fluttering rhythmical movements of the muscles of her throat. Muscular tension was also indicated by her tightly compressed lips. Motoric items were not completely rejected, but she responded so lethargically that puzzle pieces never quite met and drawings were segmented and awkward. She stopped altogether when asked to draw a picture of her parents, after which she sat absolutely still, except for a slight pulling in of her lips and flickering of her eyelids, for a full seven minutes. Her Performance IQ of 93, a twenty-point drop from her preschool level, was obviously not representative of her potential abilities.

The psychiatrist who saw her at about the same time found her equally unapproachable: "Sharon . . . is an immaculate, beautiful, doll-like little girl who, like a doll, cannot really be reached." She "initiated no activities on her own and only very passively participated in anything that I attempted to suggest."

An interview with the mother, who welcomed an opportunity to talk about her child at this point, offered some clarification of her increased and almost totally incapacitating constriction. Although Sharon was considered "a model, angel child" at school, at home she was "sassy," uncooperative, demanding, aggressive toward the younger children, and prone to cry at the slightest reproach from her mother. The mother suggested that she was probably under considerable strain at school and was perhaps reacting to insufficient attention at home (the mother was pregnant with the fifth child and was busy with plans for building a new house). She felt that Sharon had been going through a period of intense questioning and doubt, stemming partly from preparation for her first communion, which raised religious concerns about the meaning of God, church, creation, and Hell, but also from insecurity and doubt about her own worth and her fears that no one really loved her. The mother added that Sharon was relaxed only when alone with her. Mrs. J. remarked that Sharon's stiffness interfered with certain skills. Sharon was unable to handle acrobatic dancing with the ease of her younger sister and was unable to learn to skate. Mrs. J. felt that Sharon's lack of skill was caused not only by her bodily rigidity, but also by muscular weakness of the ankles.

Summary of Findings Through Latency

Weak at birth, handicapped by unusual physical vulnerabilities throughout her early development, and unable, partly because of these vulnerabilities, to cope effectively with stress, Sharon showed evidence of personality difficulties almost from her earliest days. A tendency to avoid seemed evident from infancy, as did a tendency to stiffen physically in a way that hampered her motoric development. Her early tendency toward avoidance seems to have emerged in later interpersonal behavior in part as rather massive constriction expressing a need to withdraw.

It seemed apparent that she reached preadolescence far too easily upset by everyday stress, with a tendency toward disorganization under stress, and with a well-established pattern of avoidance and constriction (ideational, verbal, and motoric) in the service of defensive withdrawal.

Sharon at Preadolescence

Sharon was almost eleven when the tests and observations of the present study were conducted. Her behavior, though less constricted than during her latency-age evaluation, seemed remarkably predictable from her earlier history.

Defense Mechanisms and General Characteristics of Ego Functioning

The rater felt that an unusually low rating on over-all ego strength was required primarily because of the almost incapacitating constriction implied by her test performances. Although he felt that her sparse responses contained reflections of suspiciousness (leading to a relatively high rating on Projection), he was most impressed by her massive over-control.

Rating Variable	Rating
Ego Strength	2
Over-all Ego Autonomy	3
Repression	10
Isolation	4
Reaction Formation	4
Projection	7
Avoidance	9
Denial	5
Acting Out–Overcontrol	10

Assignment to Sharon of the highest possible rating on Repression was clouded by the ambiguity attendant upon her limited responses. The very high rating on Avoidance seemed to parallel the impression of earlier observers that she was not simply withdrawn, but rather actively avoided participation. In one sense, such avoidance could be considered related to acting out, in which case assignment of the highest possible rating on Acting Out–Overcontrol (indicating maximal overcontrol) could have appeared incongruous. Although this may exemplify a limitation of the combination of acting out and overcontrol into one rating scale, it seemed particularly apparent in Sharon's case that the related defense mechanisms of avoidance and acting out *can* be employed to very different degrees.

Intellectual Abilities

Sharon's WISC subtest scores and IQ scores are presented below. The subtest scores are adjusted for age.

Information	9
Comprehension	9
Arithmetic	17
Similarities	12
Vocabulary	5
Digit Span	11
Picture Completion	7
Picture Arrangement	8
Block Design	11
Object Assembly	9
Coding (B)	16
Verbal IQ	104
Performance IQ	101
Full Scale IQ	103

Sharon's constriction, particularly in the area of verbal behavior, was as apparent in her WISC performance as in her other preadolescent behavior. That her Vocabulary score was so much lower than the average of her other scores could mean that it was not measured effectively, or that her long-standing constriction in this area actually limited her acquisition of words. The gross fluctuations in IQ noted at earlier ages suggested analogous hypotheses concerning her general performance. In either case, her test IQ was probably lower than her potential IQ. The range of her subtest scores (5 to 17) was remarkable and provided a further indication that her test performance, if not her verbal development itself, was marred by her withdrawal and constriction. She was capable of learning and remembering, and even of thinking in abstract terms, when she could do so without involving her own feelings (as in Arithmetic and Coding). When social interchange with the examiner or meanings derived from previous social relationships were involved, she was far less capable (as in Information, Comprehension, Picture Completion, and Picture Arrangement).

She was especially poor in Vocabulary, apparently because she experienced both written and oral forms of communication with considerable distaste and without any urge to investigate or use language. Her successful definitions were largely concrete and functional. The few times she permitted display of feelings, there were overtones of melancholy and generalized anxiety. With more difficult stimulus words, she quietly refused, apparently not as a function of strain in the ongoing interpersonal exchange, but rather as a reflection of long-standing inhibitions and blocking in communication.

As a part of her disinclination toward communication, Sharon showed a kind of lethargy or inability to mobilize her cognitive resources. For example, shift of focus was especially hard for her; each new task demanding the use of slightly different combinations of skills was met with delay and temporary vagueness. With motor items, this delay often appeared to be strategic, serving to pave the way for planned manipulation, which was then deliberate, fairly graceful and accurate, but not obsessively neat. With verbal or emotionally toned test items (such as Comprehension or Picture Arrangement), delay seemed to reflect unwillingness or inability to commit herself to a definite stand or specific plan.

It was also apparent that Sharon sometimes chose the easiest or most obvious response. This behavior could have reflected low energy level, but this was not an entirely satisfactory explanation in view of the vigor and forcefulness of her behavior at other times. One might also hypothesize low achievement drive, yet she clearly wanted to do well once she had committed herself and could be very persistent, as she was observed to be in the Object Assembly subtest.

Cognitive Controls

The consistency with which Sharon's withdrawal and constriction were reflected in relevant cognitive control principle factors was also notable.

Factor	Score	Meaning
I Scanning A	2.03	Extensive checking (to the point of doubt-riddenness?) of judgments in the size estimation tests.
II Conceptual Differentiation	1.84	High differentiation (many small groups in the sorting tests); literal, descriptive, "stimulus-bound" response to the TAT.
III Scanning B	.15	Average judgment times in the size estimation tests (in contrast to her extensive postjudgment checking).
IV Field-Articulation	.07	Average articulation.
V Constricted-Flexible Control	− .95	Difficulty in inhibiting irrelevant vocalizations in the Color-Word Test; few inadequate definitions and few spontaneous elaborations of definitions in the Object Sorting Test.
VI Spontaneity	−2.14	Unusual lack of spontaneity, evidenced by long Rorschach and TAT reaction times; literal, descriptive responses to the TAT; few elaborations of definitions in the Object Sorting Test; intolerance for unrealistic experiences.

It is intriguing that Sharon was average in her actual judgment times in the size estimation tests but unusually high in the amount of time she spent checking her judgments (without making further adjustments of the comparison stimulus). It may be, of course, that this "checking" reflected her withdrawal and her resistance to overt communications to the experimenter (in this case, indicating completion of a judgment by closing her eyes), as much as careful checking of her adjustments of the comparison stimulus. Her other two outstanding factor scores, on Conceptual Differentiation and Spontaneity, had direct implications for her generalized constriction. The Conceptual Differentiation score reflected a literal, stimulus-close approach to the sorting tests and the TAT that bespoke ideational constriction and, in the latter case, the possibility of massive repression as well.

In summary, her performances in the tests of cognitive controls showed a rather remarkable concordance to the picture of Sharon gleaned from earlier studies and from the other tests and observations of the present study. It is theoretically noteworthy that performance in laboratory size estimation and categorizing tests could be used to draw verifiable inferences about constriction, inhibition, and withdrawal. It is important to note, however, that she was much more avoidant in such tests as the TAT than in tests involving motor activity (e.g., the size estimation tests). Her greater participation in the latter type of task was also consistent with earlier observations.

Behavior in the Clinical Testing Situation

Sharon's factor scores on the six factors derived from the forty-seven ratings of the children's behavior during the WISC and TAT were, in part by virtue of their nature, even more saturated with indications of her generalized constriction. Sharon's scores are presented here, with notations as to their meaning.

	Factor	*Score*	*Meaning*
I	Active Openness to New Experience	−2.25	Extreme closedness (withdrawal, lack of curiosity, rigidity, limited range of enjoyment, dependence, etc.).
II	Unity of Identity	.51	About average clarity of identity; identification with own sex; etc.
III	Accuracy of Reality Testing	.23	Average accuracy and clarity of perception; attention to fine detail; adequacy of spatial orientation, etc.
IV	Cooperativeness	− .14	Average task-involvement, frustration tolerance, cooperation with authority, etc.
V	Compulsive Exactness	.42	About average concern with goodness and badness; about average meticulosity, determination, stubbornness, etc.
VI	Sporadic Disruption of Control	1.22	Rather high in variability, fearfulness, observable tension, etc.

It is impressive that, in keeping with many of the other findings, Sharon appeared both extremely constricted and erratically variable, although she was average on the other dimensions, particularly cooperativeness. This apparently reflected a change in her stance in the clinical testing situation from her earlier determined resistance to more adequate participation. That is, she was viewed as constricted but involved, rather than as actively avoidant. This may have reflected an important area of improvement in her preadolescent behavior.

Behavior in the Laboratory Testing Situation

Sharon's scores on the four factors derived from the twenty-three ratings of behavior in the laboratory closely parallel the other findings.

	Factor	Score	Meaning
I	Impulsive Spontaneity	−1.22	Low in warmth, friendliness, talkativeness, spontaneity, etc.
II	Anxious Dependence	2.22	Very low in confidence in own abilities; high dependence, tension, etc.
III	Explorativeness	− .29	About average in scanning, curiosity, drive toward mastery, etc.
IV	Acting upon the Environment	−2.47	Extreme overcontrol (meticulous, low in energy level and action on the environment, etc.).

In relation to a male examiner in a new setting, Sharon was seen by the observer as distantly unresponsive, excessively overcontrolled, and anxiously (if rather silently) dependent. That she was viewed as average in explorativeness may be attributable in part to her tendency to scan new situations rather carefully, and to the lack of explorativeness shown by many other children in the sample.

Cognitive Style—Aspects of Over-all Ego Organization

Sharon's scores for the six general factors are presented below.

	Factor	Score	Meaning
I	Field-Articulation	− .64	Tendency toward low articulation.
II	Spontaneity	2.10	Unspontaneous.
III	Maturity	−1.39	Low in age, autonomy, comfortable independence, ego strength, etc.
IV	Adequacy of Reality Testing	.58	Tendency toward leveling, sporadic disruption of control, inaccurate reality testing, etc.
V	Explorativeness	− .37	Tendency toward unexplorativeness, narrow categorizing, etc.
VI	Acting Out	−1.01	Catholic; low in acting out, etc.

Sharon's generalized constriction, her low ego strength and over-all ego autonomy, her inability to explore her surroundings actively, her tendency toward literality and stereotypy, and her relatively primitive reality testing, which was manifested both in weak articulation of current experience and in leveling of differences between new and old experiences, were all summarized, as it were, by her scores on these general factors. It was impressive that her score for the Maturity factor was considerably lower than the mean (about zero) in spite of the fact that she was only half a year younger than the average of the sixty children at the time she was tested. Her low score on Factor III was primarily dictated by her generalized constriction and ego weakness.

Summary of Preadolescent Findings

The outstanding features of Sharon's behavior at preadolescence—her generalized constriction, her high tension level, her tendency to avoid by withdrawing, and her depressed unspontaneity—appeared repeatedly in the various groups of tests and ratings employed. In spite of indications of some general improvement from latency to preadolescence, the appearance of these as major traits at preadolescence suggested preliminary crystallization of a personality organization with adaptive limitations and with unhappy implications for her future. Other children in the sample were more overtly disturbed, however, and showed more peculiarities of thought and perception. It seemed probable that her long-standing constriction had impaired her future intellectual potential, yet she seemed capable of more than she achieved. Her limitations were most evident in her interactions with adults.

Discussion of the Four Case Studies

We have seen how rather extensive empirical assessments of ego organization at preadolescence mesh with, supplement, clarify, and extend information available from longitudinal studies of individual children. The most important general point to make here is the apparent effectiveness of cognitive control scores, ratings of behavior in the laboratory testing situation, and the other assessments as contributors to a more comprehensive picture of personality organization at preadolescence. Even the control dimensions whose generality is least understood at this point seem to add meaningfully to the other material.

Empirical assessment of various cognitive structures can serve a function in longitudinal studies analogous to the function of diagnostic testing in the clinic. Mutually contradictory speculations about subtleties of defense organization, ego strength, and so forth are nowhere so effectively evaluated in a minimal time period as by the use of procedures that force the subject to cope with standardized sets of conditions in the presence of an examiner or observer who has had extensive experience with individuality of response to those conditions and the clinically or generally relevant behaviors associated with various forms of individuality. One of the special virtues of such an empirical approach is that the examiner can detect subtle incongruities in behavioral organization that may point to major lines of identity or role cleavage in the individual. We have seen examples of this revealing kind of incongruity in the case studies discussed in these chapters.

The other general observation to be made here is that none of the single groups of variables assessed seems regnant in terms of explanatory power concerning the life history of an individual child. To know that a child is "repressive" in the extreme explains certain key facets of his current personality organization but tells us little or nothing about a considerable number of other ego structures that have dramatically important effects on his total cognitive style and his total personality organization. To know that a child is extremely adept or extremely ineffective at field-articulation tells us much about an aspect of his personality organization that is at least partly rooted in his individual heredity and is relevant to certain aspects of his performance in a broad class of adaptive situations. To know this, however, does not allow prediction of most of his defensive armamentarium, his other cognitive controls, his verbal ability, major features of his interpersonal behavior, or a wide variety of other significant features of his personality organization. This conclusion is reinforced by the outcome of the final analysis of interrelations among major groups of structures described in Chapter 12. These two sets of findings lead to some tentative general conclusions and some further questions concerning personality organization as a whole that are discussed in Chapter 15.

15 Overview of the Study and Major Implications of the Results

THE COMPLEXITY of the controlling structures discernible in a sampling of defenses, cognitive controls, abilities, and other aspects of behavior at preadolescence and the complexity of interrelationships among these variables at a higher level of structural organization has been apparent throughout this book. The patterns of individual personality organization are much more complex and variegated. This general finding applies also to the nature of developmental curves for particular cognitive phenomena and to the relationships of cognitive structures to these phenomena and the developmental changes they undergo.

Before dealing with some of the general implications of these and related results, it should be noted that the sampling of behavioral structures was obviously incomplete. It must also be recognized, by way of orientation to the discussion to follow, that we have focused our sampling of structures primarily on a group of controlling structures that seems to fall in the middle range of the hierarchy of structures involved in personality organization. The kinds of structures sampled in this study do not provide an effective view of the totality of individual personalities, nor was the study designed to do so. Later in this chapter, we shall discuss some unresolved questions concerning the totality of behavioral individuality and some possible approaches to this grand enigma.

Before launching on a discussion of the present study as a whole, we should also reiterate that the apparent effectiveness of the concept of structure as a means of dealing with individuality does not mean that such structuring itself is fully understood, either with respect to its nature or its possible origins. In Chapter 1, we expressed our dissatisfaction with the redundant older process hypotheses concerning structure formation, including the emergence of patterned defense operations. We pointed briefly to a simpler view of controlling structures that could clarify approaches to their actual nature. More problems concerning the nature and origins of such structures remain than have been answered, however. The problem of the sequence of structure formations in early development, for example, is all but untouched. The present study was not designed to add new evidence to the bits of current knowledge relevant to these problems. The results do, however, reinforce a point of view that could be anticipated before the study was performed: the behavioral structures giving consistency to individual personality organization differ enough in kind and in developmental characteristics to indicate that extremely varied clusters of hereditary and experiential factors are involved in their evolution. It is tempting to reduce this complexity to a few simpler rules about cognitive development. It would appear more appropriate to await further evidence, rather than to oversimplify the results in the service of premature parsimony.

Structural Organization at Preadolescence

The value of the present study as a means of generating new questions concerning personality development rests in part on the degree to which critical aspects of personality organization were sampled. Although no claim can be made that the assessment was in any sense comprehensive, the major groups of variables involved, particularly the defenses and abilities, are applicable to wide varieties of adaptive behaviors and have proved their usefulness in a number of behavioral contexts. The newer concept of cognitive control also promises to play a role in future views of structural organization. With these points in mind, what has the present study told us of these important groups of structures at preadolescence?

A first answer to this question is that defense and cognitive control organization are apparently more fully and clearly developed at preadolescence than has often been assumed. Defense organization, in particular, is rather sharply discernible in terms of its recognizability, the degree of differentiation of specific defensive functions, and the interrelations among specific defenses. The *patterning* of defenses is, in fact, remarkably similar to the patterning one might anticipate in a group of adults. The notion that defense organization at preadolescence is universally global or amorphous can apparently be disposed of rather completely.

This statement about the patterning of defenses in no way denies, of course, qualitative changes in the specific defenses and the products of their operation that occur between preadolescence and adulthood.

A second answer to the general question posed above comprises one of our more important findings concerning structural organization at preadolescence: no single group of structural variables was regnant over the others assessed in predicting other important aspects of behavior. Key aspects of the child's over-all behavior in two very different types of testing situation, for example, were no more referable to his defense organization than to his ability or cognitive control organizations, although each was relevant to specific aspects of such behavior. This general result should alert us to the pitfalls for theory development of viewing individuality too exclusively through the conceptual framework provided by any single set of structural variables. The ramifications of defense operations, as explicated in the clinic, have vastly extended our understanding of cognitive behavior. But defensive structures are only one of a larger constellation of structures and in themselves provide an inadequate, and potentially distorted, view of personality organization.

The effects of similarity and difference in individuals' total cognitive styles (including defenses, controls, abilities, and other variables) on the transference, on teaching and learning, on communication, on marital compatibility, and on teamwork have been envisioned (see, e.g., Gardner *et al.*, 1959), but remain unexplored. Although the newer and broader conceptual framework that is beginning to evolve is yet in its infancy, it may not be too early to study these effects. It is questionable, for example, that a work team (therapist-patient, teacher-student, factory work group) will enjoy equal ease of communication when the members are similar or different with respect to even a single dimension of cognitive control, such as spontaneous conceptual differentiation. The general human tendency to attach evaluative labels to individuals' styles and expressive contents must play some role here. Negative evaluations of styles differing from one's own may in part be referable to the greater amount of cognitive work required for effective communication under these conditions.

Although recent progress in the study of individuality makes a third possible answer less novel than it would have been fifteen years ago, it may be worth reiteration in terms of the results of the present study: the evidences of individual consistency are impressive, although different constellations of consistency show a remarkable degree of discreteness at this general level of personality organization and although the realms of consistency range from broad to narrow. That this is true at preadolescence as well as among adults points, we feel, to the potential value of full-scale explorations of structural development from birth to adulthood.

Developmental Changes in Structural Organization

One of the advantages of the present study as an approach to developmental changes in behavioral structuring was its inclusion of a number of control and defense variables about which much is known in the case of adults. It was possible, therefore, to observe some of the varieties of developmental progression that characterize different aspects of ego functioning and, perhaps more important, to look at the controlling structures in relation to some of these progressions. The yield in this area was relatively great, we feel, and can be summarized, in terms of controlling structures, in the points discussed in the following paragraphs.

The multiplicity of developmental progressions from early to late preadolescence, as exemplified in this study, include at least the following types of change: (1) change from early to late preadolescence, with further change in the same direction from preadolescence to adulthood; (2) change from early to late preadolescence, with *no* change from preadolescence to adulthood (i.e., the structure seems to have achieved "maturity" at preadolescence) ; (3) no change from early to late preadolescence, with considerable change from preadolescence to adulthood; (4) change at both age levels in the direction of greater articulation of experience; (5) change at both levels in the direction of greater synthesis of experience; (6) change at both levels leading to progressively greater perceptual accuracy; (7) change at both levels leading to progressively lesser perceptual accuracy; (8) qualitative and quantitative change in structural products, without change in structural patterning; (9) change in different directions in two sets of attentional-perceptual phenomena, without change in the relation of a control structure to these phenomena; (10) change in the same direction in sets of attentional-perceptual phenomena, also without change in the relation of a control structure to the phenomena; (11) synthesis with age of initially disparate structures into correlated groups of structures.

Exploration of the relationships of developmental curves for particular cognitive phenomena to the structures relevant to these phenomena has produced a new kind of finding that seems, as noted before, to provide evidence that the controlling structures involved in the individual consistencies are relatively autonomous structures. These structures have predictable effects on individual consistencies with respect to cognitive products that have different types of developmental curves. This is an important finding that seems to imply stability and longevity of structural organization as an entity in and of itself. At the very least, it is now clear that the structural constellations so vividly evident at preadolescence cannot necessarily be explained in terms of the nature of the developmental curves characterizing the specific phenomena to which these structures are relevant. Here, then, is a glimpse into the *interactional* complexity of cognitive development, in terms of basic processes on the one hand and individuality of structure formation on the other.

Earlier, we noted Hartmann's point about the "change of function" of defenses, in which they come to be employed for nondefensive purposes. It is also obvious that originally nondefensive structures may generalize to encompass defensive purposes. The present results indicate that it may be appropriate to add a third concept of developmental change in structural organization: defensive and nondefensive aspects of individuality operating as discrete constellations at preadolescence may, during subsequent development, become correlated aspects of over-all adaptational style. In this case (exemplified, for example, by the relation of extensiveness of scanning to isolation and projection in adults but not in children), the ultimate correlation is not referable solely to the generalization of defensive or nondefensive structures. On the basis of such findings, we are tempted to speculate that a type of synthesis occurs in which certain structures originally formed to serve defensive and nondefensive purposes are integrated into more general adaptive structures useful for either purpose. Taken together, these three interrelated conceptions of structural change in development suggest that adult behavior is more economically and efficiently organized in part because available structures can be used more flexibly for multiple adaptive purposes. It could be that this kind of developmental synthesis with increased flexibility is one key to the grossly more adequate adaptive behavior of the adult and his greater freedom from immediate stimulus conditions. It could also be that the development of integrated structures serving as multipurpose adaptive tools is a key to one difference between the "undifferentiated" adult and the adaptively adroit adult. The latter's outstanding characteristic is often his capacity to function effectively under a wide variety of adaptive conditions.

The three related types of structural change we have postulated here could, of course, be referable to a generalized capacity for structural integration. Such a capacity could in itself be partly rooted in hereditarily given characteristics of the individual's adaptive apparatuses.

Concerning defense organization per se, we have noted that specific defense structures and the products of their operation may change more than the patterning of defenses from preadolescence to adulthood. Our results in this area thus seem to suggest that the oft-presumed revolution in defense organization at and following puberty has been overestimated, at least in the case of many normal children. It seems likely, also, that individual children differ greatly in the amount of change in defense structures and in defense patterning that occurs in this important new phase of development.

It is time to apply longitudinal methods to exploration of the aspects of preadolescent structure formation which undergo greater or lesser reorganization in adolescence. Such questions as the following suggest themselves: Are there adolescent structural changes of several kinds that differentiate individuals high and low in ego strength? What are the specific structural strengths or weaknesses associated with effective versus ineffective resolution of the problems posed by the adolescent maturational changes? Do generally constricted, conforming children change less than more actively exploratory and self-expressive children? Is a middle range of over-all control versus expressive freedom the ideal structural condition for personality growth during preadolescence? Which children are most likely to undergo gross disturbances of equilibration that lead to severe regression followed by large-scale reorganization? Such questions require careful assessment of known structural variables at preadolescence and subsequently. They imply that specific adolescent problems, such as the problem of how to deal with intensified genital sexual drives, may have their roots in specific drives and constellations of defense, but can be better understood only when a more comprehensive structural picture of the individual is achieved.

Sex Differences in Structural Organization and Their Relations to Cultural Attitudes

The general absence of sex differences in the present study is one of its most important general results. In the area of defense, of course, some sex differences were found. These could be expected; the defensive problems of boys and girls are inevitably different because of their different biological characteristics and the different cultural demands imposed upon them during their development. Differences in explorativeness were also noted (in the laboratory testing situation). In general, however, the study is remarkable for the lack of sex differences apparent in a rather wide variety of behaviors. In at least the cognitive control area, these findings are supported by earlier results with adults.

Two sets of points should be made here concerning these general observations:

1. Sex differences in certain aspects of cognitive structuring may be less prevalent in this culture and subculture than is often assumed. Apparent sex differences should be examined carefully to insure that a real sex difference in some extraneous variable is not responsible for an apparent sex difference in response to a test presumed to tap another cognitive function.

2. The general absence of apparent sex differences in this study, or any other study performed in one culture, does not imply absence of potential sex differences. The paucity of observed differences in the present study may be attributable to the similar demands this culture makes on boys and girls with respect to cognitive growth. Support for this notion is apparently contained in the results of a study of preadolescent boy-girl differences in conceptual differentiation and related aspects of concept formation reported by Mercado *et al.* (1963). Whereas boys and girls of the midwestern United States did not differ in these important aspects of concept formation, Mexican boys and girls differed widely in ways predictable on the basis of the role differences assigned to boys and girls in the Mexican culture. Like estimations of heritability, estimations of sex differences are easily oversimplified by overlooking the effects of cultural variables. An analogous point can be made about an apparent lack of heritability. Adequate evaluation of either ultimately requires intercultural studies, as do all other studies of structural development.

Some Unexplored Areas of Behavioral Individuality

A list of unexplored, or largely unexplored, areas of psychological individuality could well fill a small book in itself. A few of the areas most impressively apparent from the work on structures to date will be listed here as examples of the many important problems yet unsolved.

Among the most obvious areas of individual consistency, and high on the list of those stamping the individual as a unique entity, is that of affective style. Part of the problem here has been the general lack of agreement about the nature of affect, its origins, and its causative role in behavior. In the psychoanalytic view, affects, like ideas and structure formations, are in part by-products, as it were, of delay of drive gratification. Among the other views intertwined with, or in opposition to, this conception in the recent history of psychology is the notion that affect is more fundamental and of greater causative significance in behavior. It seems apparent that in either case—or somewhere in the realm between these emphases—feeling states, and individuality in the organization of feeling states, must in part be referable to the nature and interaction of a wide variety of behavioral structures, including defenses, cognitive controls, intellectual abilities, the little-explored patternings of motoric behavior, and others.

A second area of individuality as yet largely unexplored is that of verbal style. The extreme generality of the ability to articulate certain aspects of experience suggests the potential fruitfulness of a similar large-scale assault on the generality of verbal ability, as well as other aspects of verbal style. Individuality of language style, vocal style, and so forth have been explored to some degree, but with nothing like the thoroughness that may be possible even at the present stage of methodology in these areas.

As for the cognitive control concepts employed in this study, work to date has suggested the value of considerable numbers of additional studies, of which only a few groups can be discussed here. The further explorations of individuality in assimilation versus contrast effects referred to in Chapter 3 would seem to be of basic importance to more adequate understanding of perception, concept formation, and relations between them. Such studies could potentially provide a basis for linking work on leveling-sharpening to Helson's work on adaptation level, Piaget's extensive work on other types of perceptual contrast effects, and other work on cognitive controls already completed.

Studies of the "borderland" between assimilation and categorizing and their interaction as determinants of perceptual and memoric phenomena could also help to clarify the individual differences thus far explored.

In the area of categorizing behaviors, a number of explorations are suggested by results of the present study, including studies of the individual's conceptual "distance" from objects and persons, and his openness and explorativeness.

Among the many other groups of cognitive control studies that could clarify unsolved issues in this area is a more comprehensive study of the controls of attention. Selectivity of attention and extensiveness of scanning in perceptual decision-making situations are but two of an obviously larger number of dimensions of attentional control. The difficult problem of intensity of attention is, for example, all but untouched. This is one of several areas in which combinations of psychological and physiological methods could be most fruitfully employed.

Exploration of cognitive controls as determinants of the perception of persons has been touched on in the present study and is being extended in a current study of three controls as determinants of the organization of perceptions of both persons and objects (see Gardner, 1964b). Shrauger and Altrocchi (1964) have recently pointed out the potential fruitfulness of such an approach to person perception.

A pressing need dictated by sampling limitations common to most psychological studies, including much of the work on cognitive controls, is worthy of mention here. Our current knowledge concerning behavioral structuring is rather severely limited by the employment as subjects of adults and children who range from low average to superior in general intellectual ability. What of persons whose IQ's range downward from 90 to 70, or 50? It seems likely that various classes of limited endowment or postnatal damage affect not only the abilities measured by intelligence tests, but also the patterning of defenses, cognitive controls, and other behavioral structures included in the present study. The fact that a cognitive control dimension can be shown to be independent of commonly measured intellectual abilities in the 90–140 IQ range does not mean that these variables are independent when there are gross limits on one or more mental functions. Exploration of structure formation in this ability range could add a new dimension to our understanding of relations among such structures.

Analogous sampling extensions to older age groups or to groups of psychiatric and neurological patients would also provide valuable new information concerning cognitive control structures. The beginnings that have been made in this area (see, e.g., Mathae, 1958; Witkin *et al.*, 1962; and Silverman, 1964a, b) strongly support this point of view.

The possibility that individuals differ in the tightness or looseness of structural arrangements and in the variability of operation of specific structures is potentially amenable to investigation and is all but unexplored (cf. Murphy, 1947).

Relations between structural variables and individual differences in learning and recall have been the subject of several fruitful studies (see, e.g., the work on cognitive controls and learning phenomena referred to in Chapter 3), but the completed work deals with only a few of the variables in this important area.

Tests of the predictive implications of an individual's *pattern* of cognitive control structures (i.e., one aspect of his "cognitive style," as defined by Gardner *et al.*, 1959) for performance in complex tasks poses intriguing and challenging problems that are also largely unexplored.

Although the role of controlling structures in drive expression has been an essential component of the conceptualization of such controls (see, e.g., Klein, 1956, 1958; Holzman and Klein, 1956), motivational variables have been employed thus far in only a limited number of studies. The studies of constricted and flexible-control subjects by Klein (1954) and Holt (1960) indicate the potential value of further studies in this area. Relations between cognitive structures and individuality of drive and drive level is of critical importance to structural conceptions (cf. Murphy's 1947 discussion of the basic importance of the organization of tension systems) and would appear to require a multifaceted approach to heredity, observations of neonates, physiological and psychological measurements of drive level, and the like. Here again, general psychology seems to provide valuable stepping stones to studies of individuality. The possibility that generalized drive level acts as a "moderator variable" (see Wallach, e.g., 1962) in certain situations presents an equally challenging problem.

Relations between the structures explored in the present study and individuality with respect to speed, personal tempo, and various aspects of expressive style (e.g., as explored by Allport and Vernon, 1933) also recommend themselves as fruitful avenues of research.

Among the many other areas that could be explored, that of belief and value organizations seems of special importance. What interactions obtain, for example, between categorizing styles and belief organization? To take but one simple example from a large number of potentially relevant questions, does a conservative narrow categorizer (in neutral categorizing tasks) differentiate more than a conservative broad categorizer between individuals who are arrayed along a conservative-liberal dimension?

As stated in Chapter 1, it seems to us that certain initial features of cognitive behavior—some of them highly hereditary—serve as part of the anlage for the development of specific controls, defenses, abilities, and other specific cognitive structures and may in part determine the ultimate relationships among constellations of structures in the individual. In some instances, the cognitive control structuring may precede defense formation. Some of the basic characteristics of human behavior which are later incorporated into defense operations, such as turning away from noxious stimuli, are part of our evolutionary heritage, as are the apparatuses involved in all defense, control, ability, and other operations. The strengths of the drives to be modulated, certain aspects of temperament, and the like are also aspects of the species' heredity (cf. Diamond, 1957) which unfold in individually unique patternings via the vagaries of genetic combination. To learn, as might be learned through more extensive studies, the ways in which the total anlage leads to individually unique basic cognitive dispositions—out of which defense, control, and ability patternings evolve under particular sets of ecological conditions—would be to provide a conceptual base from which to unify our understanding of later individuality.

To proceed from preadolescent structures to structure formation in earlier childhood and infancy will require new approaches to assessment, empirical linking of these methods to methods now applicable to older age groups, and solution of a series of additional problems that are as impressively difficult as they are intriguing and challenging. It is in studies of this kind, however, combined with results of genetic (i.e., hereditary) studies, that some of the answers to questions concerning structural origins lie. The results of the present study have, we feel, sharpened our focus on this general problem a bit by making it clearer than before that over-all structural organization in late childhood is, if anything, more differentiated (i.e., less globally synthesized) than in adulthood. The additional fact that clearly articulated clusters of cognitive structures are apparent at preadolescence that are independent of defense operation exemplifies the potential complexity of total cognitive development from infancy onward.

Studies of the differential importance of heredity to the formation of particular behavioral structures are essential to any approach to the origins of such structures. A first step in this direction, which combines estimates of heritability with assessments of parental attitudes and behavior, parental structures, other ecological variables, and developmental changes, is described briefly in the next section of this chapter.

We have pointed to some of the more obvious unexplored problems suggested by the present study and those that preceded it. It should be apparent from this brief discussion that we see the problem of individual personality organization as extremely complex and the present study as but one limited step among the many that will be required in this area.

Some Current Studies of Structural Development

Certain further studies are now in progress that were stimulated by the unsolved problems pointed up in the present study. The questions approached in these studies are among those that seemed of most general importance to further explorations of individuality.

Results of the present study pointed to the usefulness of a larger study including the following: (1) investigation of the nature of the heredity-environment coaction in the development of a considerable variety of structures (a first study, with subjects in this culture); (2) a full-scale study of developmental changes in most of the variables included in the present study, plus a considerable group of additional variables highly relevant to individuality; (3) assessment of the children's parents with the same procedures administered to the children; (4) evaluation of each parent's attitudes toward child-rearing, as well as his actual behavior toward his child; (5) assessment of key features of these parent-child groups as constellations of interacting persons; (6) measurement of a larger group of ecological variables, including each parent's attitudes toward individuality in the child; (7) inclusion of measures of the perception of self and other persons, measures of some basic aspects of physiological reactivity, and measures of several other groups of potentially relevant behaviors explored by other investigators (so that these studies would also extend earlier work on the generality of various structural variables).

The guiding premises and the design of this group of studies have been outlined elsewhere (Gardner, 1964a, c; 1965). In brief, the aims above and their manifold subsidiary aims (e.g., to determine the effects of child-rearing attitudes on heritability estimates; to explore complex interactions among other variables) has led to the administration, in identical form, of large batteries of group and individual procedures to fifty identical and fifty fraternal twins ranging in age from eight to nineteen and their parents. Interviews were added to provide additional information, particularly information on parental orientations toward similarity and difference in their twins (in itself a potential source of new information concerning heritability). A group decision-making procedure has provided unique information concerning interactions within these parent-child groups. Additional batteries of psychological and physiological procedures were subsequently administered to the twins alone. These further batteries were designed to extend the earlier work on controls in several specific areas.

The potential yield of such studies is large. The interactions among structural and other variables that can be explored by this method are numerous. But this work in progress can hope to provide further orientation toward the general problem of behavioral individuality only to a limited degree. The studies referred to above and others too numerous to describe here are all highly relevant to advances in this relatively new area of psychology.

The Problem of Total Personality Organization

At the beginning of this chapter, we referred to the problem of individual personality organization as a whole and noted subsequently that several key aspects of individuality—including the structuring of affective and motoric behavior—have received relatively little attention. It would appear, however, that a larger conceptual problem awaits the explorer in this area: the problem of the most general organizing principles of individuality—the general principles that serve as a structural framework in which the component structures are arranged. That there are such general principles and that the behavioral patternings involved are relatively autonomous of the component structures seems clearly apparent from observations of the life careers of individuals (cf., e.g., Murphy, 1947, chap. xxx on "Continuity," and Bühler, 1964, on the life-course in terms of goals).

Two possibly related approaches have repeatedly emerged in both deliberate and inadvertent approaches to this problem by members of the first author's research team. We hold no strong brief for their ultimate effectiveness, but will employ them here to exemplify the unanswered question of behavioral organization at the most general level.

The first of these approaches seems to express itself most readily in terms of identity formation, particularly the early patterns of identity acquired by imitation, incorporation, and identification with respect to the parental figures. The work of Erik Erikson, referred to in Chapter 1 and elsewhere in this book, could be of particular relevance here. A guiding speculation is that the nature of the unconscious self-concepts that emerge from the interaction of the infant and young child (with his unique hereditary dispositions toward sensitivity, temperament, ability, and the like) with the parental figures is of central importance in the shaping of the total personality. It seems possible that this permanent set of unconscious concepts and images both dictates (in the peremptory fashion of unconscious thinking) the over-all facilitation of self-expression and self-actualization in certain areas of behavior and imposes powerful inhibitions upon subsequent activity and structural differentiation in other areas. It seems possible, in this connection, that areas of potential talent may be walled off from extensive further development by such deep-laid self-concepts in all or nearly all individuals. It seems possible, also, that the black-and-white quality of the primitive thinking and perception preserved in these unconscious self-concepts could, when appropriately modulated by higher-order structures, in part account for the general thematic consistency of most individual life courses, including special interests and occupational choices. Perhaps such unconscious self-concepts account in part for the relative permanence of over-all orientation toward interests, attitudes, careers, hobbies, and so forth that characterizes most persons under normal conditions.

The second way of viewing such life consistencies that has repeatedly recommended itself to us can be rather crudely expressed in terms of highly generalized life styles or "stances" toward significant aspects of reality, including the personal unconscious, other persons, and the physical world. We seemed to glimpse such a possible stance, or a product of such a stance, in our work on categorizing styles (Chapters 3, 5, and 6). The work of Rotter (e.g., 1954) and others on internal versus external control could be relevant here (and is being explored further in the study of twins and their parents referred to above). In the studies by Rotter and his associates, some persons consistently attribute the causes of their behavior to factors outside themselves, whereas others understand their behavior as products of aspects of themselves that their externalizing counterparts seem unaware of. The realm of general "stances" must be multidimensional, of course, but may be less populous than the realms of structures lower in the hierarchy of total personality organization. Eysenck's (e.g., 1952) concept of extraversion-introversion, Riesman's (1950) concept of inner- versus outer-directed persons, Rokeach's (1960) delineation of the open versus the closed mind, Harvey, Hunt, and Schroder's (1961) characterization of general attitudes that are abstract versus concrete, and Tomkins' (1964) explication of conservative versus liberal stances are among the currently available conceptions that may be relevant to this kind of approach.

On the basis of our experience with structural variables thus far, including particularly the challenging results of the present study, we would predict that the most general organizational principles of individuality—whatever their other properties—will prove to be relatively autonomous structures that are both causes and effects of all the other behavioral structures and all the other processes involved in the totality of individual personality organization. Only by investigating all these structures and their interrelationships will we ultimately achieve a more effective view of the entire equilibrational system that is the individual person.

Appendix

Definitions of Ratings of Over-all Behavior in the Clinical and Laboratory Testing Situations

Rating	*Definition*
*1. Coping I (Activeness of problem-solving)	Activeness of use of environmental demands, opportunities, obstacles in problem-solving.
*2. Coping II (Internal equilibration)	Internal balance; resources for maintaining integration under stress.
*3. Cognitive coping capacity	Effectiveness of employment of available cognitive resources.
*6. Ability to synthesize thought, affect, action	Effectiveness of coordination of ideation, feelings, and motor skills.
*8. Mobilization of resources under stress	Effectiveness of use of cognitive, affective, and motor skills under pressure of difficulty, frustration, etc.
*10. Translation of ideas into action	Adequacy in thinking through problems and acting accordingly.
*13. Clarity of perception	Sharpness and definiteness of percepts.
*14. Accuracy of perception	Adequacy in checking experience against reality; using past experiences to verify percepts.
*15. Speed of orientation	Quickness to understand, absorb directions, see implications.
*18. Clarity of identity	Definiteness and unity of self-concept.
*19. Adequacy of self-appraisal	Accuracy of self-evaluation.
*21. Concern with goodness and badness	Emphasis on naughtiness or evil, concern with religious teaching.
*22. Range of areas of enjoyment	Scope of pleasurable activities.
*23. Ability to ask for help	Freedom to ask adult for appropriate assistance.
*24. Pleasure in own body	Satisfaction with physical development, appearance, and skills.
*25. Expressive rigidity	Limitation in quantity or variety of facial expressions, gestures, postures, etc.

313

Rating	*Definition*
ª27. Accuracy of evaluations of others	Understanding of and empathy with others; recognition of others' assets and limitations.
ª29. Social insightfulness	Sensitivity to implications of social interaction; capacity to behave appropriately in social situations.
ª30. Cooperation with authority	Willingness to follow instructions given by an adult.
ᶜ31. Confidence in abilities	Experienced adequacy to deal with the demands of the situation.
ᵇ32. Observable tension	Tension apparent in verbalization, voice quality, facial expression, autonomic reaction, body-part movements, etc.
ᵇ33. Fearfulness	Apprehensiveness.
ᵇ34. Task-involvement	Involvement in the tests; satisfaction or pleasure, rather than compliance.
ᵇ35. Energy level	Vigorousness of motor activity.
ᶜ36. Friendliness	Affability, cordiality.
ᶜ37. Talkativeness	Quantity of verbal communication.
ᵇ38. Enjoyment	Pleasure and gratification in the situation.
ᵇ39. Frustration tolerance	Acceptance of frustrating circumstances without disruption of behavior.
ᵇ40. Variability	Fluctuation in performance or in quality of contact with the examiner.
ª44. Affective differentiation	Experience and expression of nuances of affect.
ª46. Clarity of fantasy-reality distinction	Differentiation of the real from the fantasied.
ª47. Flexibility	Acceptance of new ideas or reformulation of ideas already held; freedom from blocking.
ᵇ51. Warmth	Expression of positive feelings toward others, including the examiner.
ᵇ52. Trust	Faith in the integrity of people and things.
ᵇ53. Openness to new experience	Receptivity to and enjoyment of new experiences.
ᵇ54. Curiosity	Eagerness to know about people and things.
ª55. Adequacy of spatial orientation	Clarity concerning the size, direction, and distance of objects or locations; ease of finding way in new places.
ª57. Identification with own sex	Acceptance of sex-appropriate values and behavior patterns.
ᵇ62. Action upon the environment	Direction of action *toward* the environment.
ᵇ63. Independence, self-reliance	Freedom to act confidently without direction.
ᶜ64. Grasp of the situation	Grasp of directions, sequences, implications.
ᵇ65. Drive toward mastery	Drive to learn about, understand, control.

Rating	*Definition*
ᵃ66. Determination	Resolution in working toward a goal.
ᵃ67. Perseverance	Sustaining effort toward completion of a task.
ᵃ68. Stubbornness	Obstinacy; clinging to ideas and behavior whether effective or not.
ᵃ69. Attention span	Duration of attention to relevant objects or purposes.
ᵃ70. Attention to fine detail	Awareness of and focus on parts or qualities of a whole.
ᵃ71. Freedom from doubt and ambivalence	Singleness of purpose.
ᵃ72. Capacity to delay for appraisal	Waiting when necessary for effective planning.
ᵇ73. Spontaneity	Freedom of self-expression.
ᵇ74. Meticulosity	Emphasis on neatness and precision, e.g., in speech, grooming, and manipulation of objects.
ᶜ76. Avoidance	Evasion of situational demands, e.g., by ignoring them, going out of the field, etc.
ᶜ77. Acting out–Overcontrol	Inadequacy of delay leading to inappropriate expression of impulses in action at one extreme, ranging to excessive delay implying inappropriate inhibition of action at the other.
ᶜ78. Gross Scanning	Spontaneous examination or exploration of the laboratory.

[a] Rating made only in the clinical testing situation, used in factor analysis.

[b] Rating made in both the clinical and laboratory testing situations, each used in factor analysis.

[c] Rating made in the laboratory testing situation, used in factor analysis.

References

Allport, F. H. *Theories of perception and the concept of structure.* New York: Wiley, 1955.

Allport, G. W. Attitudes. In C. Murchison (ed.), *A handbook of social psychology.* Worcester, Mass.: Clark University Press, 1935, pp. 798–844.

Allport, G. W., & Vernon, P. E. *Studies in expressive movement.* New York: Macmillan, 1933.

Altman, L. L. On the oral nature of acting out. *J. Amer. psychoanalyt. Assn.,* 1957, 5, 648–62.

Barker, R. G., & Barker, Louise S. Behavior units for the comparative study of cultures. In B. Kaplan (ed.), *Studying personality cross-culturally.* Evanston, Ill.: Row, Peterson, 1961, pp. 457–76.

Barron, F. The disposition toward originality. *J. abnorm. soc. Psychol.,* 1955, 51, 478–85.

Beck, S. J. *Rorschach's Test, Vol. I, Basic processes* (2nd ed., rev.). New York: Grune and Stratton, 1949.

Beres, D. Ego deviation and the concept of schizophrenia. *Psychoanalyt. stud. Child,* 1956, 11, 164–235.

Berkowitz, L. Leveling tendencies and the complexity-simplicity dimension. *J. Pers.,* 1957, 25, 743–51.

Berlyne, D. E. *Conflict, arousal and curiosity.* New York: McGraw-Hill, 1960.

Berlyne, D. E. Uncertainty and epistemic curiosity. *Brit. J. Psychol.,* 1962, 53, 27–34.

Bibring, Grete L., Dwyer, T. F., Huntington, Dorothy S., & Valenstein, A. F. A study of the psychological processes in pregnancy and of the earliest mother-child relationship. I: Some propositions and comments. *Psychoanalyt. stud. Child,* 1961, 16, 9–72.

Binder, A., & Feldman, S. E. The effects of experimentally controlled experience upon recognition responses. *Psychol. Monogr.,* 1960, 74, No. 9 (Whole No. 496).

Bishop, Barbara M. Mother-child interaction and the social behavior of children. *Psychol. Monogr.,* 1951, 65, No. 11 (Whole No. 328).

Blos, P. The concept of acting out in relation to the adolescent process. *J. Amer. acad. child Psychiat.,* 1963, 2, 118–43.

Bolles, Mary M. The basis of pertinence: a study of the test performance of aments, dements and normal children of the same mental age. *Arch. Psychol.*, 1937, 30 (Whole No. 212).

Bossard, J. H. S., & Boll, Eleanor S. *The sociology of child development* (3rd ed.). New York: Harper, 1960.

Bowlby, J. Forty-four juvenile thieves: their characters and home-life. *Int. J. Psycho-anal.*, 1944, 25, 19–53.

Broverman, D. M. Dimensions of cognitive style. *J. Pers.*, 1960, 28, 167–85 (a).

Broverman, D. M. Cognitive style and intra-individual variation in abilities. *J. Pers.*, 1960, 28, 240–56 (b).

Broverman, D. M., & Lazarus, R. S. Individual differences in task performance under conditions of cognitive interference. *J. Pers.*, 1958, 26, 94–105.

Bruner, J. S., & Tagiuri, R. The perception of people. In G. Lindzey (ed.), *Handbook of social psychology.* Cambridge, Mass.: Addison-Wesley, 1954, Vol. II, pp. 634–54.

Bühler, Charlotte. The human course of life in its goal aspects. *J. hum. Psychol.*, 1964, 4, 1–18.

Callaway, E., III, & Band, R. I. Some psycho-pharmacological effects of atropine. *A.M.A. arch. neurol. Psychiat.*, 1958, 79, 91–102.

Cantor, Joan H., & Cantor, G. N. Observing behavior in children as a function of stimulus novelty. *Child Develpm.*, 1964, 35, 119–28.

Carroll, E. J. Acting out and ego development. *Psychoanalyt. Quart.*, 1954, 23, 521–28.

Chance, E., Arnold, J., & Tyrell, S. Communality and stability of meaning in clinical case description. *J. abnorm. soc. Psychol.*, 1962, 64, 389–406.

Chapman, S. Church schools. *J. educ. Sociol.*, 1945, 18, 340–51.

Clayton, Martha B., & Jackson, D. N. Equivalence range, acquiescence, and overgeneralization. *Educ. psychol. Measmt.*, 1961, 21, 371–82.

Cohen, J. The factorial structure of the WISC at ages 7–6, 10–6, and 13–6. *J. consult. Psychol.*, 1959, 23, 285–99.

Comalli, P. E., Jr., Wapner, S., & Werner, H. Interference effects of Stroop Color-Word Test in childhood, adulthood, and aging. *J. genet. Psychol.*, 1962, 100, 47–54.

Crandall, V. J., & Sinkeldam, Carol. Children's dependent and achievement behaviors in social situations and their perceptual field dependence. *J. Pers.*, 1964, 32, 1–22.

Cronbach, L. J. Processes affecting scores on "understanding of others" and "assumed similarity." *Psychol. Bull.*, 1955, 52, 177–93.

Diamond, S. *Personality and temperament.* New York: Harper, 1957.

Dickman, N. R. An investigation of the relationship between the cognitive organization of objective and behavioral stimuli. Unpublished master's thesis, University of Kansas, 1954.

Duffy, Elizabeth. The conceptual categories of psychology: a suggestion for revision. *Psychol. Rev.*, 1941, 48, 177–203.

Duffy, Elizabeth. *Activation and behavior.* New York: Wiley, 1962.

Ekstein, R., & Friedman, S. W. The function of acting out, play action, and play acting in the psychotherapeutic process. *J. Amer. psychoanalyt. Assn.*, 1957, 5, 581–629.

Erikson, E. H. *Childhood and society.* New York: Norton, 1950.

Erikson, E. H. The problem of ego identity. *J. Amer. psychoanalyt. Assn.,* 1956, 4, 56–121. Also in: Identity and the life cycle. *Psychol. Issues,* 1959, 1, No. 1.

Erikson, E. H. Reality and actuality. *J. Amer. psychoanalyt. Assn.,* 1962, 10, 451–74.

Erlenmeyer-Kimling, L., & Jarvik, L. F. Genetics and intelligence: a review. *Sci.,* 1963, 142, 1477–79.

Escalona, Sibylle, & Heider, Grace. *Prediction and outcome: a study in child development.* New York: Basic Books, 1959.

Escalona, Sibylle, & Leitch, Mary. *Early phases of personality development: a non-normative study of infancy behavior.* Evanston, Ill.: Child Development Publications, 1953.

Eysenck, H. J. *Scientific study of personality.* London: Routledge and Kegan Paul, 1952.

Fenichel, O. *The psychoanalytic theory of neurosis.* New York: Norton, 1945 (a).

Fenichel, O. Neurotic acting out. *Psychoanalyt. Rev.,* 1945, 32, 197–206 (b).

Fenichel, O. Ego strength and ego weakness. *Collected Papers,* 2nd series. New York: Norton, 1954, pp. 70–80.

Filer, R. J. Frustration, satisfaction, and other factors affecting the attractiveness of goal objects. *J. abnorm. soc. Psychol.,* 1952, 47, 203–12.

Fisher, S., & Cleveland, S. E. *Body image and personality.* Princeton, N.J.: Van Nostrand, 1958.

French, J. W. *The description of aptitude and achievement tests in terms of rotated factors.* Chicago, Ill.: University of Chicago Press, 1951.

Freud, Anna (1936). *The ego and the mechanisms of defense.* New York: International Universities Press, 1946.

Freud, Anna. Certain types and stages of social maladjustment. In K. R. Eissler (ed.), *Searchlights on delinquency.* New York: International Universities Press, 1949, pp. 193–204.

Freud, S. (1894). The neuro-psychoses of defense. *Standard Edition.* London: Hogarth, 1962, Vol. 3, pp. 45–61.

Freud, S. (1896). Further remarks on the neuro-psychoses of defense. *Standard Edition.* London: Hogarth, 1962, Vol. 3, pp. 159–85.

Freud, S. (1900). The interpretation of dreams. *Standard Edition,* London: Hogarth, 1953, Vols. 4–5.

Freud, S. (1901). The psychopathology of everyday life. *Standard Edition.* London: Hogarth, 1960, Vol. 6.

Freud, S. (1905). Fragment of an analysis of a case of hysteria (Dora). *Standard Edition.* London: Hogarth, 1953, Vol. 7, pp. 3–123 (a).

Freud, S. (1905). Three essays on the theory of sexuality. *Standard Edition.* London: Hogarth, 1953, Vol. 7, pp. 123–243 (b).

Freud, S. (1908). Character and anal erotism. *Standard Edition.* London: Hogarth, 1959, Vol. 9, pp. 167–75.

Freud, S. (1909). Notes upon a case of obsessional neurosis. *Standard Edition.* London: Hogarth, 1955, Vol. 10, pp. 153–318.

Freud, S. (1911). Formulations of the two principles of mental functioning. *Standard Edition.* London: Hogarth, 1958, Vol. 12, pp. 213–26 (a).

Freud, S. (1911). Psychoanalytic notes on an autobiographical account of a case of paranoia (Dementia Paranoides). *Standard Edition*. London: Hogarth, 1958, Vol. 12, pp. 3–84 (b).

Freud, S. (1913). The disposition to obsessional neurosis. *Standard Edition*. London: Hogarth, 1958, Vol. 12, pp. 311–26.

Freud, S. (1914). Remembering, repeating and working-through. *Standard Edition*. London: Hogarth, 1958, Vol. 12, pp. 145–56.

Freud, S. (1915). Repression. *Standard Edition*. London: Hogarth, 1957, Vol. 14, pp. 141–58 (a).

Freud, S. (1915). A case of paranoia running counter to the psychoanalytical theory of the disease. *Standard Edition*. London: Hogarth, 1957, Vol. 14, pp. 261–72 (b).

Freud, S. (1918). From the history of an infantile neurosis. *Standard Edition*. London: Hogarth, 1955, Vol. 17, pp. 3–123.

Freud, S. (1925). Negation. *Standard Edition*. London: Hogarth, 1961, Vol. 19, pp. 234–39.

Freud, S. (1926). Inhibitions, symptoms and anxiety. *Standard Edition*. London: Hogarth, 1959, Vol. 20, pp. 77–178.

Freud, S. (1933). New introductory lectures on psycho-analysis. *Standard Edition*. London: Hogarth, 1964, Vol. 22, pp. 3–184.

Freud, S. (1937). Analysis terminable and interminable. *Standard Edition*. London: Hogarth, 1964, Vol. 23, pp. 209–54.

Gardner, R. W. Cognitive styles in categorizing behavior. *J. Pers.*, 1953, 22, 214–33.

Gardner, R. W. Cognitive control principles and perceptual behavior. *Bull. Menninger Clin.*, 1959, 23, 241–48.

Gardner, R. W. Cognitive controls of attention deployment as determinants of visual illusions. *J. abnorm. soc. Psychol.*, 1961, 62, 120–29 (a).

Gardner, R. W. Individual differences in figural after-effects and response to reversible figures. *Brit. J. Psychol.*, 1961, 52, 269–72 (b).

Gardner, R. W. Personality organization and the nature of consciousness. Paper presented at Conference on Problems of Consciousness and Perception, Wayne State University, Detroit, Mich., 1961 (c).

Gardner, R. W. Cognitive controls in adaptation: research and measurement. In S. Messick & J. Ross (eds.), *Measurement in personality and cognition*. New York: Wiley, 1962, pp. 183–98.

Gardner, R. W. The development of cognitive structures. In Constance Scheerer (ed.), *Cognition: theory, research, promise*. New York: Harper and Row, 1964, pp. 147–71 (a).

Gardner, R. W. Cognitive control and person perception. Paper read at the annual meeting of the American Psychological Association, Los Angeles, Calif., Sept. 5, 1964 (b).

Gardner, R. W. The Menninger Foundation study of twins and their parents. Paper read at the annual meeting of the American Psychological Association, Los Angeles, Calif., Sept. 9, 1964 (c).

Gardner, R. W. Genetics and personality theory. In S. G. Vandenberg (ed.),

Methods and goals in human behavior genetics. New York: Academic Press, 1965, pp. 223–29.

Gardner, R. W. Organismic equilibration and the energy-structure duality in psychoanalytic theory: an attempt at theoretical refinement. *J. Amer. psychoanalyt. Assn.,* in press, 1967.

Gardner, R. W., Holzman, P. S., Klein, G. S., Linton, Harriet B., & Spence, D. P. Cognitive control: a study of individual consistencies in cognitive behavior. *Psychol. Issues,* 1959, 1, No. 4.

Gardner, R. W., Jackson, D. N., & Messick, S. J. Personality organization in cognitive controls and intellectual abilities. *Psychol. Issues,* 1960, 2, No. 4 (Whole No. 8).

Gardner, R. W., & Lohrenz, L. J. Leveling-sharpening and serial reproduction of a story. *Bull. Menninger Clin.,* 1960, 24, 295–304.

Gardner, R. W., & Lohrenz, L. J. Attention and assimilation. *Amer. J. Psychol.,* 1961, 74, 607–611.

Gardner, R. W., & Long, R. I. Errors of the standard and illusion effects with the inverted-*T. Percept. mot. Skills,* 1960, 10, 47–54 (a).

Gardner, R. W., & Long, R. I. Errors of the standard and illusion effects with L-shaped figures. *Percept. mot. Skills,* 1960, 10, 107–9 (b).

Gardner, R. W., & Long, R. I. Leveling-sharpening and serial learning. *Percept. mot. Skills,* 1960, 10, 179–85 (c).

Gardner, R. W., & Long, R. I. Cognitive controls as determinants of learning and remembering. *Psychologia,* 1960, 3, 165–71 (d).

Gardner, R. W., & Long, R. I. The stability of cognitive controls. *J. abnorm. soc. Psychol.,* 1960, 61, 485–87 (e).

Gardner, R. W., & Long, R. I. Selective attention and the Mueller-Lyer illusion. *Psychol. Rec.,* 1961, 11, 317–20 (a).

Gardner, R. W., & Long, R. I. Field-articulation in recall. *Psychol. Rec.,* 1961, 11, 305–10 (b).

Gardner, R. W., & Long, R. I. Control, defence, and centration effect: a study of scanning behaviour. *Brit. J. Psychol.,* 1962, 53, 129–40 (a).

Gardner, R. W., & Long, R. I. Cognitive controls of attention and inhibition: a study of individual consistencies. *Brit. J. Psychol.,* 1962, 53, 381–88 (b).

Gardner, R. W., & Schoen, R. A. Differentiation and abstraction in concept formation. *Psychol. Monogr.,* 1962, 76, No. 41 (Whole No. 560).

Gault, U. Factorial patterns of the Wechsler Intelligence Scales. *Austral. J. Psychol.,* 1954, 6, 85–93.

Giering, H. Das augenmass bei schulkindern. *Ztsch. f. Psychol.,* 1905, 39, 42–87.

Giffin, Mary E., Johnson, Adelaide M., & Litin, E. M. Specific factors determining antisocial acting out. *Amer. J. Orthopsychiat.,* 1954, 24, 668–84.

Gill, M. M., & Brenman, Margaret. *Hypnosis and related states.* New York: International Universities Press, 1959.

Glanzer, M. Curiosity, exploratory drive, and stimulus satiation. *Psychol. Bull.,* 1958, 55, 302–15.

Glover, E. The concept of dissociation. *Int. J. Psycho-anal.,* 1943, 24, 7–13.

Glover, E. Ego-distortion. *Int. J. Psycho-anal.,* 1958, 39, 260–64.

Glueck, S., & Glueck, Eleanor (1950). *Physique and delinquency.* New York: Harper, 1956.

Glueck, S., & Glueck, Eleanor. *Family environment and delinquency.* Boston: Houghton Mifflin, 1962.

Goldstein, K., & Scheerer, M. Abstract and concrete behavior: an experimental study with special tests. *Psychol. Monogr.,* 1941, 53, No. 2 (Whole No. 239).

Gollin, E. S., & Baron, A. Response consistency in perception and retention. *J. exp. Psychol.,* 1954, 47, 259–62.

Goodenough, D. R., & Karp, S. A. Field dependence and intellectual functioning. *J. abnorm. soc. Psychol.,* 1961, 63, 241–46.

Green, R. F., & Berkowitz, B. Changes in intellect with age. II: Factorial analysis of Wechsler-Bellevue scores. *J. genet. Psychol.,* 1964, 104, 3–18.

Greenacre, Phyllis. General problems of acting out. *Psychoanalyt. Quart.,* 1950, 19, 455–67.

Greenacre, Phyllis. Problems of acting out in the transference relationship. *J. Amer. acad. child Psychiat.,* 1963, 2, 144–75.

Grinberg, L. ¿Por qué negamos? *Rev. de Psicoanal.,* 1961, 18, 118–30.

Hagen, Elizabeth, P. A factor analysis of the Wechsler Intelligence Scale for Children. Unpublished doctoral dissertation, Columbia University, 1952.

Hardison, J., & Purcell, K. The effects of psychological stress as a function of need and cognitive control. *J. Pers.,* 1959, 27, 250–58.

Harman, H. H. *Modern factor analysis.* Chicago, Ill.: University of Chicago Press, 1960.

Hartmann, H. (1939). *Ego psychology and the problem of adaptation* (trans. D. Rapaport). New York: International Universities Press, 1958.

Hartmann, H. Comments on the psychoanalytic theory of the ego. *Psychoanalyt. stud. Child,* 1950, 5, 74–96.

Hartmann, H. The mutual influences in the development of ego and id. *Psychoanalyt. stud. Child,* 1952, 7, 9–30.

Hartmann, H. Notes on the theory of sublimation. *Psychoanalyt. stud. Child,* 1955, 10, 9–30.

Hartmann, H. The development of the ego concept in Freud's work. *Int. J. Psycho-anal.,* 1956, 37, 425–38 (a).

Hartmann, H. Notes on the reality principle. *Psychoanalyt. stud. Child,* 1956, 11, 31–53 (b).

Hartmann, H., Kris, E., & Loewenstein, R. M. Comments on the formation of psychic structure. *Psychoanalyt. stud. Child,* 1946, 2, 11–38.

Harvey, O. J., Hunt, D. E., & Schroder, H. M. *Conceptual systems and personality organization.* New York: Wiley, 1961.

Havighurst, R. J., Bowman, P. H., Liddle, G. P., Matthews, C. V., & Pierce, J. V. *Growing up in River City.* Chicago, Ill.: University of Chicago Commission on Human Development, 1962.

Hebb, D. O. *The organization of behavior.* New York: Wiley, 1949.

Helson, H. *Adaptation-level theory: an experimental and systematic approach to behavior.* New York: Harper and Row, 1964.

Hernández-Peón, R. Centrifugal control of sensory inflow to the brain and sensory perception. *Acta neurol. Latinoamer.*, 1959, 5, 279–98.

Hernández-Peón, R. Reticular mechanisms of sensory control. In A. Rosenblith (ed.), *Sensory communication.* New York and London: MIT Press and Wiley, 1961, pp. 497–520.

Hernández-Peón, R., & Scherrer, H. Habituation to acoustic stimuli in cochlear nucleus. *Fed. Proc.*, 1955, 14, No. 71.

Hesselbach, C. F. Superego repression in paranoia. *Psychoanalyt. Quart.*, 1962, 31, 341–50.

Hirsch, J. Individual differences in behavior and their genetic basis. In E. L. Bliss (ed.), *Roots of behavior.* New York: Harper, 1962, pp. 3–23.

Hollingworth, H. Experimental studies of judgment. *Arch. Psychol.*, 1913, 29, 44–52.

Holt, R. R. Cognitive controls and primary processes. *J. psychol. Res., Madras,* 1960, 4, 105–12.

Holtzman, W. H., Gorham, D. R., & Moran, L. J. A factor-analytic study of schizophrenic thought processes. *J. abnorm. soc. Psychol.*, 1964, 69, 355–64.

Holtzman, W. H., Thorpe, J. S., Swartz, J. D., & Herron, E. W. *Inkblot perception and personality.* Austin: University of Texas Press, 1961.

Holzman, P. S. The relation of assimilation tendencies in visual, auditory, and kinesthetic time-error to cognitive attitudes of leveling and sharpening. *J. Pers.*, 1954, 22, 375–94.

Holzman, P. S. Repression and cognitive style. In J. G. Peatman & E. L. Hartley (eds.), *Festschrift for Gardner Murphy.* New York: Harper, 1960, pp. 330–44. Also in: *Bull. Menninger Clin.*, 1962, 26, 273–82.

Holzman, P. S., & Gardner, R. W. Leveling and repression. *J. abnorm. soc. Psychol.*, 1959, 59, 151–55.

Holzman, P. S., & Gardner, R. W. Leveling-sharpening and memory organization. *J. abnorm. soc. Psychol.*, 1960, 61, 176–80.

Holzman, P. S., & Klein, G. S. Cognitive system-principles of leveling and sharpening: individual differences in assimilation effects in visual time-error. *J. Psychol.*, 1954, 37, 105–22.

Holzman, P. S., & Klein, G. S. Motive and style in reality contact. *Bull. Menninger Clin.*, 1956, 20, 181–91.

Hörmann, H. *Konflikt und entscheidung: experimentelle untersuchungen über das interferenzphänomen.* Göttingen: Verlag für Psychologie, 1960.

Houston, J. P., & Mednick, S. A. Creativity and the need for novelty. *J. abnorm. soc. Psychol.*, 1963, 66, 137–41.

Hustmyer, F. E., Jr., & Karnes, E. Background autonomic activity and "analytic perception." *J. abnorm. soc. Psychol.*, 1964, 68, 467–68.

Jacobson, Edith. The self and the object world: vicissitudes of their infantile cathexes and their influence on ideational and affective development. *Psychoanalyt. stud. Child*, 1954, 9, 75–127.

Jacobson, Edith. Denial and repression. *J. Amer. psychoanalyt. Assn.*, 1957, 5, 61–92.

Jasper, H. Reticular-cortical systems and theories of the integrative action of the brain. In H. F. Harlow and C. N. Woolsey (eds.), *Biological and biochemical bases of behavior.* Madison: University of Wisconsin Press, 1958, pp. 37–61.

Johnson, Adelaide M. Sanctions for superego lacunae of adolescents. In K. R. Eissler (ed.), *Searchlights on delinquency.* New York: International Universities Press, 1949, pp. 225–45.

Johnson, Adelaide M., & Szurek, S. A. The genesis of antisocial acting out in children and adults. *Psychoanalyt. Quart.,* 1952, 21, 323–43.

Kaiser, H. F. The varimax criterion for analytic rotation in factor analysis. *Psychometrika,* 1958, 23, 187–200.

Kaltenbach, J. E., & McClelland, D. C. Achievement and social status in three small communities. In D. C. McClelland, A. L. Baldwin, U. Bronfenbrenner, & F. L. Strodtbeck (eds.), *Talent and society.* Princeton, N.J.: Van Nostrand, 1958, pp. 112–34.

Kanzer, M. Panel report: acting out and its relation to impulse disorders. *J. Amer. psychoanalyt. Assn.,* 1957, 5, 136–45 (a).

Kanzer, M. Acting out, sublimation, and reality testing. *J. Amer. psychoanalyt. Assn.,* 1957, 5, 663–84 (b).

Karp, S. A. Field dependence and overcoming embeddedness. *J. consult. Psychol.,* 1963, 27, 294–302.

Karp, S. A., Poster, D. C., & Goodman, A. Differentiation in alcoholic women. *J. Pers.,* 1963, 31, 386–93.

Karush, A., Easser, B. Ruth, Cooper, A., & Swerdloff, Bluma. The evaluation of ego strength. I: A profile of adaptive balance. *J. nerv. ment. Dis.,* 1964, 139, 332–49.

Kaufman, I. Three basic sources for pre-delinquent character. *Nerv. Child,* 1955, 2, 12–15.

Kelly, G. A. *The psychology of personal constructs* (2 vols.). New York: Norton, 1955.

Klein, G. S. The personal world through perception. In R. R. Blake & G. V. Ramsey (eds.), *Perception: an approach to personality.* New York: Ronald, 1950, pp. 328–55.

Klein, G. S. Need and regulation. In M. R. Jones (ed.), *Nebraska symposium on motivation.* Lincoln: University of Nebraska Press, 1954, pp. 224–74.

Klein, G. S. Perception, motives and personality. In J. L. McCary (ed.), *Psychology of personality: six modern approaches.* New York: Logos, 1956, pp. 121–99.

Klein, G. S. Cognitive control and motivation. In G. Lindzey (ed.), *Assessment of human motives.* New York: Rinehart, 1958, pp. 87–118.

Klein, G. S. Semantic power measured through the interference of words with color-naming. *Amer. J. Psychol.,* 1964, 77, 576–88.

Klein, G. S., Gardner, R. W., & Schlesinger, H. J. Tolerance for unrealistic experiences: a study of the generality of a cognitive control. *Brit. J. Psychol.,* 1962, 53, 41–55.

Klein, G. S., & Schlesinger, H. J. Where is the perceiver in perceptual theory? *J. Pers.,* 1949, 18, 32–47.

Klein, G. S., & Schlesinger, H. J. Perceptual attitudes toward instability. I: Prediction of apparent movement experiences from Rorschach responses. *J. Pers.,* 1951, 19, 289–302.

Klopfer, B., & Kelley, D. *The Rorschach technique.* Yonkers, N.Y.: World Book, 1942.

Knight, R. P. Borderline states. *Bull. Menninger Clin.,* 1953, 17, 1–12.

Köhler, W. Zur theorie des sukzessivvergleichs und der zeitfehler. *Psychol. Forsch.,* 1923, 4, 115–75.

Köhler, W., & Adams, Pauline A. Perception and attention. *Amer. J. Psychol.,* 1958, 71, 489–503.

Koltuv, Barbara B. Some characteristics of intrajudge trait intercorrelations. *Psychol. Monogr.,* 1962, 76, No. 33 (Whole No. 552).

Lang, A. *Über zwei teilsysteme der persönlichkeit.* Bern: Hans Huber, 1964.

Lauenstein, O. Ansatz zu einer physiologischen theorie des vergleichs und der zeitfehler. *Psychol. Forsch.,* 1933, 17, 130–77.

Lazarus, R. S., Baker, R. W., Broverman, D. M., & Mayer, J. Personality and psychological stress. *J. Pers.,* 1957, 25, 559–77.

Lenski, G. *The religious factor.* Garden City, N.Y.: Doubleday, 1961.

Lidz, T. Discussion of "A developmental program of acting out," by G. E. Gardner. *J. Amer. acad. child Psychiat.,* 1963, 2, 19–21.

Ligon, E. M. A genetic study of color naming and word reading. *Amer. J. Psychol.,* 1932, 44, 103–22.

Lindsley, D. B., Bowden, J., & Magoun, H. W. Effect upon the EEG of acute injury to the brain stem activating system. *E.E.G. clin. Neurophysiol.,* 1949, 1, 475–86.

Livant, W. P. Grammar in the story reproductions of levelers and sharpeners. *Bull. Menninger Clin.,* 1962, 26, 283–87.

Long, R. I. Field-articulation as a factor in learning and recall. *Percept. mot. Skills,* 1962, 15, 151–58.

Lutzky, Harriet C., Schmeidler, Gertrude R. Perceptual leveling in institutional and other children. *J. genet. Psychol.,* 1963, 103, 45–51.

McGuire, C., & White, G. D. The measurement of social status. Research paper in human development No. 3 (rev.), Department of Educational Psychology, University of Texas, 1955.

McNamara, H. J., Murphy, G., & Harrell, S. N. Curiosity and reality contact: a preliminary report. *Percept. mot. Skills,* 1964, 18, 976.

Madison, P. *Freud's concept of repression and defense, its theoretical and observational language.* Minneapolis: University of Minnesota Press, 1961.

Malone, C. Some observations on children of disorganized families and problems of acting out. *J. Amer. acad. child Psychiat.,* 1963, 2, 22–49.

Marrs, C. L. Categorizing behavior as elicited by a variety of stimuli. Unpublished master's thesis, University of Kansas, 1955.

Maslow, A. H. Defense and growth. *Merrill-Palmer Quart.,* 1956, 3, 36–47.

Mathae, D. E. Figural aftereffects, weight judgment and schematizing in relation to "cortical conductivity." Unpublished doctoral dissertation, University of Kansas, 1958.

Maw, W. H., & Maw, Ethel W. Selection of unbalanced and unusual designs by children high in curiosity. *Child Develpm.*, 1962, 33, 917–22.

Mercado, S. J., Diaz Guerrero, R., & Gardner, R. W. Cognitive control in children of Mexico and the United States. *J. soc. Psychol.*, 1963, 59, 199–208.

Merrill, Barbara. A measurement of mother-child interaction. *J. abnorm. soc. Psychol.*, 1946, 41, 37–49.

Messick, S., & Fritzky, F. J. Dimensions of analytic attitude in cognition and personality. *J. Pers.*, 1963, 31, 346–70.

Messick, S., & Kogan, N. Differentiation and compartmentalization in object-sorting measures of categorizing style. *Percept. mot. Skills*, 1963, 16, 47–51.

Michaels, J. J. Character disorder and acting upon impulse. In M. Levitt (ed.), *Readings in psychoanalytic psychology*. New York: Appleton, 1958.

Moriarty, Alice. Coping patterns of preschool children in response to intelligence test demands. *Genet. psychol. Monogr.*, 1961, 64, 3–127.

Moruzzi, G., & Magoun, H. W. Brain stem reticular formation and activation of the EEG. *E.E.G. clin. Neurophysiol.*, 1949, 1, 455–73.

Moseley, E. C., Duffey, R. F., & Sherman, L. J. An extension of the construct validity of the Holtzman Inkblot Technique. *J. clin. Psychol.*, 1963, 19, 186–92.

Mulaik, S. A. Are personality factors raters' conceptual factors? *J. consult. Psychol.*, 1964, 28, 506–11.

Murphy, G. *Personality*. New York: Harper, 1947.

Murphy, Lois B. *The widening world of childhood*. New York: Basic Books, 1962.

Nunberg, H. The synthetic function of the ego. *Int. J. Psycho-anal.*, 1931, 12, 123–40.

Nunberg, H. Ego strength and ego weakness. *Amer. Imago*, 1942, 3, 25–40.

Nunberg, H. *Curiosity*. New York: International Universities Press, 1961.

Overall, J. E. Orthogonal factors and uncorrelated factor scores. *Psychol. Rep.*, 1962, 10, 651–62.

Piaget, J. *The origins of intelligence in children* (trans. Margaret Cook; 2nd ed.). New York: International Universities Press, 1953.

Piaget, J. *Les mécanismes perceptifs*. Paris: Presses Universitaires de France, 1961.

Piaget, J. The stages of the intellectual development of the child. *Bull. Menninger Clin.*, 1962, 26, 120–28.

Piaget, J., Lambercier, M., Boesch, E., & Albertini, B. Introduction à l'étude des perceptions chez l'enfant et analyse d'une illusion relative a la perception visuelle de cercles concentriques (Delboeuf). *Arch. Psychol., Genève*, 1942, 29, 1–107.

Pinzka, C., & Saunders, D. R. Analytic rotation to simple structure. II: Extension to oblique solution. Research Bulletin RB-54–31, Educational Testing Service, Princeton, N.J., 1954.

Rand, G., Wapner, S., Werner, H., & McFarland, J. H. Age differences in performance on the Stroop Color-Word Test. *J. Pers.*, 1963, 31, 534–58.

Rapaport, D. The autonomy of the ego. *Bull. Menninger Clin.*, 1951, 15, 113–23 (a).

Rapaport, D. (ed.). *Organization and pathology of thought*. New York: Columbia University Press, 1951 (b).

Rapaport, D. Cognitive structures. In *Contemporary approaches to cognition.* Cambridge, Mass.: Harvard University Press, 1957, pp. 157–200.

Rapaport, D. The theory of ego autonomy: a generalization. *Bull. Menninger Clin.,* 1958, 22, 13–35.

Rapaport, D. The structure of psychoanalytic theory. In S. Koch (ed.), *Psychology: a study of a science.* Vol. 3: *Formulations of the person and the social context.* New York: McGraw-Hill, 1959, pp. 55–183.

Rapaport, D. Psychoanalysis as a developmental psychology. In B. Kaplan & S. Wapner (eds.), *Perspectives in psychological theory.* New York: International Universities Press, 1960, pp. 209–55 (a).

Rapaport, D. On the psychoanalytic theory of motivation. In M. R. Jones (ed.), *Nebraska symposium on motivation.* Lincoln: University of Nebraska Press, 1960, pp. 173–247 (b).

Rapaport, D., Gill, M., & Schafer, R. *Diagnostic psychological testing.* Chicago, Ill.: Yearbook, 1945–46, Vols. I–II.

Rexford, Eveoleen N., & Van Amerongen, Suzanne. The influence of unsolved maternal oral conflicts upon impulsive acting out in young children. *Amer. J. Orthopsychiat.,* 1957, 27, 75–85.

Riesman, D. *The lonely crowd.* New Haven, Conn.: Yale University Press, 1950.

Rogers, C. R. Toward a theory of creativity. In H. H. Anderson (ed.), *Creativity and its cultivation.* New York: Harper, 1959, pp. 69–82.

Rokeach, M. *The open and closed mind.* New York: Basic Books, 1960.

Rorschach, H. *Psychodiagnostics* (trans. P. Lemkau & B. Kronenberg). Bern: Verlag Hans Huber, 1949.

Rotter, J. B. *Social learning and clinical psychology.* New York: Prentice-Hall, 1954.

Santos, J. F., Farrow, B. J., & Haines, J. R. How attention influences what is perceived: some experimental evidence. *Bull. Menninger Clin.,* 1963, 27, 3–14.

Santostefano, S. A developmental study of the Delboeuf illusion. *Percept. mot. Skills,* 1963, 17, 23–29.

Santostefano, S. A developmental study of the cognitive control "leveling-sharpening." *Merrill-Palmer Quart.,* 1964, 10, 343–60.

Schachtel, E. G. *Metamorphosis.* New York: Basic Books, 1959.

Schafer, R. *The clinical application of psychological tests.* New York: International Universities Press, 1948.

Schafer, R. *Psychoanalytic interpretation in Rorschach testing: theory and application.* New York: Grune and Stratton, 1954.

Schalock, H. D. Observation of mother-child interaction in the laboratory and in the home. Unpublished doctoral dissertation, University of Nebraska, 1956.

Schlesinger, H. J. Cognitive attitudes in relation to susceptibility to interference. *J. Pers.,* 1954, 22, 354–74.

Schwartz, F., & Rouse, R. O. The activation and recovery of associations. *Psychol. Issues,* 1961, 3, No. 1 (Whole No. 9).

Secord, P. F., & Berscheid, Ellen S. Stereotyping and the generality of implicit personality theory. *J. Pers.,* 1963, 31, 65–78.

Shapiro, D. Aspects of obsessive-compulsive style. *Psychiat.,* 1962, 25, 46–59.

Shrauger, S., & Altrocchi, J. The personality of the perceiver as a factor in person perception. *Psychol. Bull.*, 1964, 62, 289–308.

Siegal, R. S., & Ehrenreich, G. A. Inferring repression from psychological tests. *Bull. Menninger Clin.*, 1962, 26, 82–91.

Silverman, J. The problem of attention in research and theory in schizophrenia. *Psychol. Rev.*, 1964, 71, 352–79 (a).

Silverman, J. Scanning-control mechanism and "cognitive filtering" in paranoid and non-paranoid schizophrenia. *J. consult. Psychol.*, 1964, 28, 385–93 (b).

Sloane, H. N. The generality and construct validity of equivalence range. Unpublished doctoral dissertation, Pennsylvania State University, 1959.

Sloane, H. N., Gorlow, L., & Jackson, D. N. Cognitive styles in equivalence range. *Percept. mot. Skills*, 1963, 16, 389–404.

Smith, G. J. W., & Klein, G. S. Cognitive controls in serial behavior patterns. *J. Pers.*, 1953, 22, 188–213.

Smith, G. J. W., & Nyman, G. E. Psychopathological behavior in a serial experiment: investigations of neurotic, psychotic, psychopathic, and normal subjects. *Lund Univer. Arsskr.*, Avd. 2, 1959, 56.

Solley, C. M., & Murphy, G. *Development of the perceptual world.* New York: Basic Books, 1960.

Spaeth, J. L. Value orientations and academic career plans: structural effects on the careers of graduate students. Unpublished doctoral dissertation, University of Chicago, 1961.

Spivack, G., Levine, M., & Sprigle, H. Intelligence test performance and the delay function of the ego. *J. consult. Psychol.*, 1959, 23, 428–31.

Steiner, I. D. Ethnocentrism and tolerance of trait "inconsistency." *J. abnorm. soc. Psychol.*, 1954, 49, 349–54.

Strodtbeck, F. L. Family interaction, values, and achievement. In D. C. McClelland, A. L. Baldwin, U. Bronfenbrenner, & F. L. Strodtbeck (eds.), *Talent and society.* Princeton, N.J.: Van Nostrand, 1958, pp. 135–94.

Stroop, J. R. Studies of interference in serial verbal reactions. *J. exp. Psychol.*, 1935, 18, 643–62 (a).

Stroop, J. R. The basis of Ligon's theory. *Amer. J. Psychol.*, 1935, 47, 499–504 (b).

Stroop, J. R. Factors affecting speed in serial verbal reactions. *Psychol. Monogr.*, 1938, 50, No. 5 (Whole No. 225), 38–48.

Szurek, S., Johnson, Adelaide M., & Falstein, E. Collaborative psychiatric therapy of parent-child problems. *Amer. J. Orthopsychiat.*, 1942, 12, 511–16.

Tajfel, H., Richardson, A., & Everstine, L. Individual consistencies in categorizing: a study of judgmental behavior. *J. Pers.*, 1964, 32, 90–108.

Thurstone, L. L. *A factorial study of perception.* Chicago, Ill.: University of Chicago Press, 1944, pp. 5–148.

Tomkins, S. Left and right: a basic dimension of ideology and personality. In R. W. White (ed.), assisted by Katherine F. Bruner, *The study of lives.* New York: Atherton Press, 1964.

Van Amerongen, Suzanne T. Permission, promotion, and provocation of anti-social behavior. *J. Amer. acad. child Psychiat.*, 1963, 2, 99–117.

Vandenberg, S. G. The hereditary abilities study: hereditary components in a psychological test battery. *Amer. J. hum. Genet.*, 1962, 14, 220–37.

Wallach, M. A. Commentary: active-analytical vs. passive-global cognitive functioning. In S. Messick, & J. Ross (eds.), *Measurement in personality and cognition.* New York: Wiley, 1962, pp. 199–218.

Walters, J., Connor, Ruth, & Zunich, M. Interaction of mothers and children from lower-class families. *Child Develpm.*, 1964, 35, 433–40.

Wapner, S., & Krus, D. M. Effects of lysergic acid diethylamide, and differences between normals and schizophrenics on the Stroop Color-Word Test. *J. Neuro-psychiat.*, 1960, 2, 76–81.

Warner, W. L., & Srole, L. *The social systems of American ethnic groups.* New Haven, Conn.: Yale University Press, 1945.

Wechsler, D. *Manual, Wechsler Intelligence Scale for Children.* New York: The Psychological Corporation, 1949.

Werner, H. *Comparative psychology of mental development.* Chicago, Ill.: Follett, 1940.

Wertheimer, M. Figural aftereffect as a measure of metabolic efficiency. *J. Pers.*, 1955, 24, 56–73.

Witkin, H. A. Individual differences in ease of perception of embedded figures. *J. Pers.*, 1950, 19, 1–15.

Witkin, H. A., Dyk, R. B., Faterson, H. F., Goodenough, D. R., & Karp, S. A. *Psychological differentiation.* New York: Wiley, 1962.

Witkin, H. A., Karp, S. A., & Goodenough, D. R. Dependence in alcoholics. *Quart. J. stud. Alcohol.*, 1959, 20, 493–504.

Witkin, H. A., Lewis, Helen B., Hertzman, M., Machover, Karen, Meissner, Pearl B., & Wapner, S. *Personality through perception.* New York: Harper, 1954.

Wohlwill, J. F. Developmental studies of perception. *Psychol. Bull.*, 1960, 57, 249–88.

Wulf, F. Über die veränderung von vorstellungen (gedächtnis und gestalt). *Psychol. Forsch.*, 1922, 1, 333–73.

Zunich, M. Study of relationships between child rearing attitudes and maternal behavior. *J. exp. Educ.*, 1961, 30, 231–41.

Name Index

Adams, Pauline A., 39
Albertini, B., 68n
Allport, F. H., 11
Allport, G. W., 7, 307
Altman, L. L., 173
Altrocchi, J., 306
Arnold, J., 134

Baker, R. W., 51
Band, R. I., 53
Barker, Louise S., 29
Barker, R. G., 29
Baron, A., 45
Barron, F., 56
Beck, S. J., 125
Beres, D., 4, 13
Berkowitz, B., 130n, 131
Berkowitz, L., 40
Berlyne, D. E., 151
Berscheid, Ellen S., 134
Bibring, Grete L., 167, 168
Binder, A., 8
Bishop, Barbara M., 206
Bishop, Gail, 135n
Blos, P., 174
Boesch, E., 68n
Boll, Eleanor S., 207
Bolles, Mary M., 90
Bossard, J. H. S., 207
Bowden, J., 46
Bowlby, J., 173
Bowman, P. H., 207
Brenman, Margaret, 10, 15, 156, 177, 178, 179
Broverman, D. M., 51, 53
Bruner, J. S., 134
Bühler, Charlotte, 310

Callaway, E. III, 53
Cantor, G. N., 151
Cantor, Joan H., 151
Carroll, E. J., 174
Chance, E., 134
Chapman, S., 208

Clayton, Martha B., 55
Cleveland, S. E., 124
Cohen, J., 130, 131, 132, 133
Comalli, P. E., Jr., 53
Connor, Ruth, 206
Cooper, A., 180
Crandall, V. J., 45
Cronbach, L. J., 134

Diamond, S., 308
Diaz Guerrero, R., 29
Dickman, N. R., 54
Duffey, R. F., 128
Duffy, Elizabeth, 39, 62, 144n
Dwyer, T. F., 168
Dyk, R. B., 24

Easser, B. Ruth, 180
Ehrenreich, G. A., 160, 162
Ekstein, R., 174
Erikson, E. H., 3, 10, 15, 16, 18, 28, 182, 183, 310
Erlenmeyer-Kimling, L., 21
Escalona, Sibylle, 27
Everstine, L., 59
Eysenck, H. J., 311

Falstein, E., 173
Farrow, B. J., 8
Faterson, H. F., 24
Feldman, S. E., 8
Fenichel, O., 13n, 158, 165, 168, 169, 173, 180
Filer, R. J., 134
Fisher, S., 124
French, J. W., 44
Freud, Anna, 17, 18, 28, 121, 157, 158, 164, 166, 167, 168, 169, 170, 174, 175, 180
Freud, S., 4, 5, 6, 8, 11, 12, 13, 14, 15, 20, 47, 150, 155, 157, 158, 159, 162, 163, 164, 165, 166, 168, 169, 170, 172, 176, 181
Friedman, S. W., 174
Fritzky, F. J., 45

Subject Index